Presidential Campaigns in Latin America

Electoral Strategies and Success Contagion

How do presidential candidates in new democracies choose their campaign strategies, and what strategies do they adopt? In contrast to the claim that campaigns around the world are becoming more similar to one another, Taylor C. Boas argues that new democracies are likely to develop nationally specific approaches to electioneering through a process called success contagion. The theory of success contagion holds that the first elected president to complete a successful term in office establishes a national model of campaign strategy that other candidates will adopt in the future. He develops this argument for the cases of Chile, Brazil, and Peru, drawing on interviews with campaign strategists and content analysis of candidates' television advertising from the 1980s through 2011. The author concludes by testing the argument in ten other new democracies around the world, demonstrating substantial support for the theory.

Taylor C. Boas is assistant professor of political science at Boston University and has been a Visiting Fellow at the Kellogg Institute for International Studies, University of Notre Dame.

CAMBRIDGE
UNIVERSITY PRESS

32 Avenue of the Americas, New York, NY 10013-2473, USA

Cambridge University Press is part of the University of Cambridge.

It furthers the University's mission by disseminating knowledge in the pursuit of education, learning, and research at the highest international levels of excellence.

www.cambridge.org
Information on this title: www.cambridge.org/9781107131149

© Taylor C. Boas 2016

First published 2016

A catalog record for this publication is available from the British Library.

ISBN 978-1-107-13114-9 Hardback

To Helen, Julian, and Evelyn

Contents

Figures

Tables

Acknowledgments

This book has been many years in the making, and I have incurred a number of debts along the way. The study began as my doctoral dissertation at the University of California, Berkeley. David Collier and Ruth Berins Collier, the co-chairs of my committee, shaped the project in innumerable ways, from my initial formulation of ideas, to fine-tuning logical steps in the argument, to offering support and encouragement as I prepared the manuscript for submission. Henry Brady provided key insights from the subfield of American politics, and Susan Rasky offered the perspective of someone with close ties to the world of campaigning and electoral politics. I am grateful for their support and guidance.

A number of institutions generously offered financial support for this research. I am grateful to the National Science Foundation, the Fulbright-Hays Doctoral Dissertation Research Abroad program, the Institute of International Studies and the Center for Latin American Studies at the University of California, Berkeley, the Alpha of California Chapter of Phi Beta Kappa, and Boston University. Thanks also to the institutions that provided an academic base for my field research: the Instituto de Ciencia Política of the Universidad Pontificia Católica de Chile, the Instituto de Estudios Peruanos, and the Political Science Department of the Universidade de São Paulo. The Kellogg Institute for International Studies at the University of Notre Dame, where I was a visiting fellow from 2009 to 2010, provided an intellectually stimulating environment to work on the manuscript.

Throughout the various phases of this project, I have benefited enormously from colleagues, both at home and abroad, who provided advice, feedback, contacts, or logistical support. These include Alessandra Aldé, Jorge Almeida, David Altman, Will Barndt, Mauricio Benítez, Maxwell Cameron, Vera Chaia, Tomás Chuaqui, Adam Cohon, Miguel de Figeuiredo, Patricio

Dussaillant, Tasha Fairfield, Natalia Ferretti, Marcus Figueiredo, Jordan Gans-Morse, Candelaria Garay, John Gerring, David Glick, Matt Grossmann, Frances Hagopian, Sam Handlin, Veronica Herrera, Danny Hidalgo, José Miguel Izquierdo, Maiah Jaskoski, Alfredo Joignant, Diana Kapiszewski, David Karol, Chappell Lawson, Juan Pablo Luna, Jim Mahoney, Cristóbal Marín, Lindsay Mayka, Cynthia McClintock, Patricio Navia, Beth Neitzel, Aldo Pan-fichi, Mauro Porto, Neal Richardson, Cynthia Sanborn, Tim Scully, Ana Maria Stuart, Mariela Szwarcberg, Martín Tanaka, Sergio Toro, Fernando Tuesta Soldevilla, Mekoce Walker, Francisco Weffort, and Deborah Yashar. For able research assistance, I am grateful to Karla León Espinosa, Stephanie Mulhern, and Julia Sendor.

The primary data sources for this study include interviews and the content analysis of television advertising. I am particularly grateful to all those who agreed to be interviewed for this book. The content analysis component would have been impossible without the help of a number of institutions and individuals that generously allowed me to make copies of their video collections. In Chile, sources included the Consejo Nacional de Televisión, the journalism school of the Pontificia Universidad Católica de Chile, the Corporación Justicia y Democrácia, the Fundación Frei, the Government of Chile's Secretaría de Comunicación y Cultura, the Stanford University Bing Overseas Study Program in Santiago, the library of the Universidad Diego Portales, Juan Enrique Forch of Visión Comunicaciones, and the personal collections of Eduardo Bustos, Patricio Dussaillant, and Cristóbal Marín. In Peru, thanks go to the Communication Department of the Universidad de Lima, the Instituto Prensa y Sociedad, Ricardo Ghibellini of Amazonas Films, Alfonso Maldonado of Cinesetenta, Rubén Bonilla of Corporación Internacional de Comunicaciones, and Abel Aguilar. In Brazil, I obtained material from the Doxa communication research lab at the Instituto de Estudos Sociais e Políticos and from the Fundação Perseu Abramo of the Partido dos Trabalhadores. A copy of the entire video collection is archived at the Qualitative Data Repository (QDR) at Syracuse University; thanks to Colin Elman and Diana Kapiszewski for inviting me to participate in the QDR pilot project.

At Cambridge University Press, I am grateful to my editor, Lewis Bateman, and also to two anonymous reviewers who provided exceptional feedback. Portions of some chapters appeared previously in Taylor C. Boas, "Varieties of Electioneering: Success Contagion and Presidential Campaigns in Latin America," *World Politics* 62, no. 4: 636–675, copyright 2010 by Cambridge University Press.

Finally, I am thankful for the love and support of my family. My wife, Helen Oliver, accompanied me during fieldwork in Chile and Peru, where we had many exciting times together, squeezed in between interviews and chasing down campaign advertising videos. The dissertation upon which this book is based was dedicated to Helen, "as we embark upon our next adventure." As it turns out, two wonderful children, Julian and Evelyn, have joined us in that adventure. During a recent campaign in Massachusetts, when a canvasser for Senator Ed Markey visited our door, Julian asked me afterwards, "Daddy, what's an election?" Hopefully this book provides some answers.

Success Contagion and Presidential Campaigns in Latin America

In the campaign for Chile's 2005 presidential election, one of the first policy issues center-left candidate Michelle Bachelet mentioned in her television advertising was the problem of youth unemployment. "What is this craziness of want ads asking for youth with experience?" she asked indignantly. "Dear employers: the only way your youth can get experience is by working." Bachelet did not say much about her proposed solution to the problem, beyond a vague reference to subsidies that might help young people enter the labor market. Rather, her focus was on empathizing with the youth and on underscoring their value to society. "Let's take advantage of the contribution of new perspectives," she continued. "They are a source of energy and creativity that we cannot waste."

In Brazil's 2002 presidential election, center-left candidate Luiz Inácio Lula da Silva took a very different approach to the same policy issue. Like Bachelet, Lula expressed empathy with unemployed youth and their families: "I'm very familiar with this problem. I have 5 children, and I know how much Marisa and I suffered during this phase of our lives." Yet Lula's appeal went much further. After initially framing the problem in human terms, his ad outlined the proposed First Job Program: any business creating a new job for a sixteen- to twenty-one year old with no prior work experience would receive a subsidy equal to the minimum wage, to be paid during the first twelve months of employment. The segment spent nearly a minute explaining how the policy would work, offering examples to help viewers understand the fine details.

Why did Lula's campaign focus on the details of his proposed solution to the problem of youth unemployment, while Bachelet's simply sought to convey how much she cared about the issue? Both candidates *had* proposals for this particular policy area; ironically, Bachelet's government program spelled out her ideas in greater detail than did Lula's (da Silva 2002: 23–24; Bachelet 2005: 21–22). Yet Lula still chose to portray himself as a capable technocrat – in this policy area, as well as many others – whereas Bachelet sought to come across as a "feel-your-pain" empathizer. The difference seems to contradict what we would expect based on common stereotypes about the two countries: Chile is often thought of as the poster child of good governance and economic stability, whereas Brazil has long struggled with clientelism and corruption. It also seems odd when we consider that the audience for each message was much more highly educated in Chile (where the median voter had finished secondary school) than in Brazil (where she had only an incomplete primary education).[1]

This book seeks to explain cross-national differences in the campaign strategies of presidential candidates in new democracies, such as the contrast between Lula and Bachelet's approaches to youth unemployment in 2002 and 2005. I argue that candidates adopt the first victorious electoral strategy that was subsequently legitimated by a successful term in government. In Chile, this was the strategy of the "No" campaign in the 1988 plebiscite, which privileged direct ties to voters, avoided divisive appeals, and stressed empathy with popular concerns rather than specific proposals to solve them. In Brazil, it was the approach of Fernando Henrique Cardoso's campaign in 1994, which also pursued direct ties and eschewed divisive appeals but was heavy on policy details. In subsequent elections, the strategies of these initial campaigns spread more broadly across the ideological spectrum, either because candidates explicitly imitated their predecessors or because they heeded the advice of campaign professionals who recommended such an approach. As a result, left- and right-wing candidates have adopted similar strategies in recent elections in both Chile and Brazil. Between the two countries, however, the dominant approach to electioneering differed.

While major presidential candidates in Brazil and Chile have converged on nationally specific campaign strategies over time, a third country, Peru, illustrates a different pattern. Peruvian candidates have retained a heterogeneous mix of strategies, and those within the same party or political sector have sometimes altered their approaches dramatically over time, even within the course of a single campaign. I argue that in cases like Peru, where victorious campaign strategies are continually delegitimated by the poor governing record of elected presidents, candidates will not converge upon a common approach because they are wary of adopting strategies that voters associate with discredited politicians. Rather, each candidate is likely to choose his or her strategies through an inward-oriented process of reacting to prior errors.

The theory developed in this book, success contagion, argues that candidates' electoral strategies often converge within countries, but that cross-nationally,

---

[1] Data are drawn from Brazil's Superior Electoral Court (profile of the electorate in September 2002, at www.tse.jus.br/eleicoes/estatisticas/estatistica-do-eleitorado-por-sexo-e-grau-de-instrucao, visited March 3, 2015) and from the Centro de Estudios Público's October–November 2005 survey of Chileans.

significant differences tend to persist. This claim runs counter to most existing arguments about the evolution of campaign strategies, which tend to emphasize cross-national convergence. Theories of campaign modernization, Americanization, professionalization, or the rise of political marketing all draw primarily on the experiences of the United States and Western Europe, but scholars of Latin America have tended to adopt these existing perspectives with little modification. I argue that the development of campaign strategies in third-wave democracies should follow a different path, one that allows for much greater cross-national diversity.

Candidates' electoral strategies carry great import for the quality of democracy in cases of recent transition from authoritarian rule. Campaigns are crucial moments in which citizens are asked to take part in democracy, by casting a vote and often by participating more actively. The nature of this participatory experience – heavily influenced by the strategies of competing candidates – can have implications for popular satisfaction with democracy itself, as well as the degree to which people support authoritarian alternatives. Campaigns are also a chance for citizens to ponder the important decision of who will best represent their interests once elected to office. In this regard, candidates' electioneering styles influence whether clear proposals are placed on the table for voters to consider before choosing their representatives. Finally, campaign strategies matter for the quality of democracy because of their implications for a particular politician's approach to governing once in office. The intense several months prior to an election often inaugurate a political style that is maintained throughout the ensuing presidential term.

Democracy promoters around the world explicitly recognize these ways in which electoral strategies matter for important substantive outcomes, and training politicians in campaign strategies and techniques has been a key element of aid to new democracies in Latin America and elsewhere (Carothers 1999, 2006). Scholars have been slower to appreciate the real-world importance of campaign strategies. Electoral campaigns have received little attention in the academic literature on the quality of democracy, apart from a few mentions of the rules by which they are conducted or the origin of the funds that finance them (Lijphart 1999; Altman and Pérez-Liñán 2002; O'Donnell 2004; Diamond and Morlino 2005). This book aims to contribute to filling this gap.

DIMENSIONS OF CAMPAIGN STRATEGY

When Bachelet and Lula appealed to their respective electorates about the issue of youth unemployment, not everything about their approaches differed. Neither candidate dwelled on something that is a basic fact of life in highly unequal societies like Brazil's and Chile's: lower- and even middle-class youth are far more likely to struggle on the job market than those whose class background gives them access to quality education and whose social connections give them a foot in the door. In general, Bachelet and Lula both chose not to campaign in the divisive manner that has become common in some other Latin American countries, where politicians routinely seek votes by mobilizing resentment between haves and have-nots. Moreover, both candidates made a personal appeal on the issue of youth unemployment, rather than emphasizing their parties' plans to tackle this issue in Congress or conveying the endorsement of relevant interest groups such as student confederations. And both relied heavily on television – the candidate-centered medium *par excellence* – to communicate their message.

In this book, I argue that the crucial similarities and differences among presidential campaign strategies in Latin America since the 1980s, including those of Bachelet and Lula, can be characterized in terms of three separate dimensions of campaign strategy: cleavage, linkage, and policy focus. In this section, I introduce these concepts and discuss how my definitions relate to those offered by other scholars. I also examine how cleavage, linkage, and policy focus matter for a country's quality of democracy via their implications for several of its component parts: participation, representation, and patterns of future governance (O'Donnell 2004; Diamond and Morlino 2005). I then go on to explain how different types of campaign strategy can be characterized in terms of these three dimensions.

Cleavage

I define cleavages as the fundamental lines of division in society that form the bases of political identity and have historically structured competition among parties and candidates. Candidates may choose to emphasize or "prime" particular cleavages during campaigns to gain strategic advantage over opponents or appeal to a particular segment of the electorate (Johnston et al. 1992). Alternatively, candidates may avoid emphasis on any cleavage, focusing instead on national unity and reaching out to the electorate as a whole. Unlike some scholars, I do not limit the category of cleavage to societal divides that are "active" in the sense of structuring voting behavior or political mobilization. Rather, I am concerned with politicians' *attempts* to activate or reinforce cleavages by priming them during electoral campaigns.

The most restrictive definitions of cleavage, all arising out of the study of Europe, specify that they must be based on social differentiation, provide distinct identity to those on alternate sides of the cleavage, and have institutional expression via a party, union, church, or other organization (Bartolini and Mair 1990; Gallagher, Laver, and Mair 1992; Knutsen and Scarbrough 1995; Whitefield 2002). Less stringent definitions drop one or more of these components, applying the term to sociological distinctions that make little difference for political identity or organization (Di Palma 1972; Baloyra and Martz 1979) or to groups defined by their support of a particular set of issues (Inglehart 1984).

I situate myself between the most restrictive and the least stringent definitions, applying the term "cleavage" to societal divides that serve as a distinct source of group identity and generally have a sociological basis but do not necessarily have institutional expression. Common cleavages include traditional social divides such as class, language, ethnicity, and religion, as well as the division between "the people" and "the political class" that is the subject of neopopulist appeals (Roberts 1995; Weyland 1996). "The people" may be an amorphous rhetorical category, but neopopulists effectively seek to unite specific sociological groups – primarily the urban informal sector and rural poor – against a ruling oligarchy that includes not only those in power but also the interests they serve and the system that perpetuates their rule (Collier 2001). The "political class" that neopopulists demonize is much broader and more permanent than current officeholders, and neopopulist discourse is clearly distinct from mere anti-incumbent language. Populism may seek to unify, but it also divides; without a clear group that can be cast as the enemy of "the people," populist appeals have little resonance (Hawkins 2003).

I also consider that cleavages can be formed around long-standing partisan divides not grounded in sociological distinctions as long as these generate a cultural sense of belonging or exclusion that leaves little room for societal indifference. As argued by Duverger (1959: 390), particularly sectarian parties tend to "introduce into public opinion irreducible cleavages which are not to be found in real life." Such parties socialize multiple generations of militants into unique partisan subcultures through membership in youth leagues, women's clubs, and other ancillary organizations, creating a political identity that may cut across class or other sociological categories (Ostiguy 1997). They also often convey a "for us or against us" discourse that profoundly alienates those on the outside. For these reasons, partisan cleavages are deeper and more durable than position with respect to particular issues or loyalty to a certain individual.

Cleavage priming during presidential campaigns can matter long after the election has been decided because of its implications for future governability and the terms of political debate. Politics is inherently about both conflict and compromise, but too much of either during a campaign can create problems in the future. A politician who wins an election with divisive rhetoric may encounter difficulties when it comes time to establish a majority governing coalition and pass legislation. On the other hand, candidates who inflame the public with cleavage-priming appeals may see fervent supporters become vehement opponents if they proceed to govern in a more conciliatory fashion and quash base-level expectations of radical change. Unity-oriented appeals may be a safer electoral strategy than cleavage priming, but ignoring the fundamentally divergent interests of societal groups may mean that important substantive issues remain absent from political debate. Addressing social and economic inequality through redistributive policies is difficult when political discourse denies the validity or even existence of basic divides among social classes.

Linkage

A second dimension of campaign strategy – linkage – can be defined as the channels between citizens and political elites that allow for mobilization and vote
seeking during campaigns. The key feature of linkages that concerns me is their
degree of organizational mediation (Eulau and Prewitt 1973: 365–366; Poguntke 2002). Intermediated linkages, which include unions, churches, and social
movements, connect politicians and citizens via an organization that plays a
key role in mobilizing its members and aggregating individual preferences into
a set of group demands. Direct linkages, which include television advertising
and candidates' personal interaction with voters during visits to public places,
connect politicians to citizens as individuals with individual interests and concerns. Several forms of linkage, such as networks of campaign volunteers or
candidate-centered support groups like Women with Bachelet in Chile's 2005
election, occupy a middle position with respect to organizational mediation;
they constitute intermediary groups but have no *raison d'être* apart from the
candidate's campaign.

Parties themselves also constitute a form of linkage that candidates may utilize to a greater or lesser extent during a campaign. All candidates formally
belong to parties, but these parties vary greatly in their age, permanence, membership, national presence, and degree of organization. Some are potentially
useful tools for reaching the electorate during the campaign, while others barely
have any presence beyond a national office and a handful of leaders. Even
those candidates who do belong to well-organized parties with militants and a
national structure may choose to circumvent their party during a campaign in
favor of direct linkages, either to gain a non-partisan or anti-party image or to
handle the logistics of campaigning in a more independent fashion.

The definition of linkage I employ is most similar to that developed in classic as well as contemporary research on American politics (Key 1961; Luttbeg
1968; Eulau and Prewitt 1973; Oppenheimer 1996; Hill and Hurley 1999;
Maggiotto and Wekkin 2000; Hurley and Hill 2003). However, it differs in
important ways from the conceptualization of linkage in many recent works
of comparative and Latin American politics. Following Lawson (1980, 1988),
a number of scholars have defined linkages not as the form of interconnection
between political elites and society but rather as the nature of the political bargain or exchange relationship between the two – what citizens get in return
for their support of a particular politician or party, such as clientelistic pay-
offs or programmatic policy commitments (Posner 1999, 2004; Kitschelt 2000;
Hawkins 2003, 2010; Mainwaring et al. 2006; Kitschelt et al. 2010; Morgan
2011; Luna 2014; Roberts 2014).

Conceptually separating the form of interconnection and the type of bargain
between citizens and elites allows for examining the effect of the former on the
latter, which has important implications for the quality of democracy. Linkages affect the degree to which citizens have bottom-up input into the political

agenda, versus being asked to decide among two or three options presented to them in a top-down, plebiscitarian fashion. Intermediated linkages through labor unions, churches, or social movements allow for collective action and pressure politics to ensure politicians' compliance with their part of the bargain. Programmatic modes of political exchange are thus more feasible when intermediated linkages prevail. In contrast, when politicians make exclusively direct appeals to voters, campaigns do not empower citizens in the same fashion, and clientelism becomes more likely.

Patterns of campaign linkage are also important because of their potential influence on the future governing style of politicians elected to office. Direct linkage strategies often involve distancing oneself from established intermediaries, including political party structures. They can thus leave a president bereft of allies once in office and dependent upon fickle public opinion for support. On the other hand, a heavy campaign debt to organized intermediary groups can limit a president's strategic maneuverability, potentially contributing to governing stalemate.

Policy Focus

A third dimension of campaign strategy is the degree to which a candidate's appeals focus on policy. A campaign message can be seen as policy focused to the extent that it provides insight into what the candidate intends to do in office. When not focusing on policy, candidates may appeal to voters on the basis of their image, personality, partisan affiliation, or numerous other criteria. Emphasizing one's own proposals scores highest in terms of policy focus, but other types of appeals, such as listing prior achievements or criticizing an opponent's platform, can also give insight into what type of policies a candidate would implement if elected. Within the range of policy-relevant appeals, I consider those that are future-oriented to constitute greater policy focus than those that look to the past, and those making acclaims about the candidate to be more policy-focused than those criticizing an opponent. The least policy-focused way of discussing substantive issues involves diagnosis – identifying problems or stating the importance of an issue without mentioning plans, describing prior achievements, or placing blame for others' failures.

It is important to distinguish policy focus from position on a left–right ideological continuum. By some measures, a candidate whose campaign emphasized a series of detailed yet centrist policy proposals might be thought of as less "programmatic" than one who was clearly leftist, but who denounced class inequalities without proposing solutions. Yet in the present measurement scheme, the leftist candidate would receive a high score only on the cleavage-priming dimension; the centrist candidate would be considered to have greater policy focus.

The degree to which candidates emphasize policy in their electoral appeals matters greatly for their accountability in office, an important component of

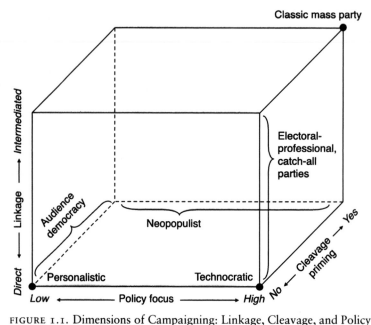

FIGURE 1.1. Dimensions of Campaigning: Linkage, Cleavage, and Policy Focus.

democratic representation. Politicians routinely depart from their campaign promises, sometimes for justifiable reasons (Stokes 2001). However, the costs to deviating from voters' expectations are lower if a candidate makes only vague statements about future policy and can argue that he or she was elected with a mandate of "change" rather than a specific and detailed platform. Campaigns that adopt a low policy focus, therefore, heighten the risk of unpleasant surprises under an ensuing government. Moreover, policy-vague campaigns facilitate the problem of delegative democracy. As described by O'Donnell (1994: 59), "delegative democracies rest on the premise that whoever wins election to the presidency is thereby entitled to govern as he or she sees fit, constrained only by the hard facts of existing power relations and by a constitutionally limited term of office." Maintaining this style of governance is much easier when citizens, media, and public opinion leaders have no basis for taking a president to task over a clear mandate violation.

Characterizing Campaign Strategies

By arraying cleavage, linkage, and policy focus along a continuum and treating each as separate dimensions of electoral campaigning, one can characterize a variety of distinct political strategies. The reference point for this discussion is Figure 1.1, a cube in which the height corresponds to direct versus intermediated linkage, the width represents the degree of policy focus in a candidate's appeals, and the depth describes the presence or absence of cleavage priming.[2]

Several types of parties identified in the study of European politics occupy the right-hand face of the cube in Figure 1.1. The upper-right rear corner represents the type of electoral campaign conducted by the classic mass party, which embodied one side of a social cleavage and devoted substantial effort – both inside and outside of campaigns – to priming that cleavage through the political education of its members (Duverger 1959: 63, 378). Electoral campaigns run by classic mass parties also had high policy content and drew heavily upon party militants to mobilize voters (Duverger 1959: 109–110, 378; Epstein 1967: 111–122, 261–262). In contrast, the campaigns of catch-all or electoral-professional parties, located at the right front edge, de-emphasize cleavages and seek to appeal to a large cross-section of voters by proposing policies that resonate broadly (Kirchheimer 1966; Panebianco 1988). Such parties connect with voters in a variety of ways, including interest groups and television, though the party itself, with a smaller membership, is not so crucial a form of linkage during campaigns.

While not identified in the literature as a separate form of party organization, it is useful to assign the label *technocratic* to the campaign strategy that combines high policy focus, direct linkages, and an avoidance of cleavage priming. The concept of technocracy is generally used to describe a governing elite whose qualifications include their technical skills and specialized academic training, as well as a policy-making style emphasizing efficient, rationalist decisions based on a single paradigm (Centeno 1993, 1994). Technocrats are obsessed with policy making and reject the idea that zero-sum social conflict is inherent in politics, so a technocratic campaign is policy-focused and avoids cleavage priming. Technocracy also implies a belief that the maximum social benefit can be achieved when the relationship between government and citizens does not pass through intermediary organizations that represent particular interests. Candidates adopting a technocratic approach may not actually have traditional technocratic backgrounds, but their appeals stress their policy-making qualifications, prior successes, and plans for the future, and they offer broad-based solutions for society in general rather than specific social groups.

Neopopulism, a particularly prominent electoral strategy in several Latin American countries, can be located at the lower rear edge of the cube. Neopopulism involves priming cleavages (typically the cleavage between the people at the political class) and also circumventing existing forms of intermediated linkage to appeal directly to voters (Roberts 1995; Weyland 2001; Boas 2005).

---

[2] The geometric metaphor is somewhat inexact, in that these separate dimensions of campaigning are not necessarily orthogonal. The use of intermediated linkages, for instance, is likely to imply a cleavage-priming campaign. As a result, the cube contains distinct clusters of campaign strategies as well as "empty space" with fewer empirical referents.

A particular level of policy focus is not inherent in the definition of neopopulism, though most instances of neopopulists coming to power in Latin America involved campaigns that were vague with respect to policy.

Neopopulism has received much attention in recent studies of Latin American politics, but I argue that the lower-left front corner of the cube – combining low policy focus, direct linkages, and minimal cleavage priming – is equally important. Candidates adopting this strategy, which I describe as *personalistic*, tend to portray themselves as likable individuals rather than results-oriented executives (a common technocratic appeal) or charismatic leaders engaged in a struggle against established interests (as with neopopulists). Often, their campaigns are heavy on empathy appeals, arguing that they understand the problems of various social groups and are prepared to implement largely unspecified policies once in office. If a neopopulist promises that "I will fight for you," and a technocrat says "I will solve your problems," a personalistic politician claims to "feel your pain." Personalistic strategies fall within the range of "audience democracy" as described by Manin (1997) – a phenomenon that is defined by low policy focus and the use of direct linkages.

The term "personalistic" is often used in a more general sense – for example, to describe party systems that center around individual politicians or parties that are invented for a particular candidate's campaign. In this book I use alternative terms, such as "personality-centered party system" or "personal electoral vehicle," to refer to concepts such as these, reserving "personalistic" for the campaign strategy outlined above.

THEORIES OF CONVERGENCE, EVIDENCE OF DIVERSITY

Existing arguments about the evolution of campaign strategies tend to posit that countries either move in parallel along one or more dimensions of campaigning or converge upon common scores on all three dimensions. Contrary to such predictions, the evolution of campaign strategies has followed very different trajectories in Chile, Brazil, and Peru since their transitions from authoritarian rule. In Chile and Brazil, candidates of Left and Right have converged on distinct national models that differ from one another with respect to policy focus. And in Peru, strategic heterogeneity has persisted over several decades; candidates' strategies were no more similar in 2006 than in 1980.

Classic theories of change in parties' electoral strategies predict either crossnational convergence on particular values of linkage, cleavage, and policy focus or a process of parallel evolution along one or more of these dimensions. Duverger (1959: 25) argued that conservative and middle-class parties were imitating the electorally successful structure and techniques of mass parties, in particular the use of party branches as a form of intermediated linkage. Epstein (1967: 257–260) countered this "contagion from the left" thesis with a claim of "contagion from the right," arguing that parties in Western democracies were adopting the successful media-centric (i.e., direct linkage) campaign techniques initially implemented by conservative parties. Kirchheimer's (1966) and Panebianco's (1988) arguments about catch-all and electoral-professional parties made similar claims of a broad transformation toward declining emphasis on cleavage and more use of direct linkages. Katz and Mair (1995) maintain that party change in Western democracies has followed a dialectical process through stages in which cadre, mass, catch-all, and finally cartel parties have been the dominant form. Likewise, Manin's (1997) notion of audience democracy is the final stage in a process of evolution through which a variety of Western democracies are expected to pass.

More recent theories of change in the nature of electoral campaigns also advance claims of convergence or parallel evolution across countries. Scholars embracing the notion of campaign modernization have described a series of stages, such as premodern, modern, and postmodern, through which all Western democracies are thought to pass (Blumler and Kavanagh 1999; Norris 2000). This process involves declining emphasis on cleavage and a shift from intermediated to direct linkages. A variant of the modernization thesis, Americanization, makes similar claims but identifies U.S.-style campaigns as the cause of transformation or the endpoint toward which other countries are progressing. Arguments about the professionalization of political campaigns (Farrell 1996; Mancini 1999) draw upon Panebianco's notion of the electoral-professional party and similarly emphasize a broad, cross-national transformation. Claims about the rise of political marketing (Scammell 1999) argue that the use of opinion polls and focus groups allows candidates to map the preferences of the electorate and craft a broadly resonant political appeal – generally, de-emphasizing cleavages. While some scholars have criticized the extreme notion of convergence inherent in these arguments and suggested that countries will only selectively implement "modern" or American techniques (Negrine and Papathanassopoulos 1996; Plasser and Plasser 2002), there have been no arguments explicitly theorizing why particular countries should end up with one style of campaigning versus another.

Most of the literature on changing campaign practices focuses on advanced democracies in Europe and the United States, but scholars of Latin America who have addressed the topic have generally adopted the same theoretical perspectives, including Americanization, modernization, and professionalization (Angell et al. 1992; Mayobre 1996; Waisbord 1996; Silva 2001; Tironi 2002; Rottinghaus and Alberro 2005). For the most part, these studies examine single countries or even single candidates, so they are not well suited to empirically assessing whether campaign practices are converging cross-nationally. Nonetheless, by adopting convergence-centric theoretical frameworks, they add to the impression that campaigns around the world are becoming more similar to one another.

The evolution of presidential campaign strategies in Chile, Brazil, and Peru tells a different story from the claims of the existing literature. Figure 1.2 illustrates how campaigns in the first two countries have evolved since the 1980s

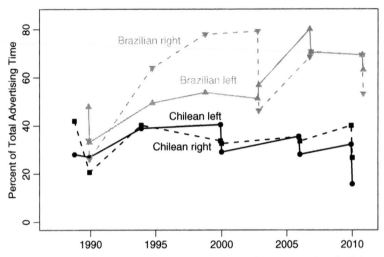

FIGURE I.2. Television Advertising Devoted to Policy in Brazil and Chile.

in terms of policy focus.[3] In the last several elections, Brazilian presidential candidates on both sides of the political spectrum devoted a roughly similar proportion of their television advertising to policy content, as did Chilean candidates. In 2005–2006, in particular, the Left and Right within each country differed by no more than a few percentage points. However, there were large differences – 39 percentage points in 2005–2006, and 35 percentage points in 2009–2010 – between the average policy focus of Chilean candidates and that of Brazilian candidates. Rather than converging cross-nationally, presidential candidates from Chile and Brazil devoted a similar proportion of their advertising to policy content in the late 1980s and have diverged in subsequent years.

Strategic contagion has also come from opposite sides of the ideological spectrum in Chile and Brazil. Table I.I scores six presidential campaigns in each country with respect to all three dimensions of campaign strategy. In Chile, the Left was the first to avoid cleavage priming, emphasize direct linkages, and campaign with a low policy focus. It has consistently adhered to this approach except in the first round of the 1999 and 2009 elections. The Right, however, fully embraced this strategy only starting in 1999. In Brazil, by contrast, strategic contagion has gone from Right to Left. In 1994, the Right was the first to utilize direct linkages, avoid cleavage priming, and focus heavily on policy. Right-wing candidates continued with this strategy in subsequent elections, while the campaigns of Workers' Party (PT) leader Luiz Inácio Lula da Silva steadily gravitated toward it.

---

[3] Data are drawn from content analysis of television advertising, as described in the section on Data Sources and Indicators and in Appendix A.

TABLE 1.1. *Contagion from the Left in Chile and the Right in Brazil*

CHILE		1988	1989	1993	1999	2005	2009
Left	Cleavage	No	No	No	Yes/No	No	No
	Linkage	Direct	Direct	Direct	Direct	Direct	Direct
	Policy	Low	Low	Low	High/Low	Low	High/Low
Right	Cleavage	Yes	Yes	No	No	No	No
	Linkage	Direct	Direct	Direct	Direct	Direct	Direct
	Policy	Medium	Low	High	Low	Low	Low

BRAZIL		1989	1994	1998	2002	2006	2010
Left	Cleavage	Yes	Some	No	No	No	No
	Linkage	Intermediated	Intermediated	Both	Both	Direct	Direct
	Policy	Medium	Medium	High/Low	High	High	High
Right	Cleavage	Yes	No	No	Some	No	Some
	Linkage	Direct	Direct	Direct	Direct	Direct	Direct
	Policy	Low	High	High	High	High	High

Note: Score1/Score2 represents a major strategic shift within a single campaign. Dark shading indicates a strategy fully consistent with the national model; light shading indicates one that is partially consistent. Scoring of policy focus is based on the data in Figure 1.2 as well as other indicators.

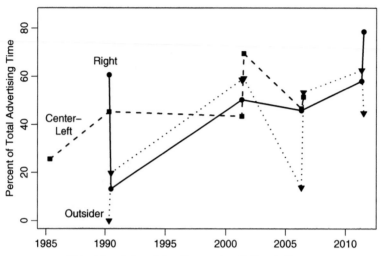

FIGURE 1.3. Television Advertising Devoted to Policy in Peru.

In contrast to Chilean and Brazilian candidates' convergence on unique national models of campaign strategy, presidential candidates in Peru have continued to employ very different approaches from one another. Figure 1.3 shows the policy focus of major candidates in Peru's 1985, 1990, 2001, 2006, and 2011 elections.[4] Candidates from different political sectors have not converged over time on either high or low policy focus. The range of this variable, from 0 to 78.5 percent, is much larger than in Chile or Brazil. None of these parties or political sectors illustrates anything resembling a stable trend over time. On the contrary, candidates have tended to implement major changes in campaign strategy vis-à-vis their predecessors and even the previous rounds of their own campaigns.

Table 1.2, which scores Peruvian candidates' strategies on all three dimensions, shows that there has also been no clear convergence over time with respect to linkage and cleavage.[5] The shifting back and forth between alternate strategic extremes has affected not only the policy dimension, but also cleavage priming (on the center-left between 1980 and 1990, and on the right during the 1990 campaign) and linkage (on the right after 1990).

In sum, the cases of Chile, Brazil, and Peru display nationally distinct patterns of campaigning in presidential elections that can be only partially accounted for

---

[4] I was unable to obtain television advertisements from the 1980 election, and from one major candidate, Barrantes, in the 1985 election. I also excluded the 1995 and 2000 elections from the content analysis portion of the study, since they occurred under Alberto Fujimori's authoritarian regime and involved widespread fraud and corruption (Conaghan 2005). However, the analysis of Peru in Chapter 4 does discuss each of these elections based on secondary literature.

[5] I score the campaigns of major candidates in the 1980 election based on secondary literature. There were no major outsiders prior to 1990, and no major right-wing candidates in 1985.

TABLE 1.2. *Continued Heterogeneity in Peru*

PERU		1980	1985	1990	2001	2006	2011
Center-Left	Cleavage	Yes	No	Yes	No	No	
	Linkage	Intermediated	Both	Intermediated	Both	Both	
	Policy	High	Low	High	High	High	
Right	Cleavage	No		No/Yes	No	No	No
	Linkage	(Direct)		Direct	(Intermediated)	Direct/Intermediated	Intermediated
	Policy	(Low)		High/Low	High	Low/High	High
Outsider	Cleavage			Yes	Yes	Yes	No
	Linkage			Direct	Direct	Direct	Direct
	Policy			Low	High	Low/High	High

Note: Score1/Score2 represents a major strategic shift within a single campaign. Parentheses indicate a higher degree of uncertainty because of limited data. Blank cells mean there was no major candidate from that sector. Scoring of policy focus is based on the data presented in Figure 1.3 as well as other indicators.

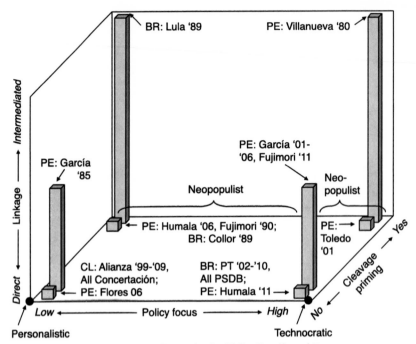

FIGURE 1.4. Major Campaign Strategies in Chile, Brazil, and Peru.

by theories emphasizing broad, parallel changes or cross-national convergence over time. Figure 1.4 depicts the linkage, cleavage, and policy focus positions of various presidential campaigns from these countries (vertical bars are used to locate the candidates in three dimensions; each candidate's point is at the top of the bar). Since the transitions to democracy, candidates have abandoned the top half of the cube, a space corresponding to campaigns that privilege intermediated linkage via political parties, interest groups, and social movements. This pattern accords with Katz and Mair's (1995) description of how parties are decreasingly serving as channels of representation, and also with the linkage-related claims of arguments about the professionalization and modernization of electioneering. Perspectives that emphasize broad transformations and convergence over time, however, cannot account for candidates in Chile, Brazil, and Peru ending up in such different places after they abandoned highly intermediated campaigns – nor can they explain why Chilean and Brazilian candidates have tended to converge on similar national styles of campaigning while Peruvian candidates have not.

Institutional, Structural, and Spatial Explanations

Institutional differences among Chile, Brazil, and Peru cannot easily account for these distinct patterns of campaigning. All three countries use the majority runoff formula in presidential elections and had compulsory voting during the period under study. They also have held concurrent legislative contests, with only a few exceptions (Brazil in 1989 and Chile in 1999). Brazil differs from the others in that it has allowed immediate presidential reelection for most of the period; incumbents might naturally focus on their prior accomplishments and thus run more policy-focused campaigns. However, similarly policy-centric appeals prevailed in 1994, 2002, and 2010 when no one was running for a second term.

Major structural differences among countries also do not provide a compelling explanation for the different patterns of campaigning. As noted at the outset of the chapter, average levels of education are much higher in Chile than in Brazil, making it somewhat counterintuitive that Chilean candidates focus much less on the details of their policy proposals. Likewise, despite substantial structural inequalities among different social classes and ethnicities in both Brazil and Peru, cleavage-priming appeals remain common only in the latter. Chile and Peru differ substantially in the size of their informal sectors (31.9 percent of the urban workforce in Chile in 2003, and 54.9 percent in Peru in 2005), and this aspect of the Peruvian economy has been advanced as an explanation for Fujimori's electoral success in 1990 (Cameron 1994, 1997). However, Brazil is close to Peru on this metric (49.1 percent in 2005) without having developed similar campaigning or party system dynamics (ILO 2006: 60–64). Moreover, at the time when both countries first experienced the election of neopopulist outsiders, levels of informality were much further apart (41.8 percent in Brazil and 60.2 percent in Peru in 1990).

Potential explanations for within-country convergence in electoral strategies also cannot distinguish between the very different forms that this process has taken in Chile and Brazil. One might be tempted to invoke structural explanations for the moderation of the Left – the end of the Cold War, economic globalization, and changes in the composition of the workforce – to explain contagion from Right to Left in Brazil. But such arguments cannot account for convergence in the opposite direction in Chile. Nor can the spatial tradition associated with Downs (1957) differentiate between these outcomes. Changes in electoral strategies in both Brazil and Chile have certainly involved shifts to the center; major left- and right-wing candidates in each country are now quite similar in their programmatic stances. But a theory predicting convergence on the policy preferences of the median voter does not explain why Brazilian candidates should campaign by emphasizing their essentially identical policy proposals while Chilean candidates campaign with a low policy focus.

Finally, the evolution of presidential campaign strategies in Chile, Brazil, and Peru does not appear to involve a "constant cause" (Stinchcombe 1968) in which candidates respond, perhaps at different rates, to societal conditions present across multiple elections. The threat of destabilizing the transition to democracy influenced the strategy of the Chilean opposition in the 1988 plebiscite, but such concerns had almost certainly ceased to affect candidates' decision-making by 1999, when convergence actually occurred. In Brazil, the context of hyperinflation that influenced candidates' strategies in 1989 and

1994 has long since faded. In Peru, the major societal problems that facilitated Fujimori's dark horse victory in 1990 – hyperinflation and terrorism – were effectively solved in subsequent years, and macroeconomic performance was positive in the 2000s. Yet new political outsiders have continually emerged as major contenders to replace unpopular incumbent presidents.

In sum, Chile, Brazil, and Peru exhibit no cross-national convergence in campaign strategies, contradicting the claims of existing theories. Structural and institutional differences among countries do not readily correspond to the distinct patterns of electioneering that have emerged, and potential explanations for within-country convergence cannot distinguish the different forms this process has taken in Chile and Brazil. Hence, a new theory is necessary to explain why Chile, Brazil, and Peru have adopted such distinct varieties of electioneering in the decades since democratization.

THE THEORY OF SUCCESS CONTAGION

This book develops a new theory, *success contagion*, that can account for distinct national patterns of electioneering in new democracies. The theory of success contagion holds that major candidates, regardless of ideological orientation, are likely to adopt the first victorious campaign strategy subsequently legitimated by a successful term in office for the elected president. The contagion of this model can occur both directly, with politicians explicitly imitating the strategies of previous candidates, and indirectly, with a national community of campaign professionals playing a key mediating role. Success contagion also implies a corollary: failure avoidance. Strategies that lead to electoral victory may be delegitimated by ensuing failure in office, prompting future candidates to avoid them. And when one president after another proves to be highly unpopular, candidates are likely to choose strategies through an inward-oriented process of reacting to previous errors within their own political camp.

In cases of success contagion, candidates' convergence on national models of campaign strategy creates isomorphic outcomes, just as organizations often converge upon forms and procedures that are similar to those of their peers (DiMaggio and Powell 1983). A central claim of the isomorphism literature is that actors are motivated to seek legitimacy, particularly when faced with uncertainty about the consequences of their actions. Legitimate strategies and behaviors are those that are most common in one's organizational field or employed by the most prestigious or successful organizations. Non-profit organizations and government bureaucracies are often motivated by legitimacy concerns, but such behavior has also been identified in studies of competing firms, where straying from established norms may negatively impact upon a company's performance (Lieberman and Asaba 2006). Even when there are competitive pressures to deviate from an industry's standard operating procedure, the space in which firms choose to do so may be bounded by legitimacy concerns (Deephouse 1999).

I argue that legitimacy is likely to play at least as large a role in presidential elections as in competition among firms. As with firms worried about customers' reactions to their behavior, performance and legitimacy can be intimately connected in the political realm if candidates perceive legitimacy concerns as influencing voters' decisions. During the compressed time frame of a campaign, with heightened media attention and a smaller number of relevant actors than in most competitive markets, the appropriateness of candidates' actions is likely to be more highly scrutinized. If voters disapprove of candidates' deviation from the informal rules of the game, the punishment they enact will be much more immediate than the similar effect of public opinion on a firm's sales. While pursuit of legitimacy is often seen as inimical to the pursuit of interests, in the present theoretical perspective they are linked by candidates' expectations of voter behavior.

Like firms entering a new marketplace, presidential candidates in a new democracy face uncertainty about the unwritten rules of the game and the strategies that might bring electoral victory. When taking part in a "founding election," many political actors have no prior campaign experience, while others are competing in a context far removed from that of previous democratic episodes. All candidates are confronted with new technologies – in the 1980s, primarily television advertising and opinion polls – that had scarcely been used in the past. Given this uncertainty, initial campaign strategies are likely to be heterogeneous, responding to the whims of candidates, the long-buried instincts of older democratic actors, and existing endowments such as a large volunteer labor force. Strategic diversity is likely to decline, however, once the strategy of a particular candidate is demonstrated to be effective at winning elections and also gains legitimacy among relevant campaign actors.

Of the three sources of institutional isomorphism identified by DiMaggio and Powell (1983), mimetic and normative mechanisms are most relevant to a theory of candidates' strategic behavior.[6] Mimicry involves actors voluntarily modeling themselves on their peers. In the management literature, mimetic isomorphism plays a central role in theories of bandwagons (Abrahamson and Rosenkopf 1993), managerial fads (Abrahamson 1991), follow-the-leader strategies (Haveman 1993), and the existence of strategic groups whose business models resemble one another (Deephouse 1999). Imitating the actions of other firms is particularly common when undertaking highly uncertain moves such as overseas expansion (Henisz and Delios 2001; Guillén 2002; Delios et al. 2008; Xia, Tan, and Tan 2008). Often the targets of mimicry, or those that set the pattern in motion, are the largest, most visible, most successful, or most prestigious firms (Burns and Wholey 1993; Haveman 1993; Haunschild and Miner 1997; Henisz and Delios 2001).

---

[6] The third source of isomorphism, coercion, involves pressure from an external actor and is thus less relevant to candidates' choices of electoral strategies.

Presidential candidates in a new democracy are also likely to imitate the behavior of those among their peers who have been most successful and prestigious – namely, the winners of prior presidential elections who went on to maintain a positive public image while in office. The combination of electoral and governing success confers legitimacy on a former candidate's campaign strategy and encourages others to copy it in subsequent elections. For instance, if the current president was elected on a pledge of national reconciliation and then maintained popularity for uniting a fractious country around a common national project, future candidates are likely to emulate these unity appeals not only because they helped win an election but also because they are associated with a prestigious incumbent.

For its part, the normative mechanism of isomorphism focuses on standard operating procedures that develop within professional communities and come to influence the behavior of organizations throughout a particular field. Normative isomorphism is distinct from outright mimicry because of the intermediary role played by these professional communities, who are often able to package recommended changes in more palatable terms than simply copying the tactics of successful competitors. For instance, in a study of accounting firms in Alberta, Canada, Greenwood et al. (2002) argue that the provincial and national accountants' associations played a key role in the expansion of their members' business models to include consultancy services. Large, internationally oriented firms initiated this change, but smaller firms were reluctant to follow suit. The role of the professional organizations "was to couch and frame the entrepreneurial movement in terms that nullified any emergent reluctance or opposition" (Greenwood et al. 2002: 74), presenting the change as a legitimate and necessary transformation of the industry.

In a similar fashion, the professionalization of campaign management can contribute to a process whereby particular norms and practices are spread as consultants work on the campaigns of different candidates. Political consultants in new democracies often sponsor training seminars and annual conferences or publish how-to books conveying the wisdom of their craft to colleagues and potential clients. As a result, strategies that were successful and became associated with prestigious politicians are likely to become institutionalized as standard operating procedures within the professional community. Such strategies can then readily spread across the political spectrum as these professionals are employed by candidates of varying ideological stripes. Where the diffusion of norms is the mechanism of contagion, candidates do not explicitly copy the tactics of a predecessor. Rather, they adhere to the recommendations of professionals whose standard approach incorporates a strategy introduced by the other side.

As with Greenwood et al.'s (2002) study of Canadian accounting firms, professional norms may play an important role in success contagion when those who have not yet adopted a particular strategy see themselves as fundamentally different from the politician or party who introduced it. Perceived differences limit the willingness to explicitly copy one's predecessors, so professional communities may need to help justify strategic change. For instance, candidates or parties with strong ideological profiles may be reluctant to reach across the political spectrum and adopt the tactics of their arch enemies, even if these tactics have been legitimated by both electoral and governing success. In such a context, campaign professionals may be able to recommend the same strategic changes in a more depoliticized and palatable fashion.

The normative mechanism of success contagion is also more likely to matter when a country has developed a strong professional community of political consultants. Among new democracies, federal systems with frequent elections at multiple levels of government generate the necessary demand for campaign expertise to help sustain a growing industry. Previous experience with electoral contestation – either during prior democratic episodes, or in the form of restricted elections under authoritarian rule – may mean there is already a nascent community of professionals waiting to expand. Larger economies and higher levels of economic development allow for a more diverse array of career options among the well educated, including niche occupations like political consultant. In new democracies that do not meet these conditions, campaign consultants may still exist, but they will be fewer in number and less likely to be organized into strong professional communities.

The development of norms within national communities of campaign professionals does not imply that all consultants think alike. Dissidents often emerge within campaign teams, recommending strategies that go against the conventional wisdom. Yet once a successful and legitimate model of campaign strategy exists, its proponents are typically able to prevail in internal disputes. Studies of firms have found that the success of particular strategies tends to empower those who crafted them and to weaken dissidents, making future repetition more likely (Miller and Chen 1994). Similarly, victorious campaign strategists are likely to be put in charge of the same party's future campaigns, and if they repeat a previously successful approach, they should have an easier time marginalizing those who disagree with it. The candidate may ultimately have the last word in factional disputes among advisers, but the arguments marshaled by those trying to win his or her confidence are important for the outcome.

Stability can be just as important as change for explaining isomorphic outcomes; strategies can only become more similar over time if the first ones to adopt a new approach stick with it while others subsequently join their camp. In the management literature, satisfactory prior performance has been highlighted as an incentive to maintain the status quo and not experiment with alternative approaches (Levitt and March 1988; Miller and Chen 1994). As Baim et al. (2000: 769) argue, "[g]iven initial success with an activity (i.e., few immediate negative consequences), organizations are likely to repeat it because they know increasingly well how to."

As with isomorphism among firms, political actors' convergence on a common strategy requires that the party or political sector to introduce the model not deviate from it in the future. There is often little incentive to alter an approach that brought victory for a candidate from the same party in the last election. Even when continued recourse to a previously successful strategy leads to an electoral loss, candidates and their advisors may not be motivated to change their approach. This is especially the case if losers view their opponent as having beaten them at their own game – that is, more effectively employing the strategy with which they themselves achieved victory in the past. Because strategic inertia of this sort involves the replication of a strategy by different candidates in successive elections, it can also be considered a mechanism of success contagion, albeit one that operates over time within a single party or group of parties rather than across the ideological spectrum.

Failure Avoidance

If presidential candidates are likely to adopt campaign strategies associated with prestigious incumbents, they also will tend to avoid those that were subsequently delegitimized by a president's abysmal record in office. For instance, if the current president was elected based on specific policy proposals and then failed miserably to deliver, the next round of candidates will be wary of appearing as "politicians who promise too much." Conversely, a governing failure following a campaign that was image- rather than policy-centric will encourage future candidates to be specific about their policy intentions. Candidates will not necessarily adopt the polar opposite strategy on all three dimensions, but they are likely to distance themselves from their predecessor with respect to those that were most salient during the campaign. What matters is the perception of how the electorate will respond to a new candidate whose tactics are reminiscent of a disgraced incumbent. As explained by one Peruvian political consultant, "voters' evaluation of the previous government's performance and the situation of the country has an important influence on the decision to vote for or against the government *or a candidate who has similar characteristics*" (Ventura Egoávil 2002: 10, emphasis added).

Why might a candidate's advisers expect voters to remember the prior campaign strategy of an unpopular president? In the new democracies to which the theory applies, the first several elections after a political transition tend to be dramatic, foundational moments in which major issues are at stake, including economic stabilization, human rights abuses under military regimes, or even the durability of democracy itself. The relevant electorate in these initial elections is quite distinct from the unengaged citizens of advanced democracies where "politics is boring."[7] Instances of governing failure also tend to be spectacular, involving extensive political corruption, inflation as high as 10,000 percent per year, and sometimes even terrorist violence.

Presidents in new democracies also frequently govern in a manner that is consistent with their campaign styles, so public memories of an incumbent's

---

[7] Engagement with electoral politics may, of course, decline significantly in later elections, as it has in Chile.

electoral strategy may be much fresher than the previous campaign. Reasons for this congruence between campaigning and governing strategies include habit, the elevation of campaign advisers to cabinet positions, and the constraints that a particular campaign strategy places upon the president's strategic maneuverability. For instance, one who campaigns as an anti-establishment outsider cannot easily change course once in office and make deals with the organized interests alienated during the election.

Even if public recollection of prior campaigns has grown fuzzy, a candidate who seeks to woo voters with the playbook of a disgraced predecessor is likely to find his or her opponents more than willing to point out the similarities. In Brazil's 2014 presidential election, for instance, Dilma Rousseff's television advertising drew explicit parallels between outsider Marina Silva, who was leading the polls with a vague message of "change," and Fernando Collor, who won the 1989 election with a similar approach before being impeached and resigning the presidency in disgrace. Flashing images of mass protests and newspaper headlines surrounding Collor's impeachment – as well as the resignation of Jânio Quadros, another "lone wolf" president from the 1960s – the spot intoned, "two times in our history, Brazil elected 'saviors of the homeland' ... and we know how that turned out."[8]

In countries where one president after another is unsuccessful in office, candidates are unlikely to converge upon a single campaign strategy. Lacking an attractive external model, they will instead tend to choose their strategies through an inward-oriented process of reacting to prior errors within their own party or political camp, rather than the outward-oriented search that generates contagion across the ideological spectrum. Drawing different lessons from these previous efforts, the candidates of different political tendencies may move in opposite directions from one campaign to the next, even leapfrogging each other in successive elections. Over time, these reactions and counterreactions can generate a zigzag trajectory in which candidates alternate between distinct strategies.

The lack of a dominant model of campaign strategy implies that strategic disputes within a campaign team are unlikely to be resolved in a common manner. Rather than being marginalized for going against a professional consensus about how campaigns should be run, advisors hawking alternative strategies will often convince the candidate to change course, especially when proposing a shift after a drop in the polls or some other indicator of poor performance. Hence, strategic zigzags may emerge not only from one election to the next, but also over the course of a single campaign.

As governing failures accumulate in a new democracy, it becomes less likely that a successful presidency will generate strategic convergence in the future. Uncertainty decreases as successive candidates learn to choose their strategies by reacting against the perceived errors of their predecessors. Looking across the ideological spectrum for an example of how to campaign is more natural

---

[8] Evening free electoral advertising program, September 2, 2014.

in the second election after democratization than in the seventh. Thus, there may be a limited window of time in which success contagion can occur in any country before a pattern of inward-oriented reactions is set in place.

The Expected Duration of Success Contagion

In cases where major candidates have converged on a common approach to electioneering, it is important to consider how long into the future this model should remain in place. Short of another prolonged episode of authoritarian rule, strategic convergence is most likely to be dislodged by a significant change in a country's party system, such as realignment or collapse, that affects the organizational continuity of the major actors competing in presidential elections. Outsiders often have little prior experience in politics, and they may enter the race with entirely new ideas rather than taking their cues from previous patterns of success and failure. With the demise of one or more established parties, one loses a group of political leaders who have internalized the lessons of prior campaigns and have often formed durable relationships with the national community of campaign professionals.

If a country's electoral dynamics are not interrupted by authoritarian rule or severely altered by party system realignment or collapse, the processes set in motion by success contagion should continue at least into the medium term, despite the occasional failed presidency. Once politicians have converged upon a single approach to electioneering and numerous successful presidencies have become associated with that strategy, candidates' uncertainty is greatly reduced. It is unlikely that one unsuccessful presidency would lead them to deviate from an established approach, unless that failure also contributed to significant party system change. One can think of the process as involving Bayesian updating, where multiple prior successes weigh more heavily than a single recent failure.

As democracies age, and voters who experienced a country's first post-transition elections are replaced by those who did not, one might expect candidates to be freer to stray from established models of campaigning. Yet the development of standard operating procedures among campaign professionals and political parties means that these models may survive generational turnovers in the electorate. The same mechanisms that contribute to the diffusion of campaign strategies among a national community of consultants also facilitate their perpetuation over time. In the United States, for instance, the lessons that consultants learned from the Kennedy–Nixon campaign in 1960 have persisted in an era when fewer and fewer voters actually participated in that election and none of the relevant campaign professionals are still actively advising candidates. Where the same parties present major candidates in successive presidential elections, a similar process of norm consolidation may take place among party leaders, perpetuating present-day patterns.

Despite the likelihood of strategic continuity in the short to medium term, it would be a mistake to extrapolate present-day patterns of electioneering into the indefinite future, even barring major party system changes or a reversion to authoritarian rule. Prevailing theories of the evolution of political institutions and public policies allow not only for major episodes of change brought on by exogenous shocks, but also for gradual change over time (Thelen 2003, 2004; Hacker 2004; Pierson 2004; Boas 2007). Patterns of political campaigning may be even more subject to incremental transformation than institutions or policies, since they do not carry the same logic of network effects and lock-in through increasing returns to scale. Hence, long-term sociological and technological transformations – for example, the demise of traditional intermediary organizations such as labor unions, the emergence of television as a new medium of campaigning, or their twenty-first-century equivalents – are likely to produce gradual changes in a country's dominant form of electioneering.

What Success Contagion Is Not

It is important to distinguish the theory of success contagion from several alternative models of candidate behavior or campaign dynamics. First, success contagion does not require that all major candidates converge upon the appropriate national model at the first opportunity, but rather that their strategies more closely adhere to this model over time. Change should be slower among certain types of candidates, such as those from parties with highly institutionalized internal rules and procedures (Panebianco 1988). In such organizations, candidates and their close confidants may favor strategic changes but confront internal obstacles, such as rules that prevent a candidate from hand-picking the campaign team. Some institutionalized parties also have greater sunk costs that can slow the pace of change, such as cadres of militants whose available volunteer labor predisposes candidates toward the use of intermediated linkages.

Success contagion does not mean that candidates and their advisors behave irrationally. Candidates are purposive actors, and in most cases, the top contenders are seriously trying to win the election. However, elections are complicated strategic terrain, and there is rarely a single, unambiguous course of action that will maximize one's chances of victory. Different groups of advisors often disagree about the best moves at particular choice points, and viable arguments are often marshaled in support of both sides. Such disagreement is particularly likely when the race is close or when a candidate is declining in the polls. Success contagion predicts that when making tactical decisions among two or more plausible alternatives, candidates will choose the option that is consistent with the established national model of campaigning. Whether such decisions ultimately help or harm the candidate's electoral chances does not change the decision-making logic that went into them. In demonstrating success contagion, therefore, it is less important to show that a candidate made an irrational or "wrong" decision than to show that he or she repeatedly chose the same course of action when faced with plausible alternatives.

Success contagion does not imply that candidates adhere mechanically to a single model of campaigning without trying to compensate for their own weaknesses, attack an opponent's vulnerabilities, or take advantage of opportunities arising during the campaign. In some instances, responding to these sorts of candidate-specific or conjunctural incentives may constitute partial deviations from the predominant national model of campaign strategy. Such deviations, however, are almost always small in magnitude when compared to differences across countries or to differences within a single country before and after convergence. The "anchoring heuristic" is likely to discourage actors from significantly altering established models of campaign strategy, just as it does with policy models (Weyland 2006a). Moreover, the causes of such deviations tend to be candidate- or election-specific factors that are unlikely to recur over time.

Nor does success contagion mean that candidates do not seek to distinguish themselves from their opponents. Within a given model of campaign strategy, there is plenty of room for differentiation: one cleavage-priming candidate may emphasize ethnicity while another focuses on religion, or one policy-focused candidate may stress social protection while another says more about public works. Competition, even bitter competition, will surely take place even when the range of strategies on the table has been limited.

Finally, the theory of success contagion should be distinguished from a model in which multiple candidates settle upon a largely predetermined style of campaigning through individual trial-and-error processes, randomly sampling different strategies until they find the one that is best suited to a country's structural conditions, electoral institutions, or political culture. In initial elections, the strategies of major candidates may tend to differ from one another, but neither the victorious nor unsuccessful candidates choose their approaches haphazardly. Heterogeneity in these initial elections arises from uncertainty and the fact that there are multiple plausible ways to choose purposively in an effort to win. The strategy that is victorious will probably be well suited to current conditions, but those conditions – the state of the economy, recent cases of political corruption, and so on – are likely to differ in subsequent elections. Moreover, the possibility of a country's first successful campaign strategy being delegitimized by poor performance in office – which could occur for any number of reasons – suggests that there is a great deal of initial contingency in where candidates eventually end up.

Delimiting the Scope of Success Contagion

In addition to distinguishing between success contagion and alternative models of candidate behavior or campaign dynamics, it is important to specify certain limits to the theory's scope. First, given the winner-take-all nature of presidential elections, minor candidates are usually playing a different game than major candidates – acting as spoilers, positioning themselves to trade a second-round endorsement for political deals with a new government, or simply pursuing media exposure to improve their future electoral prospects. For this reason, the theory of success contagion should only apply to candidates with a realistic chance of winning the election – a criterion that I operationalize below.

Certain characteristics of a country's party system may influence how well the theory of success contagion applies. The mechanisms described above tend to work best when there is broad organizational continuity over time – the same candidates, parties, or political coalitions competing in each election, or the same professional consultants participating in subsequent campaigns. When entirely different sets of political actors take part in successive electoral contests, each one may bring new ideas rather than experience to the table, making it difficult for anyone's strategy to converge on a model.

The theory of success contagion is also most applicable to countries that have recently experienced transitions to democracy, such that particular approaches to campaigning have not yet developed into stable routines and there is still uncertainty about what strategies will lead to victory. A model of successful and legitimate campaigning demonstrated during the first or second presidential election after democratization is thus more likely to lead to success contagion than one that does not emerge until much later on.

A final limitation is that the theory of success contagion should apply to scenarios in which actors can choose freely among alternative strategies, subject only to internal constraints such as power struggles among advisors or party rules and procedures that limit strategic flexibility. The theory is therefore less applicable to cases of electoral or competitive authoritarianism (Schedler 2006; Levitsky and Way 2010), where elections are routinely won through fraud, bribery, and intimidation of the opposition, and the campaign strategies of candidates on both sides are largely determined by the nature of the regime.

Absent external constraints, it is generally possible for candidates to adopt any strategy falling within the cube depicted in Figure 1.1. In any country where cleavages exist, candidates can decide whether or not to focus on them. Which specific cleavages they choose to emphasize may depend upon their ideological orientation – class cleavages tend to work against the Right, which may prefer to emphasize religious or regional divides (Gibson 1992) – but generally there is some plausible way that a candidate can divide the electorate in his or her favor. Cleavage-priming strategies may be more viable in multiparty systems, where one can profit from appealing to a minority of the electorate. Yet under majority runoff rules, these incentives also vary across rounds of the election; cleavage priming may work in a first round even if it is less advisable in the runoff.

Similarly, any candidate with proposals or past accomplishments can choose whether to structure a campaign around policy. An incumbent seeking a second term may naturally tend to focus on prior policy achievements because of the plebiscitary nature of reelection, but challengers have the option of running a similarly policy-focused campaign by criticizing the incumbent on policy grounds or stressing their own record of accomplishment in other offices. Challengers may also have an incentive to focus on their own proposals, arguing in favor of a new policy approach versus the incumbent's continuity of existing policies. In terms of a campaign's overall level of policy focus, it also should not matter whether candidates think voters are prospective or retrospective in their assessments, or whether one candidate has a greater incentive to criticize an opponent by virtue of being behind in the polls.

The only partial exception to the notion of freely chosen campaign strategies concerns the dimension of linkage. Candidates from parties with a well-developed structure and ties to interest organizations such as labor unions have the option of either utilizing these intermediaries during a campaign or circumventing them in favor of direct linkages. Candidates without well-organized parties or ties to established interest groups will probably not be able to construct these sorts of linkages in the course of a single campaign. Yet they may be able to build campaign-specific networks of volunteers or establish intermediated linkages via alternative organizations, such as churches, that have not previously been active in national politics.

Just because it is possible for a major candidates to adopt different strategies does not mean that in any given election, each strategic option will be equally plausible. Even when they are not subject to environmental constraints, candidates may have particular endowments that predispose them toward certain approaches. Those who are members of a structurally disadvantaged ethnic group that is large in number have the ability to prime ethnic cleavages, while other may not. Those with a technocratic background will surely have an easier time making convincing policy-centric appeals. There are more degrees of freedom in the strategic decisions of some candidates versus others. At the level of the individual candidate, one can account for these factors only in the course of a detailed case study. However, when choosing countries in which to examine instances of success contagion, one can select those in which a wide range of strategies are plausible, even if not equally likely for every candidate.

RESEARCH DESIGN

This study is a variant of nested analysis (Lieberman 2005) in which model-building small-N analysis is combined with subsequent model testing. My approach departs from the canonical example of nested analysis, where a researcher begins with a baseline theory and assesses its validity through large-N analysis before proceeding to conduct small-N comparisons. First, as in Lieberman's (2009) study of AIDS policy, there is little extant theory on the topic of interest; most discussions of the evolution of presidential campaign strategies in new democracies simply adopt frameworks from the literature on the United States and Western Europe. Second, no existing datasets score the outcome – campaign strategies as measured in terms of linkage, cleavage priming, and policy focus – in any way that would allow for an initial large-N analysis. A necessary first step, therefore, was to build a theory inductively based on the in-depth examination of a small number of country cases. The bulk of the analysis of Chile, Brazil, and Peru serves to illustrate the mechanisms and processes involved in the theory of success contagion as described above.

Testing the theory of success contagion takes two forms: a medium-N analysis of ten additional cases based on secondary literature, as well as examining presidential elections in Chile, Brazil, and Peru that occurred after the theory's formulation. Field research for the model-building small-N analysis was conducted in 2005–2006, and the initial version of this study (Boas 2009) was completed prior to the next round of presidential elections in 2009–2011. The theory of success contagion presented here has not been modified post-hoc to account for these recent elections, so in this sense they serve as a test of an argument that was formulated in advance. On its face, this test may not seem like a particularly strong one – the continuity of prior patterns for one more electoral cycle could be consistent with other explanations as well – so it is important also to test the theory's predictions in out-of-sample cases and over a longer period of time. Here, I have chosen to examine nearly every country falling into the same universe as Chile, Brazil, and Peru: third-wave presidential democracies with enough elections since their transitions that one could expect clear patterns to emerge.[9] Large-N analysis was not feasible for this model-testing stage, both because of the lack of existing datasets to score campaign strategies and because the number of cases (ten in addition to Chile, Brazil, and Peru) is too small.

Model-Building Case Selection

Country cases for this study's small-N analysis were chosen to approximate the strategy of achieving maximum variation on the dependent variable, an important goal for small-N comparative research designs (Collier and Mahoney 1996; Collier et al. 2004). Unlike with many qualitative studies, which often seek to explain puzzling outcomes known to the researcher in advance, fully scoring candidates' strategies in terms of linkage, cleavage, and policy focus was impossible prior to data collection. However, structural and party system features of Chile, Brazil, and Peru mean that candidates at least have the potential to choose a wide range of different campaign strategies. An additional justification for these cases is their similarity in terms of major electoral institutions, such as majority runoff, which helps to rule out alternative explanations for cross-national differences in campaign strategies.

---

[9] Restricting the theory to presidential systems is important in order to identify cases where a single elected official (as opposed to a majority party) is likely to bear responsibility for governing performance.

With respect to linkage, all major candidates in Chile, Brazil, and Peru have the option of crafting direct ties to voters, and at least some political actors could also plausibly draw upon intermediated linkages. The percentage of households with access to television, the main medium candidates use to make direct appeals to voters, is particularly high in Chile and Brazil, ranging from 78 percent at the beginning of the 1990s to 90 and 91 percent, respectively, in 2005 (World Bank 2008). This figure is well above the regional average for Latin America and the Caribbean, which ranged from 64 to 79 percent during the same period. Peru is someone below the mean on this variable, increasing from 61 percent in 1993 to 71 percent in 2005. However, the other major form of direct linkage – traveling around the country to campaign in person – is more feasible in Peru because distances between locations are not as great as they can be in Brazil and Chile.

The use of intermediated linkages is also plausible for at least some major political actors in Chile, Brazil, and Peru. One major party in each country is (or has been) a populist or class-based mass party with a well-developed national structure and important ties to labor unions. Brazil's PT also enjoys a relationship with a number of social movements, such as the Landless Rural Workers' Movement. Chile's Socialist Party has failed to maintain many of its ties to unions and social organizations during the new democratic period, though several other Chilean parties – the Christian Democratic Party and the Independent Democratic Union – have a well-organized national structure and important ties to the popular sectors (Pollack 1999; Huneeus 2001, 2003; Morales and Bugueño 2002; Barozet 2003; San Francisco 2003).

Priming cleavages during their electoral appeals is also a plausible strategy for presidential candidates in Chile, Brazil, and Peru. As countries that historically had labor-mobilizing party systems, they include one or more parties initially organized around either the class or populist cleavage. Relatedly, these three countries have relatively high levels of income inequality. In 2006, Brazil and Chile's GINI coefficients – 0.57 and 0.55, respectively – placed them higher than average in a region that is already the most unequal in the world. Peru's GINI coefficient (0.52) was slightly lower than the regional average, though it is also somewhat poorer than the other two.[10] These characteristics mean that priming class or populist cleavages is a plausible political strategy for those at the center or on the left of the political spectrum. In Peru and Brazil, non-white minorities make up about 45 percent of the population, suggesting that appeals to ethnic or racial cleavages are also strategic options for certain candidates. Finally, as I will argue in the respective country chapters, priming religious cleavages has at times been a viable strategy for right-wing politicians in each country.

In addition to these societal divides rooted in sociological differentiation, Chile and Peru have additional party- or regime-based divides that meet this

---

[10] Peru had a per capita GDP of $7,092 in 2006, versus $8,949 for Brazil and $13,029 for Chile (World Bank 2008).

study's definition of a cleavage. In Chile, the division between supporters and opponents of the prior military regime constitutes an important cleavage (Auth 1994; Tironi and Agüero 1999; Navia and Joignant 2000; Tironi 2002; Torcal and Mainwaring 2003). Prior to Pinochet's coup, political parties were deeply embedded in Chilean society, generating distinct and enduring partisan "subcultures" (Valenzuela and Valenzuela 1986; Garretón Merino 1993; Valenzuela 1995). Afterward, these multiple group identities were essentially collapsed into two: opposition to and support for authoritarian rule. As a result, Chile's once high levels of party identification have declined since the transition, while identification with the two electoral coalitions representing alternative sides of the 1988 plebiscite campaign has remained high (Tironi and Agüero 1999).[11]

In a similar fashion, the division between supporters and opponents of the American Popular Revolutionary Alliance (Alianza Popular Revolucionaria Americana, APRA) in Peru constitutes a long-standing cleavage that is deeply embedded in the country's political culture. The shared suffering of APRA partisans during the harsh repression of the 1930s, combined with a cult-like reverence for its charismatic founder Víctor Raúl Haya de la Torre, created an almost religious devotion to the party among its supporters. Out of this experience emerged an often sectarian, exclusionary "us versus them" discourse that tended to provoke intense opposition to the party among nonmembers and made it difficult for anyone to maintain a neutral stance. The APRA/anti-APRA cleavage sometimes transcended other, more traditional divides, with the Communist Party forming anti-APRA alliances with the political Right (Graham 1992: 13–14, 26–27, 36).

Elections and Candidates

Within each country, this study examines all direct presidential elections, starting with the transition from authoritarian rule and ending with those held during 2009–2011. As discussed above, the most recent round of presidential elections in each country is treated as a test of the theory, which was formulated based on those up through 2005–2006. The sample includes elections that occurred as part of the transition itself – Peru's 1980 presidential election and Chile's 1988 plebiscite and 1989 presidential election. I do not examine the 1985 "founding election" of Brazil's new democracy because the president was chosen indirectly by existing legislators. I also treat the Peruvian elections of 1995 and 2000 in a secondary manner, given that they took place under an authoritarian regime and involved widespread manipulation and fraud (Kay 1996; Schmidt 2000; Youngers 2000; Levitsky and Cameron 2003; Conaghan 2005).

---

[11] In a December 2006 survey conducted by Chile's Centro de Estudios Públicos, a majority of identifiers with each of Chile's five main political parties said they identified more closely with the corresponding coalition than with the actual party.

In order to focus on the political actors who are most likely to adhere to the logic of success contagion, I examine only the major presidential candidates – those whose performance in the first round suggests that they had a reasonable chance of winning the election. I define major candidates as the first- and second-place finishers, plus any third candidate that received over 20 percent of the valid vote.[12] This decision rule can be considered a Latin American presidential-election equivalent to Sartori's (1976: 122) criterion that parties have "governing potential" in order to be relevant to party system dynamics. To the best of my knowledge, no candidate receiving less than 20 percent of the valid vote in the first round of a Latin American presidential election has both qualified for and been victorious in the runoff.

The candidates and elections under consideration are listed in Table 1.3. In the chapters that follow, I focus on the campaigns and specific elements of campaign strategy that are most important for illustrating the mechanisms of success contagion. For campaigns establishing a strategic model that later diffused across the ideological spectrum – the "No" campaign in Chile's 1988 plebiscite, and Cardoso's 1994 campaign in Brazil – I explicitly discuss all three dimensions of campaign strategy. I do the same for their unsuccessful competitors ("Yes" in Chile in 1988, and Lula in Brazil in 1994), as well as for Collor's 1989 campaign in Brazil, a model I argue was not adopted due to governing failure. Fully scoring these baseline campaigns is necessary for assessing subsequent convergence or lack thereof. For future campaigns in Brazil and Chile, and for all campaigns examined in Peru, I focus on those dimensions that best illustrate mechanisms of the theory of success contagion as well as those representing deviations that call for explanation. I pay less attention to other strategic dimensions of these campaigns, as well as to several campaigns for which I had difficulty obtaining data (e.g., Belaúnde 1980 in Peru) or which are less useful overall for characterizing the evolution of campaign strategy in each case (e.g., Barrantes 1985 in Peru, Cardoso 1998 in Brazil).

Model-Testing Case Selection

As formulated above, the theory of success contagion should apply to presidential election strategies in other cases of third-wave transition from authoritarian rule. To test the theory beyond the empirical context in which it was formulated, I draw on secondary literature to examine the evolution of presidential campaign strategies in ten additional countries: Argentina, Benin, Ecuador, Ghana, Honduras, Mali, Nicaragua, the Philippines, South Korea, and Uruguay.

---

[12] The valid vote excludes null and blank ballots, and is the baseline used to determine whether a candidate wins outright in the first round (by receiving more than 50 percent) or whether a second round is held.

TABLE 1.3. *Scope of the Book: Elections, Candidates, and First-Round Valid Vote*

		1st Place	%	2nd Place	%	3rd Place > 20%	%
Brazil	1989	Fernando Collor	30	L. I. Lula da Silva	17		
	1994	F. H. Cardoso	54	L. I. Lula da Silva	27		
	1998	F. H. Cardoso	53	L. I. Lula da Silva	32		
	2002	L. I. Lula da Silva	46	José Serra	23		
	2006	L. I. Lula da Silva	49	Geraldo Alckmin	42		
	2010	Dilma Rousseff	47	José Serra	33		
Chile	1988	"No" option	56	"Yes" option	44		
	1989	Patricio Aylwin	55	Hernán Büchi	29		
	1993	Eduardo Frei	58	Arturo Alessandri	24		
	1999	Ricardo Lagos	48	Joaquín Lavin	48		
	2005	Michelle Bachelet	46	Sebastián Piñera	25	Joaquín Lavín	23
	2009	Sebastián Piñera	44	Eduardo Frei	30	M. Enríquez-Ominami	20
Peru	1980	Fernando Belaúnde	45	Armando Villanueva	27		
	1985	Alan García	53	Alfonso Barrantes	25		
	1990	Mario Vargas Llosa	33	Alberto Fujimori	29	Luis Alva Castro	23
	1995	Alberto Fujimori	64	J. Pérez de Cuéllar	22		
	2000	Alberto Fujimori	50	Alejandro Toledo	40		
	2001	Alejandro Toledo	37	Alan García	26	Lourdes Flores	24
	2006	Ollanta Humala	31	Alan García	24	Lourdes Flores	24
	2011	Ollanta Humala	32	Keiko Fujimori	24		

Source: Georgetown Political Database of the Americas, http://pdba.georgetown.edu. In some cases valid vote was given; in others it was calculated by excluding blank and null ballots.

To choose cases for model testing, I first sought to identify present-day democracies, which I defined as countries whose Freedom House scores for political rights were no higher than 3 for any year between 2000 and 2006 (the most recent year available at the time of initial case selection). I then restricted the sample to countries that had experienced a transition from authoritarian rule after 1974 and adopted a presidential system of government.[13] Of the resulting group of countries, I focused on those that had held four or more presidential elections since their transition to democracy or resolution of civil war, given that convergence in both Chile and Brazil did not occur until the fourth election. Finally, I eliminated one country (the Seychelles) for lack of sufficient secondary literature. Several countries experienced backsliding after 2006, earning scores of 4 or higher in subsequent years, and Honduras and Mali suffered military coups in 2009 and 2012, respectively. However, all of these countries continued to hold elections – in the case of Mali, with a delay – so I have retained them in the sample.

Operationalizing Governing Success

In order to apply the theory of success contagion consistently across countries, it is important to operationalize governing success in a way that can be objectively scored based on readily available data yet also accounts for the subjectivities of national politics and public opinion. Based purely on economic and social indicators such as GDP growth or poverty reduction, Alan García would easily be judged a more successful president of Peru in the 2000s than Fernando Henrique Cardoso was of Brazil in the 1990s. Yet Peruvian and Brazilian public opinion would tend to disagree with this assessment.

I define a successful presidential term as one in which the incumbent has more public approval than disapproval at the start of the next electoral campaign (or, for those presidents who leave prematurely, at the end of their time in office). Presidential approval data are readily available for numerous countries and leaders, allowing for an objective characterization of each term in office. Yet these figures themselves also take into account the vagaries of national public opinion, allowing for a president to be judged unsuccessful because of personal scandals or leadership failures that are not reflected in national statistics. I focus on presidential approval just prior to the start of the next electoral campaign, when candidates are formulating their strategies and taking public attitudes into account, yet campaign dynamics themselves are unlikely to have had much impact on the numbers. Table 1.4 summarizes the end-of-term approval and disapproval ratings for the relevant incumbents in Chile, Brazil, and Peru, along with a summary judgment of success. I characterize presidents for the model-testing cases in Chapter 5.

---

[13] I thus exclude Bolivia from consideration, which employed a hybrid system of "parliamentarized presidentialism" until 2009 (Linz 1994: 85–86; Mayorga 1997; Centellas 2007).

TABLE 1.4. *Measuring Success: End-of-Term Approval Ratings*

	Date	President	Approve	Disapprove	Success
Brazil	March 1992	Fernando Collor	15%	35%	No
	July 1998	F. H. Cardoso	38%	19%	Yes
	July 2002	F. H. Cardoso	31%	26%	Yes
	July 2006	L. I. Lula da Silva	38%	21%	Yes
	July 2010	L. I. Lula da Silva	78%	4%	Yes
Chile	July 1993	Patricio Aylwin	54%	28%	Yes
	May 1999	Eduardo Frei	32%	40%	No
	July 2005	Ricardo Lagos	61%	18%	Yes
	August 2009	Michelle Bachelet	72%	15%	Yes
Peru	January 1985	Fernando Belaúnde	20%	–	No
	January 1990	Alan García	18%	–	No
	January 1995	Alberto Fujimori	64%	–	Yes
	January 2000	Alberto Fujimori	55%	–	Yes
	November 2000	Alberto Fujimori	24%	–	No
	January 2001	Alejandro Toledo	13%	82%	No
	January 2006	Ollanta Humala	30%	65%	No

Note: Approval ratings are the last figures available prior to the start of the next presidential campaign or the president's removal from office.
Sources: Datafolha (Brazil), Centro de Estudios Públicos (Chile), Datum (Peru: Belaúnde), and Apoyo Opinión y Mercado (Peru: all others). Peru figures prior to 2001 are for Lima residents only. Survey questions for Chile and Brazil also include an in-between option ("so-so" performance, or "neither approve nor disapprove").

DATA SOURCES AND INDICATORS

The argument of this book draws upon four original data sources: content analysis of campaign advertising, interviews with key political actors, coverage of each campaign in local print media, and, for the 2005–2006 electoral cycle, direct observation of campaign events. The first source examines candidates' advertisements aired on broadcast television. I assembled a collection of television advertisements for nearly all of the candidates and campaigns listed in Table 1.3, a total of sixty-nine hours of video. I then coded segments of advertising according to a number of common categories, such as acclaims versus criticism and the presence of cleavage priming. Appendix A describes the format of televised campaign advertising in each country, the population and sample analyzed, the basic coding procedure, the calculation of summary statistics, and the results of inter-coder reliability testing. The coding instructions and coding sheet used in inter-coder reliability testing are reproduced in Appendices B and C.

A second data source involves semi-structured interviews with key participants in each of the campaigns through 2005–2006. I conducted more than 170 interviews, primarily during five months of field research in each country during or shortly after its 2005 or 2006 campaign. Many of the interview subjects had participated in multiple presidential campaigns, so these interviews covered 236 "campaign-jobs," or an average of six per campaign. I sought to interview three different types of actors: those responsible for overall campaign direction and strategy, such as campaign managers or party leaders; those specifically in charge of communication, media, and advertising strategy; and those dealing with mobilization, the coordination of volunteers, and the organization of campaign events. In particular, my interviews sought to gain insight into a campaign's internal strategic disputes, such as when one faction advocated attacking an opponent's prior governing record and another favored a strictly positive appeal. I always tried to interview individuals on both sides of these disputes and was generally successful in doing so.

A third source of data consists of newspaper and magazine articles on the various campaigns. In Chile, I consulted an archive of campaign-related articles from a variety of newspapers and magazines during the year before each election. In Brazil and Peru, I reviewed daily coverage of the campaign in major newspapers (*Folha de São Paulo* in Brazil, *El Comercio* and *La República* in Peru) during the 4–6 months prior to each election. I also reviewed weekly coverage of each election in Peru's major newsmagazine, *Caretas*. The review of print media sought to assess what the campaigns were doing beyond the television screen, including such activities as rallies, canvassing by volunteers, or negotiations with allied party leaders.

Throughout the book, I triangulate between content analysis, interviews, and print media coverage to characterize campaign strategies and assess why candidates and their advisors adopted a particular approach. To score policy focus, I rely primarily on the content analysis, focusing on indicators such as the percentage of a candidate's total advertising time that is devoted to policy in general (the metric depicted in Figure 1.3) as well as to more specific purposes such as criticizing an opponent's performance in prior office. Evidence of cleavage priming draws on the content analysis as well as print media coverage and interviews. Some candidates remain strictly positive in their television advertisements but engage in confrontational discourse when speaking to a crowd, so it is important to examine multiple areas of campaign communication. I score linkage based primarily on interviews and print media coverage, with some additional evidence drawn from television advertising, such as candidates seeking to minimize party symbols and appear alone on screen rather than surrounded by allies. Finally, interviews are the primary source of evidence about the mechanisms involved in strategic choices – inertia, imitation, professional norms, and inward-oriented reactions.

For the 2005–2006 presidential campaigns, a final source of data consists of direct observation of campaign events. I attended most candidates' first- and second-round closing rallies in Santiago, Lima, and São Paulo, as well as a handful of events in these cities at earlier points in the campaign. I also accompanied four candidates – Michelle Bachelet and Sebastián Piñera in Chile, and Lourdes Flores and Ollanta Humala in Peru – on campaign trips to smaller towns outside of the capital. As a result of these efforts, I was able to see every candidate at a major rally at least once, and several of them many more times.

I rely on the direct observation of campaign events as a reality check to assess the validity of measurements drawn from other, more distant sources of data. Thus, for instance, I compared information gleaned from interviews and print media coverage of the campaign with my own observations regarding the relative importance of rallies versus other campaign events, the role of volunteer labor versus professionals in logistical work, how many people attend rallies and how many party flags are prominently displayed, whether there is an obvious presence of labor unions or other organized civil society groups, and how the candidate's speeches differ from the messages communicated via television advertising.

THEORETICAL INSIGHTS: CAMPAIGNS, CONSULTANTS, DIFFUSION, AND PROGRAMMATIC COMPETITION

This book seeks, first and foremost, to fill an important gap in the study of Latin American and comparative politics. For many comparativists who follow current events in their countries of interest, campaign strategies are inherently fascinating. But beyond brief post-election reports in *Current History*, *Journal of Democracy*, and *Electoral Studies*, sustained attention to electioneering has been rare in comparative politics, especially in the study of new democracies.

Among Latin Americanists, most scholarship has taken campaign strategies as an independent rather than dependent variable, seeking to explain their effects on voting behavior and public opinion rather than variation in these strategies themselves. The consensus of this literature is that campaigns in Latin America, in the form of candidates' direct communication to the public or of electoral coverage by commercial news media, can have substantial effects on attitudes and on action at the polls. A first reason is that relatively low levels of mass partisanship make voters more susceptible to persuasion than in advanced democracies. A second factor is that voters tend to have more limited preexisting stores of political information – in part, because of routinely biased media coverage – which leaves them liable to be influenced by new information gleaned during a campaign (Boas 2005, 2015; Lawson and McCann 2005; Baker et al. 2006; Greene 2011).

That campaign strategies potentially matter for voting behavior – and, by extension, electoral outcomes – is an important reason to study the choice of strategies in the first place. Yet Latin Americanists have devoted much less attention to the latter question. For example, the edited volumes emerging out of the Mexico Panel Studies project have examined the presidential elections of 2000, 2006, and 2012 in great detail (Domínguez and Lawson 2004; Domínguez et al. 2009; Domínguez et al. 2015). Yet their empirical and theoretical emphasis is on the question of campaign effects rather than campaign strategy. A few chapters in these volumes do examine parties' and candidates' strategic choices in each election (Bruhn 2004, 2009, 2015; Langston 2009; Shirk 2009). However, the focus is on describing the election at hand rather than explaining strategic change and continuity over time or drawing broader comparisons. Moreover, these chapters make little use of proximate data sources, such as content analysis of television advertising or interviews with campaign advisors, to characterize campaign strategy.

Given the limited research, much of what we know (or think we know) about campaign strategies in Latin America comes from nonacademic sources – journalistic or autobiographical accounts of political consultants' activities abroad (Séguéla 2000; Harding 2008; Greenberg 2009), as well as films such as *No* (a 2012 drama about the 1988 Chilean plebiscite) and *Our Brand is Crisis* (a 2005 documentary about Bolivia's 2002 election). Each of these accounts conveys elements of truth but also presents a distorted picture of the campaign as a whole, overstating the importance of campaign professionals and modern techniques such as television advertising. If we believe that campaign strategies can matter for election outcomes in new democracies – not to mention democratic quality – we should have a better understanding of how they are chosen.

Political Consultants

In addition to filling a gap with respect to research on campaign strategies in new democracies, this book aims to contribute to a number of related literatures that have attracted more scholarly attention. A first concerns the role of political consultants. Research on American politics has long recognized the important role of consultants in campaigns for all levels of government (Sabato 1981; Herrnson 1988; Thurber and Nelson 2000; Johnson 2001; Dulio 2004; Johnson 2012). Much of this literature's conclusions jibes with my arguments about Latin American consultants' work in their own countries, especially Brazil. American political consultants form an increasingly well-developed professional community, with high levels of consensus regarding ethical standards, norms of appropriate campaigning, and best practices (Grossmann 2009). As they work on the campaigns of different candidates, U.S. consultants facilitate the diffusion of particular approaches with respect to negative advertising, risk taking, and choosing which policy issues to emphasize (Francia and Herrnson 2007; Grossmann 2012; Nyhan and Montgomery 2015). Some predict that consultants' professional norms will prompt within-country convergence in campaign strategies (Grossmann 2009), though others expect increasing similarities only along party lines, given U.S. consultants' tendency to work exclusively within Republican or Democratic Party networks (Nyhan and Montgomery 2015).

For all the work on political consultants in the United States, however, scholars have virtually ignored their counterparts in other democracies. Rather, comparative research on campaign professionals has focused almost exclusively on the international activities of American consultants, with a few mentions of Europeans who have also conducted campaigns abroad (Swanson and Mancini 1996; Farrell 1998; Bowler and Farrell 2000; Plasser 2000; Plasser and Plasser 2002; Sussman and Galizio 2003; Sussman 2005). Only in the case of Russia has there been any English-language scholarship examining a national community of campaign consultants outside of the United States (Wilson 2005; Ledeneva 2006).

I argue that, in many democracies, local campaign professionals are likely to be more influential than those from abroad. Prominent international consultants certainly steal the spotlight. American and European "spin doctors" working their magic around the world make for more compelling headlines than the role of lesser-known locals, even when the latter are more influential (Kramer 1996; McFaul 1996). For their part, academics may be drawn to a focus on globe-trotting consultants because of normative concerns about this phenomenon (e.g., Sussman 2005). Yet there are many reasons why candidates in other countries might rely heavily or exclusively on domestic campaign professionals. Consultants from Europe and the United States typically charge similar rates for work around the world, placing them out of reach for less wealthy candidates. Language and cultural barriers can discourage hiring international consultants or limit their influence when advising the campaign team. Candidates may also be wary of a nationalist backlash if word gets out about their reliance on foreign "hired guns" (Farrell 1998). Among the campaigns examined in this study, hiring a foreign consultant was the exception rather than the rule.[14] Even where they did participate, foreign consultants – who typically come and go during the campaign season as they attend to clients around the world – often had to compete for influence with local strategists who were constantly on the ground offering advice.

This study's focus on national communities of campaign professionals in Latin America offers a complement to research on the professionalization of consultants and their role in the diffusion of campaign strategies in the United States. In particular, it highlights that the assumptions, norms, and standard operating procedures of American political consultants are not universal to the profession, and that very different notions may develop in other national contexts. For example, the prevailing opinion among American campaign consultants, repeatedly confirmed in surveys and studies of the industry, is that negative advertising is both ethical and effective (Sabato 1981: 165–166; Kern 1989: 25–26; Perloff and Kinsey 1992; Thurber and Nelson 2000: 191–192; Dulio 2004: 36; Mark 2006; Grossmann 2009). A very different belief prevails in

---

[14] In only four of forty-five campaigns examined in this study – Vargas Llosa 1990, Flores 2006, and Humala 2011 in Peru and Lagos 1999 (first round) in Chile – did foreign campaign consultants constitute a major source of strategic advice. Foreign consultants played a more limited role in the "Yes" 1988, "No" 1988, and Büchi 1989 campaigns in Chile and the Cardoso 1994 campaign in Brazil.

Chile, rooted in a distinct historical experience. In the words of Eugenio Tironi (2002: 78), one of Chile's most influential political communication consultants, "organizing a campaign around a denunciation of the system, the government, or one's opponent generates more rejection than support – which is proven in Chile ever since the campaign for the 'No' in the 1988 plebiscite, whose stroke of genius was precisely to avoid falling into that temptation."

Policy Diffusion

A second area of literature to which the book contributes concerns the international and subnational diffusion of public policies. Like campaign strategies within a country, the public policies employed at distinct levels of government often become more similar over time, and political scientists have sought to document and explain these patterns of change across numerous different policy areas. I have chosen to ground the theory of success contagion in the sociological and management literature on isomorphism rather than the political science literature on policy diffusion because I consider political candidates more akin to competing firms than to the technocrats who typically make public policy decisions. However, the present study holds several insights for the policy diffusion literature.

First, this study suggests that the diffusion literature's sharp theoretical distinction between learning and imitation is overstated. Typologies of diffusion mechanisms routinely distinguish between learning, which involves a clear goal-oriented effort to adopt the most effective policy based on demonstrated success or failure, and imitation or emulation, in which norms, legitimacy, and standard operating procedures come into play (Elkins and Simmons 2005; Holzinger and Knill 2005; Meseguer 2005, 2009; Weyland 2005, 2006a; Braun and Gilardi 2006; Karch 2007; Shipan and Volden 2008; Simmons et al. 2008; Gilardi 2012; Graham et al. 2013; Maggetti and Gilardi 2015). Learning is not always fully rational – policymakers may rely on cognitive heuristics that lead them to make suboptimal decisions – but it is always purposive (Meseguer 2005, 2009; Weyland 2005, 2006a). Scholars sometimes admit that these distinctions are less clear in practice, or that multiple mechanisms may be at play in any one diffusion process (Simmons et al. 2008; Graham et al. 2013), but success-driven learning and legitimacy-driven imitation are thought to be theoretically distinct.

In line with Glick (2013), I argue that learning from success and seeking legitimacy should not be seen as inimical strategies, especially when performance depends upon avoiding sanctions from an external monitor, such as voters or regulators. Behavior that falls outside of the mainstream may be more likely to alienate a candidate's electoral supporters. In this case, conforming to standard operating procedures matters for an actor's success because it is a criterion valued by the monitor. This insight is relevant not only to campaign and corporate strategies but also for public policies. Gilardi (2010) has sought to broaden the definition of success-driven learning – arguing that politicians may also consider a policy's implications for their reelection prospects – while still considering this mechanism distinct from imitation. Yet if voters care whether a policy falls outside of the mainstream – such as, for example, a zero-tolerance policing policy that is effective but also unusually draconian – the clear distinction between imitation and learning breaks down.

A second, and related, theoretical insight stems from an apparent puzzle: why should we observe little cross-national convergence in campaign strategies when there has been so much cross-national convergence in public policies, both in Latin America and beyond (Heichel et al. 2005; Holzinger and Knill 2005; Weyland 2005, 2006a; Simmons et al. 2008; Meseguer 2009)? In the policy diffusion literature, rational learning predicts convergence on models that have been demonstrated to be successful anywhere in the world. Bounded learning and imitation also imply cross-national convergence, albeit on a smaller, often regional scale. Yet none of these mechanisms predicts the pattern we observe with campaign strategies in Chile and Brazil – greater cross-national differentiation over time, and increasing similarity only within countries.

An answer is suggested by research on policy diffusion at the subnational level, particularly across states or provinces within a federation. The literature on policy diffusion among U.S. states has often assumed that rational learning is the primary mechanism – the United States is conceived of as a "laboratory of democracy" in which states experiment with different policy approaches and those that prove most successful are eventually adopted more broadly (Boushey 2010). Yet, to my knowledge, this literature has never looked systematically at whether U.S. states consider adopting state-level policies in other federal democracies around the world, as the rational learning perspective insists that they should. Presumably this practice is uncommon, but not because successful policies are rarely developed in other federations. Rather, U.S. state policymakers are probably more aware of the policies of, say, California than those of Ontario or Bavaria – a bounded reasoning explanation – or else they assume that foreign solutions are less appropriate for their own reality – a legitimacy-driven thought process.[15]

As with policy diffusion among U.S. states, I argue that presidential candidates in new democracies are more likely to turn to successful examples within their own countries than those that come from abroad. The clustering of policy innovations along geographical lines, or among countries with similar history, cultural background, political regimes, or socioeconomic conditions, is often attributed either to the availability heuristic, in which more proximate policy innovations are better known and thus more influential (Elkins and Simmons

---

[15] The few examples I have encountered of subnational governments considering or adopting policies from abroad involve similarities that would be consistent with heuristic- or legitimacy-driven reasoning. For example, Washington State looked to the bordering Canadian province of British Columbia when studying policies for forest fire prevention and management (Glick and Friedland 2014). Likewise, Switzerland's smoking ban, copied from Italy, was first implemented in an Italian-speaking Swiss canton on the border between the two countries (Gilardi 2012).

2005; Weyland 2005, 2006a), or else to what Simmons et al. (2008: 37) dub the contingency hypothesis – that policy solutions from similar countries are considered more appropriate to local conditions and more likely to succeed. In contrast to most national policymakers, but similar to those at the state level, presidential candidates have multiple examples of alternative strategies in their own country, drawn from current or recent elections. These domestic models are as proximate as possible – they were employed in the exact same national context – so they are likely to be more "available" than foreign models and also to be considered more appropriate to local conditions. Strategies that debuted during dramatic political moments such as the founding election of a new democracy are even more likely to be influential in this regard.

Programmatic Party Competition

A final distinct literature to which this study contributes concerns programmatic modes of party competition. As noted above, an expanding research agenda has sought to characterize parties and party system in terms of the bargain or exchange relationship between voters and politicians. In the case of programmatic exchange, citizens' post-electoral payback consists of public goods allocated according to transparent rules, as opposed to particularistic benefits given informally to copartisans (Kitschelt 2000, 2012; Kitschelt and Wilkinson 2007; Hagopian et al. 2009; Kitschelt et al. 2010; Morgan 2011; Kitschelt and Kselman 2013; Stokes et al. 2013; Luna 2014; Roberts 2014; Hagopian forthcoming).

This book makes several contributions to the literature on programmatic party competition. First, it challenges the criteria used to measure this concept, suggesting that the analysis of campaign messages should play a much more central role. Nearly every definition of a programmatic party system implies or explicitly requires that parties' appeals during electoral campaigns specify the details of their proposed policies (Kitschelt et al. 2010: 3; Morgan 2011: 39, 80; Kitschelt 2012: 16; Kitschelt and Kselman 2013: 1454; Luna 2014: 4; Roberts 2014: 26; Hagopian forthcoming). Yet no research of which I am aware has used a primary source of data on campaign appeals, such as the present study's content analysis of campaign advertising, to operationalize this criterion. Instead, scholars have relied on qualitative assessments, mass and elite surveys, and expert ratings to measure more distant proxies, such as the congruence of elite and mass issue opinions, the coherence of policy positions among a party's elected representatives, and the ideological polarization of parties within a party system (Mainwaring et al. 2006: 27–28; Kitschelt and Wilkinson 2007: 323; Kitschelt et al. 2010: 59–64; Morgan 2011: 114–115; Kitschelt 2012: 16–18; Kitschelt and Kselman 2013: 1463–1464; Luna 2014: 15; Roberts 2014).[16]

---

[16] Morgan (2011) does use content analysis of legislation to directly measure a separate component of programmatic representation, government responsiveness to popular concerns.

In many cases, the result is likely to be measurement error that overstates parties' programmatic nature. For instance, expert coders may agree on a party's policy stance because of their familiarity with its legislative activity, even if its candidates avoid emphasizing policy during campaigns. Hagopian et al. (2009) and Hagopian (forthcoming) improve upon the status quo by using newspaper coverage and elite surveys to characterize candidates' campaign messages as clientelistic or programmatic. Yet journalistic accounts are still filtered through an intermediary that often has its own political biases (Boas 2013), and politicians' self-reports may measure how they view their campaigns in retrospect or how they would like to be perceived.

Second, this book raises questions about the appropriate unit of analysis for the study of programmatic politics. Existing literature has examined the degree to which individual parties as well as entire party systems can be classified as programmatic (Kitschelt 2000, 2012; Mainwaring et al. 2006; Kitschelt and Wilkinson 2007; Kitschelt et al. 2010; Morgan 2011; Kitschelt and Kselman 2013; Luna 2014; Roberts 2014; Hagopian forthcoming). However, this designation is much less frequently applied to individual politicians or their campaigns (Hagopian et al. 2009; Hagopian forthcoming). Moreover, in operationalizing programmatic effort at the party level, scholars have focused almost entirely on legislators and legislative candidates. Doing so makes sense in parliamentary democracies, but it is less defensible in Latin America's presidential systems, where the executive often wields outsize influence. Some Latin American presidents, including those of Chile and Brazil, enjoy exclusive authority to initiate legislation in key policy areas, the ability to issue decrees that require no congressional approval, and a host of other law-making powers (Shugart and Carey 1992: 139–144). Moreover, some Latin American parties have no *raison d'être* beyond the presidential ambitions of their founders. By virtue of being *primi inter pares* within their parties, presidents and presidential candidates deserve greater attention than the literature on programmatic competition has afforded them to date.

In part because of its different unit of analysis and more proximate measure of campaign strategies, this book suggests different conclusions than much of the existing literature about change over time in programmatic competition. Rather than playing out over multiple decades in response to historical processes or broad structural or institutional changes (e.g., Kitschelt et al. 2010; see Hagopian forthcoming for a review), I find that consequential shifts toward (or away from) policy-focused campaigning can happen much more rapidly, over the course of a few electoral cycles or even during a single campaign. Moreover, I identify significant change over time in the policy focus of parties, such as Brazil's PT, that are often viewed as programmatic since their inception (Roberts 2014; Hagopian forthcoming). Policy focus as employed in this study is not identical to programmatic competition, and other definitional components of the latter, such as voters considering proposals when choosing candidates or parties sticking to their mandates once elected, may take longer to emerge. However, it is also possible that the focus on more slow-moving proxies for programmatic competition, such as opinion congruence between legislators and citizens, has led to misleading conclusions about how quickly it can change.

In sum, this study aims not only to fill a gap in the existing literature on campaigns in new democracies but also to contribute to other topics – programmatic party competition, policy diffusion, and the professionalization of political consultants – that have spawned more extensive research agendas. In Chapter 5, I draw upon evidence presented throughout the book to summarize implications for an additional area of research, the quality of democracy in Latin America.

PLAN OF THE BOOK

The bulk of this book draws on the theory of success contagion to explain why Chilean and Brazilian presidential candidates have converged on unique national models of campaign strategy while Peruvian candidates continue to campaign in very different ways from one another. I argue that Chile and Brazil are both cases of contagion, with candidates settling upon a personalistic strategy in the former and a technocratic strategy in the latter. In each country, different background conditions at the time of the first or second election meant that different styles of campaign strategy were established as models and were subsequently legitimated by successful terms in office for the elected president. In later elections, these strategies diffused to other candidates through a combination of the mechanisms discussed above – imitation, professional norms, and strategic inertia. In Peru, by contrast, convergence has not occurred because every president since democratization has suffered dismal approval ratings at the start of the election that would replace him. As a consequence, most candidates have chosen their strategies through inward-oriented approaches, reacting to prior errors from within their own political camp.

Chapter 2 analyzes the consolidation of the *personalistic* model of campaign strategy in Chile, which was initially introduced by the center-left Concertación in the 1988 plebiscite that ended authoritarian rule. This campaign, which differed substantially from that of the incumbent military government, circumvented parties in favor of direct linkages to voters, called for unity and national reconciliation rather than priming cleavages, and de-emphasized policy content. In subsequent elections, Concertación candidates have continued with this strategy largely through strategic inertia, reinforced by the norms against cleavage-priming that have developed among Chilean campaign professionals.

On the right, the first clear instance of contagion in Chile was in 1999, when Joaquín Lavín embraced the Concertación's prior approach of campaigning with direct linkages and minimal policy focus. Imitation was the crucial mechanism of success contagion in this case. The centrist position of the governing

Concertación and the depoliticized nature of its personalistic campaign strategy meant that the Right could mimic this approach without betraying its ideological roots. Professional norms also played a role; right-wing candidates avoided priming religious cleavages in both 1999 and 2005 because of the strong taboo against divisive appeals.

Chapter 3 examines Brazilian candidates' convergence on a *technocratic* strategy, which differs from the Chilean model because of its emphasis on policy. The first Brazilian candidate to employ this approach was Fernando Henrique Cardoso, who won the 1994 election by casting himself as a capable administrator and emphasizing the inflation-taming effects of the Real Plan he had implemented as finance minister. Brazil's well-developed community of campaign professionals, who quickly adopted Cardoso's approach as their standard operating procedure, played the crucial role in its contagion across the ideological spectrum. The PT's status as a left-wing mass party made its leaders unlikely to explicitly copy a campaign strategy identified with Cardoso, who presided over numerous privatizations and governed in concert with the Right. Political consultants, who were able to package the strategy in a more depoliticized fashion, somewhat eased the transition. While the PT was reluctant to follow the advice of its consultants during Lula's 1998 presidential campaign, the first opportunity for contagion, it did so wholeheartedly in 2002, embracing a technocratic strategy similar to that of Lula's competitor.

Brazil also demonstrates that governing success is necessary to legitimate a victorious campaign strategy. After Fernando Collor was removed from office in 1992 amidst hyperinflation and corruption charges, the next set of candidates avoided strategies that might identify them with Collor's style of politics.

Chapter 4 turns to the case of Peru, showing that the convergence of campaign strategies is unlikely to occur without a clear example of governing success. Since Peru's transition to democracy in 1980, every elected president has been highly unpopular by the start of the campaign that would replace him. Hence, no single electoral strategy has been more broadly legitimated. Lacking a clear model to emulate, Peruvian candidates have instead taken a variety of distinct approaches. In both the 2001 and 2006 elections, a political outsider employed a neopopulist strategy in an effort to occupy the anti–status quo space left open by the seemingly permanent demise of Peru's partisan Left. However, candidates with ties to the political establishment, including those from APRA and the Right, have chosen their strategies through inward-oriented approaches, reacting to prior errors within their own party or political camp.

Though Peru is a case of heterogeneity over the long term, it also provides an example of short-term strategic convergence during the 1990s. At a time when Fujimori was enjoying high levels of popularity, candidates challenging his reelection in 1995 and 2000 imitated his organizational strategy, crafting personal electoral vehicles that privileged direct linkages.

In the final section of each case-study chapter, I argue that the predictions of success contagion hold up well in that country's recent elections. Major Chilean and Brazilian candidates in 2009–2010 continued to run personalistic and technocratic campaigns, respectively. In Brazil, José Serra adhered to the dominant national strategy even though he had been unsuccessful with a similar approach in 2002. In Chile, third-place candidate Marco Enríquez-Ominami campaigned much as others had done in the past, despite having been highly critical of this approach when working as a strategist for another candidate in 1999. In Peru, the two major candidates continued the zigzag pattern in which campaign strategies change radically from one election to the next. Humala abandoned his former neopopulist stance to emphasize national unity and specific proposals, while Keiko Fujimori, candidate of an historically anti-party political movement, relied on intermediated linkages to a significant degree.

In Chapter 5, I first review the theory of success contagion and examine alternative explanations for campaign strategies in Chile, Brazil, and Peru. I then conduct a medium-N analysis of ten additional cases to test the theory beyond the empirical context in which it was formulated. Though this exercise, drawing on secondary literature, is more limited than the analysis presented in Chapters 2–4, the results are encouraging. In seven of ten countries, the evolution of campaign strategies is consistent with the predictions of the theory of success contagion, and an eighth country provides partial support. The major exceptions – South Korea and the Philippines – serve to confirm several limitations to the scope of success contagion that were posited above. Finally, the book concludes with a review of the implications of candidates' campaign strategies for the quality of democracy in Chile, Brazil, and Peru.

2

Convergence on a Personalistic Strategy in Chile

In the first week of free television advertising (the *franja*) during Chile's 1999 presidential election campaign, Socialist candidate Ricardo Lagos ran a spot designed to "unmask" his right-wing opponent Joaquín Lavín, who had once been a supporter and functionary of the military regime but was now casting himself as a non-ideological public servant. The spot showed previously broadcast television news footage of Lavín speaking at a rally in support of former dictator Augusto Pinochet, in which he criticized Pinochet's recent arrest in London on human rights charges. Other than ironically juxtaposing Lavín's appearance at the rally with his saintly public image and campaign message of "change," the spot made no commentary about the candidate.

By the standards of most present-day campaigns, the Lagos campaign's criticism of Lavín in the Pinochet spot would barely have qualified as an attack. In this instance, however, it ignited a mini-controversy in the media and among the Chilean political class. One of Lavín's communication strategists retorted that, in contrast to his opponent, Lavín would not be resorting to "defamation and hatefulness" in his bid to get elected. Lavín himself responded that his own *franja* "does not injure or offend anyone – its message is one of peace, like the peace that you want for Chile." And in the campaign for the runoff, Lagos shifted course, abandoning all criticism of his opponent in favor of a positive and forward-looking message. Second-round communication strategist Eugenio Tironi (2002: 62) later commented that the aggressiveness of the first-round *franja* "broke with the style established by the Concertación since its storied campaign for the No in the 1988 plebiscite," and that the runoff campaign wisely returned to this tried-and-true model.

The reaction to Lagos's criticism of Lavín in the first round of the 1999 election and the abandonment of this approach in the second round illustrate one of three defining elements of the personalistic strategy that has come to dominate

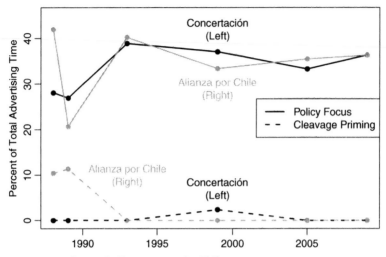

FIGURE 2.1. Strategic Convergence in Chile.

electoral campaigns in Chile. First, as shown by the above example, candidates who adopt this strategy avoid priming cleavages, such as the divide between supporters and opponents of Pinochet's former military regime. Instead, they favor a broadly resonant, inclusive, and positive message. Second, their appeals have a relatively low policy focus. Candidates aim primarily to demonstrate their empathy with the electorate by arguing that they understand the problems of various social groups and will implement largely unspecified solutions once in office. Finally, candidates employing personalistic strategies seek to circumvent intermediated linkages, such as political parties and interest groups, in favor of direct ties to the electorate.

The personalistic strategy that predominates in Chile was first introduced by the center-left Concertación in the 1988 plebiscite that ended authoritarian rule. In subsequent elections, candidates from the Concertación have continued to rely on this formula, while right-wing presidential candidates have gravitated toward it over time. As a result, campaigns from opposite sides of the ideological spectrum, which were radically different from one another in the plebiscite, have become very similar in recent elections. Figure 2.1 illustrates this process of strategic convergence with respect to the two dimensions that can be measured through an analysis of television advertising. In both the 1988 and the 1989 elections, candidates of the right-wing alliance devoted over a tenth of their *franja* time to priming ideological cleavages. In subsequent years, however, the Right has adopted the nondivisive appeals initially introduced by the Left. Likewise, the amount of television advertising that the two sides devoted to policy content differed by 14 percentage points in 1988 but only by a few percentage points from 1993 to 2009.

In this chapter, I argue that the choice of electoral strategies by Chilean presidential candidates of both Right and Left has been driven by a process of success contagion. In the context of uncertainty surrounding the campaign for Chile's 1988 plebiscite, the first presidential election in eighteen years, the strategies of the two sides differed substantially from one another. The democratic opposition's choice of a personalistic strategy in this campaign was based on a process of learning about the most effective way to bring down the dictatorship, as well as the recommendations of a group of Chilean social scientists based on surveys and focus groups. The strategy of the military government's "Yes" campaign differed markedly from that of the "No" campaign in terms of both cleavage priming and policy focus.

In subsequent elections, candidates of the center-left Concertación have continued to employ the personalistic strategy first introduced in the plebiscite campaign. This process has largely been driven by strategic inertia – sticking with a strategy that provided positive results in the past even when there are plausible reasons to behave differently. In most cases, repeating this previously successful formula has been a noncontroversial decision that has not been questioned by any of the candidate's major campaign advisors. The key exception concerns the first round of Lagos's 1999 campaign, when a new cadre of campaign strategists intentionally deviated from the personalistic model. Long-term strategic continuity was maintained, however, when a different group of advisors who had participated in the original plebiscite campaign convinced Lagos to return to this tried-and-true approach in the second round.

Most importantly, success contagion has led right-wing candidates in Chile to converge on personalistic strategies. Here, imitation of the Concertación's prior example has been a key mechanism. Joaquín Lavín's campaign in 1999 explicitly sought to adopt techniques previously employed only by the Left, such as communicating one's empathy with popular concerns and prioritizing direct contact with the people. Imitation could serve as a mechanism of success contagion because Lavín's campaign strategists saw the Concertación, which had governed for ten years with the Right's own economic model, as more of a political than a philosophical adversary. Hence, strategic emulation was considered a wise tactical move, not a betrayal of the Right's ideological roots.

The influence of professional norms has also played a role in success contagion in Chile. Campaign strategists are not organized into as tight a professional community as in Brazil, but they do share certain ideas about appropriate campaigning – most notably, that cleavage-priming appeals are off limits. Given the relationship between partisan and religious identification in Chile, one would have expected right-wing candidates in both 1999 and 2005 to devote much greater attention to the cleavage between Christians and nonbelievers. The taboo against divisive campaigning has thus arguably led to missed opportunities for right-wing presidential candidates.

In the first section of this chapter, I examine Chile's 1988 plebiscite, particularly the campaign for the "No" option, which established the personalistic model that would subsequently be adopted by candidates of both Right and Left. The second section discusses how candidates of the center-left Concertación have continued to employ personalistic strategies, primarily through strategic inertia. The third section examines candidates of the Right, showing how imitation and professional norms have both served as mechanisms of strategic contagion across the ideological spectrum. In the fourth section, I examine two partial deviations from the personalistic ideal type, arguing that the increased policy focus of Michelle Bachelet's and Joaquín Lavín's 2005 campaigns is better understood as variation within personalism than a shift to a different type of campaign strategy. The final section tests the argument by examining the campaigns of major candidates in the 2009–2010 election. Here, I find that candidates continued to employ a personalistic approach, as expected.

THE CAMPAIGN FOR THE "NO," 1988: ORIGINS OF THE PERSONALISTIC STRATEGY

The personalistic model that has come to dominate presidential election campaigns in Chile was first employed by the campaign for the "No" vote in the October 5, 1988 plebiscite that brought an end to the Pinochet dictatorship. Chile's plebiscite was a special election organized by the military government of General Augusto Pinochet, in which voters were asked to choose between an additional eight-year term for the dictator (the "Yes" option) and open presidential elections to be held the next year (the "No" option). The "No" option won the plebiscite by a margin of 55–43 percent, leading to open elections in December 1989 and the inauguration of a civilian president in 1990.

As a referendum on a single candidate taking place under authoritarian rule, Chile's 1988 plebiscite differs from a normal presidential election in important ways. In particular, key elements of campaign strategy might seem largely predetermined by the electoral context. No electoral competition had taken place since 1973, and parties had been in recess or operating clandestinely during the interim, so their participation in the campaign as organized intermediaries might seem unlikely. Without an opposition candidate to promote, the campaign might naturally avoid focusing on policy, and given the need to unify forces against a powerful dictator, unity rather than cleavage-priming appeals would seem a logical choice. In other words, Chile's 1988 plebiscite might seem to run afoul of one of the scope conditions for the theory of success contagion, that it should not apply to elections held under authoritarian rule because there is much less freedom of choice in campaign strategy.

I argue that, for several reasons, the 1988 plebiscite is the appropriate starting point for applying the theory of success contagion to Chile. First, success contagion makes claims about the strategies that candidates adopt *after* a successful model has been established, not about the election in which that strategy debuts. A plebiscite held under authoritarian rule might be inappropriate for testing predictions about strategic convergence, but it is not inherently problematic to claim that such an election establishes the model that other candidates later adopt. Second, given the short elapsed time between the plebiscite and the following year's presidential election, the opposition essentially treated the two as separate phases of a single campaign. Starting the analysis with Patricio Aylwin's presidential campaign in 1989 would miss the crucial "Act I" in which key elements of opposition strategy were established.

Third, a close examination of the "No" campaign shows that its strategic choices were not inevitable. The decision to adopt a personalistic strategy resulted not only from a previously determined factor – opposition politicians' prior experience in combating the military regime – but also from a fairly contingent one: the efforts of Chilean social scientists to "sell" to politicians a series of strategic recommendations based on surveys and focus groups. With respect to each dimension of campaign strategy, there was substantial debate within the opposition as to the appropriate course of action; the strategy of the "No" campaign was never a foregone conclusion. Moreover, the military government's "Yes" campaign adopted a very different strategy with respect to the dimensions of cleavage and policy focus. The common belief that the "No" campaign chose correctly in this election, and the "Yes" campaign erred, has been highly influential in subsequent electoral contests in Chile.

Circumventing Intermediaries and Establishing Direct Linkages

The decision by opposition politicians to privilege direct ties to voters during the 1988 plebiscite was largely a reaction to an earlier failed effort by grass-roots organizations to bring down the regime by force. Following a severe economic crisis in 1982, labor unions and shantytown-based popular associations initiated a series of anti-government protests designed to weaken the regime (Garretón M. 1989). While initially seeming to gain some traction, the popular mobilization strategy ultimately bore little fruit. Pinochet proved unwilling to make substantive political concessions, and the increasingly violent tactics of the opposition's more radical wing – including an assassination attempt on Pinochet in 1986 – prompted an increase in state repression.

Responding to the failed effort to weaken the regime through popular mobilization, most opposition party leaders eventually embraced the goal of defeating Pinochet at the ballot box, using a strategy that would bypass intermediary organizations in favor of direct appeals to voters. Chile's 1980 constitution called for a 1988 plebiscite in which voters would approve or reject an eight-year presidential term for a single candidate chosen by the military junta. The majority of opposition forces ultimately decided to participate in this plebiscite as a unified front, the fourteen-party Concertación de Partidos por el No (Coalition of Parties for the No). In shifting to a strategy of electoral opposition, party leaders aimed to bypass and marginalize the organizations that had led that

protest movement (Roberts 1998: 139). Politicians needed the votes of shantytown dwellers, but they ultimately sought their support as individuals rather
than members of an organized movement, since this movement had acquired
an intransigent and violent image (Oxhorn 1994).

In preparation for the 1988 plebiscite, leaders of the "No" campaign also
made an effort to circumvent the national structure of political parties themselves, establishing an alternative structure of municipal campaign headquarters (*comandos comunales*) as the basic organizing unit of the campaign
(Almarza 1989; Montes 1989). Doing so brought the campaign as close as
possible to unorganized individuals, and it facilitated a relatively new activity –
door-to-door campaigning in place of mass rallies and protests. Ultimately, the
territorial structure devised for the campaign created a new generation of political intermediaries that "replaced the previous system of political leadership of
the masses, the organizing of protests" (Montes 1989: 42).

The Strategic Recommendations of Chilean Social Scientists

The failed protest effort of the 1980s led opposition leaders to embrace participation in the plebiscite and prioritize direct linkages, but it did not determine
what message the "No" campaign would convey. The communication strategy
that was ultimately adopted is largely attributable to the strategic recommendations of a group of Chilean social scientists from the research consortium CIS
(Sunkel 1989, 1992; Puryear 1994; author's interviews, Tironi and Valdés).[1]
Their recommendations were noteworthy in two respects. First, the campaign
sought to convey an inclusive, nonconfrontational, future-oriented message of
happiness and reconciliation, avoiding any emphasis on cleavages. Second, the
campaign avoided stating the policy objectives of a future democratic government and limited itself to a diagnosis of the social problems resulting from the
military regime's policies.

Avoid Cleavage-Priming Confrontation

The principal recommendation of CIS social scientists was that the campaign
avoid a confrontational message of retribution for past injustices and instead
convey a positive, forward-looking, integrative appeal that all Chileans come
together in support of democracy. Based on focus groups conducted in August
1987, CIS scholars had detected an overwhelming sense of fear regarding the
potential for social conflict and the government's likely response (Tironi 1990:
19–25). Likewise, a CIS survey found that those who opposed Pinochet were
reluctant to register to vote or participate in the plebiscite because of fear and
skepticism. In response to these findings, CIS (1987) recommended a unifying

---

[1] CIS is an acronym of acronyms; it brought together the three think tanks CED (Centro de Estudios del Desarrollo), ILET (Instituto Latinoamericano de Estudios Transnacionales), and SUR
(Centro de Estudios Sociales y Educación).

and positive campaign message and a strategy focused on the notion of regaining dignity.

Conveying a positive and integrative appeal meant that the "No" campaign would avoid any emphasis on cleavages. References to divisions between Left and Right, workers and capitalists, or popular sectors and the economic elite were completely absent from the campaign's television advertising. Aversion to cleavage priming was so strong that the campaign avoided mention of the very cleavage that defined the plebiscite – between the democratic opposition and the military regime. Rather than criticizing the military government as a whole, the "No" campaign focused its opposition on Pinochet as an individual, stressing that his supporters and members of the military would have a place in a future democratic Chile (Correa 1989: 162). One prominent example concerns the *franja* episode of September 9, 1988, which depicted footage of Chile's paramilitary national police beating an unarmed civilian at a protest. As the camera alternated its focus between the protester and a baton-wielding officer, a voice repeated, for each one in turn, "this man wants peace; this man is Chilean; this man fights for what he believes." The spot concluded with the message "Chile will be a great country when everyone has a place in the homeland, so that this never happens again."

Minimize Policy Content

A second key recommendation of CIS social scientists was that the campaign eschew statements about the policy objectives of a future democratic government and avoid criticism of current government policies. In the interest of maintaining the broadest possible support base for the "No" vote, and to avoid threatening the interests of the military and economic elite or exacerbating middle-class fears of a return to the economic chaos of the Allende years, CIS social scientists recommend postponing any discussion of a common program of government until after the plebiscite. Strategist Tironi (1990: 29) argued in January 1988 that the advantage of unifying a heterogeneous group of political forces around a common goal "is lost when one tries to attach 'content' to the No [campaign]."

The CIS social scientists argued that any discussion of policy issues in the campaign should be diagnostic rather than prescriptive. CIS's studies detected a widespread frustration that common people were not benefiting from Chile's economic growth. Hence, their strategic memos recommended that opposition politicians "convey an attitude that brings them closer to the people's problems" (CIS 1988). But because they had ruled out specific proposals, the effort to get close to the people would be limited to diagnosing symptoms and communicating the generic notion that things would be better under a future democratic government. As summarized in Table 2.1, diagnosis occupied 15.1 percent of the "No" campaign's *franja*, over half of the amount devoted to policy in general. Discussion of specific proposals or general acclaims about future policy took up a comparatively minuscule share of time.

TABLE 2.1. *Television Advertising in Chile's 1988 Plebiscite*

	"No" Option	"Yes" Option
Policy focused	28.1	41.9
Specific proposals	0.3	0.5
General proposals	1.4	3.4
Achievements	0.4	10.6
Criticism	10.8	20.5
Diagnosis	15.1	7.0
Not policy focused (jingles, image, or other)	71.9	58.1
Cleavage priming	0.0	10.4
No cleavage priming	100.0	89.6

Note: Entries are percentages of total advertising time.

The Contrary Instincts of Politicians

While the "No" campaign was successful in its effort to defeat Pinochet, its choice of strategy was hardly inevitable. Rather, this approach ran counter to politicians' basic instincts and met with initial resistance, and parties ultimately accepted it "with great sacrifice to their political culture" (Correa 1989: 159). Concertación leaders were initially skeptical when presented with the campaign's "Happiness is Coming" slogan, rainbow logo, positive television advertising, and campaign jingle built around the message of national reconciliation (Puryear 1994: 158; Otaño 1995: 57–58). A number of political leaders called for a very different approach – a confrontational campaign centered on issues like human rights or government corruption and playing upon feelings of indignation (Sunkel 1992: 43; Puryear 1994: 156). Politicians also tended to favor more rational and policy-oriented arguments than the emotional appeals recommended by CIS scholars (Arriagada 1989). Finally, political party leaders resisted the decision to circumvent party structures and organize the territorial campaign around a new system of municipal campaign headquarters (Almarza 1989; Montes 1989).

In the face of such resistance, the "No" campaign's choice of strategy is ultimately attributable to two factors: proximity between the academic realm of campaign advisors and the political world of party leaders, and the demonstrated success of the personalistic strategy in the campaign's early phases. Academia and opposition politics were closely intertwined in Chile during the Pinochet years. Ricardo Lagos, a Socialist leader and founder of the Party for Democracy (PPD), held a PhD in economics from Duke. Likewise, Gabriel Valdés, outgoing president of the Christian Democratic Party (PDC), had founded one of the research institutes that made up CIS and was the father of Juan Gabriel Valdés, an academic and key CIS advisor. Personal backgrounds thus predisposed many Concertación leaders to embrace recommendations from social scientists (Puryear 1994).

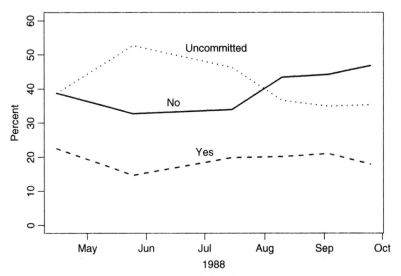

FIGURE 2.2. Intended Vote in Chile's 1988 Plebiscite.

Once opposition politicians had begun to follow the recommendations of CIS social scientists, their commitment to this strategy was reinforced by CIS's own survey data on vote intention in the plebiscite (Figure 2.2). Four months before the October election, the "No" option was winning by a substantial margin, but the large number of uncommitted voters made it possible that the election could go either way. Starting in July, however, intended "No" vote began to increase sharply, while the number of uncommitted voters fell and support for the "Yes" option remained stagnant. During the final month before the vote – the period in which the *franja* was being broadcast – support for the "No" option increased at the expense of the "Yes." These data strongly suggested that CIS's recommended strategy was achieving its desired effect.

The Contrasting Strategy of the "Yes" Campaign

With respect to both cleavage priming and policy focus, the strategy of the military government's "Yes" campaign contrasts markedly with that of the opposition. First and foremost, the "Yes" campaign sought to instill fear in the population of the consequences of an opposition victory. It did so by painting the opposition as ideologically extremist and dominated by undemocratic leftist groups, such as the Communist Party and Movement of the Revolutionary Left, that had utilized violent tactics against the regime in recent years. As summarized in Table 2.1, 10.4 percent of the "Yes" campaign's television advertising was devoted to priming left–right cleavages, either associating the opposition with an image of violence and chaos or charging that it was dominated by communists.

The "Yes" campaign was also more focused on policy than the "No" campaign. In addition to extensive policy critiques of the Allende government, it placed emphasis on the economic development that had been achieved under military rule and the continued gains that Chileans could expect from another term for Pinochet. On the whole, 41.9 percent of the "Yes" campaign's television advertising was devoted to policy, versus 28.1 percent for the "No" campaign. The government allocated a substantial amount of time to praising its achievements and advancing proposals for the future. It also devoted nearly twice as much time as the opposition to policy-related criticism, primarily with respect to the failings of the Allende government.

The main similarity between the "Yes" and the "No" campaigns concerns their use of direct linkages. Since its inception, the military government had looked negatively upon all forms of organized political intermediation, including Chile's traditional Right parties. During the plebiscite, leaders of the Independent Democratic Union (Unión Democrática Independiente, UDI), the more pro-Pinochet of the two major right-wing parties, played an important role in formulating campaign strategy (Berrier Sharim 1989; Pollack 1999: 99–102). In terms contact with voters, however, the state apparatus under the direct control of Pinochet took the lead. Local campaign operations were run by the military government's appointed governors and mayors (Allamand 1999: 153–154), and Interior Minister Sergio Fernández served as campaign manager.

SUCCESS CONTAGION ON THE LEFT

In five presidential elections following the victory of the "No" campaign, Concertación candidates have continued to rely on the personalistic strategy that was introduced in the 1988 plebiscite. This outcome is consistent with the theory of success contagion, given the high approval ratings enjoyed by Patricio Aylwin, the Christian Democrat who succeeded Pinochet as president of Chile. Aylwin had been spokesman for the "No" campaign, and during 1989, he led negotiations with the outgoing military government over the rules of transition. His performance during this period met with broad public approval; in a June 1989 survey by the Centro de Estudios Públicos, Aylwin received the highest feeling thermometer rating among twenty-six Chilean politicians. Following his election as president in December 1989, Aylwin maintained high approval ratings throughout his four-year term (Figure 2.3). Given this combination of electoral and governing success, the theoretical expectation is that future Concertación campaigns would employ a similar approach.

The primary mechanism of success contagion on the left has been strategic inertia. An uninterrupted, multidecade period of governing helped established strong confidence among candidates and their advisors in what is now the traditional way of running campaigns in Chile. In the presidential elections of 1989 and 1993 – both easy victories for Concertación candidates – no major campaign advisors seriously considered departing from a personalistic strategy. Much the same can be said of Michelle Bachelet's 2005 campaign.

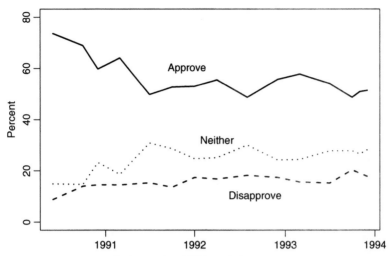

FIGURE 2.3. Approval of President Patricio Aylwin.

The 1999 campaign of Ricardo Lagos shows that long-term strategic inertia can overcome short-term disturbances. In the first round of the 1999 election, Lagos intentionally deviated from the personalistic approach, both by priming cleavages and by emphasizing policy. This strategy was recommended by a new team of advisors that had not participated in previous campaigns for the Concertación. However, a group of strategists from the 1988 plebiscite campaign successfully lobbied for a return to personalism in the runoff. As the architects of the Concertación's tried-and-true strategy, they ultimately were able to marginalize those who had implemented an unorthodox approach in the first round.

The consistent recourse to a personalistic approach, despite plausible reasons to behave differently, constitutes evidence of success contagion within the Concertación. Both Aylwin and Frei had incentives to focus more on policy than the "No" campaign had done in 1988. In Lagos's campaign, numerous campaign advisors argued that he should continue with a policy-centric and confrontational campaign in the second round rather than switching back to personalism. And in Bachelet's case, her constant efforts to circumvent political parties during the campaign created serious tensions with important political leaders from her own coalition.

Patricio Aylwin, 1989: The "Second Round" of the Plebiscite Campaign

With presidential elections scheduled for barely a year after the 1988 plebiscite, the campaign of Christian Democrat Patricio Aylwin was largely a continuation of the previous year's "No" campaign (Tironi 1990; author's interviews, Figueroa, Forch, and Salcedo). Many of the same individuals occupied key roles

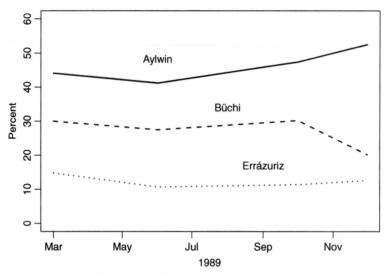

FIGURE 2.4. Intended Vote in Chile's 1989 Election.

in both contests. CIS continued its focus groups, electoral surveys, and transmission of strategic recommendations via regular memos, and the team involved in the production of television advertising remained largely the same. Because of the continuity of personnel, the minimal elapsed time between the two campaigns, and the successful result of the previous year's plebiscite effort, little changed in terms of the opposition's campaign strategy.

As with the "No" campaign, Aylwin's 1989 presidential campaign sought to avoid cleavage priming and de-emphasize policy. The first of these decisions could just as easily be attributed to conjunctural incentives as to an unquestioning repetition of what had worked well in the past. Given his comfortable lead throughout the 1989 campaign (Figure 2.4), there was little reason for Aylwin to criticize his opponents or the military government in any fashion.

Aylwin's decision to minimize the policy focus of his campaign can be more unambiguously attributed to strategic inertia. Compared to the plebiscite, the 1989 presidential election gave Aylwin both the ability and the incentive to place more emphasis on policy. While the parties of the Concertación intentionally produced no government program for the plebiscite campaign, they did agree upon a detailed program for the 1989 election. Moreover, the political context was one in which voters might have had legitimate doubts about the Concertación's ability to govern. The last time the opposition was in power, the fractious nature of Allende's Popular Unity coalition contributed to a sense that the country, gripped by economic chaos and widespread social protest, was ungovernable. As discussed below, the campaign of right-wing candidate Hernán Büchi sought to raise doubts about accountability within a seventeen-party coalition and the difficulties it might encounter in governing.

TABLE 2.2. *Patricio Aylwin's Television Advertising, 1989*

Policy focused	26.9
Specific proposals	3.1
General proposals	7.6
Achievements	1.3
Criticism	1.9
Diagnosis	13.0
Not policy focused (jingles, image, or other)	73.1
Cleavage priming	0.0
No cleavage priming	100.0

Note: Entries are percentages of total advertising time.

Conveying detailed, concrete policy proposals during the campaign could be an effective way to combat such doubts.

Despite the ability and incentive to emphasize policy, Aylwin's campaign avoided doing so. As shown in Table 2.2, the share of Aylwin's television advertising devoted to policy (26.9 percent) was similar to that of the "No" campaign (28.1 percent). Also similar was the fact that policy discussion most frequently involved a diagnosis of current problems without specifically assigning blame to the government (13 percent). Aylwin's advertising director insisted that the campaign "practically had no promises. Everything that had to do with proposals was entirely general, and did not focus on details" (author's interview, Salcedo). In Aylwin's television advertising, generic statements about policy priorities were much more common than specific proposals. For example, on December 5, 1989, economics advisor Alejandro Foxley explained to viewers: "If you ask me ... 'how are you going to manage the economy in the Aylwin government,' I can summarize by saying: We are going to keep the doors open to everyone. We are always going to speak the truth. And we are going to manage the economy in a serious, responsible manner, based on the problems that affect you today."

Aylwin's 1989 presidential campaign thus provides evidence of success contagion through strategic inertia. Given the electoral context, Aylwin had both an incentive and a greater capacity to focus on policy, and in particular, specific proposals. Yet Aylwin's campaign avoided a focus on policy just as the "No" campaign had done. This outcome makes more sense when one considers the continuity of personnel between the two campaigns, the Concertación's success in the plebiscite, and Aylwin's positive public image at the time of the campaign – factors which would predict strategic inertia.

Eduardo Frei, 1993: Strategic Continuity in a New Era

As with Aylwin's campaign, the 1993 presidential campaign of Eduardo Frei Ruiz-Tagle is an example of strategic inertia in a context where there were

TABLE 2.3. *Eduardo Frei's Television Advertising, 1993*

Policy focused	38.9
Specific proposals	0.0
General proposals	0.0
Achievements	1.4
Criticism	0.0
Diagnosis	37.5
Not policy focused (jingles, image, or other)	61.1
Cleavage priming	0.0
No cleavage priming	100.0

Note: Entries are percentages of total advertising time.

clear incentives to act differently. Part of the reason for choosing Frei as candidate was change rather than continuity; it was thought that Frei could most effectively signal a new, more apolitical approach to governance for the Concertación. A businessman during the dictatorship, Frei had been elected senator in 1989 and PDC president in 1991 but was still not widely viewed as part of the traditional political class. Frei's communication strategists sought to emphasize his engineering background and portray him as a competent administrator who could lead the country into a new era of growth and efficiency now that Aylwin had completed the "political work" of the democratic transition (author's interviews, Figueroa and Toloza). The campaign itself "tried to establish a symbolic break between the past, the transition, and what was to come" (author's interview, Cortés). In light of this strategy, the concept of modernity occupied a central place in Frei's campaign – particularly in his forward-looking slogan "For the New Times."

Given the candidate's technocratic background and the campaign's goal of portraying him as a competent administrator, as well as the effort to achieve a symbolic break with the past, it would be logical to emphasize policy more than prior Concertación campaigns had done. Yet Frei's campaign was similar to the "No" and Aylwin campaigns in terms of its vagueness on policy details. While Frei devoted a somewhat higher percentage of his *franja* to policy issues (38.9 percent), nearly all of this discussion (37.5 percentage points) involved a generic diagnosis of challenges for the future (Table 2.3). Frei always framed policy discussion in terms of "we need to" rather than "I will" – avoiding commitments, yet conveying the notion of an ongoing project that had done well in the past and simply needed to be renewed to meet with continued success.

While a vague approach to policy seemingly contradicted the strategy of portraying Frei as a capable technocrat, this approach is consistent with the argument that prior success leads to strategic inertia. The campaign's communication director characterized the decision to avoid specific proposals in precisely such terms: "There was an inertia coming from the past, and it was an inertia of growth ... in the percentage of votes. Hence, there was not much that we had to do – in fact, we had to do very little . . . Why take a risk if you are not going to win a single additional vote by making promises?" (author's interview, Salcedo).

Rather than advancing specific proposals, Frei resorted to the tried-and-true Concertación strategy of communicating familiarity with people's problems. One method for doing so was to travel around the country, visiting small groups of people in their communities and gathering information about their concerns. This program, known as Listen to Chile (Escucha a Chile), was also a form of direct linkage that involved putting the candidate in immediate contact with the people. Listen to Chile was publicly characterized as providing input into the candidate's program, but in reality, the form of this activity was more important than any substantive feedback obtained. According to the campaign's executive secretary, the "idea was to generate participation, and nothing more; the result didn't matter much" (author's interview, Pérez Yoma).

In sum, Frei's campaign, like Aylwin's, marked continuity with the personalistic strategy that the Concertación introduced in the 1988 plebiscite. There were incentives for both candidates to deviate from the strategy of the "No" campaign by placing greater emphasis on policy. The conditions that had inspired that strategic choice during the plebiscite – the difficulty of uniting a diverse coalition around a common program, and a desire to avoid threatening the interests of the military or economic elite – were a much less relevant factor during the 1989 election and an even smaller concern after four years of consensus-oriented governing by the Concertación. Rather than emphasizing policy, however, both Aylwin and Frei resorted to personalistic strategies because there was little reason to alter an approach that had delivered successful results in the past.

Ricardo Lagos, 1999: The Triumph of a Personalistic Approach

The 1999 campaign of Socialist Ricardo Lagos marks a contrast with earlier Concertación presidential campaigns. At the start of his campaign, Lagos placed substantial emphasis on policy proposals and sought to prime the cleavage between supporters and opponents of the former military regime. This strategy arguably delivered positive results. Lagos did not win the first round outright, but he still received more votes than his opponent, despite representing the continuity of a governing coalition whose popularity had been battered by economic downturn. However, a dissident group of advisors that had participated in the plebiscite successfully maneuvered to take control of Lagos's campaign and alter the strategy. During the second round, they spearheaded a return to the Concertación's traditional approach.

Lagos's campaign is important for the theory of success contagion because it shows that short-term deviations from an established campaign strategy do not necessarily alter long-term strategic inertia. Power struggles may emerge among strategists with competing visions, but those who implemented an initially

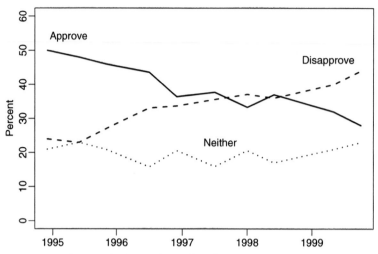

FIGURE 2.5. Approval of President Eduardo Frei.

successful course of action tend to gain the upper hand in internal arguments. In this particular case, the normative preference for a personalistic approach to campaigning and the fact that Lagos's cleavage priming was seen as breaking a taboo played a role in the campaign's return to the Concertación's tried-and-true strategy.

Lagos's departure from a personalistic approach in the first round of the 1999 election owes much to the presence of a new team of strategists that had not participated in Chile's previous presidential elections. First-round advisors Carlos Ominami, Manuela Gumucio, and Marco Enríquez-Ominami (author's interviews) had worked closely with Lagos in the past, particularly during his campaign for the 1993 presidential primary. However, they did not participate in the 1988 plebiscite or the campaigns of Aylwin in 1989 or of Frei in 1993. Lagos also hired French political consultant Jacques Séguéla to advise his campaign in 1999, thus bringing in a key outsider's perspective.

Chile's 1999 presidential election occurred in a context in which economic crisis and increasing frustration with the governing Concertación combined to produce the first real possibility of a right-wing victory. Evaluations of president Frei's performance at the outset of the campaign were the poorest they had been since the transition to democracy, with more Chileans disapproving than approving (Figure 2.5). Moreover, the spillover effects of the East Asian and Russian financial crises had contributed to an unemployment rate of 11 percent and the likelihood of negative growth for the year (Angell and Pollack 2000). Given the combination of unfavorable economic circumstances and the fact that the Concertación had held the presidency for nearly ten years, right-wing candidate Joaquín Lavín had been making gains in opinion polls (Figure 2.6). Also capitalizing on discontent with the government, the Communist Party made a strong showing in the 1997 congressional elections, winning 7 percent

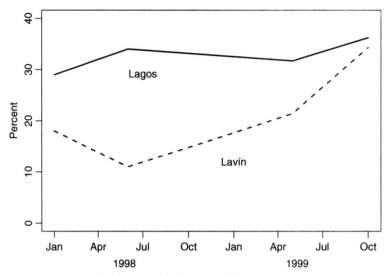

FIGURE 2.6. Intended Vote in Chile's 1999 Election.

of the vote. In 1999, there was concern that Communist presidential candidate Gladys Marín would take away left-wing votes from Lagos, facilitating an outright victory or at least a strong first-round showing for Lavín (author's interview, Ominami).

Cleavage-Priming and Policy Focus in the First Round

In light of the more precarious situation for the Concertación, Lagos's first-round advisors recommended a strategy that departed from the personalistic approach in two key ways. First, the campaign sought to reaffirm the core Concertación vote by politicizing the authoritarian–democratic cleavage – in the words of Enríquez-Ominami (author's interview), to "Pinochet-ize the election." In addition to the spot depicting Lavín at the pro-Pinochet rally (described at the outset of this chapter), the campaign team produced two additional advertising segments in this vein – one showing Lavín's endorsement of the "Yes" option in the 1988 plebiscite, and another noting that as a young man, he had been publicly honored by Pinochet for embodying the values of the military regime. These cleavage-priming spots took up 3.4 percent of Lagos's total advertising time (Table 2.4), a much smaller share than the 10.4 percent that the "Yes" campaign devoted to cleavage priming in 1988. Yet they were prominently displayed at the beginning of each *franja* episode in which they appeared, and both critics and supporters of the cleavage-priming strategy considered these spots a key component of Lagos's first-round campaign.[2]

---

[2] Séguéla (2000: 52–53), for instance, singles out these three spots for specific mention when discussing the Lagos campaign in his memoirs.

TABLE 2.4. *Ricardo Lagos's Television Advertising, 1999*

	Round 1	Round 2
Policy focused	40.4	29.1
Specific proposals	10.7	4.2
General proposals	6.2	7.5
Achievements	4.5	7.8
Criticism	4.3	0.0
Diagnosis	14.7	9.6
Not policy focused (jingles, image, or other)	59.6	70.9
Cleavage priming	3.4	0.0
No cleavage priming	96.6	100.0

Note: Entries are percentages of total advertising time.

A second key element of Lagos's first-round strategy was to adopt a more policy-oriented campaign than in the past, focused not only on the diagnosis of problems remaining at the end of the Frei government but also specific policies intended to resolve them. The slogan for the first round, "Grow with Equity" (*Crecer con Igualdad*), stands out as the only policy-oriented slogan adopted by a major presidential candidate in Chile in the years since democratization. By several measures, Lagos's first-round television advertising was the most policy-oriented presidential campaign that Chile had yet seen. His *franja* included many more specific proposals (10.7 percent of the total time) than did previous Concertación presidential campaigns (an average of 1.1 percent), and it devoted a higher percentage of time to policy content in general (40.4 percent, versus an average of 31.3 percent).

Embracing Personalism in the Second Round

Following a close result in the first round of the election – Lagos received 48 percent of the valid vote, compared to Lavín's 47.5 percent, triggering Chile's first-ever presidential runoff – Lagos announced major changes in his campaign team and strategy. Concertación stalwarts who had played key roles in the "No" campaign were put in charge of the runoff, while the first-round strategists were effectively marginalized. The new team completely overhauled the campaign strategy with respect to both cleavage priming and policy content. Head communication strategist Eugenio Tironi (author's interview) described the second round as being "much more affective, much more emotional, less argumentative, and, above all, with a much more optimistic vision." The effort to "unmask" Lavín by identifying him with the prior authoritarian regime was abandoned in favor of a strictly future-oriented, positive campaign message. None of the second-round *franja* engaged in cleavage priming; indeed, there was virtually no mention of Lavín at all.

The first-round's focus on policy content and specific proposals was also reduced in favor of a somewhat generic, optimistic vision for the future – epitomized by the new slogan "A Much Better Chile" (*Chile Mucho Mejor*). A typical statement from the second-round *franja* (broadcast the evening of January 6) explicitly contrasted these two approaches and signaled Lagos's new stance:

> I know that there are urgent problems. I will focus on them immediately as president. But today we are in a new millennium. We have to look to the long term. We have to think big. Let's not let the urgent keep us from thinking about the future. I invite you to join me in building this great, modern, generous Chile. A nation that is the star of a new millennium. A much better Chile.

On the whole, Lagos's second-round *franja* discussed policy only 29.1 percent of the time, nearly as little as the "No" campaign in 1988 (28.1 percent).

In describing the strategic shift between the first and second rounds of the election, those from the second-round team stressed the influence of norms about appropriate campaigning that had been established during the 1988 plebiscite. Eugenio García (author's interview), creative director of the second-round *franja*, said that his team's strategy involved "returning to that Concertación aesthetic...it was [the 'No' campaign's] 'Happiness is Coming' ten years later." Strategist Carlos Montes (author's interview) also acknowledged the effort to recapture the sentiment of "No" campaign, and he pointed out that the plebiscite experience had created a particular school of campaign strategy that was still very present in Chile. Tironi (author's interview) offered a similar explanation: "starting with the plebiscite, a certain local 'know-how' was created, and this has been fairly important...because it has given a certain tone to the campaigns and a certain style to Chilean democracy."

Those who participated in the first round of Lagos's campaign similarly emphasized the persistence of norms established during the plebiscite campaign and the difficulty that they encountered in trying to break the taboo against divisive appeals. Enríquez-Ominami (author's interview) maintained that "since the coup, there has been such a strong reaction against conflict and confrontational language." Gumucio (author's interview) noted that "the *franja* was accused of being 'confrontational'...[but] no one questions what is so criminal about being confrontational." And Carlos Figueroa (author's interview), the campaign's communication director and something of a neutral party in the debate between the first- and the second-round teams, explained that "this country is still traumatized by the confrontation of the dictatorship years...it is not ready for attacks. Does it want what Séguéla wanted? No, this country is not the United States or France...it is a very sensitive country."

There were plausible reasons for Lagos to have maintained his first-round strategy in the runoff rather than changing advisors and shifting course. Ominami (author's interview) and Séguéla (2000) advised Lagos that shifting to the center or depoliticizing the campaign in the second round would be dangerous because it would risk alienating the 3 percent of voters who had supported Communist candidate Gladys Marín. Given the unfavorable economic context in which the Concertación was seeking another presidency, the result of the first round could easily have been seen as a victory for Lagos, who outpolled his contender and had a clear prospect of winning the runoff. Returning to the tried-and-true model of campaigning in Chile was not an inevitable product of the close result in the first round of the election. Rather, it was a choice that was influenced by norms about appropriate campaigning in Chile – norms that Lagos had expressed reluctance about violating even at the start of the first-round campaign (author's interview, Enríquez-Ominami).

In sum, Lagos's 1999 campaign is an example of strategic inertia, yet in a different fashion from the Concertación's presidential campaigns in 1989 and 1993. Rather than a successful prior strategy never really being questioned, a new team of advisors who had not worked with previous Concertación candidates devised a first-round strategy that differed from personalism with respect to both cleavage priming and policy focus. However, a second group of strategists who had participated in the plebiscite campaign and disagreed with Lagos's unorthodox first-round approach successfully imposed their preferred strategy in the second round. The fact that Lagos's first-round strategy fell outside of the established norm for Concertación campaigns facilitated the return to a personalistic approach in the runoff.

Michelle Bachelet, 2005: The Direct Linkage Strategy of a "Citizen" Candidate

Whereas Lagos's 1999 campaign illustrates strategic inertia in terms of cleavage priming and policy focus, the 2005 campaign of Michelle Bachelet is an example of continuity with respect to the use of linkages. Bachelet's campaign emphasized that she was embracing a "new style of politics" – one that was close to the people rather than political parties. But the particular strategies Bachelet employed in this effort were similar to those utilized in prior Concertación presidential campaigns. As in the campaign for the 1988 plebiscite, Bachelet circumvented political parties in favor of direct, campaign-specific linkage structures, despite the fact that these efforts created very public tensions with the leaders of Concertación parties. The alternative forms of linkage that she established – citizen networks and citizen dialogues – were similar to previous efforts by Frei and Lagos. Given the centrality of direct linkages to the established model of campaign strategy in Chile, adopting this strategy in 2005 was a logical step.

Circumventing Parties: The "Remote Control" Campaign

Bachelet's campaign argued that her path to the nomination – amassing popular support rather than jockeying for position within the Socialist Party leadership – made her a "citizen" rather than "party" candidate. A former minister of health and defense under President Lagos, Bachelet had been steadily gaining ground in public opinion surveys for several years before the 2005 election

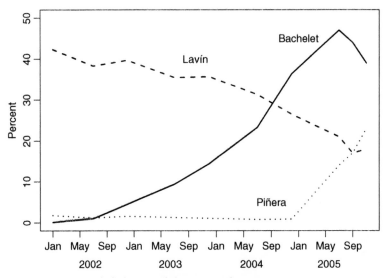

FIGURE 2.7. Intended Vote in Chile's 2005 Election.

(Figure 2.7). For Bachelet, being a citizen candidate also meant explicitly distancing herself from parties and adopting something of an anti-party discourse. Several months before the election, Bachelet said that she had "a critical vision of the form of politics that we are doing in our parties" and argued that political parties were becoming increasingly distant from society.[3] Bachelet's "citizen campaign" effectively sought to breach this distance by establishing direct linkages between the candidate and voters – a strategy epitomized by her campaign slogan "I am with you" (*Estoy contigo*).

In keeping with her direct linkage strategy, Bachelet's campaign often neglected or sought to circumvent political parties, provoking constant tensions between the campaign leadership and major Concertación politicians. The president, general secretary, and vice president of the Socialist Party all publicly criticized the presidential campaign on separate occasions for not allowing Bachelet to do enough party-supported territorial campaigning.[4] Pablo Lorenzini (author's interview), a Christian Democratic senator and Bachelet campaign manager for the Maule region, denounced the "remote control" campaign being directed from Santiago without the input of party leaders in rural areas and smaller towns.[5] In particular, Lorenzini complained that the national campaign leadership did not organize much door-to-door campaigning by party

---

[3] *El Mercurio*, October 5, 2005.
[4] *La Tercera*, June 19, 2005; *El Mercurio*, October 26, 2005; *El Mercurio*, November 17, 2005; *El Mercurio*, December 18, 2005.
[5] *El Mercurio*, October 29, 2005.

members. Sergio Bitar (author's interview), a top PPD politician, said that people wanted to get involved during the first round but that there was no organized way to channel the enthusiasm because there was little door-to-door campaigning or activist work.

Alternative, Campaign-Specific Linkage Structures

Rather than reaching out to voters through the political parties of the Concertación, Bachelet sought to promote alternative, campaign-specific forms of linkage. The most prominent of these were the "citizen networks," a series of semiautonomous support groups organized into a loosely coordinated structure that could provide logistical support for Bachelet's candidacy. The first and largest of these groups, Women with Bachelet, grew to be a network of 8,000 members, with some 3,000–4,000 in the Santiago metropolitan area (author's interview, Galleguillos). Another network, Youth with Bachelet, signed up approximately 2,000 people (author's interview, Krauss). As the election approached, the official campaign team sought to unify the citizen networks into something of a confederation, with a formal link to the campaign headquarters, and to encourage on-the-ground campaigning. Typical activities included distributing pamphlets on the weekends, as well as organizing "citizen parties" – carnival-like campaign events held in public plazas that offered games for children, entertainment and music, and services such as haircuts or free medical checkups.

While Bachelet's citizen networks brought together supporters with common interests and a common political orientation, these networks were designed to be very different from traditional intermediary organizations. They provided as direct and unmediated a connection as possible between Bachelet and her supporters, and their entire *raison d'être* was to support the presidential campaign. The networks did not operate like an interest group, articulating the preferences of their members into a set of demands that the candidate could pledge to satisfy in return for the organization's support. As Youth with Bachelet's coordinator explained (author's interview, Krauss), "the relationship is Michelle with the electorate...there is no spokesperson for the youth. Michelle is the spokeswoman; there are no intermediaries."

In creating an alternative linkage structure emphasizing the concept of citizenship, Bachelet was taking a page out of Lagos's book. The first "citizen network" was introduced during the Concertación's primary campaign in 1999, in which Lagos confronted Christian Democrat Andrés Zaldívar. Lagos was reluctant to rely on party networks for mobilizing primary voters. Instead, the Lagos campaign sought to establish a network of supporters connected by existing family or friendship ties, where one Lagos supporter would serve as a link to other close contacts. Lagos's citizen network was also similar to Bachelet's in that it was designed solely for the election. When Bachelet asked for the Lagos citizen network database at the start of her 2005 campaign, its organizer was unable to pass along any useful information because the network had not been maintained since 1999 (author's interview, Solis).

Bachelet also sought to reach out directly to individual voters around the country through a series of meetings known as "citizen dialogues" – a technique that had been introduced in previous Concertación presidential campaigns. Bachelet's citizen dialogues consisted of town hall–style meetings of about 300 people held regularly around the country, with the stated purpose of soliciting popular input into her government program. From the time they debuted in January 2005 until the official start of the campaign in September, citizen dialogues were Bachelet's principal campaign activity (author's interview, Benado). Bachelet emphasized that citizen dialogues were part of her "different style" of campaigning, but Lagos had employed an identical strategy with the same name during the 1999 campaign.[6] Frei's "Listen to Chile" program from 1993 was also similar in its design and inspiration. Essentially, both the citizen dialogues and the citizen networks repeated a direct linkage strategy that had worked well for previous Concertación candidates and was consistent with the approach to the 1988 plebiscite campaign.

A Partial Embrace of Partisan Image

Beginning several weeks before the election, and accelerating during the second round, the Bachelet campaign did shift its orientation toward political parties. While Bachelet's communication strategists had initially insisted that the *franja* would highlight her connection with the people rather than political parties,[7] the last two weeks of first-round television advertising included endorsements from a number of prominent Christian Democrats, including former presidents Patricio Aylwin and Eduardo Frei. At the start of the second round, Bachelet brought in senior politicians Andrés Zaldívar from the PDC and Sergio Bitar from the PPD to publicly head up the campaign's operations and convey an image of party support. The second round also featured more use of intermediated linkages – in Bitar's words (author's interview), "much greater party organization, more coordinated work by all structures of elected leaders, and also a more active connection with social organizations."

In contrast to the dramatic reversal in strategy between the first and second rounds of Lagos's 1999 campaign, the change in Bachelet's strategy is better understood as a modification or complement. The director of Bachelet's television advertising characterized the change in the *franja* in mid-November as a slight correction, noting that the inclusion of party endorsements did not imply any other shift in the first-round advertising strategy (author's interview, Vinacur). For a Socialist candidate, featuring endorsements from Christian Democrats is more a strategy of protecting one's center flank than an embrace of

---

[6] *El Mercurio*, May 30, 2005; *La Hora*, August 12, 1999.
[7] *Cosas*, October 25, 1999.

a partisan image. Campaign communication strategists also described these segments as communicating the personal support of popular party figures rather than official party support (author's interviews, Díaz and Vinacur). Finally, there was no wholesale replacement of campaign strategists as there had been in 1999 (author's interview, Díaz).

The increased territorial work of parties in the second round is also best seen as a correction rather than a major reversal in campaign strategy. Bitar (author's interview) characterized his effort to stimulate party participation as a complement to the citizen campaign, a way to "free up [the candidate] from the work of coordination and direction, and leave her directly in contact with the people, which is her forte." And Bachelet's head of territorial operations claims the campaign agreed to an increase in activists' door-to-door canvassing in mid-November mainly as a political concession to the parties that were pressing for it (author's interview, Jofré).

In sum, despite the common claim that Bachelet's campaign represented a new style of politics, the strategies by which she sought to circumvent established intermediary institutions and create new, direct linkages were quite similar to those of prior Concertación presidential candidates. In this sense, her campaign represents success contagion through strategic inertia.

SUCCESS CONTAGION ON THE RIGHT

For right-wing candidates in Chile, success contagion has meant convergence over time on the personalistic strategy employed by the "No" campaign in 1988. Given the severity (and for many on the right, the unexpectedness) of Pinochet's defeat in the plebiscite, a partial form of convergence occurred relatively quickly. The 1989 campaign of Hernán Büchi was personalistic in terms of its minimal policy focus, and it also started out with a message of national reconciliation similar to that of the "No" campaign. However, at the urging of a foreign consultant, Büchi shifted to a cleavage-priming approach in the final weeks of his campaign.

Success contagion among the Chilean Right began in earnest with the 1999 campaign of Joaquín Lavín, and it continued in 2005 with the presidential bids of Lavín and Sebastián Piñera. Imitation of prior left-wing strategies and the consolidation of norms within the community of campaign professionals both played a role in these processes. In 1999, Lavín explicitly modeled his campaign on prior electoral strategies of the Concertación, particularly with respect to policy focus and linkage. His strategy of communicating closeness to the common people involved an effort to empathize with their problems (though not propose specific solutions) and also circumvent political parties in favor of multiple forms of direct contact.

The contagion of a personalistic strategy has also discouraged right-wing candidates – Lavín in 1999, and both Lavín and Piñera in 2005 – from priming religious cleavages. Emphasizing their own Catholic faith and stance on

TABLE 2.5. *Hernán Büchi's Television Advertising, 1989*

Policy focused	20.7
Specific proposals	2.5
General proposals	3.3
Achievements	1.1
Criticism	3.4
Diagnosis	10.4
Not policy focused (jingles, image, or other)	79.3
Cleavage priming	11.2
No cleavage priming	88.8

Note: Entries are percentages of total advertising time.

moral issues while criticizing the secularism and agnosticism of their Socialist opponents could have been a valuable strategy in both elections. But Lavín consistently avoided priming religious cleavages in both campaigns, and Piñera did so only in a very limited fashion in 2005. In both instances, campaign strategies were influenced by the strong norm against confrontational and divisive campaign appeals in Chile.

Hernán Büchi, 1989: A Partial Embrace of the Personalistic Approach

Coming only a year after the 1988 plebiscite, the presidential campaign of Hernán Büchi already showed some signs of convergence on the successful strategy introduced by the "No" campaign. Büchi was a technocrat who had served as finance minister for the military government from 1985 to 1989 but had no background as a politician and did not belong to a political party. These characteristics made him particularly appealing to the economic Right, which was interested in a candidate identified with the government's economic model but not right-wing party politics or the regime's human rights record (author's interview, González).

Despite the stated intention of associating Büchi with his policies as finance minister, his campaign was actually much more focused on the candidate as an individual. In stark contrast to previous year's "Yes" campaign, Büchi's television advertising was *less* policy focused than that of his opponent, with barely a fifth of his *franja* devoted to policy issues (Table 2.5). The majority of this policy-related content was diagnostic in nature, with only 5.8 percentage points focused on general or specific proposals and a strikingly low 1.1 percentage points devoted to policy accomplishments. Instead, the campaign focused largely on Büchi's personal image and the myriad ways in which he differed from Pinochet as an individual, such as his youth, personal appearance (he sported a shaggy haircut), and obsession with fitness.

Büchi's campaign also started out similar to the Concertación's "No" campaign by avoiding confrontation and conveying a message of national reconciliation. During the first two weeks of Büchi's *franja*, the song "I Don't Want War" (sung by children) was repeated in nine consecutive episodes, and a segment from the November 20 program embraced the human rights rallying cry "Never Again." Attacks on the opposition were designed to be light and humorous in nature; they were done as parodies, focusing on the potential lack of accountability among a coalition of seventeen different parties and the difficulties it might encounter in governing.

In the final weeks before the election, however, Büchi's campaign hardened the tone of its attacks, returning to the cleavage-priming appeals of the 1988 plebiscite. A three-minute-long segment, repeated multiple times in the last two weeks of the *franja*, reported on the high percentage of Concertación party leaders who were former officials of the Allende government or belonged to parties with a Marxist ideology. Cleavage-priming criticism of this sort occupied a total of 11.2 percent of Büchi's *franja*, similar to the 10.4 percent of the previous year's "Yes" campaign. These attacks were implemented at the suggestion of American political consultant Mark Klugmann, a former speechwriter for Ronald Reagan who had not been involved in the plebiscite, so in this sense, they were a new idea rather than a repetition of the plebiscite strategy. In part, such a suggestion may have been welcomed because Büchi's team had decided that there was little chance of winning the presidency, and it was focused on supporting right-wing candidates in the legislative election (author's interviews, Baraona and González).

In sum, Büchi's campaign illustrates partial convergence on the personalistic strategy employed by the Concertación in the 1988 plebiscite. This move may have been an inward-oriented negative reaction to the previous year's "Yes" campaign, as Büchi sought to differentiate himself from Pinochet as an individual. But explicitly imitating the approach of the "No" campaign might also have been a factor. In a roundtable discussion held at Chile's Centro de Estudios Públicos, a prominent think tank, in October 1989, several right-wing intellectuals expressed grudging admiration for the Concertación's plebiscite strategy and argued that the Right had to learn from this example so as to effectively convey its project for society in an era of television campaigning (Méndez et al. 1989). Büchi's campaign may well have come to the same conclusions.

Joaquín Lavín, 1999: A Strategy of Closeness Inspired by the Left

Among right-wing presidential candidates in Chile, the first full-fledged instance of success contagion concerns the 1999 campaign of Joaquín Lavín, who embraced personalism by specifically imitating strategies that had previously been employed only by the Left. The primary objective of Lavín's campaign was to communicate closeness to the common people and an empathy with their problems – an idea that was central to the Concertación's strategy in prior elections but had not previously been a major concern for the Right.

Lavín's closeness strategy implied a relatively low policy focus for the campaign, as well as an effort to circumvent parties and other forms of intermediated linkage in favor of direct contact with the people. The former mayor of Las Condes, a large and wealthy municipality in metropolitan Santiago, Lavín capitalized upon the image of a public servant who regularly mingled with his constituents and worked hard to solve their problems rather than getting mired in partisan disputes. He merged this message of closeness with a call for change, asking voters to elect someone who was not a traditional politician and did not belong to the coalition that had governed for the past ten years. Rather than emphasizing policy proposals, Lavín concentrated on the diagnosis of current problems such as crime and unemployment, as well as on "empathy appeals" – arguing that he understood the concerns of various social groups because of his direct contact, and would be prepared to implement unspecified solutions once in office.

Media-Centric Campaign Trips and Empathy Appeals

Lavín's efforts to circumvent party intermediation in the 1999 election are particularly noteworthy because he was the first right-wing presidential candidate from a party with substantial organizational presence. Lavín's UDI is considered one of Chile's most institutionalized and best-disciplined parties (Pollack 1999; Huneeus 2001; Morales and Bugueño 2002; Barozet 2003; San Francisco 2003). Thanks to a long tradition of organizing in poor neighborhoods, it also has substantial support and institutional presence in geographic areas traditionally dominated by the Left. This party structure is a significant resource during electoral periods, and both UDI and its coalition partner National Renewal (Renovación Nacional, RN) were involved behind the scenes in providing logistical support for Lavín's campaign. Nonetheless, both RN and UDI played a subordinate role in terms of the public face of the campaign and the structures that provided an actual linkage between Lavín and his potential voters. Party flags were prohibited from appearing at any of Lavín's rallies, for instance, in order to project an independent image (author's interviews, Moreno and Sepúlveda).

In place of party intermediation, Lavín crafted a "doubly direct" linkage strategy that involved making personal contact with individuals and then ensuring that images of this contact were broadcast directly to the nation via television news. Lavín's campaign was intensely territorial – he visited all 345 *comunas* in the country, and various neighborhoods in each, for a total of over 1,500 distinct locales (author's interview, Guzmán) – but he did so in a manner that was particularly innovative with respect to the mass media. One common technique involved Lavín spending the night in the house of a shantytown dweller, something that was repeated approximately every fifteen days during the campaign. While appearing as a spontaneous gesture of solidarity with the poor and an opportunity to connect personally with an individual voter, these visits were carefully orchestrated by the campaign's production specialist, who was also in charge of organizing mass events such as the campaign's closing rally (author's interview, Mackenna). According to Lavín's chief of staff, "he focused all of his activities on the television images that were going to be broadcast in

TABLE 2.6. *Joaquín Lavín's Television Advertising, 1999*

Policy focused	33.4
Specific proposals	2.6
General proposals	8.7
Achievements	5.3
Criticism	4.7
Diagnosis	12.1
Not policy focused (jingles, image, or other)	66.6
Cleavage priming	0.0
No cleavage priming	100.0

Note: Entries are percentages of total advertising time.

the evening" (author's interview, Moreno). In this fashion, Lavín could extend his direct contact with one shantytown dweller to the thousands of others who saw him spending the night in the house of someone just like them.

Lavín also sought to communicate a message of closeness to the common people through his television advertising, which privileged "man in the street" testimonials and diagnosis of problems rather than specific proposals for solving them. During Lavín's travels around the country, campaign staff filmed thousands of short comments from people who attended his events. Over two hundred of these clips were ultimately used in Lavín's television advertising, taking up a fifth of the total time. Although these testimonials often mentioned policy issues, they rarely discussed Lavín's proposals; rather, a testimonial might bemoan the terrible state of crime and express confidence that Lavín would somehow solve the problem. As shown in Table 2.6, Lavín's advertising privileged generic discussion of future policy (8.7 percent) over specific proposals (2.6 percent), and it devoted a large share of time to the diagnosis of current problems (12.1 percent).

Lavín's *franja* also sought to convey closeness to the common people through explicit empathy appeals, in which the candidate stressed his intimate understanding of people's challenges. This strategy is essentially identical to that of the "No" campaign in the 1988 plebiscite, though Lavín took it to new lengths. One such appeal was initially broadcast on the first day of the *franja* and repeated seven times during the campaign. As images from Lavín's campaign trips and direct contact with individuals flashed across the screen, Lavín said:

I've been a miner in Chuquicamata … I was a fisherman in Los Vilos … I was moved by unemployment … I ate in soup kitchens. I saw poverty in the shantytowns. I met with youth who feel that they have no opportunity … After traveling thousands of kilometers, embracing and sharing the feelings of thousands of people, I truly have Chile under my skin. Today I *know* what a miner or a fisherman feels. Today I *know* what it is like to have no job or nothing to eat.

Empathy appeals of this sort were also conveyed through testimonials, such as a university student opining that Lavín understands the problems of today's youth.

Success Contagion by Imitation

Lavín's 1999 campaign is an example of success contagion by imitation because his strategy of conveying closeness and empathy with the common people explicitly copied prior efforts by the Concertación. The producer of Lavín's *franja* said that the campaign borrowed various "secret weapons from the Left" such as using "testimonials from the Chilean people, the poor people of Chile, which was their natural market" (author's interview, Iriarte). Another advertising strategist specifically mentioned the "No" *franja* as an inspiration for the emotional tone of Lavín's campaign and its efforts to convey a grand project of change that could unify the country (author's interview, Subercaseaux). And Lavín's campaign manager said that taking the campaign to the streets to establish direct connections with the common people was something that only the Concertación had done previously. "In 1999, we copied them in that regard," he argued. "The closeness [strategy] originated on the left" (author's interview, de la Maza).

Imitation was able to serve as the main mechanism of success contagion in Chile because copying the Left's electoral strategy was not a difficult ideological pill for the Right to swallow. The Concertación's centrist governing style during the 1990s meant that the coalition, while a political adversary of the Right, was not a philosophical adversary. De la Maza (author's interview) noted that the first instance of copying across the ideological spectrum involved the Concertación maintaining the Right's economic model when it came to power in 1990. In comparison, borrowing campaign strategies was a relatively minor affair. Moreover, the personalistic approach was a particularly easy strategy for the Right to copy. De-emphasizing cleavages and appealing directly to individuals is a classic electoral tactic for the Right, which typically needs to unify distinct segments of the electorate in order to be competitive (Gibson 1992). Likewise, stressing empathy rather than grand proposals help to depoliticize Lavín's image and cast him as being above partisan disputes, which could help win votes across the ideological spectrum.

The Rarity of Religious Appeals among Right-Wing Candidates

Another aspect of right-wing presidential campaigns in Chile has been influenced by a normative process in which the taboo against cleavage priming has become widely accepted within Chile's community of campaign professionals. In both the 1999 and 2005 elections, major candidates on the right were reluctant to prime religious cleavages even though their major left-wing opponent was an acknowledged nonbeliever. Lavín, a member of Opus Dei with impeccable Catholic credentials, steadfastly avoided pointing out his rivals' agnosticism, their stance with respect to moral issues, or even his own religious identity. And while Sebastián Piñera did flirt with such a strategy in 2005, these attacks were fairly limited.

The correlation between religious and political identification in Chile suggests that priming cleavages between the country's Catholic and secular subcultures could be a viable electoral strategy for the Right. In the 1995–1996 World Values Survey, supporters of the centrist PDC scored significantly higher on several measures of religion and religiosity than those who identified with the left-wing parties of the Concertación. On both religious identity and stance on moral issues, Christian Democrats cluster with those who support the Right (Mainwaring and Scully 2003). The PDC is also perceived as being closer to UDI's and RN's positions on abortion and same-sex marriage – as well as to the average voter's stance on these issues – than to the stance of the other Concertación parties (Raymond and Feltch 2014). During the pre-dictatorship period, the PDC sometimes cooperated with right-wing parties, but since the transition to democracy, it has remained solidly allied with the secular Left. Given the discrepancy between religious identity and parties' electoral alliances, one might expect frequent efforts by right-wing candidates to realign the bases of competition by priming the religious–secular cleavage.

In the 2005 election, the right-wing electoral pact Alliance for Chile (Alianza por Chile) failed to agree upon a single presidential candidate; Lavín ran for a second time with the support of UDI, and Sebastián Piñera competed as the candidate of RN. Piñera, who had publicly supported the "No" option in the plebiscite and whose father had been a Christian Democrat, was positioned to make a more legitimate play for centrist votes than Lavín. Piñera's electoral appeals emphasized his centrist identity, arguing that he could lead a new, broader coalition combining the Right with segments of the Center and the PDC. Meanwhile, Lavín's popularity had declined after four unsuccessful years as mayor of Santiago, and he was seen as more mired in right-wing party politics than in 1999. These aspects of his public image, combined with Piñera's candidacy, meant that Lavín's efforts in 2005 would focus more on mobilizing core right-wing voters for UDI's legislative campaign than on winning the presidency (author's interviews, Cordero and Larroulet).

In neither the 1999 election, when he was making a play for the center, nor in 2005, when he was more focused on the right-wing vote, did Lavín seek to prime the religious–secular cleavage. In a total of over five-and-a-half hours of television advertising from both elections, Lavín never once made reference to Lagos's or Bachelet's agnosticism or stance on moral issues such as divorce and abortion. On the whole, Lavín devoted less than two minutes from a single episode of the 2005 *franja* to his own religious image, his position with respect to moral issues, or endorsements from religious figures.

During the 2005 presidential campaign, Sebastián Piñera did place some emphasis on the contrast between his opponent's agnosticism and his own Christian faith. In the first few weeks of the campaign for the runoff, Piñera publicly embraced the values of Christian humanism closely identified with the social positions of the Catholic Church and the philosophy of the PDC. In laying claim to this Christian Democratic tradition, Piñera specifically contrasted his Catholicism with Bachelet's secularity. In comments to the media, Piñera said that "she accuses me of political cross-dressing for invoking and convoking the world of Christian humanism ... such criticism coming from an agnostic or atheist like Michelle Bachelet seems like a total contradiction to me" (Campusano S. 2005). A week later, when the Catholic Bishops requested that the two candidates spell out their positions on a number of values-related issues, Piñera similarly underscored his opponent's lack of Christian faith.[8] Toward the end of the month, Piñera attempted to reignite public debate on moral issues, sending a letter to bishops and evangelical pastors reaffirming his position against abortion, gay marriage, and euthanasia.[9]

Piñera's religious campaigning in 2005 marks a partial deviation from the established model of campaign strategy in Chile. Yet these instances of cleavage priming were quite limited in scope. Members of the campaign team clearly perceived the potential strategic benefit of priming the religious–secular cleavage.[10] But Piñera's attacks on his opponent's agnosticism consisted only of a handful of comments in the first two weeks of the second-round campaign. Piñera's campaign manager characterized these comments to the press as slip-ups, saying that the second-round campaign strategy was to emphasize Christian humanism but in a nonconfrontational manner (author's interview, Hinzpeter). No discussion of religious identity, either in the form of self-praise or criticism of his opponent, made its way into Piñera's second-round *franja*, and only one twenty-four-second clip mentioned the values of Christian humanism that he was supposedly trying to invoke. The few instances of direct criticism of Bachelet in the second round *franja* focused on her lack of preparation for office rather than her lack of Christian faith.

The taboo against cleavage priming that has been perpetuated since the 1988 plebiscite has discouraged right-wing candidates from making serious efforts to divide Chilean politics along religious–secular lines. The normative preference for nondivisive appeals has spread broadly among Chilean campaign professionals, including those who typically work for the Right. During Lavín's 1999 campaign, the main member of his advertising team favoring an attack strategy was marginalized and overruled by other advisors who preferred a nonconfrontational approach (author's interview, Subercaseaux). The producer of Lavín's 1999 *franja* explained that a positive campaign message had been

---

[8] *El Mercurio*, December 22, 2005.
[9] *El Mercurio*, December 30, 2005.
[10] As chief of staff Ignacio Rivadeneira (author's interview) explained after the fact, "if the scenario was democracy–dictatorship, they would win. If it was rich or poor, they would win. If it was Concertación–Alianza, they would win. All of the possible scenarios, except for one, which was Christian humanism–secular humanism ... that scenario could benefit us."

appropriate because "we lived through sixteen years of dictatorship." Interviewed several days before the January 2006 runoff election, at a point when polls were predicting a victory for Bachelet, he went on to opine that "the great error that definitely cost Piñera the presidency was this confrontation of the past week, in which he was very aggressive" (author's interview, Iriarte). The ineffectiveness of divisive appeals, a conclusion drawn from the 1988 plebiscite, has become a conventional wisdom in Chilean politics, even in the absence of strong evidence that might reconfirm it.

PARTIAL DEVIATIONS FROM PERSONALISM: POLICY FOCUS IN 2005

As illustrated by Piñera's brief recourse to cleavage priming in the second round of the 2005 campaign, candidates do sometimes respond to conjunctural incentives by deviating from the ideal-typical personalistic strategy. However, such instances are quite limited in comparative perspective. Even when explicitly seeking to deviate from a personalistic approach, Chilean presidential candidates never come close to adopting a fundamentally different model of campaign strategy.

In this section, I discuss two partial deviations from the personalistic model of campaign strategy – the emphasis on policy in the campaigns of Lavín and Bachelet in 2005, which was somewhat greater than that of previous Chilean candidates. While both candidates had incentives to increase the policy focus of their campaigns, in neither case did the candidate's strategy approach the technocratic style of campaigning that dominates in Brazil. And Bachelet's campaign, while focusing more on future policy than the campaigns of prior Concertación candidates, nonetheless was consistent with personalism in its effort to limit the details of proposals.

Michelle Bachelet, 2005: Emphasizing Policy, Avoiding Details

As the first serious female contender for the presidency in Chile, Bachelet had to confront an unusually high degree of skepticism and negative press coverage regarding her qualifications for office (Valenzuela and Correa 2007). This adverse scenario offered a clear incentive to emphasize her prior accomplishments as health and defense minister, as well as specific future policy initiatives that would showcase her mastery of the issues. In an effort to demonstrate that Bachelet was prepared to govern, her communication strategists highlighted her government program more than previous candidates had done, devoting 20.3 percent of the *franja* over both rounds to the discussion of current or future policy. Such segments not only occupied a comparatively large portion of her advertising but were also prominently set apart. Each segment began with a "person on the street" holding a sign in front of the camera that said "Government Program, Michelle Bachelet." The explicit focus on future policy was

TABLE 2.7. *Michelle Bachelet's Television Advertising, 2005*

Policy focused	33.3
Specific proposals	4.6
General proposals	15.7
Achievements	3.8
Criticism	0.0
Diagnosis	9.2
Not policy focused (jingles, image, or other)	66.7
Cleavage priming	0.0
No cleavage priming	100.0

Note: Entries are percentages of total advertising time.

complemented by segments designed to emphasize Bachelet's leadership qualifications – images of her reviewing troops as defense minister or fluently speaking English, French, and German at a press conference.

The effort to communicate Bachelet's preparedness to govern, however, entered into conflict with the desire to minimize policy focus in a manner consistent with the Concertación's traditional style. Among the campaign communication strategists, specific policy commitments tended to be cast in the category of "big offers" (*ofertones*) that were considered unrealistic, unbelievable, and an element of the "old politics" of promises that are never fulfilled (Gerber 2006). According to communication director Ricardo Solari, "rather than a campaign of programmatic offers, it had to be a campaign where the dimensions of style, production, and all of the discourse were permanently tied to a different way of doing things" (Gerber 2006: 33).

In effect, the tension between communicating preparedness and avoiding "big offers" was resolved by focusing Bachelet's policy discussion on generalities. Specific proposals took up only 4.6 percent of her *franja* across both rounds of the campaign, whereas generic discussion of future policy accounted for 15.7 percent (Table 2.7). A typical "government program" segment would involve Bachelet talking about how important a particular issue was to her and how much she would worry about it as president, but saying very little about the measures she proposed to implement. Bachelet also spent a substantial amount of time conveying the same sort of empathy appeals that had been a hallmark of Lavín's strategy in 1999. Across both rounds of the election, about a sixth of her advertising was primarily oriented toward demonstrating her empathy with people's everyday concerns.

In sum, Bachelet did place somewhat more emphasis on future policy than is the norm for Concertación candidates, but her campaign was still consistent with personalism in that it sought to avoid policy details and specific commitments. Adhering to the established model of campaigning in Chile was an important reason for adopting this strategy. When asked why the campaign made so few major policy commitments, Solari (author's interview) responded

TABLE 2.8. *Joaquín Lavín's Television Advertising, 2005*

Policy focused	38.2
Specific proposals	9.4
General proposals	7.0
Achievements	4.7
Criticism	0.8
Diagnosis	16.2
Not policy focused (jingles, image, or other)	61.8
Cleavage priming	0.0
No cleavage priming	100.0

Note: Entries are percentages of total advertising time.

that "that is a tradition of the Concertación; in terms of its programmatic offerings, the Concertación emphatically resists making very big...promises." The two major communication strategists working for Bachelet, Solari and Pablo Halpern, had both participated in previous presidential campaigns for the Concertación and thus had direct experience with this approach.

Joaquín Lavín, 2005: Policy Emphasis without Wholesale Change

Like Bachelet, Joaquín Lavín had incentives to emphasize policy more than usual in his 2005 campaign. In 1999, when Lavín had just completed a successful term as mayor of Las Condes, communicating his understanding of people's problems was considered sufficient to convince voters that he could solve them. In 2005, however, Lavín was coming off a much less successful term as mayor of Santiago, and his advisors worried that voters would not entrust him with running the country merely because of his closeness to the people (author's interview, de la Maza). Campaign strategists also recognized that Lavín could not compete against Bachelet on the basis of empathy alone (author's interview, Cordero).

One of the major objectives of Lavín's 2005 campaign, therefore, was to present him as more of a statesman than in 1999. In pursuit of this goal, Lavín's television advertising included numerous segments in which the candidate, dressed in a suit and standing in front of a podium, discussed specific policy issues and offered detailed proposals for addressing them. Lavín's *franja* included the most overall policy discussion of any of the candidates in the first round (38.2 percent, versus 35.5 percent for Bachelet and 32.6 percent for Piñera). It also devoted a substantial amount of time (9.4 percent) to specific proposals (Table 2.8). Lavín's move away from a personalistic approach in 2005 was thus less ambivalent than Bachelet's; he not only increased his focus on overall policy when compared to the 1999 campaign but also devoted a substantial proportion of time to specific details.

Despite Lavín's shift in strategy, his 2005 campaign still remains more consistent with personalism than with any other ideal-typical model of campaign strategy. The overall level of policy focus in Lavín's 2005 television advertising was much closer to that of other Chilean candidates than to those in Brazil who have converged upon the technocratic model of campaign strategy. As discussed in the next chapter, Brazilian candidates not only focus more of their policy discussion on specifics rather than generalities but also devote as much as 70–75 percent of all advertising time to policy discussion. By this measure, Lavín's 2005 campaign (or for that matter, Lagos's first-round campaign in 1999) would be the second least policy-focused campaign since democratization if it had been conducted in Brazil. While clearly a strategic response to conjunctural incentives, Lavín's 2005 campaign still represents variation within the personalistic category rather than a wholesale shift to a fundamentally different model of campaign strategy.

TESTING THE ARGUMENT: STRATEGIC CONTINUITY IN 2009

As discussed in Chapter 1, the theory of success contagion was formulated inductively based on campaigns in Chile, Peru, and Brazil through 2005–2006. More recent presidential elections thus constitute a test of the theory's predictions for each country. In this section, I examine the campaigns of the three major candidates in Chile's 2009–2010 presidential election: Marco Enríquez-Ominami, Eduardo Frei Ruiz-Tagle, and Sebastián Piñera. Each of them employed a personalistic strategy that was similar to those of prior presidential candidates on both the right and the left. The one partial deviation from personalism in 2009–2010, Frei's somewhat greater emphasis on policy in the first round, was both limited in scope and corrected in the runoff with a return to the tried-and-true model of campaigning in Chile.

For the first time since democratization, Chile's 2009–2010 presidential election pitted a divided Left against a united Right. Former president Eduardo Frei of the PDC was chosen as candidate of the Concertación. However, Marco Enríquez-Ominami, a first-term Socialist legislator, ended up resigning from his party and launching an independent bid for president after party elites blocked him from competing in the Concertación's primary. Enríquez-Ominami finished third in the first round, with 20.1 percent of the vote, helping push the contest into a runoff. On the right, Sebastián Piñera was supported by the Coalition for Change, which consisted of RN, UDI, and several fledgling centrist movements led by Concertación defectors. Despite the Bachelet government's record approval rating – as high as 80 percent during the campaign – the Concertación was unable to translate her personal popularity into another presidential victory. Piñera won the first-round vote, with 44.1 percent compared to Frei's 29.6 percent, and he went on to defeat Frei in the runoff by a margin of 51.6–48.4 percent.

Each of the three major candidates ran a campaign that was broadly consistent with the personalistic style. None of them emphasized cleavages in any way, and they often denounced mildly critical comments from their opponents as inappropriate, divisive, and reminiscent of the "Yes" campaign in the 1988 plebiscite. For example, at an event commemorating the victory of the "No" campaign in 1988, Frei said that "the arrogance of the Right…is going to bring us social conflict and problems, because whenever they have governed the country, they have only looked after the interests of a minority." In response, Piñera denounced Frei's "terror campaign," saying "Chileans want nothing to do with campaigns like that." Enríquez-Ominami sounded a similar note: "I'm sorry to see them running a terror campaign…the same discourse as Pinochet."[11]

Enríquez-Ominami's rejection of divisive campaigning in 2009 is particularly striking, given that, as a strategist for Ricardo Lagos's first-round campaign in 1999, he had strenuously defended a cleavage-priming approach. While critical of establishment politicians, Enríquez-Ominami's 2009 campaign was explicitly inclusive with respect to Chilean society. Parts of his television advertising even copied scenes from the "No" campaign's *franja*, such as a segment urging Chileans to vote for him "without hatred, without violence, without fear."

Piñera also avoided priming religious cleavages in 2009, even more so than in his previous campaign. Though Frei, a Catholic and member of a confessional party, was not as vulnerable to religious attacks as his agnostic predecessors, he did come out in support of civil unions for same-sex couples and greater societal acceptance of lesbians and gays. Piñera might have been expected to criticize Frei for being pulled to the left on this issue by his coalition partners, and to stake out the opposite position (Raymond and Feltch 2014). Instead, Piñera mirrored Frei's stance, even prominently featuring a gay couple in his television advertising after Frei had included a lesbian couple in his. Piñera's stance caused great consternation within his coalition, especially among members of the more conservative UDI.[12]

The three major candidates also privileged direct linkages to voters, emphasized their closeness to the people, and sought to circumvent or minimize the role of parties. For Enríquez-Ominami, who ran explicitly as an outsider, emphasizing his distance from political parties was a natural move. But Piñera and Frei, despite their status as party candidates, also sought to circumvent party intermediation (Navia 2009: 32). For Frei, as with Bachelet in 2005, the critical stance toward parties generated tensions within the coalition that spilled out into the open during the first round. During the first presidential debate, for instance, the Frei campaign refused to allow the leaders of Concertación parties to be seated in the main room so as to keep them from appearing in

[11] *El Mercurio*, October 7, 2009.
[12] *El Mercurio*, November 21, 2009.

TABLE 2.9. *Television Advertising in Chile's 2009 Election*

	Enríquez-Ominami Round 1	Piñera Round 1	Piñera Round 2	Frei Round 1	Frei Round 2
Policy focused	19.2	40.0	27.7	45.2	15.7
Specific proposals	3.1	3.4	1.8	13.8	1.8
General proposals	4.0	7.1	18.2	0.0	4.6
Achievements	0.0	0.4	0.0	5.2	3.5
Criticism	0.1	0.2	0.0	0.0	0.0
Diagnosis	12.0	28.9	7.7	26.1	5.8
Not policy focused (jingles, image, or other)	80.8	60.0	72.3	54.8	84.3
Cleavage priming	0.0	0.0	0.0	0.0	0.0
No cleavage priming	100.0	100.0	100.0	100.0	100.0

Note: Entries are percentages of total advertising time.

television coverage of the event.[13] Throughout the campaign, party leaders openly criticized symbolic snubs of this sort as well as a lack of input into campaign decision-making.[14] Tense relations between Frei and party leaders may have been partially responsible for the tepid support from Concertación legislative candidates, many of whom refused to appear alongside Frei in their campaign posters.[15]

Finally, the campaigns were consistent with previous efforts in terms of their minimal policy focus. Enríquez-Ominami's campaign was primarily focused on the candidate as a person. Image-oriented content, including a long, six-part biography of the candidate, took up a quarter of Enríquez-Ominami's television advertising time; jingles, entertainment-oriented content, and opening, closing, and transitional segments took nearly an additional third. As shown in Table 2.9, discussion of policy issues occupied only 19.2 percent of the total time. The majority of this content (12 percentage points) simply conveyed a diagnosis of current problems. As with his campaign's reluctance to prime cleavages, the minimal policy focus is striking when contrasted with Enríquez-Ominami's strong preference for emphasizing policy when advising Lagos's campaign in 1999.

Piñera's campaign was also relatively light on policy. His television advertising prominently reported on the "Tantauco Groups," a series of discussions among policy experts that had been used to generate proposals for the government program prior to the campaign. Yet the emphasis in the *franja* was

---

[13] *El Mercurio*, September 25, 2009.
[14] *El Mercurio*, September 27, 2009; *El Mercurio*, September 28, 2009; *El Mercurio*, October 18, 2009.
[15] *El Mercurio*, October 14, 2009; *El Mercurio*, October 15, 2009.

more on the diversity of ideas that went into these sessions, and the expertise of those who participated, than on specific proposals that emerged. Other advertising segments showed Piñera listening to the concerns of particular groups – retirees, women, middle-class families – and then empathizing with their plight but saying little about specific solutions. In the first round, 40 percent of Piñera's advertising was devoted to policy, slightly more than the long-term average for Chile, but the majority of this content (28.9 percentage points) was diagnostic. In the second round, only 27.7 percent of his *franja* focused on policy.

Like Bachelet's and Lavín's campaigns in 2005, Frei's first-round campaign in 2009 represents a partial deviation from the ideal-typical personalistic strategy in that it conveyed a somewhat greater policy focus. Based on initial survey and focus group research, Frei's strategists determined that he could not compete with Piñera on personal attributes, and they opted to shift the focus away from Frei as an individual. The approach "was to show Frei more as a 'container' than as 'content'" (Tironi 2010: 78) – part of which meant emphasizing that a Frei government would continue and improve upon the Concertación's popular policies in areas such as social protection. Television advertising from the first round thus included a number of segments describing specific policy gains under Bachelet, along with Frei's proposals for further progress in the same area. Frei's first-round *franja* devoted 45.2 percent of its total time to policy, and much of this content – 13.8 percentage points – involved specific proposals. These figures are the highest of any Chilean campaign examined in this study.

For several reasons, however, Frei's greater policy focus in the first round is best considered variation within the category of personalism rather than a wholesale abandonment of this approach. First, the most important part of the first-round strategy was to convey "citizen histories" – life stories of common people that were often relevant to a particular policy area but focused much more on the human interest factor than on proposals or policy achievements (Tironi 2010: 147–151). As a result, the largest share of policy content in Frei's first-round advertising was devoted to diagnosis (26.1 percentage points), and the *franja* retained an "empathy" feel similar to that of prior Concertación campaigns. Second, as with Lagos's campaign in 1999–2000, the higher policy emphasis in the first round was abandoned in the runoff, in part thanks to a change in advisors.[16] The second-round *franja* devoted only 15.7 percent of its total time to policy, the lowest figure of any Chilean campaign examined in this study. Finally, as with Lavín and Bachelet's 2005 campaigns, the greater-than-normal policy focus of Frei's first-round campaign in 2009 was still closer to the long-term trend in Chile than to the policy-centric campaigns of recent candidates in Brazil.

On the whole, therefore, there is substantial evidence of strategic continuity during Chile's 2009–2010 presidential election, as predicted by the theory of success contagion. In some ways, this election presents a relatively weak

---

[16] *El Mercurio*, November 29, 2009.

test of the theory: two of the three major candidates had run previously, and their major advisors had also participated in prior presidential campaigns, so one might naturally expect a similar approach. Yet Enríquez-Ominami's choice of strategy is more telling. Having advocated so strongly for a policy-focused, cleavage-priming campaign for Lagos in 1999 – not merely in an effort to win, but also out of principled opposition to a depoliticized campaign style – one might expect him to follow his own advice when he became the candidate. However, Enríquez-Ominami ultimately embraced the tried-and-true, personalistic model of campaigning in 2009.

CONCLUSION

In the years since democratization, Chilean presidential candidates have converged upon common campaign strategies because of a process of success contagion. Left-wing candidates have repeatedly employed the personalistic model of campaign strategy first introduced in the 1988 plebiscite and legitimated by Patricio Aylwin's successful term in office. Their campaigns have placed a relatively low emphasis on policy, favored direct over intermediated linkages, and avoided priming cleavages. Meanwhile, right-wing candidates have gravitated toward this model of campaign strategy over time, with Lavín being the first to fully embrace it in 1999.

Among candidates on the left, the consistent recourse to personalism has resulted primarily from strategic inertia. Repeating a previously successful strategy has often been the first instinct of candidates and their advisors, and it occurred without much question in the campaigns of Aylwin, Frei (1993), and Bachelet. Lagos's 1999 campaign involved strategic inertia for a different reason – advisors who had been responsible for the Concertación's strategy in prior elections were able to impose their vision in the second round and marginalize those who had favored an unorthodox approach. The particular outcome of this power struggle was facilitated by the strong taboo against confrontational campaigning in Chile. Frei's 2009 campaign involved a similar mid-course correction, emphasizing policy more than usual in the first round but returning to a low policy focus in the runoff.

On the right, imitation has played an important role in candidates' convergence on a strategy initially introduced by the Left. In 1999, Lavín's advisors designed a strategy of closeness to the common people that was specifically inspired by prior campaigns of the Concertación. Imitation of a previously successful example thus led Lavín to circumvent political parties, privilege direct ties to the electorate, emphasize his familiarity with people's problems, and avoid discussing the details of proposed solutions. The limited ideological distance between the governing Concertación and the right-wing opposition facilitated this mimetic process. Lavín's advisors had no qualms about copying campaign strategies from a Center-Left that had previously borrowed policy models from their side of the ideological spectrum.

The campaign strategies of the Right have also been influenced by the norm against cleavage priming in Chilean elections. In both 1999 and 2005, right-wing candidates engaged in few cleavage-priming attacks against their secular, agnostic opponents, despite the potential to woo centrist Christian Democrats who have tended to vote for the Concertación. The same thing occurred in 2009, when Piñera opted to mirror Frei's inclusive stance toward gays and lesbians.

Success contagion in Chile does not mean that candidates adhere to identical campaign strategies without responding to conjunctural incentives, differentiating themselves from their opponents, or playing up their own strengths. Lavín and Bachelet in 2005, and Frei in 2009, all had reasons to emphasize policy somewhat more than the Chilean norm. Likewise, Piñera did not completely ignore the opportunity to criticize his opponent's agnosticism in 2005. But "deviations" such as these are small in magnitude, especially when compared to the strategies employed by presidential candidates from other Latin American countries such as Brazil. As such, they are better considered variation within the category of personalism than the adoption of an entirely different approach.

3

Convergence on a Technocratic Strategy in Brazil

In a contest that pitted a working-class incumbent against a physician and governor of Brazil's richest state, the appeals of Luiz Inácio Lula da Silva and Geraldo Alckmin were strikingly similar. During two rounds of the 2006 election, both Lula and Alckmin's free television advertising programs (the *Horário Gratuito de Propaganda Eleitoral*, HGPE) spent about 70 percent of their time discussing policy, often at a high level of detail. Lula's advertising described a litany of social programs implemented during his first term – conditional cash transfers via Bolsa Família, subsidized medications through the People's Pharmacy, improved nutrition thanks to Zero Hunger, and scholarships and job training under ProUni and ProYouth.[1] In-depth reporting segments explained how these policies worked, how they had boosted social indicators, and how they improved lives. Likewise, Lula's program specified how many airports and seaports had been expanded with federal government funding, how far biofuels research had advanced during his term, and how he had facilitated information-sharing among different police and security agencies.

Alckmin's television program was quite similar. It presented a parallel list of social programs that he implemented as governor of São Paulo – cash transfers via Citizen Wage, subsidized medications through the Right Dose program, better nutrition thanks to Long Live Milk and Good Plate Restaurants, and job training through Youth Action.[2] It also featured a long list of Alckmin's public works, such as building ninteen new hospitals in the state, overseeing the largest public housing project in Latin America, and directing the most extensive flood-control effort in Brazil. The two candidates even disputed the authorship of

---

[1] In Portuguese, the latter four are Farmácia Popular, Fome Zero, ProUni, and ProJovem, respectively.

[2] In Portuguese, these are Renda Cidadã, Dose Certa, Viva Leite and Restaurantes Bom Prato, and Ação Jovem, respectively.

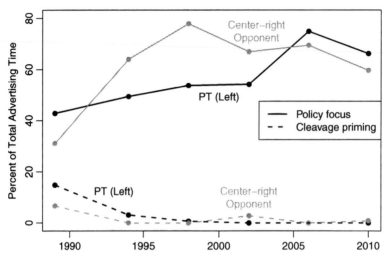

FIGURE 3.1. Strategic Convergence in Brazil.

some of the same policies – Alckmin pointed out that the individual components of Bolsa Família were first introduced by a former president from his
own party, while Lula argued that the federal government funded São Paulo's
Right Dose program and that the state merely administered it. In an article published after the first day of television advertising, columnist Kennedy Alencar
(2006) opined that "Lula's consultant could have done Alckmin's advertising,
and vice-versa."

The extensive policy focus of Lula's and Alckmin's 2006 campaign advertising illustrates one of three characteristic elements of the technocratic strategy
that has come to dominate presidential campaigns in Brazil. Like the personalistic model in Chile, candidates using a technocratic strategy eschew cleavage
priming and privilege the use of direct linkages. The technocratic model differs
from personalism, however, in its emphasis on specific policy proposals and
prior accomplishments. If Chilean candidates argue that they can "feel your
pain," Brazilian candidates specify how they have alleviated people's pain in
the past and how they plan to do so in the future.

Candidates' convergence on technocratic strategies in Brazil differs from the
pattern in Chile because it has involved contagion from the right rather than
the left. The technocratic model of campaign strategy was first introduced in
Brazil by Fernando Henrique Cardoso, who occupied the center-right position
in the 1994 election. As illustrated in Figure 3.1, Cardoso was the first major
presidential candidate in post-democratization Brazil to avoid priming cleavages and focus heavily on policy issues. In subsequent elections, the campaigns
of five-time Workers' Party (Partido dos Trabalhadores, PT) candidate Luiz
Inácio Lula da Silva gravitated toward this technocratic model. Meanwhile,
candidates from Cardoso's Party of Brazilian Social Democracy (Partido da

Social Democracia Brasileira, PSDB) have continued to implement the same basic strategy introduced in 1994.

The theory of success contagion also helps explain why Brazilian candidates did not converge on a strategy of neopopulism, despite a neopopulist outsider winning the first direct presidential election after democratization. Fernando Collor de Mello was elected in 1989 with a campaign that primed cleavages, circumvented existing forms of political intermediation, and focused more on the candidate's image than on policy. Despite Collor's electoral victory, neopopulism did not become a recurrent phenomenon in Brazil, largely because his governing experience was such a failure. After Collor was impeached and removed from office on corruption charges, thoroughly disgraced in the eyes of the public and with virtually no allies to stand by him, it was unlikely that any serious contender in the next election would repeat his campaign strategy. The Brazilian case thus illustrates that a victorious electoral strategy must be legitimated by a successful term in office if future candidates are to adopt it.

The principal mechanism of success contagion in Brazil has involved the country's campaign professionals embracing a technocratic approach. Political consultants in Brazil form a much tighter professional community than in either Chile or Peru, and many of those who have advised Lula or his PSDB opponent have particularly close professional ties to one another. In the years since Cardoso's 1994 campaign, a policy-centric approach to electioneering has become the standard operating procedure within this community of campaign professionals. Consultants working for both major candidates in 1998, 2002, and 2006 recommended a high policy focus for the campaign. On the right, these campaign professionals have consistently enjoyed the candidate's confidence and have been able to marginalize dissidents within the campaign team, facilitating strategic continuity.

In contrast to Chile, direct imitation of the other side's tactics has not played a major role in strategic contagion across the ideological spectrum in Brazil. Rather, the PT has converged on the technocratic model of campaigning in an indirect fashion, as it has given greater weight to the recommendations of outside professionals whose standard advice adheres to technocratic norms. Cardoso, a former left-wing sociologist and onetime political ally of Lula and the PT, was considered a traitor to the Left for allying with the right-wing Liberal Front Party (Partido da Frente Liberal, PFL) during his presidency and privatizing many of Brazil's state-owned firms. This factor meant that explicitly copying the strategy of the other side would have been much more difficult for Lula than it was for Lavín in Chile. Even the prospect of hiring a political consultant who had previously worked with the Right provoked substantial opposition within the PT, where many party leaders were reluctant to symbolically abandon their left-wing roots in an effort to win elections. Yet Lula and his close allies were ultimately willing to accept consultants' recommendation of a technocratic strategy, which they enthusiastically embraced in 2002. While not exactly an easy pill for the PT to swallow, following the strategic advice of a campaign professional was more palatable than copying that same strategy from a bitter foe.

In the first section of this chapter, I examine Fernando Collor's successful neopopulist campaign but failed presidency, focusing on why his electoral strategy was not more widely adopted. The second section contrasts the leading candidates' approaches to the 1994 election: Lula, who ran a traditional mass party campaign, versus Cardoso, who introduced a technocratic, policy-centered approach. In the next three sections, I examine the professionalization of Brazilian political consulting as a mechanism of success contagion, consultants' role in the adoption of a technocratic approach by PSDB candidates in 2002 and 2006, and the contagion of this approach across the ideological spectrum to Lula's campaigns in 1998 and 2002. The sixth section examines limited instances of cleavage priming in Serra's 2002 campaign and Lula's 2006 campaign, arguing that these strategic deviations are better understood as variation within the technocratic model than as the embrace of a fundamentally different campaign strategy. The final section tests the argument by examining presidential campaigns in 2010. Here, I show that major candidates continued to employ a technocratic approach – including Serra, who lost the 2002 election with a very similar strategy.

FERNANDO COLLOR DE MELLO: THE FAILURE OF A NEOPOPULIST OUTSIDER

The 1989 campaign of Fernando Collor de Mello constitutes the only major instance of neopopulism in Brazilian presidential elections. Collor initiated his campaign for president in early 1989, surged rapidly in the polls during the first half of the year (Figure 3.2), and was ultimately elected president in a runoff with Workers' Party (PT) candidate Luiz Inácio Lula da Silva. As governor of the state of Alagoas, Collor had first gained national prominence for his efforts to fire 15,000 state employees (known disparagingly as *marajás*, or maharajahs, a term for Indian princes) who were seen as doing little work in exchange for generous salaries and perks. The maverick stance he had taken as governor allowed Collor to cast himself during the presidential campaign as a political outsider and opponent of incumbent José Sarney, whose government was evaluated as "poor" or "terrible" by 68 percent of voters in September 1989. Sarney's administration was plagued by charges of corruption and failed attempts to stabilize hyperinflation, which reached 44.3 percent per month during November 1989 (Weyland 2002: 98).

Collor crafted a presidential campaign with three key characteristics. First, he emphasized his independence from all established forms of political intermediation, relying instead on direct linkages to the people and a personal electoral vehicle cobbled together solely for the campaign. Second, Collor also engaged in cleavage priming – principally the populist cleavage juxtaposing the interests of "the people" with those of elites or "the political class." In addition to these

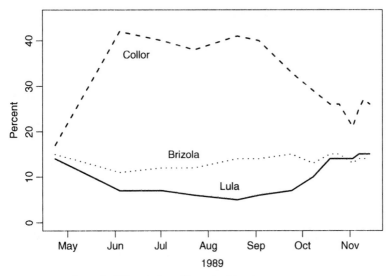

FIGURE 3.2. Intended Vote in Brazil's 1989 Election.

two defining characteristics of neopopulism, Collor's campaign was vague with respect to policy, focusing much more on the candidate's charismatic personal image. With respect to the dimensions of cleavage and policy focus, Collor's strategy differed substantially from the technocratic approach that would later come to predominate in Brazil.

Collor's campaign went to extreme lengths to circumvent established forms of intermediation and craft direct linkages to the people. First, his National Reconstruction Party (Partido da Reconstrução Nacional, PRN) had little identity or *raison d'être* beyond his candidacy and did not serve as a form of linkage during the campaign. The party's name was chosen on the advice of Collor's polling firm in order to best suit his intended campaign message (author's interview, Vasconcelos), and the party president acknowledged during the campaign that its structure was solely dependent upon Collor's candidacy.[3] Existing legislators were recruited into the party indiscriminately in order to maximize Collor's free television advertising time – calculated based on the size of one's congressional delegation.

Collor's campaign message also emphasized direct connections and a commitment to the unorganized "people." In a typical message from his television advertising during the second round, Collor reassured his supporters that "we are the majority, my people. We won, and we're going to win again. Just us, without groups, without conspiracies – just me, and you close to me." According to the campaign's main pollster, the common refrain "don't leave me alone

[3] *Folha de São Paulo*, November 23, 1989.

in this journey," used in both stump speeches and television advertising, "was a direct appeal to the voter without institutional mediation, without a party, without any form of interest aggregation like a union or association...He had an image of a sort of Lone Ranger that was going to be able to solve the country's problems" (author's interview, Coimbra).

Closely related to Collor's use of direct linkages was a discourse that sought to prime cleavages by juxtaposing the interests of the people with those of the economic and political elite. When São Paulo's major business confederation endorsed his candidacy in the second round, he responded by denigrating the group as "a businessmen's ghetto representing what is most backward about this country" (Figueiredo and Figueiredo 1990: 121). Most significantly, Collor sought to attack the vaguely defined but much reviled "political class." In his HGPE broadcast the evening of September 26, for instance, Collor made reference to a popular soap opera about a king and his corrupt kingdom, which was widely understood at the time as a metaphor for the Brazilian state (Sluyter-Beltrão 1992):

The kingdom of Avilan declared war against me and my candidacy...The kingdom of the corrupt, the thieves, the speculators, the tax evaders, the kingdom of the *marajás*. They, whom we are going to throw in jail, have definitively declared war against us, you and I who are going to reform this country...Why? Because they know that when I am President of the Republic I will not be defending their interests, I will be defending your interests.

In the second round, with Collor squaring off against a much more authentic anti-establishment candidate, he began to place greater emphasis on the basic ideological cleavage that distinguished him from his left-wing opponent Lula. One segment, first aired on December 8 and repeated several times thereafter, showed the yellow, green, and blue Brazilian flag slowly fading to white, as an off-camera voice stated, "Lula's radical ideas would bring violence to our countryside. Lula's radical ideas would drive investments out of Brazil. Lula's radical ideas don't allow for any stars other than his red star. Lula's radical ideas would bring strikes and chaos. Lula's radical ideas would send the country back to the past."

Finally, Collor's campaign placed a relatively low emphasis on policy. The director of television advertising for most of Collor's campaign maintains that the focus "was not proposals. I think it was a more impressionistic thing, his impact with the people...The proposals were vague, [such as] 'we're going to get rid of the *marajás*'" (author's interview, Ribeiro). Concocting a style that would resonate with the public was a more important part of campaign strategy than orienting the campaign toward specific policy issues. According to the campaign's head pollster, strategic planning focused not on the major policy concerns uncovered in internal surveys but rather on the values that respondents found to be important, such as youth, change, and dynamism (author's interview, Coimbra).

TABLE 3.1. *Fernando Collor's Television Advertising, 1989*

Policy focused	31.1
Specific proposals	5.0
General proposals	7.2
Achievements	4.4
Criticism	7.5
Diagnosis	7.0
Not policy focused (jingles, image, or other)	68.9
Cleavage priming	6.6
No cleavage priming	93.4

Note: Entries are percentages of total advertising time.

As summarized in Table 3.1, Collor's television advertising reflects the relatively low importance that his advisors assigned to policy, as well as his use of cleavage-priming appeals. Only 12.2 percent of his total advertising time focused on proposals, and most of this discussion did not convey specific details. On the whole, Collor's television advertising devoted only 31.1 percent of its total time to policy, a figure in line with most campaigns in Chile. For its part, cleavage priming occupied 6.6 percent of Collor's television advertising – less than the "Yes" campaign in Chile, but enough to make an impression.

Why Collor's Neopopulism Did Not Generate Success Contagion

Collor's 1989 campaign for the presidency of Brazil is widely considered the country's first "modern" presidential campaign, and Brazilian political consultants took notice of his successful example. If contagion were solely generated by successful *electoral* strategies, one might expect major candidates in 1994 to adopt elements of neopopulism. Yet Collor's neopopulist campaign was instead a onetime occurrence because his presidency turned out to be a spectacular failure. In the lead-up to the 1994 election, Brazilian campaign professionals detected the widespread popular rejection of Collor's political style, and they recommended against repeating such an approach.

In the years immediately following Collor's electoral victory, Brazilian campaign professionals expressed a clear admiration for his campaign strategy. Ney Lima Figueiredo characterized Collor's decision to demonstrate independence from organized interests by attacking the São Paulo State Federation of Industries (Federação das Indústrias do Estado de São Paulo, FIESP) as a move that showcased his "rare talent for political marketing." Figueiredo also spoke positively of Collor's decision to prime ideological cleavages by casting his opponent as a radical Marxist (Figueiredo and Figueiredo 1990: 29, 34). Other books by Brazilian campaign professionals published around the same time (e.g., Grandi et al. 1992; Manhanelli 1992: 51) show a similar admiration for Collor's successful campaign strategy.

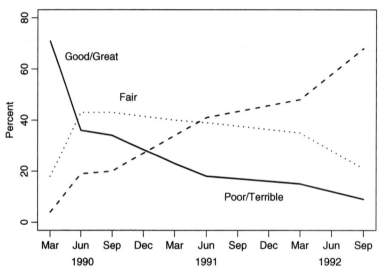

FIGURE 3.3. Evaluation of President Fernando Collor.

Collor's success as a politician, however, was short-lived; his presidency ulti-mately became synonymous with governing failure. After winning an election amidst hyperinflation and corruption, Collor ended up exacerbating both of these problems as president. Several stabilization plans temporarily reduced inflation during his first year and a half in office, but the inflation rate climbed back to more than 20 percent per month in 1992 (Weyland 2002: 218). More-over, Collor plunged the country into a crisis of morality and public ethics much worse than the one that he had promised to defeat in 1989. In May 1992, the president's brother exposed a corruption scheme, involving bribes for state con-tracts, that had been masterminded by the head of fundraising for Collor's 1989 campaign. A congressional inquiry discovered that Collor had knowledge of the scheme and that proceeds had gone to pay for personal expenses, such as land-scaping for his private mansion. These charges eventually led the Congress to impeach Collor and remove him from the presidency in October 1992. By the time he left office, Collor's approval rating had fallen to 9 percent (Figure 3.3).

The spectacular failure of Brazil's neopopulist president had an impact on public opinion, leading potential voters in the 1994 election to be wary of any candidate who appeared similar to the disgraced former president. Brazil-ian campaign professionals detected this shift in public opinion and recom-mended against any approach that would remind voters of Collor. Based on a series of surveys and focus groups, a report prepared for the FIESP in Novem-ber 1993 (Figueiredo 2002 [1994]: 187) maintained that "the ideal candidate should not...have a profile that is reminiscent of the ex-president." Ney Lima Figueiredo (2002 [1994]: 187), who had expressed so much admiration for Collor's campaign strategy shortly after the 1989 election, argued in 1994 that the best presidential candidate would be one with "the capacity to bind people together, in contrast to the strategy used by Collor in '89." In a seminar prior to the 1994 election, pollster Carlos Matheus (1998: 82–83) recommended against a repeat of Collor's strategy because he felt that voters' sense of responsibility for their poor choice in 1989 "is now beginning to come to the surface and will certainly influence the final selection process."

In accordance with the theory of success contagion, therefore, the negative feedback effect of Collor's disastrous presidency took neopopulism off the table as a viable campaign strategy in 1994. Prior to even contemplating the particular candidates involved in the 1994 election and the circumstances in which they found themselves at the start of the campaign, we can say that any major candidate with a realistic chance of winning the presidency would be unlikely to adopt a strategy similar to Collor's. Such candidates would not necessarily choose a polar opposite strategy, but they would be likely to distance themselves from Collor on one or more dimensions.

CAMPAIGN STRATEGIES IN 1994: THE CONTRASTING APPROACHES OF CARDOSO AND LULA

With neopopulism no longer viable as an electoral strategy, there was not yet any single model of campaigning that candidates in the 1994 election were likely to adopt. As a result, the strategies of the two major candidates, Fernando Henrique Cardoso and Luiz Inácio Lula da Silva, were very different from one another. Cardoso's approach, crafted by a team of campaign professionals, took advantage of his having recently designed an effective inflation-control program while serving as finance minister. Building upon this policy success, Cardoso ran a technocratic campaign that emphasized his proposals for the future, conveyed a message of national unity, and relied upon direct rather than intermediated linkages. Lula's strategy, designed by a group of party leaders representing many of the PT's internal factions, was very different. A classic mass party campaign, it drew upon intermediated linkages and primed cleavages between the people and the economic elite. It also focused on Lula's empathy with popular concerns rather than his proposed solutions. Structural characteristics of the campaign team and party, along with a positive assessment of Lula's prior electoral strategy, contributed to strategic inertia and a repetition of many aspects of the 1989 campaign.

Fernando Henrique Cardoso: Professionals Design a Technocratic Campaign

Fernando Henrique Cardoso was a former senator from São Paulo and one of the founders of the PSDB. When Collor was replaced by his vice president Itamar Franco in 1992, Cardoso left the Senate to become Franco's foreign minister, and in May 1993, he was appointed finance minister. His primary task

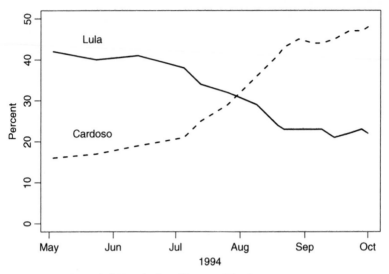

FIGURE 3.4. Intended Vote in Brazil's 1994 Election.

was to solve the country's inflation problem, something that five stabilization plans and nine of his predecessors had failed to do. Cardoso's Real Plan, which launched a new currency, the *real*, on July 1, 1994, ended the recurrent bouts of hyperinflation that had plagued Brazil since 1985.

During Cardoso's term as finance minister, the PSDB decided to choose him as its presidential candidate in the hopes that he could ride a successful stabilization plan to victory. According to the PSDB president at the time, the Real Plan "was the very justification for his candidacy. Six months before, Fernando Henrique never could have been a presidential candidate, [but] he was the candidate that conceived and coordinated that plan, so it became the flagship" of the campaign (author's interview, Pimenta da Veiga). Resigning his position as finance minister in April 1994, Cardoso prepared a campaign that would focus on his success at taming inflation and the technocratic competence that he would bring to numerous other policy areas. He scored an easy victory in the first round of the election, defeating Lula by a margin of 54–27 percent (Figure 3.4).

Cardoso's 1994 campaign stands out from the efforts of prior Brazilian candidates in terms of the influence of campaign professionals – actors who would later play a major role in the contagion of Cardoso's technocratic approach. In 1989, Collor had relied heavily on paid labor, but few of the individuals making key decisions were campaign professionals. Rather, they were Collor's close associates, all of whom had little or no prior campaign experience. Major strategic decisions thus depended on the shifting influence of different factions of advisors (author's interviews, Ribeiro and Rosa e Silva). By contrast, public opinion and advertising specialists played major decision-making roles in

TABLE 3.2. *Fernando Henrique Cardoso's Television Advertising, 1994*

Policy focused	64.0
Specific proposals	12.6
General proposals	16.2
Achievements	4.5
Criticism	1.5
Diagnosis	29.2
Not policy focused (jingles, image, or other)	36.0
Cleavage priming	0.0
No cleavage priming	100.0

Note: Entries are percentages of total advertising time.

Cardoso's 1994 campaign, and there were no shifts in direction based on a new faction suddenly gaining the candidate's ear. The marketing team was given free reign over the production of Cardoso's television advertising, with no one besides the candidate and his campaign manager exercising veto power (Filho 1994; Suassuna and Novaes 1994). Survey-based strategic recommendations determined nearly every move; one journalist went so far as to describe the campaign as a "survey dictatorship" (Suassuna and Novaes 1994).

Technocratic Policy Competence and the Real Plan

The most prominent feature of the campaign designed by Cardoso's professional strategists was to focus on the candidate's policy competence and ability to solve Brazil's problems. In a strategic document prepared for Cardoso after he left the Finance Ministry, head pollster Antônio Lavareda pointed out that the former professor was perceived as an aloof intellectual who was distant from the people and did not understand their problems. However, the report also noted that focus group participants who supported the Real Plan were not concerned about this perceived distance. "Comments of this sort," Lavareda maintained, "only reinforce FHC's dependence on the success of the Plan. If he is successful in controlling inflation, it is possible that the 'distance from the people' will cease to be a negative factor" (Filho 1994: 80). According to another of the campaign's pollsters, this strategy achieved the desired effect: "By the end of the campaign, Lula only had the empathy with the working class and the poor, but he was not seen as anyone that provided any results. So I think that was a major thing: establish a very clear program, a result-oriented program ... Fernando Henrique was perceived as solving poor people's problems more than Lula" (author's interview, Olsen).

A focus on the ongoing success of the Real Plan was a major priority for the campaign, though Cardoso also spoke extensively about his proposals in other policy areas as well. The campaign adopted an open hand as its symbol, and each of the fingers represented a policy area – employment, health, education, security, and agriculture. As summarized in Table 3.2, 64 percent of the total time was devoted to policy issues, a large share of which involved proposals (28.8 percentage points). These figures are more than double those for Collor in 1989, and also substantially higher than those for Lula's campaign in 1994. Cardoso's advertising also devoted a large amount of space (29.2 percent) to diagnostic content, much of it focused on the positive results of the Real Plan (11.8 percentage points). Finally, in both his television advertising and his stump speeches, Cardoso often contrasted his own detailed policy proposals with his opponent's lack of clear alternatives. In a July 18 rally in Fortaleza (Graziano 1995: 33), he argued:

There is one Brazil that knows what the people want, that talks with them, that has a proposal and a roadmap. And there is another Brazil that only knows how to criticize, that takes potshots, that attacks everything about the Plan, but is incapable of advancing any concrete proposal. No one has ever proposed any alternative to what we are doing to end inflation.

A Call for National Unity

A second key feature of Cardoso's campaign was that it avoided cleavage priming. The notion of national unity was a key feature of Cardoso's appeals (Miguel 1998, 2000). His choice of the open hand as a campaign symbol was intended as a symbolic contrast with the clenched fist of radicalism and cleavage politics, and one of the campaign's slogan's described him as "the hand that is uniting Brazil" (Miguel 2000: 184). In a message first delivered in his August 19 television program and repeated several times thereafter, Cardoso underscored his call for national unity and contrasted it with a cleavage-priming approach:

After so many years of crisis and chaos, we can sense that people have a great, positive inclination to come together and carry Brazil forward. I have traveled around this entire country, I have spoken with many people, and I have not met anyone who thinks that we will find solutions to our problems with anger, with conflict, with radicalism, pitting boss against worker, one region against another, the country dweller against the city dweller.

As suggested by the above quote, Cardoso's campaign also sought to criticize Lula's anger and outrage at Brazil's social and economic problems, describing his positions as pessimistic and anti-patriotic and even suggesting that he was critical of the Real Plan because inflation would help his electoral prospects. By casting his opponent as being against what was good for the entire nation, Cardoso reinforced his own image of unity as well as the existing stereotype of Lula as being a divisive candidate.

Privileging Television and Other Direct Linkages

Finally, Cardoso's campaign favored direct over intermediated linkages, emphasizing television and not making much use of party structures for campaigning. Formed by an elite split from the Party of the Brazilian Democratic Movement (Partido do Movimento Democrático Brasileiro, PMDB) rather than a process of bottom-up institutional-building, the PSDB has always been a top-heavy and regionally concentrated party, with prominent leaders in the states of São Paulo and Minas Gerais but less presence in other regions and few base-level militants. For this reason, Cardoso's 1994 alliance with the PFL is often interpreted as a move designed to compensate for his own party's weakness, particularly in the Northeast where the PFL has a strong, clientelistic presence (Miguel 2000). But in reality, Cardoso's campaign had early access to survey data indicating that he could win the election on his own without any sort of alliance (Filho 1994: 67–68). Several major PSDB politicians and close aids to Cardoso described the pact with the PFL as more oriented toward gaining television time in the current election and a coalition partner for a future government than winning votes through the PFL's party machine (author's interviews, Abrão, Caldas Pereira, and Pimenta da Veiga).

Television was central not only in Cardoso's electoral alliances but also in the allocation of his agenda as candidate, which privileged electronic over territorial campaigning. Cardoso's scheduling advisor reports that he spent half of every week in São Paulo recording clips for the HGPE programs (Graziano 1995). In 138 days of campaigning, Cardoso did only fifty-three rallies (Graziano 1995), and the party played very little role in their organization (author's interview, Caldas Pereira). Rather, campaign events were the responsibility of the same marketing team that handled Cardoso's television advertising. The production specialist in charge of organizing these events had previously put on massive spectacles such as Madonna's show in Brazil (Dimenstein and Souza 1994). For places the candidate could not visit, the campaign organized a traveling "electronic rally" known as Pé na Estrada ("On the Road"), which involved trucks with video screens traveling to small towns around the country and delivering a pre-recorded message from Cardoso. To neutralize the effects of Lula's physical campaign trips, the campaign would send a Pé na Estrada truck to the same locations a few days later.[4]

Cardoso's technocratic strategy in the 1994 campaign reflected a variety of influences, from the success of the Real Plan to the on-the-ground weakness of the PSDB's party structure, but the crucial factor is the influence of campaign professionals who based their strategic recommendations upon an interpretation of survey and focus group data. Cardoso's pollsters and advertising strategists did not favor a technocratic strategy merely by virtue of being campaign professionals. As discussed in Chapter 2, professional influence in Chilean elections has facilitated convergence on a distinct model of campaign strategy, with low rather than high policy focus. Rather, Cardoso's professional advisors designed a strategy that was well-suited to the specific context of the 1994 election, which was particularly fortuitous for a candidate who could credibly claim a high degree of policy competence.

---

[4] *Folha de São Paulo*, September 26, 1994.

Luiz Inácio Lula da Silva, 1994: Strategic Inertia and a Mass Party Campaign

Lula's approach to the 1994 election responded to a very different set of influences than the campaign of his opponent, with a result that was nearly the polar opposite in strategic terms. While professional pollsters and advertising strategists were the key players for Cardoso, Lula's campaign was run by his party, purposely including representatives of different internal factions to ensure that the campaign reflected the diversity of views within the PT. This top-heavy campaign leadership limited strategic flexibility and contributed to structural inertia, making it more likely that Lula would repeat the approach that he had adopted in his first presidential contest. The relative success of the 1989 campaign also made inertia more likely. Lula had not won the 1989 election, but he performed much better than initially expected by most of his campaign team. Moreover, a standard interpretation within the PT was that Lula's second-round loss was due not to a strategic error but rather to the media's favoritism toward Collor.

In the absence of an attractive external model of campaign strategy, Lula largely repeated his approach from 1989. Lula's 1994 campaign was much less policy focused than Cardoso's, stressing his empathy with people's problems rather than specific proposals for solving them. He also relied to a significant extent upon intermediated linkages, in contrast to Cardoso's direct linkage strategy. With respect to cleavage priming, Lula's campaign does reflect some inward-oriented learning; the candidate's appeals were less divisive than in 1989, and he claimed to represent the people against the interests of the economic elite rather than the workers against the "dominant class." Yet by continuing to embrace the notion of conflicting economic interests as a fundamental fact of political life, Lula's campaign still differed markedly from Cardoso's message of national unity.

Party Factions without Campaign Professionals

In contrast to Cardoso's campaign, where authority was concentrated in the candidate and a small number of campaign professionals, numerous leaders of the PT shared responsibility for Lula's electoral effort. Formed as the union of leftist groups ranging from labor leaders to progressive Christians, the PT has always been internally diverse, and leaders are selected through internal elections in which different factions (*tendências*) present slates of candidates (Keck 1992; Azevedo 1995; Samuels 2004). In 1993, far-left factions won majority control of the party leadership, but more centrist factions also retained key posts. In an effort to accommodate this diversity, nineteen different party leaders were given decision-making power over different aspects of the 1994 campaign, a number that was later expanded to twenty-five to include representatives from each of the other parties in the electoral coalition (Medeiros

1994).[5] Similarly, the president and two vice presidents of the PT, each from a different faction, were named campaign comanagers. This unwieldy structure of authority, made up of leaders with different ideological preferences, complicated decision-making and implementation (Medeiros 1994; Kotscho 2006).

In addition to placing multiple party leaders in positions of authority, the choice of a head advertising strategist for Lula's campaign was made largely on ideological grounds. Early on, Lula had expressed an interest in hiring Duda Mendonça, a well-known Brazilian political consultant and advertising strategist who had previously worked for right-wing politician Paulo Maluf (Mendonça 2001: 197–205; Kotscho 2006: 194–195). Because of his prior affiliation with the Right, however, much of the party and campaign leadership opposed Mendonça's participation, fearing that he would "depoliticize" Lula's campaign (Kotscho 2006: 194). The preferred strategist among the PT's left wing was Paulo de Tarso Santos, a trusted figure who had been in charge of the advertising for Lula's more radical, cleavage-priming campaign in 1989. Efforts to hire Mendonça ultimately failed due to the opposition of key figures such as communication coordinator Markus Sokol and campaign comanagers Rui Falcão and Luiz Eduardo Greenhalgh; the latter threatened to resign if Mendonça were chosen (author's interviews, Falcão, Greenhalgh, and Sokol).

Finally, Lula's campaign relied much less than Cardoso's on the recommendations of professional pollsters. Jorge Almeida (2002: 23–24), an academic and party leader from one of the PT's leftist factions, commissioned a handful of surveys and focus groups to evaluate Lula's image and the reaction to his television programs. However, Almeida was also in charge of evaluating this research and passing along recommendations to the campaign team. In contrast to Cardoso's campaign, no professional pollster had any input into Lula's communication strategy (author's interview, Kotscho).

Policy Focus: Many Problems, Few Solutions

The strategy designed by Lula's party-dominated campaign team differed from that of Cardoso in several respects. First and foremost, Lula's campaign emphasized his understanding of people's problems rather than specific proposals for solving them. More than a year before the official start of the campaign, Lula and his advisors had decided upon an empathy-oriented approach. The cornerstone of this strategy was a series "Citizenship Caravans," which ran intermittently from April 1993 to July 1994 and involved visits to a total of 653 small towns around the country (Suassuna and Novaes 1994; Kotscho 2006). According to Lula's media advisor, "the principal objective of the caravans was to put the candidate in contact with the reality of Brazil, to showcase the reality of Brazil and talk to the people" (author's interview, Kotscho). Initially, one of

---

[5] *Folha de São Paulo*, August 10, 1994.

TABLE 3.3. *Lula's Television Advertising, 1989 and 1994*

	1989	1994
Policy focused	42.8	49.4
Specific proposals	4.9	3.3
General proposals	6.8	10.3
Achievements	2.5	4.6
Criticism	14.3	14.4
Diagnosis	14.4	16.8
Not policy focused (jingles, image, or other)	57.2	50.6
Cleavage priming	14.8	3.1
No cleavage priming	85.2	96.9

Note: Entries are percentages of total advertising time.

the major plans for Lula's television advertising was to feature video footage of the Citizenship Caravans, though this plan was foiled when the Congress passed a law prohibiting external scenes from being used in the HGPE (Kotscho 2006; author's interviews, Azevedo and Falcão).

Though video from the Citizenship Caravans could not be included, Lula's television advertising sought to convey a similar message of empathy with people's problems, in addition to strong criticism of the Real Plan. While the PT's economists viewed the Real Plan as an electoral swindle that would fail within months, none of them could come up with a coherent alternative. Rather than conveying proposals, therefore, "the strategy of the television program...was to juxtapose the Real Plan with the 'real Brazil' and to say that the Real Plan would not solve the problems of the real Brazil" (author's interview, Santos).[6] As a result, diagnosis and policy criticism took up 16.8 percent and 14.4 percent of Lula's television advertising, respectively – both of which exceeded the amount of time devoted to proposals (13.7 percent). If not for the change in electoral legislation, Lula probably would have spent even less time discussing policy because more of the HGPE could have been devoted to scenes from the Citizenship Caravans.

Lula's emphasis on diagnosis and policy criticism rather than proposals is an instance of strategic inertia with respect to his prior presidential campaign. Then-PT president Luiz Gushiken (author's interview) described the 1989 campaign as involving a "generic...position with respect to programmatic policy." Similarly, Lula's 1989 campaign manager characterized the party program in that election as more of a long-term plan for social transformation than a set of policies that could be realistically accomplished in a presidential term (author's interview, Pomar). As summarized in Table 3.3, television advertising from Lula's 1989 and 1994 campaigns had a very similar profile in terms of the

---

[6] The pun is the same in Portuguese as in English – *real* is the name of the currency, but it also means "authentic."

percentage of time devoted to different types of policy content. In both cases, most policy discussion consisted of either criticism or diagnosis. According to the director of television advertising in the two elections, "we went into [the 1994] campaign without proposals...there were [only] poor, underdeveloped proposals, a bit of a repetition of 1989" (author's interview, Azevedo).

A Continuing Role for Intermediary Institutions

Lula's 1994 campaign also differed from that of Cardoso in its use of interme-diated linkages. The Citizenship Caravans may have been an effort to estab-lish direct contact with people outside of the PT, but the party was intimately involved in their planning and execution, organizing activists and suggesting certain activities in various locales (author's interview, W. Prado). PT militants and members of various unions received specific instructions on how to par-ticipate in the campaign, including promoting the formation of some 10,000 "Lula for President People's Committees."[7] Vicente Paulo da Silva, president of the PT-affiliated Unified Workers' Central (Central Única dos Trabalhadores, CUT), was a regular participant at Lula's rallies. The CUT also helped create the National Forum for Struggle, which grouped together other popular asso-ciations, took an official stance in support of Lula's candidacy, and organized protest marches against the Real Plan (author's interview, da Silva).

As with his approach to policy focus, Lula's use of intermediated linkages in the 1994 campaign repeated a strategy that had been deployed in his first campaign. In 1989, the production and distribution of campaign advertising material such as posters and T-shirts was the responsibility of small groups of PT militants working through the party's base nuclei or campaign-specific support groups. At rallies, militants were in charge of numerous tasks, includ-ing setting up the stage, providing security, and mobilizing people to attend. Union participation in the campaign was restricted by law, but leaders of the CUT and its affiliated unions pushed the limits of these regulations, collecting money for Lula's campaign and holding impromptu rallies immediately outside factory doors (author's interviews, Bom, da Silva, Pereira da Silva, Pomar, and W. Prado).

Lula's recourse to intermediated linkages in both 1989 and 1994 most likely reflects structural inertia, given the established role for unions and party mil-itants in the campaigns of a mass party candidate. In 1994, Lula was seeking to appeal more broadly than in 1989, reaching out beyond organized labor and the PT's membership base. Yet the principal manner of doing so involved an activity – the Citizenship Caravans – that drew substantially upon the sup-port of the party. While Lula's 1994 campaign is sometimes described as less actively involving base-level militants than in 1989 (Medeiros 1994; Miguel 2000), there is no evidence that the candidate sought to circumvent or marginal-ize party- or union-mediated linkages.

---

[7] *Folha de São Paulo*, June 6, 1994, and September 2, 1994.

Cleavage Priming: Less Radical, Still Confrontational

In keeping with the effort to appeal to a broader segment of society than in 1989, Lula did somewhat change his cleavage-priming approach between the two elections. In his first presidential campaign, Lula focused extensively on the divide between workers and the economic elite. His television advertising often featured excerpts from radical, cleavage-priming rally speeches, such as one in the working-class city of São Bernardo do Campo, where Lula said that "capitalism has created much more misery here than any socialism that they criticize. It's easy for them to praise the strikes in Poland because it's far away, but they criticize ours...our dominant class is a bunch of hypocrites!"[8] Appeals identifying Lula with the interests of the workers or criticizing the "dominant class" took up a large portion (14.8 percent) of the candidate's television advertising in 1989.

In 1994, Lula's campaign was much less dependent on cleavage priming than in 1989, yet it was still quite distinct from Cardoso's unity-oriented effort. Lula devoted only 3.1 percent of his television advertising to cleavage-priming appeals in 1994. These appeals tended to identify Lula with the interests of "the people" in general rather than those of organized labor. Lula's 1994 campaign was also less overtly ideological than in 1989. Rather than promising to build Brazilian socialism, Lula denied having a Marxist discourse and likened his philosophy to that of Henry Ford, who wanted his workers to be paid well enough to purchase the cars they made.[9] Yet in contrast to Cardoso, who emphasized national unity and criticized the notion of cleavages, Lula often embraced a conflict of interest between the people and the elite as an inherent fact of life. In his television program on the evening of August 24, for instance, Lula argued that "we have a commitment to our people. Now, he who is on the side of the big landowners, the bankers, and the big economic groups may say the same thing...but many people who won elections speaking in the name of the people end up governing for the rich."

In terms of cleavage priming, therefore, Lula's campaign represents both an inward-oriented modification of the candidate's prior strategy and important elements of strategic inertia. In 1994, Lula did seek to broaden his appeal, siding with "the people" rather than organized workers as he had tended to do in 1989. He also engaged in significantly less cleavage priming overall. However, Lula did not abandon an emphasis on cleavages entirely, even though divisive rhetoric tended to play into the hands of his opponent by reinforcing Cardoso's claim to be the only one who could guarantee unity and social stability. Cleavage priming was still somewhat instinctual for the PT, and it was seen as having worked fairly effectively in 1989; for these reasons, the campaign team did not abandon it. As head advertising strategist Paulo de Tarso Santos (author's interview) explained with respect to the decision to criticize Cardoso for his

---

[8] Evening HGPE, November 6, 1989.
[9] *Folha de São Paulo*, June 30, 1994.

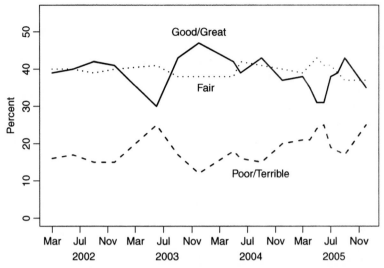

FIGURE 3.5. Evaluation of President Fernando Henrique Cardoso (First Term).

alliances with the Right and the economic elite, "I ended up paying the price of the success in 1989; I repeated some formulas that ended up not working out."

In sum, in the absence of a model of successful and legitimate campaign strategy, the two major candidates in the 1994 election ran very different campaigns that responded to a diverse set of influences. In Cardoso's case, a small group of campaign professionals designed a technocratic campaign strategy, which focused heavily on policy, conveyed a message of national unity, and relied upon direct rather than intermediated linkages. Lula's campaign, designed by representatives from numerous different factions of his party, differed with respect to each of these characteristics. Repeating many elements of his 1989 electoral strategy, Lula drew upon the support of the PT's party structure and affiliated unions, cast himself as a defender of the people against the interests of the economic elite, and sought to communicate empathy with people's problems rather than specific proposals for solving them.

PRESIDENTIAL CAMPAIGNS AFTER 1994: THE CONTAGION
OF A TECHNOCRATIC STRATEGY

In contrast to that of his predecessor, the presidential term to which Cardoso was elected in 1994 can be counted as a clear example of governing success. While this period was not without its difficulties, Cardoso's approval rating remained steady throughout the course of his first term, ending only slightly lower than when he took office in January 1995 (Figure 3.5). The percentage that evaluated his government as "poor" or "terrible" never rose above the percentage that considered it "good" or "great," even at the relative low points of his popularity. Largely due to the positive evaluation of his first term as president, Cardoso was easily reelected in 1998, when he again defeated Lula in the first round by a substantial margin of 53–32 percent.

Cardoso's combination of a victorious electoral strategy with a positively evaluated term as president achieved what Collor's neopopulism was unable to do – initiate a process of strategic contagion in Brazil. In the years since the 1994 election, presidential candidates in Brazil have converged upon technocratic campaign strategies like the one first used by Cardoso. PSDB politicians have continued to implement this successful formula in subsequent elections, while the campaigns of five-time PT candidate Lula have steadily gravitated toward it. The increasing similarity of the specific policies discussed by Lula and his major opponent on the center-right has meant a striking convergence in campaign appeals, with candidates even arguing at times over the authorship of their essentially interchangeable prior accomplishments and proposals for the future.

Campaign Consultants and Professional Norms

Unlike in Chile, where the contagion of personalism to the opposite side of the political spectrum involved Lavín's imitation of the Concertación's prior approach, Lula and his close advisors never explicitly sought to emulate Cardoso's campaign strategy. Doing so would have been anathema to PT leaders because their perceived distance from Cardoso and his government, in both personal and ideological terms, was much greater than that of Lavín with respect to the Concertación. Cardoso began his political career on the left – he opposed the military regime alongside Lula, founded the PSDB as a leftist splinter from the centrist PMDB, and even had several discussions with Lula in 1993 about a possible PT–PSDB coalition in the presidential election (Suassuna and Novaes 1994). Yet Cardoso ended up running against Lula, in coalition with the right-wing PFL, a traditional bête noir of the PT. Moreover, as president, Cardoso oversaw a market-oriented economic reform agenda that the PT bitterly opposed, including the privatization of numerous state-owned firms. As someone who came from similar political origins, yet campaigned and ultimately governed as an adversary of the PT, Cardoso was seen by party leaders as a traitor to the Left. This personal and ideological distance between Lula and Cardoso served as an impediment to strategic mimicry. Deliberately copying Cardoso's approach to the 1994 campaign would have been a difficult pill for the PT to swallow, especially when contesting the president's bid for reelection in 1998 or running against José Serra, another former leftist and minister in the Cardoso government, in 2002.

In place of direct imitation, the most important mechanism of success contagion in Brazil concerns norms that have developed among campaign professionals. Rather than explicitly copying their opponents' tactics, Lula and his advisors converged on the technocratic model of campaign strategy in an indirect fashion, by giving greater weight to the advice of campaign consultants who recommended an approach similar to Cardoso's. Granting outside professionals substantial input into campaign strategy was never an easy or natural move for the PT. In 1994, as discussed above, left-leaning party leaders vetoed the involvement of advertising strategist Duda Mendonça. In 1998, Lula and his advisors started out following their consultants' recommendations but changed course midway through the campaign. However, heeding the advice of campaign professionals was less ideologically fraught than outright mimicry. In 2002, Mendonça was brought on as a consultant and granted substantial influence over campaign strategy, facilitating the contagion of Cardoso's approach across the ideological spectrum.[10]

Political consultants in Brazil are by far the most professionalized among the three cases examined in this study, and standardized approaches to campaigning are developed and reinforced through a variety of mechanisms. The Brazilian Association of Political Consultants, founded in 1991, conducts regular training seminars for campaign managers and candidates as well as conferences for the community of campaign professionals. Consultants are also involved in designing and teaching a growing number of university extension courses in political marketing (Scotto 2004: 42–44). Since the mid-1980s, Brazilian political consultants have published a wealth of books and articles on campaign strategies and tactics, including numerous practical, how-to manuals. As a result of all of this professional interaction, Brazilian consultants learn from one another and also pass their ideas along to newcomers. In a preface to a campaign manual by Francisco Ferraz (2003: 4), veteran advertising strategist Nelson Biondi says, "I, who have had the privilege of sharing campaign leadership with talented and brilliant professionals such as Duda [Mendonça] and Nizan [Guanaes], can say that their strategies and creativity are not the result of brainstorming from scratch. In reality, they are born out of the organization and information that professionals like Ferraz put on paper."

Since 1994, the majority of consultants who participated in the campaigns of major presidential candidates have had even closer professional ties to one another, facilitating the development of standard operating procedures for electioneering. Duda Mendonça and Nizan Guanaes, who advised candidates on opposite sides of the 2002 campaign, originally worked together at the firm DM9 in the 1980s, where Guanaes (2001: 11) considered Mendonça to be his "professional father." After Mendonça left DM9 and Guanaes took over its operations, the firm was responsible for each of the PSDB presidential campaigns from 1994 to 2002. Luiz Gonzalez, head communication strategist for the PSDB presidential campaigns in 2006 and 2010, had also been involved in Cardoso's reelection effort in 1998; his firm GW handled much of the

---

[10] As discussed in Chapter 1, success contagion does not require that candidates embrace a successful and legitimate model of campaign strategy at the first available opportunity – which would have been 1998 in Lula's case – but rather than they move closer to this model over time.

production work for Cardoso's television program (Ferreira [1998]: 168). On the PT side, presidential campaign advertising in 2006 and 2010 was handled by João Santana, Mendonça's former partner who had worked with him on several projects for the PT in 2000–2001 (Mendonça 2001: 235–236, 251).

The close professional ties among Brazilian campaign consultants have facilitated the spread of a common understanding that campaign communication should emphasize policy, often at a high level of specificity. All of the recent "how-to" books characterize policy content as an essential component of campaign strategy (Mendonça 2001: 114; Santa Rita 2001: 32–33; Iten and Kobayashi 2002: 19; Ferraz 2003: 60, 64; Oliveira 2006: 50, 61). Iten and Kobayashi (2002: 19), for instance, insist that "the voter . . . demands a demonstration of specific capacity for administrative accomplishments . . . and public policies oriented toward solving his problems." Consultants' publications also frequently highlight specific proposals that their candidates emphasized during prior campaigns (Santa Rita 2001: 32–33; Iten and Kobayashi 2002: 195–207). Reflecting on the state of the industry, consultant Malfitani (2001) argues that "today what I see everywhere is a standardization . . . of campaigns – you just create the School Fund, the Work Fund, Let's Begin Again, Project Singapore, the Health Care Plan – give this thing a name, expand that [program] over there, and the people eat it up."[11]

As argued previously in this chapter, Cardoso's strategy in the 1994 election responded to the prevailing political context; the necessity of emphasizing detailed proposals was not yet conventional wisdom within the Brazilian community of campaign professionals. Indeed, Brazilian campaign manuals published prior to 1994 do not consistently emphasize policy like more recent ones do.[12] In subsequent elections, however, the recommendation of a technocratic approach to campaigning has become the norm. Hence, Cardoso's 1994 campaign played an important role in consolidating norms within the community of campaign professionals. A different successful campaign in a distinct political context could have led to the emergence of a very different conventional wisdom, as has occurred in Chile.

Given the wealth of experienced and capable political consultants from their own country, Brazilian candidates have almost never relied on foreign advice. James Carville's very limited participation in Cardoso's 1994 presidential bid (author's interviews, Caldas Pereira, Figueiredo, Olsen, and Rodrigues) is the only example among the campaigns examined in this chapter; the furor surrounding the revelation of his involvement probably discouraged future

---

[11] In Portuguese: Bolsa Escola; Bolsa Trabalho; Sim, Começar de Novo; Singapura; Plano de Atendimento à Saúde (PAS).

[12] Kuntz (1985) and Lima (1988) do emphasize proposals and offer specific recommendations for communicating them; Manhanelli (1988, 1992) and Prado and Albuquerque (1987) consider proposals to be important but say little about how they should be crafted or conveyed; and Torquato do Rego (1985) and Markun (1989) say essentially nothing about the policy content of campaigns.

candidates from doing likewise.[13] Hence, standard approaches to electioneering within Brazil's community of campaign consultants remain essentially unchallenged by outsiders who might advocate for different approaches.

SUCCESS CONTAGION IN PSDB PRESIDENTIAL CAMPAIGNS

In the three presidential elections that followed Cardoso's victory in 1994, the major candidate on the center-right has been a member of the PSDB, and each one has implemented a technocratic campaign strategy. To a large extent, this continuity has occurred because the structure of authority established in Cardoso's first campaign has been reproduced in subsequent elections, with campaign professionals exerting substantial influence over strategic decisions and enjoying a direct line of communication with the candidate. Major party leaders – even the presidents of allied parties and of the PSDB itself – have been given little decision-making power in presidential election campaigns. The campaign's political council, the official structure that brings together the leaders of all parties in the campaign coalition, is primarily responsible for formalizing alliances and making sure that state-level party leaders are supporting the presidential campaign. Its members are not regularly asked for input into campaign strategy, and major advisors often do not sit on this council (Figueiredo and Ribeiro 1999; author's interview, Bornhausen). Commenting on this process of professionalization, the coordinator of focus group and survey research for Alckmin's 2006 campaign explained (author's interview, A. Prado):

The leadership of the team that personally runs the campaign, since 1994 in Brazil, is uncontested. That's how it is – you have a leader of a team that plans and does things that may or may not be wise, may or may not be the right decisions, but [those decisions] are what matter…whether it is Fernando Henrique in 1994, Fernando Henrique in 1998, Serra in 2002, or Geraldo Alckmin in 2006. The team may be different, but [its authority] is something that in Brazil is absolutely assured.

Strategic inertia in the PSDB's presidential campaigns has occurred not because a previously successful approach was never questioned, but because campaign professionals favoring continuity were able to marginalize others – primarily party leaders – who suggested a change of course. Given their lack of formal input into the formulation of campaign strategy, dissenting politicians are often forced to air their disagreements to the press, almost always with little effect on the strategic decisions itself. Individual consultants with opposing views are also easily overruled if their recommendations go against the technocratic model of campaign strategy supported by the majority of campaign professionals.

Below, I discuss two examples that show how the recurrent use of a technocratic approach by PSDB candidates has been due to professional norms favoring policy-centric campaigns and campaign consultants' ability to impose their preferred strategy on internal dissidents. In 2002, José Serra sought to distance

---

[13] *Folha de São Paulo*, September 3, 1994.

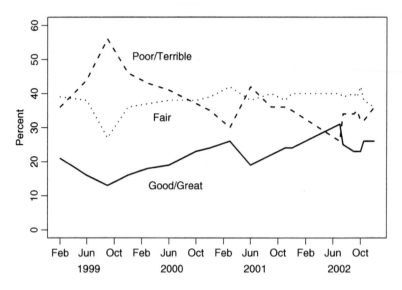

FIGURE 3.6. Evaluation of President Fernando Henrique Cardoso (Second Term).

himself from incumbent president Cardoso and to emphasize specific proposals in the area of employment, which was considered the greatest unresolved problem during Cardoso's second term. In 2006, Geraldo Alckmin focused extensively on his prior accomplishments as governor of São Paulo, and he resisted attacking Lula on corruption charges until a scandal arising during the campaign made the issue impossible to ignore. In both instances, the PSDB candidate stuck steadfastly to a strategy recommended by his principal consultant, against the vehement objections of major politicians from his own party as well other members of the electoral coalition. In each case, the alternative strategy would have ended up reducing the policy focus of the campaign.

José Serra, 2002: In Search of "Continuity without Continuism"

The 2002 presidential campaign of PSDB candidate José Serra faced a difficult scenario. Serra had been health minister during Cardoso's second term, winning renown for his policies against AIDS and in favor of generic medications, but Cardoso's own government had become increasingly unpopular during the same period. Major problems included the devaluation of the *real* in 1999, an energy crisis that led to electricity rationing in 2001–2002, and the government's inability to reduce higher-than-normal levels of unemployment during the previous four years. For these reasons, Cardoso's approval rating was consistently lower during his second term than during his first, with more negative than positive evaluations of his performance throughout almost the entire four-year period (Figure 3.6). These problems, combined with weakening of the party coalition that had supported Cardoso in 1994 and 1998, meant

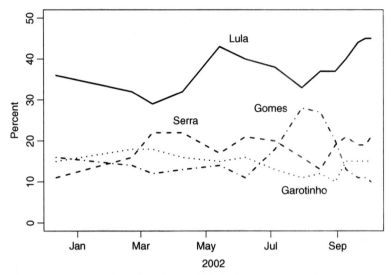

FIGURE 3.7. Intended Vote in Brazil's 2002 Election.

that Serra remained far below Lula in the polls throughout the first round and was even stuck in third or fourth place during a decent portion of the campaign (Figure 3.7).

Given the difficult context of the election, Serra's marketing team mapped out a strategy with two key features. First, the candidate should distance himself from the government he had previously served as minister, emphasizing that his candidacy provided "change with security" or "continuity without continuism." Cardoso himself appeared only once on Serra's evening television program, giving a short and generic endorsement. Advertising producers actually filmed many more statements of Cardoso expressing his support, and initially intended to use them, but the surveys "didn't allow it" (author's interview, Berni). Serra also personally sought to distance himself from Cardoso. Interviewed on a political talk show in May 2002, he characterized Cardoso's government as "good" but not great, rating it 7 out of 10 (Almeida 2006: 178). Similarly, the president rarely campaigned alongside Serra and did not appear onstage at one of his rallies until the week before the first-round vote.[14]

A second key component of Serra's strategy was a focus on policies to address unemployment, which 37 percent of voters considered the greatest unresolved problem during the president's second term.[15] In his television advertising, Serra spoke extensively about employment policy, devoting 20.4 percent of his total time to the issue of employment and 15.6 percent to job creation proposals. Beyond the specific issue of job creation, Serra's television program focused

[14] *Folha de São Paulo*, September 28, 2002.
[15] The next-highest category, violence and crime, was mentioned by only 13 percent of voters as the most serious problem (Almeida 2006: 28).

TABLE 3.4. *José Serra's Television Advertising, 2002*

Policy focused	66.9
Specific proposals	21.1
General proposals	14.4
Achievements	13.1
Criticism	3.4
Diagnosis	14.8
Not policy focused (jingles, image, or other)	33.1
Cleavage priming	2.8
No cleavage priming	97.2

Note: Entries are percentages of total advertising time.

heavily on proposals in general (Table 3.4). It devoted 35.5 percent of all advertising time to a discussion of future policy, the majority of which (21.1 percentage points) concerned specific proposals. Both of these figures are well above
those of any other major Brazilian presidential candidate in the period under
study. In response to a reporter's question about the serious and somewhat boring tone of Serra's television advertising, a campaign advisor said that "the voter
doesn't want catchy music, he wants to know how the candidate will improve
his life."[16]

Serra's campaign strategy might seem logical given the state of public opinion, but numerous politicians and one member of Serra's advertising team disputed these decisions, in part based on a different reading of the survey data.
A number of PSDB leaders with important positions in the campaign hierar-
chy, including political coordinator João Pimenta da Veiga and operational
coordinator Milton Seligman (author's interviews), disagreed with the decision
to adopt a critical stance vis-à-vis the current president. Eduardo Jorge Caldas Pereira (author's interview), a top former official in the Cardoso government who participated in strategic discussions about campaign communication,
explained that with respect to the president's approval ratings, "you can also
read the survey another way. Even being poorly evaluated, the government has
a core support base of 25 percent. Look, that 25 percent support base could
carry anyone to the second round." Consultant José Roberto Berni sided with
the politicians in this debate, arguing that by not emphasizing his ties to the
Cardoso government, Serra risked losing the votes of Cardoso supporters. Yet
Serra and head pollster Lavareda steadfastly resisted bowing to criticism of this
sort from within the campaign team (author's interview, Berni).

The alternative course of action favored by politicians was a long-term strategy that would have reduced the emphasis on Serra's proposals and defended
the image of Cardoso's government with an eye toward improving the PSDB's
prospects in future presidential elections. Such a strategy was arguably more in

[16] *Folha de São Paulo*, October 8, 2002.

the long-term interests of the party, and possibly even those of Serra himself. Serra's chances of defeating Lula in 2002 were never particularly strong, even after he made it to the second round. This fact was clearly indicated by survey data; Lavareda routinely expressed the opinion in strategy meetings that the election would be difficult to win. In such circumstances, a superior long-term strategy might have been to defend Cardoso's performance in various problem areas, such as the energy crisis, corruption allegations, and the privatization of state firms, so that the reputation of his government would not continue to weigh negatively upon the PSDB in future elections (author's interviews, Berni and Caldas Pereira).[17]

In sum, the campaign professionals working for Serra in 2002 recommended that he distance himself from the image of the president and emphasize specific job creation proposals. This recommendation was consistent with the preference for policy-centric campaign appeals that has developed among Brazilian campaign professionals, as well as with the presidential campaigns that the same marketing team had designed in 1994 and 1998. Hence, the professionals working on Serra's campaign were both repeating a previously successful strategy and adhering to a standard operating procedure within the professional community. Yet campaign professionals had to confront opposition from a number of influential party leaders, who preferred an alternative, long-term strategy that would have reduced the focus on Serra's own proposals by defending the Cardoso's government's accomplishments. Consultants' ability to win the candidate's confidence and marginalize dissenting politicians was thus an important factor in Serra's use of a technocratic campaign strategy in 2002.

Geraldo Alckmin, 2006: Resisting the Call for Attacks

Geraldo Alckmin's 2006 presidential campaign similarly illustrates the importance of professional norms and the ability of pollsters and advertising strategists to marginalize dissenting politicians and win the candidate's support. The choice of Alckmin rather than Serra as PSDB candidate in 2006 brought in a different team of professionals than the one that had been in charge of the campaigns of 1994, 1998, and 2002. However, Alckmin's head consultant Luiz Gonzalez had participated in Cardoso's reelection effort in 1998 (Ferreira [1998]: 168) and had also worked with Alckmin in his 2002 campaign for governor of São Paulo. As part of the same professional community as prior campaign strategists for the PSDB, Gonzalez and his team ended up implementing a technocratic approach quite similar to the campaigns of Serra and Cardoso.

---

[17] Indeed, in the 2006 campaign for his reelection, Lula took advantage of the continued unpopularity of Cardoso's government by contrasting his own four years in office with those of his predecessor. Cardoso thus continued to be a liability for the PSDB.

TABLE 3.5. *Geraldo Alckmin's Television Advertising, 2006*

Policy focused	69.5
Specific proposals	10.0
General proposals	8.2
Achievements	33.7
Criticism	7.3
Diagnosis	10.3
Not policy focused (jingles, image, or other)	30.5
Cleavage priming	0.0
No cleavage priming	100.0

Note: Entries are percentages of total advertising time.

The communication strategy of Alckmin's 2006 campaign shows that Brazilian campaign professionals instinctively follow the standard operating procedure of emphasizing policy, even when they claim to be pursuing a different approach. Focusing Alckmin's campaign on policy issues was *not* the stated goal of his marketing team. As Gonzalez explained (author's interview), "the strategy that I had in mind ... was to shift the agenda of the election to a discussion of personalities, and not engage in a discussion of issues ... my idea [was] that [Alckmin] become known for his biography and his personal attributes."

However, even when intending to make the election a contest of personalities, Gonzalez ended up designing a campaign that focused heavily on policy. The main image-related feature of Alckmin's television advertising was his administrative competence, which was documented by showcasing his policy achievements as governor of São Paulo. Only a small share of Alckmin's advertising focused on the candidate's personal image per se. However, Alckmin devoted 69.5 percent of his advertising time to policy, more than Serra in 2002. His achievements accounted for 33.7 percent of the total, with another 18.2 percent focused on proposals (Table 3.5).

In addition, Alckmin's campaign was surprisingly positive given the context of the 2006 election, in which the issue of government corruption could easily have become a much more central theme. While the PT had always campaigned against political corruption, in office, it succumbed to many of the same temptations as its predecessors. From 2005 to 2006, top party and governing officials were implicated in a vast series of scandals related to campaign finance and bribery. The most famous of these, the *mensalão* ("big monthly payment") scandal, involved cash stipends paid to legislators from allied parties in exchange for voting on legislation favored by the PT. While the scandals were never directly linked to the president, many of Lula's closest advisors were forced to resign. Then, two weeks before the first round of the 2006 election, the "Dossier" scandal erupted when several individuals linked to Lula and the PT were arrested in possession of a large bag of cash intended as payment for information supposedly implicating Serra in a corruption scheme. This effort

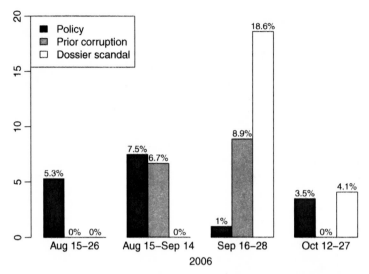

FIGURE 3.8. Criticism in Geraldo Alckmin's Television Advertising.

backfired on the PT, however, given that illegally acquired funds were being used for the dossier's purchase.

Despite the seemingly attractive opportunity to focus the campaign on the PT's corruption scandals, the strategy of emphasizing Alckmin's policy achievements meant avoiding attacks on Lula. During the first two weeks of free electoral advertising, there was little criticism of Lula at all, and none of it focused on corruption (Figure 3.8). Even when Alckmin began to step up criticism of his opponent during the first half of September, the majority of these attacks focused on policy issues such as a poorly maintained federal highway in the state of Maranhão or the weak policing of Brazil's national borders. The initial criticism was thus consistent with a technocratic campaign strategy.

Only after the outbreak of the Dossier scandal two weeks before the first round vote did Alckmin significantly increase criticism of Lula, with respect to both the PT's illegal campaign tactics (18.6 percent of the advertising during this period) and the previous year's corruption scandals (8.9 percent). In the second round, Alckmin returned to a more positive campaign, with only 4.1 percent of his time devoted to criticism of the Dossier scandal, and no references to prior corruption cases.

From the start, the strategy of running a positive campaign and avoiding attacks on Lula generated vehement objections from some of the most important leaders of the PSDB and its coalition partners. Following the first several days of Alckmin's television advertising, several top politicians from the allied PFL publicly criticized the lack of attacks on Lula.[18] After the first mention of

---

[18] *Folha de São Paulo*, August 19, 2006; *Folha de São Paulo*, August 24, 2006.

corruption in Alckmin's television advertising, his campaign coordinators from the PSDB and PFL both said they would like to see more corruption-related criticism in the future.[19] Once the Dossier scandal broke, numerous politicians, including the PSDB party president, began calling for additional attacks, to be delivered personally by Alckmin rather than a third party.[20] According to the campaign's operational coordinator, virtually all of the important PSDB and PFL politicians preferred more criticism of Lula than was being implemented (author's interview, Caldas Pereira).

Despite the public as well as internal pressures to step up the attacks on Lula, the marketing team's original plan for Alckmin's television advertising was never altered in response to these demands from politicians. The increase in attacks following the outbreak of the Dossier scandal was not in the original plan, but even this decision did not respond to pressure from political advisors. Rather, with the Dossier scandal so omnipresent in media coverage of the campaign and in voters' minds during the last several weeks, campaign professionals felt there was no way to avoid it (author's interviews, Bornhausen, Gonzalez, Guerra, and A. Prado). Throughout the various internal debates, Alckmin retained confidence in the decisions of his marketing team despite criticism from allied politicians. According to Caldas Pereira (author's interview), "there was no disputing Gonzalez's power."

The trajectory of Lula's approval rating during his first term suggests that the alternative strategy being proposed by politicians might well have borne fruit. Between Lula's inauguration in 2003 and the revelation of the first scandal in May 2005, approval of Lula was substantially higher than disapproval (Figure 3.9). Only once the scandals began to implicate close advisors and important government ministers did Lula's popularity begin a notable decline. Yet as the various corruption schemes failed to implicate the president himself and began to fade from the headlines, Lula's approval rating returned to where it had been before the scandals. During the week after free television advertising began, Lula scored his highest approval rating ever. These data suggest that Lula's greatest vulnerability lay in the corruption charges rather than the policies he implemented as president.[21] Focusing more on corruption and less on policy might well have been a more productive strategy for Alckmin.

In sum, Alckmin adopted a technocratic strategy because policy-centric appeals had become the standard operating procedure among Brazil's campaign professionals, and because these professionals were successful at marginalizing dissenting party leaders and earning the candidate's confidence. Even when intending to make the campaign a contest of personalities, Alckmin's marketing team instinctively resorted to a policy-centric strategy, casting the candidate as a successful administrator and emphasizing his prior accomplishments as

[19] Josias de Souza blog, *Folha de São Paulo*, September 1, 2006.
[20] *Folha de São Paulo*, September 21, 2006.
[21] Hunter and Power (2007) reach a similar conclusion regarding the reasons for Lula's reelection.

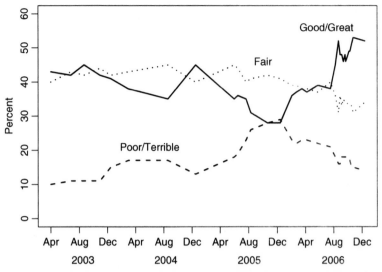

FIGURE 3.9. Evaluation of President Luiz Inácio Lula da Silva (First Term).

governor of São Paulo as well as his proposals for the future. This strategy also implied minimizing criticism of Lula on corruption charges. The corruption-related attacks that politicians were demanding would have reduced the policy focus of the campaign, but Gonzalez's strategy kept the television advertising squarely focused on Alckmin's administrative accomplishments and, during most of the campaign, concentrated its limited criticism on Lula's administrative failures.

Alckmin's campaign differs from Serra's in that the strategy defended by politicians was not a long-term strategy; rather, it was an alternative recommendation for winning the current election. In each case, however, campaign research in the form of surveys and focus groups did not indicate a single, unambiguous course of action. Rather, the candidate had to choose among competing strategic recommendations based on different interpretations of the same data. In both instances, the decision was to adhere to the recommendations of the campaign professionals whose authority had been established by Cardoso's successful campaign in 1994. This recurrent use of a technocratic approach, in the face of plausible alternatives, is evidence of success contagion among PSDB candidates in Brazil.

SUCCESS CONTAGION IN LULA'S PRESIDENTIAL CAMPAIGNS

In contrast to the PSDB, the PT's adoption of a technocratic approach to campaigning has come more slowly over time. As illustrated in Figure 3.1 at the outset of this chapter, cleavage priming disappeared from Lula's television advertising after 1994, and his campaigns became substantially more policy focused.

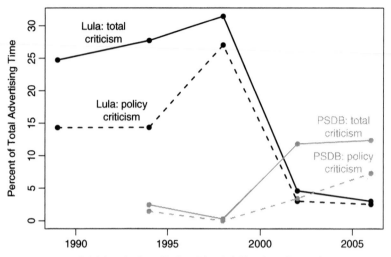

FIGURE 3.10. Criticism in Brazil's Presidential Election Campaigns.

In 2006, Lula's television program emphasized policy more than that of his opponent for the first time since 1989.

Even more significant than Lula's overall increase in policy focus has been a substantial reduction in negative content and an effort to focus all remaining criticism on policy issues. Figure 3.10, showing the proportion of television advertising that Lula and his PSDB opponent devoted to overall criticism and to policy-specific criticism, illustrates this pattern quite clearly. While attacks took up between a quarter and a third of Lula's television program in his first three elections, and increased from 1989 to 1998, they dropped to only 4.6 percent in 2002 and 3 percent in 2006. Likewise, the share of that criticism devoted to policy issues has increased from a low of 51.8 percent in 1994 to a high of 84.3 percent in the 2006 election. When Lula chose to criticize his opponents in 2002 and 2006, he did so largely with respect to their administrative failures, not by pegging them as members of the "dominant class" or denouncing their unfair campaign tactics.

Part of the reduction in criticism in Lula's campaigns might be attributed to his being an incumbent in 2006 and the leading candidate throughout the 2002 race, versus a challenger in 1994 and 1998. However, such an explanation cannot account for the magnitude of this change over time. In 2002 and 2006, when PSDB candidates were either behind in the polls or challenging Lula's reelection, they engaged in much less criticism than when Lula was in a similar situation. If there is a general "challenger" effect on campaign criticism in Brazil, it is likely to be on the order of 11 percentage points, the difference between the average criticism of PSDB candidates in 2002 and 2006 versus 1994 and 1998. The difference for Lula in these same elections is more than double this amount, at 26 percentage points.

In addition, an emphasis on specific proposals, prior accomplishments, and the administrative capacity of the candidate and his advisors has replaced an approach originally oriented toward demonstrating familiarity with the plight of everyday Brazilians. Analyzing the 1994 election, Luis Felipe Miguel (2000, emphasis in original) explained that "the PT's temptation has always been to substitute the candidate's *biography* for his *program*...the PT's discourse encouraged people to put in power someone who, because he was *the same* as the people, would solve their problems." In the years since, according to a PT pollster, "being intimately familiar with people's problems was not considered sufficient to resolve them. I think that is the perception that has changed" (author's interview, Venturi).

The PT's adoption of a technocratic approach to campaigning has implied a substantial, multidimensional strategic change since Lula's first presidential election campaign in 1989. However, this change has occurred more slowly and has been subject to more internal obstacles than in the case of the PSDB. Ever since Cardoso's 1994 victory, professional norms about campaigning have prompted the PT's consultants to recommend a technocratic approach. In the 1998 election, Lula started off embracing their advice, placing substantial emphasis on proposals. However, he abandoned this strategy midway through the campaign. Not until 2002 did Lula embrace the technocratic model of campaign strategy on a level similar to that of his major opponent, giving greater weight to the advice of his consultants.

The accumulation of the PT's subnational executive governing experience helps to explain the difference in outcomes between 1998 and 2002. Prior experience in city and state governments played a role in predisposing Lula's 2002 campaign advisors to emphasize policy competence. It also helped to ensure that their primary goal would be to win the election rather than adhere to the party's historical commitments – something that emerges as an important facilitating condition for success contagion in Brazil.

Lula, 1998: Abandoning Proposals, Denouncing the Economic Crisis

Two key factors distinguished Lula's 1998 campaign from the one in 1994. In the PT's 1995 and 1997 internal elections, leftist factions had lost the majority control of party leadership that they enjoyed in 1994 – a victory for the centrist group closely allied with Lula. In addition, Lula insisted that he be allowed to designate the leadership of his campaign, rather than accepting a team that was representative of the PT's various factions (Samuels 2004).[22] Having won this internal power struggle, Lula and his team were able to make a second change vis-à-vis the previous campaign – hiring mainstream campaign professionals. While the choice of Lula's advertising strategist in 1994 fell largely upon ideological lines, one of the two codirectors of his 1998 television advertising

[22] *Folha de São Paulo*, June 3, 1998.

had previously worked for a variety of parties across the ideological spectrum, including the right-wing PFL (Godoy et al. 2000: 285). The 1998 campaign also relied more heavily on internal surveys and focus groups than in 1994, though funds did not allow for extensive campaign research (author's interview, Venturi).

In keeping with the emerging professional norm in their community, Lula's consultants recommended a strategy centered on specific proposals, and the campaign started out following this approach. However, Lula and the politicians in charge of his campaign were not fully committed to an "electoral" rather than "political" strategy in 1998. When an economic crisis hit Brazil about six weeks before the election, they made an executive decision to abandon the proposals and focus instead on criticizing the government's handling of the crisis. Hence, professional norms prompted an initial move in the direction of a technocratic strategy in 1998, but they were ultimately not sufficient to bring about a major change in Lula's approach.

At the time of the 1998 campaign, Lula faced an uphill battle in his efforts to defeat Cardoso, whose performance as president was generally well evaluated. Nonetheless, Cardoso's approval rating was reduced to a near low for his first term (Figure 3.5) in the first half of 1998, offering Lula some hope of at least pushing the election to a second round. The government's major problem was unemployment, which reached 7.8 percent in Brazil's six largest cities in the first half of 1998, after having remained steady between 4–6 percent from 1990 to 1997 (IBGE 1998). Given this and several other problems, Cardoso's vote intentions dropped sharply after April 1998, and Lula's began to rise, to the point that the two were in a statistical tie in late May and early June (Figure 3.11).

Based on survey research showing that Lula had the greatest advantage over Cardoso when discussing social issues, campaign professionals mapped out a strategy in which Lula would concentrate on proposals in the five policy areas of education, health, agrarian reform, employment, and industrial policy (Godoy et al. 2000; Almeida 2002: 151; author's interviews, Cotrim and Godoy). Macroeconomic policy, an area in which Cardoso enjoyed a credibility advantage, was conspicuously absent from Lula's discourse at the start of the campaign. Both his official government program and a shorter "Commitment Letter" released in July 1998 made no mention of specific policies regarding interest rates or monetary stability (Almeida 2002: 150).[23] In the terrain of social policy, however, the campaign initially focused on concrete solutions to people's problems. In late July and early August, campaign manager Luiz Gushiken (author's interview) began using a tactic known as "Thematic Weeks," in which Lula would focus his campaign events and comments to the press on a different social policy area each week, presenting proposals

---

[23] *Folha de São Paulo* July 7, 1998.

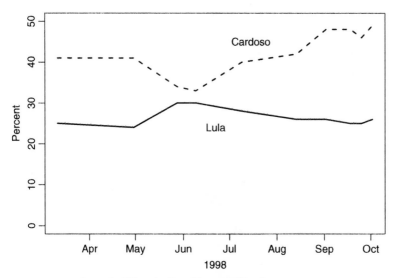

FIGURE 3.11. Intended Vote in Brazil's 1998 Election.

from his government program. Similarly, the campaign's communication director announced in early July that Lula's television advertising would focus on
proposals when it debuted in mid-August.[24]

The strategy of emphasizing social policy proposals was clearly borne out
during the start of the free electoral advertising period. During the first five
evening programs, from August 18 to August 27, Lula devoted 64.1 percent of
his advertising to policy in general, with only about one-seventh of this policy
content (9.4 percentage points) focused on macroeconomic issues or the economic crisis (Figure 3.12). A very large proportion of the advertising from this
period – 15.2 percent of the total – was devoted to specific proposals, primarily
with respect to job creation and fighting malnutrition. By both of these measures, Lula's television advertising in 1998 started out substantially more policy
focused than in 1994, when 49.4 percent of all television time was devoted to
policy, and only 3.3 percent to specific proposals.

Lula's initial strategy of emphasizing social policy proposals changed dramatically once the effects of the August 1998 Russian economic crisis began to
be felt in Brazil. As foreign investors began to pull their money out of developing economies, Brazil lost $11 billion of its $75 billion in reserves during
the month of August, and $2.1 billion on August 21 alone (Ferreira [1998]). In
an attempt to stave off a devaluation of the *real*, Cardoso announced drastic
and unpopular increases in Brazil's already high domestic interest rates – from
19 percent to 29.75 percent in early September, and then to 49.75 percent on
September 10.

[24] *Folha de São Paulo*, July 11, 1998.

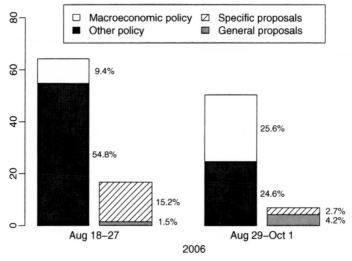

FIGURE 3.12. Lula's Television Advertising in 1998: Over-Time Variation.

In response to these events, the politicians in charge of Lula's campaign decided to shift direction, abandoning the emphasis on social issues and focusing squarely on the government's handling of the economic crisis. From August 29 through the end of the campaign, more than half of the total discussion of policy in Lula's television advertising addressed macroeconomic policy and the crisis. Since the PT lacked a coherent solution to the economic crisis, this phase of the campaign was much less focused on proposals than the first ten days of advertising. Only 6.8 percent of Lula's advertising after August 27 dealt with future policy, and less than half of this discussion concerned specific proposals. The closest Lula came to a proposed solution to the economic crisis involved a list of "emergency measures" that he called on Cardoso to implement – not actually a plan for how Lula would manage macroeconomic policy if elected.

The debate about whether to focus on the economic crisis pitted Lula's marketing team against the politicians running the campaign, and in contrast to Serra's 2002 campaign, the PT party leaders were successful at imposing a long-term "political" strategy over a short-term "electoral" one. Advertising strategist Godoy argued in these internal debates that "we have to be technically competent, we have to emphasize the social sphere" (Godoy et al. 2000: 266). Yet as soon as economic conditions began to worsen in Brazil, the PT politicians in charge of the campaign were convinced that the proper course of action was to focus on the crisis and blame the government. "You have to seriously consider the opinion of the advertising specialists and the surveys," explained Lula's campaign manager from the PT, "but politics is the realm of politicians...A political party exists to win the election, but also to discuss politics. A country that was living through a crisis as serious as that one...the party had to respond" (author's interview, Gushiken). The PT president and campaign's political coordinator similarly argued that Lula had a responsibility to address the economic crisis even if he lacked specific proposals to solve it (author's interview, Dirceu). Effectively, top party leaders made a decision that contradicted the surveys and would almost certainly lose votes for Lula, but might well reap dividends in the next election, when Lula would be able to point out that he had warned the country about the impending crisis (author's interview, Dias). As Godoy explained, "we lost votes, we lost time, and we knew that. We had surveys saying that the best person to solve the crisis was Fernando Henrique, but we were committed to announcing that the crisis was here" (Godoy et al. 2000: 266).

The 1998 presidential election was the first in which the centrist faction of the PT had reestablished control over the party and the group running Lula's campaign favored hiring mainstream advertising strategists. In its focus on specific proposals, the approach mapped out by these strategists was consistent with the technocratic model that had become the norm among campaign professionals. Yet Lula and his close political advisors were not ready to fully embrace a technocratic strategy. When the deepening of Brazil's economic crisis in mid-August forced them to choose between a short-term strategy for optimizing performance in the current election and a long-term approach that might preserve the best interests of the party, they opted for the latter. A weak commitment to winning the election thus acted as a clear impediment to success contagion in 1998.

Lula, 2002: Ideological Pragmatism, National Unity, and Policy Competence

At the time of Lula's fourth bid for the presidency in 2002, many of the same conditions were in place as during his 1998 campaign. The PT's centrist factions had further increased their share of party leadership in the 1999 and 2001 internal elections, at the expense of the more left-wing groups. Lula again insisted that he would accept the nomination only if he was allowed to designate the members of his campaign team, and a very similar group of his close allies was chosen. As in 1998, a mainstream consultant was hired for the 2002 campaign – Duda Mendonça, whom Lula had unsuccessfully attempted to bring onboard in 1994. In addition to designing Lula's television advertising and offering strategic advice on numerous aspects of campaign communication, Mendonça and his team conducted extensive surveys and focus groups throughout the campaign period.

Mendonça's recommendation for Lula and the PT was quite similar to the advice offered by campaign professionals in 1998: focus on concrete proposals rather than vague visions of the future, and avoid criticizing your opponent. In his 2001 book, at a time when he had already begun working with the PT in the lead-up to the 2002 election, Mendonça (2001: 43) argued:

It is necessary to talk about dreams, but also about reality. Instead of saying 'together we will change Brazil,' start to speak more objectively about what will be done to change Brazil…The PT needs to alter its discourse a little, communicating more clearly with the population, presenting concrete proposals for Brazil's problems, so that society can understand and trust in its project.

Mendonça's belief was that the PT's campaign communication tended to suffer from a problem of form rather than content. Its programmatic positions had moderated over the years as the party matured and gained governing experience, but it still engaged in excessive criticism and resorted to the language of social struggle in a way that frightened and alienated depoliticized voters.

Mendonça's recommendations may have been similar to the advice of prior campaign professionals, but only in 2002 were Lula and his allies fully committed to embracing this technocratic approach. While many factors played a role in this change of heart, including Lula's more favorable standing in the polls and frustration at having lost three prior elections, the PT's accumulated experience governing states and municipalities was a crucial factor. From 1982 to 2000, the PT went from having essentially no executive experience to governing 187 cities, including São Paulo, Brazil's largest. During this period, the PT also won gubernatorial elections in three states, including Rio Grande do Sul, one of the wealthiest in the country. With the party increasingly in charge of some of Brazil's most important cities and states, more and more politicians were put in a position of having to implement policies rather than merely criticize the approach of the incumbent government (Samuels 2004). This experience helped to justify campaign strategies focused on proposals. A taste of power from administering cities and states also helped convince many PT leaders that it was worth embracing strategies primarily designed to win elections, even if it meant sacrificing long-held party principles.

In 2002, the PT's subnational executive experience was directly incorporated into Lula's campaign team for the first time, with the choice of Antônio Palocci, a two-time mayor of Riberão Preto, as the coordinator of his government program. Palocci joined the campaign after the initial program coordinator – Celso Daniel, three-time mayor of the São Paulo industrial suburb of Santo André – was killed in January 2002. The involvement of these politicians in Lula's campaign brought a particular appreciation for pragmatic approaches and an emphasis on policy competence. In addition, Palocci had already shown a willingness to work with campaign professionals, having hired Mendonça in his bid for a second mayoral term in 2000.

Campaign Communication: National Unity and Policy Competence

Given the PT's willingness in 2002 to focus on policy and work with mainstream campaign professionals, Mendonça's strategic recommendations met with little resistance. One particularly important characteristic of Lula's 2002 campaign was its emphasis on national unity and compromise. The campaign's television advertising not only avoided priming cleavages; it also specifically emphasized Lula's desire to bring together disparate parties in pursuit of common national goals. Lula's television program on the evening of October 20, for instance, reported on his recent meeting with the country's most important businessmen, bankers, union leaders, and representatives of NGOs to discuss his proposals for an economic and social development council. In a speech at the event, one of the participants argued that "we need to set aside our individual interests – not forgetting them, but aligning them with a greater project."

This notion of compromise and ideological pragmatism was also reflected in the decision to offer the vice presidential slot to José Alencar, owner of one of Brazil's largest textile firms and ex-president of the Minas Gerais State Federation of Industries. Mendonça was a strong defender of putting Alencar on the ticket, and under his direction, the campaign's television advertising sought to portray their joint candidacy as the union of responsible labor and productive capital (author's interview, Dirceu). When Lula first approached Alencar, he was a PMDB senator, and his party probably would not have allowed him to become Lula's running mate.[25] Alencar thus agreed to switch his affiliation to the Liberal Party (Partido Liberal, PL), which would then formally join Lula's electoral coalition. Incorporating the PL, a small, right-wing party that had previously supported Cardoso's government, was a particularly controversial move within the PT, which had always previously allied with left and center-left parties. In the second round, Lula sought to broaden his support base even further, with endorsements from figures as historically anathema to the PT as Paulo Maluf (Miguel 2003: 307). Defending these sorts of pragmatic moves in a speech to militants in his political birthplace of São Bernardo do Campo, Lula said he did not want any ideological vetoes of second-round alliances because left and right are ultimately irrelevant when people go to vote.[26]

In addition to a message of national unity and ideological pragmatism, Lula's campaign placed substantial emphasis on the candidate's specific proposals and the qualifications of his advisors, and it engaged in very little of the policy criticism that had previously been the PT's hallmark. The overall percentage of time devoted to policy increased only minimally from 1998, from 53.8 percent to 54.2 percent, but the nature of this policy content changed dramatically.[27] Proposals took up 16.8 percent of Lula's television advertising, the highest this figure has ever been for his campaigns, and most of this discussion conveyed specific details (Table 3.6). Even more significantly, criticism virtually disappeared – only 3 percent of Lula's advertising blamed the government for current

---

[25] The PMDB ended up allied with the PSDB in the 2002 election and provided Serra's vice presidential candidate.

[26] *Folha de São Paulo*, October 9, 2002.

[27] Overall policy content would surely have been higher in 2002 if not for Mendonça's penchant for symbolic appeals, such as one segment in which a group of pregnant women dressed in white marches across a field to symbolize change and rebirth.

TABLE 3.6. *Lula's Television Advertising, 2002*

Policy focused	54.2
Specific proposals	10.3
General proposals	6.5
Achievements	6.3
Criticism	3.0
Diagnosis	28.1
Not policy focused (jingles, image, or other)	45.8
Cleavage priming	0.0
No cleavage priming	100.0

Note: Entries are percentages of total advertising time.

problems, and none of it sought to criticize his opponent's policies. Much of what previously took the form of attacking the incumbent became a simple diagnosis of policy challenges (28.1 percent) with no mention of Cardoso or the government. In addition, Lula's television advertising prominently emphasized the technical qualifications of his advisors, an idea contributed by Mendonça (author's interview, Dirceu). Many of Lula's broadcasts began with him walking through a room surrounded by a team of experts poring over charts and computer screens. After Lula introduced the issue of the day, an off-camera voice would explain in detail the relevant experience of three or four advisors for that policy area.

In sum, Lula's 2002 campaign was the first in which both the candidate and his close advisors from the PT fully embraced a technocratic strategy. Unlike 1994, those in the PT who opposed the involvement of the "apolitical" consultant Mendonça had essentially no voice in the campaign leadership. And in contrast to 1998, the close circle of Lula's allies who were running the campaign did not seek to overrule their consultant's "electoral" recommendations. Numerous factors may have played a role in this change of heart, but the PT's accumulated subnational executive experience and the presence of two-time mayor Antônio Palocci as government program manager arguably contributed to the campaign's predisposition toward policy emphasis and ideological pragmatism. The example of the PT thus highlights that a primary commitment to winning the election, rather than defending the party's long-term interests or historical commitments, can be a crucial enabling factor for success contagion.

DEVIATIONS FROM TECHNOCRATIC STRATEGIES: CLEAVAGE PRIMING IN 2002 AND 2006

The process of success contagion in Brazil has not meant that candidates always adhere perfectly to the technocratic model of campaign strategy when there are opportunities to profit by doing otherwise. As in the Chilean case, there are several examples in recent elections of candidates partially deviating from

Brazil's dominant style of campaigning. In each case, however, these deviations have been limited in scope or duration, either occupying only a small portion of a much longer campaign or constrained to less visible venues such as speeches at rallies. Alckmin's decision to take advantage of the Dossier scandal in the 2006 election and substantially increase criticism of Lula in the final weeks before the first-round vote is one such short-term deviation, in that it involved temporarily reducing the discussion of policy in order to focus on Lula's campaign tactics.

In this section, I examine two other partial deviations from a technocratic strategy, involving cleavage priming by Serra in 2002 and Lula in 2006. Both of these examples demonstrate that, while candidates may choose to strategically emphasize societal divisions during particular portions of a campaign, they come nowhere near the level of cleavage priming in Brazil's 1989 election before the technocratic model had been introduced. In addition to being limited in magnitude, occasional cleavage-priming deviations do not respond to a common, cross-case mechanism like the influence of professional norms. Rather, they involve candidates taking advantage of various opportunities that arise in the course of the campaign. What has caused Brazilian candidates to become more similar to one another is a systematic process; what occasionally pushes them apart is contingent.

Toward the end of the first-round campaign in 2002, when Serra had retaken second place and it seemed likely that he would enter the runoff, his television advertising began to engage in limited cleavage-priming attacks on Lula. One of these attacks showed a clip of Lula's campaign manager, PT president José Dirceu, speaking during a 2000 São Paulo teachers' union strike in a manner more reminiscent of Lula from 1989: "More and more mobilization! More and more strikes! More and more street demonstrations!" The program then went on to report that the PSDB governor of São Paulo had been wounded by street demonstrators a week later, implying that Dirceu's comments had stirred them to violence.

In the campaign for the runoff in October, Serra's advertising attacked Lula more frequently. Several segments argued that the PT was hiding old allies such as the CUT and Landless Rural Workers' Movement (Movimento dos Trabalhadores Rurais Sem Terra, MST) because of their radical image, and suggested that they would have a more prominent role in Lula's government if he won the election. In the sample of Serra's advertising examined for the 2002 campaign, cleavage-priming attacks of this sort took up 2.8 percent of the total time, and 4.8 percent in the second round.

In a somewhat similar fashion, Lula's reelection campaign in 2006 also engaged in a number of cleavage-priming appeals – though these appeals were intentionally kept off the television screen. Under attack by the center-right opposition since the first corruption allegations against his government in 2004, Lula sometimes used his stump speeches in 2006 to cast himself as a victim of elite conspiracies. At a rally in Olinda in July, Lula argued that "the same elite that carried Getulio [Vargas] to his death, that dragged Juscelino [Kubitschek] through the worst process of accusations and lies, that overthrew João Goulart, that same elite tried to get rid of me."[28] Harkening back to language not used since the 1994 campaign, Lula occasionally cast himself as a representative of the people, the poor, or the working class in opposition to the privileged and powerful. Appearing before supporters in Sorocaba, he said that "this campaign is not about one candidate versus another. This is a campaign of the working people against an aristocratic elite."[29]

In some ways, Serra and Lula's priming of cleavages in the 2002 and 2006 elections constitutes a departure from the model of technocratic campaign strategy. However, the fairly limited emphasis on social divisions in these two campaigns was hardly a return to the cleavage-priming politics of 1989. Serra did not construct his entire candidacy around social divisions in the same manner that Collor did with his anti-elite, populist discourse. Rather, his appeal to ideological cleavages in 2002 was confined to a fairly limited portion of the campaign – primarily the three weeks of the second round. Distancing himself from Cardoso's legacy and emphasizing job creation policies were both fundamental elements of campaign strategy conceived well in advance; criticizing Lula and the PT's radicalism was simply embraced in a somewhat desperate attempt to close the gap toward the end of the campaign.

Similarly, in contrast to Lula's frequent and instinctual resort to cleavage priming in 1989, divisive appeals were used entirely as a tactical tool in the 2006 campaign, and they were employed quite sparingly. Lula sought to prime cleavages only occasionally during rallies, and they were kept off of television entirely. During the second round, the campaign filmed at least one television commercial with a message similar to the cleavage-priming language that Lula was using in rallies, but ultimately decided not to air it because doing so would be too risky. Instead, strategists kept the on-camera criticism focused on policy issues, charging that Alckmin had plans to privatize cherished national institutions such as the post office, the Bank of Brazil, the Federal Savings Bank (Caixa Econômica Federal), and the state oil firm Petrobras. While tapping into similar sentiments as cleavage-priming discourse, policy-focused criticism of this sort was considered a much safer option.[30]

In sum, while both Serra and Lula partially diverged from technocratic strategies in their respective campaigns in 2002 and 2006, such moves were limited in either scope or duration. Even allowing for these deviations, Lula and Serra's campaign strategies in these elections were still much closer to the technocratic ideal type than they were to Collor's neopopulist strategy or Lula's mass party campaign in 1989.

[28] *Folha de São Paulo*, July 24, 2006.
[29] *Folha de São Paulo*, September 24, 2006.
[30] *Folha de São Paulo*, October 30, 2006.

TABLE 3.7. *Television Advertising in Brazil's 2010 Election*

	Dilma Round 1	Dilma Round 2	Serra Round 1	Serra Round 2
Policy focused	69.3	63.2	69.2	53.2
Specific proposals	11.8	13.0	16.0	10.9
General proposals	6.0	6.7	2.9	3.0
Achievements	30.0	18.3	33.3	13.2
Criticism	0.1	12.4	6.7	11.4
Diagnosis	21.4	12.9	10.3	14.6
Not policy focused (jingles, image, or other)	30.7	36.8	30.8	46.8
Cleavage priming	0.0	0.0	0.0	1.4
No cleavage priming	100.0	100.0	100.0	98.6

Note: Entries are percentages of total advertising time.

Testing the Argument: Strategic Continuity in 2010

Brazil's 2010 presidential campaign presents strong evidence of strategic continuity, with major candidates of Left and Right adhering to the dominant technocratic model of campaign strategy. Lula, with an approval rating of over 80 percent at the end of his second term, sought to transfer power to his former chief of staff and chosen successor, Dilma Rousseff (hereafter referred to by her first name, following Brazilian practice). On the right, the PSDB-led coalition supported José Serra, the candidate from 2002. Marina Silva, a former PT member who served as Environmental Minister in Lula's government before defecting to the Green Party, placed third with 19.3 percent of the first-round vote, helping push the election to a runoff. Dilma won the first round of the election, with 47 percent of the vote to Serra's 33 percent, and she defeated him in the runoff by a margin of 56–44 percent.

On the PT side, Dilma's campaign sought to claim co-responsibility for the policies that had made the Lula government so popular, and she pledged to continue them during her presidency. The campaign underscored that Dilma had been in charge of programs such as Light for Everyone (rural electrification), My House My Life (subsidized housing), and the Growth Acceleration Program (large-scale public works), and that she had headed up the Administrative Council of Petrobras, which had recently discovered massive offshore oil deposits. Her television advertising spoke about the accomplishments of "the government of Lula and Dilma," and it described ongoing projects – especially infrastructure investment such as the diversion of the São Francisco River to arid parts of Brazil's Northeast – that "cannot be interrupted in any way." As shown in Table 3.7, policy content occupied 69.3 percent of Dilma's television advertising time in the first round. Proposals accounted for 17.8 percent of the total time, on par with Lula's campaign in 2002, and most of the discussion involved specific details (11.8 percentage points).

Serra's campaign was also heavily focused on specific policies. As with Alckmin in 2006, Serra boasted of specific accomplishments during his tenure as mayor and governor of São Paulo, including infrastructure investments such as the São Paulo beltway. He disputed the authorship of Lula government policies such as Light for Everyone or a public housing complex built in a São Paulo slum, saying that they originated in earlier PSDB programs or that his state and municipal government deserved the credit.[31] He pledged to expand the Lula government's conditional cash transfer program Bolsa Família, and he proposed ProTec, a vocational training scholarship fund modeled on the federal government's ProUni. Serra also criticized policies for which Dilma sought to claim credit, arguing that many infrastructure projects were stalled and that public-funded emergency medical clinics were poorly run. His first-round advertising focused on policy 69.2 percent of the time, with 16 percent devoted to specific proposals – a profile similar to that of Dilma's campaign.

As in 2006, events arising during the campaign sometimes led the candidates to deviate from their focus on policy. In particular, both candidates sought to woo religious voters in the second round, following a grassroots religious campaign against Dilma's ill-defined position on abortion and an unexpectedly strong first-round result for Marina Silva, an evangelical Christian.[32] As a result, the runoff campaign focused more on candidates' values than usual, with Dilma appealing to "the defense of life" and Serra invoking "the values of the Brazilian family." Policy focus in both candidates' second-round advertising was somewhat lower than in the first round (63.2 percent for Dilma and 53.2 percent for Serra), but still within the range of normal for recent Brazilian campaigns. Indeed, the central clash between candidates in the second round was not about values but about policy. Dilma sought to tie Serra to unpopular privatizations under Cardoso and charged that he would privatize Petrobras's claims to the newly discovered oil reserves; Serra countered by pointing out concessions for gas exploration that the PT government had granted to the private sector.

Candidates also largely avoided opportunities to prime cleavages. The most obvious concerned the religious cleavage that had been made salient in the first round by the grassroots campaign against Dilma. In Serra's television advertising, references to religion or the issue of abortion were almost always positive and used coded language – talking about a "new Brazil that is being born" with Serra's candidacy, for instance. In the content analyzed, the only explicit criticism of Dilma's stance on abortion involved a short clip from the candidates'

---

[31] *Folha de São Paulo*, August 6, 2010.
[32] Several years prior to the election, Dilma had come down in favor of decriminalizing abortion. During the campaign, she said that she preferred it be treated as a public health rather than criminal matter but that she still supported the existing (very strict) legislation.

debate. When the press turned up allegations that Serra's wife had gotten an abortion, Dilma's campaign did not take up this opportunity to prime the religious cleavage to her own advantage.[33] As in 2002, Serra did engage in some very limited priming of the class cleavage in the second round. Following a campaign event in which Serra was hit by an object thrown by a protester (allegedly from the PT), his campaign aired a segment attacking the PT and its labor union allies for their violent tendencies, using some of the same footage as in similar attacks in 2002. This segment accounted for 1.4 percent of Serra's advertising in the second round and was clearly in response to an unexpected event, not part of the original plan for campaign strategy.

For Serra in particular, the decisions of campaign professionals were crucial to the strategy that was implemented, as they had been in previous campaigns. Luiz Gonzalez, the head communication strategist for Alckmin in 2006, advised Serra in a similar capacity in 2010. As in 2006, Gonzalez won the loyalty of the candidate, who adhered to his recommendations in spite of open criticism from some of the top figures in his party and coalition, including former presidents Cardoso and Itamar Franco. Politicians were consistently calling for a more aggressive campaign against Dilma and less of a positive focus on Serra's accomplishments and proposals. While it is possible that some of the attacks on Dilma came as a result of this pressure, press coverage emphasized the numerous times that Serra and Gonzalez resisted their urgings.[34]

Brazil's 2010 election is thus consistent with the predictions of success contagion, in that candidates of both Left and Right continued to rely on technocratic strategies. In some ways, this election may seem like a relatively weak test of the theory, given the continuity of the political actors involved. Yet Serra's prior presidential campaign had been unsuccessful, and in a different context, one might expect a negative reaction against his earlier tactics, seeking to do something different from what had failed in the past. As discussed in the next chapter, such inward-oriented reactions are quite common among Peruvian candidates, where a single approach to campaigning was never legitimated by a successful presidency. In Brazil, by contrast, Serra employed the dominant model of campaign strategy in 2002 and again in 2010, despite his loss in the earlier contest.

CONCLUSION

Brazilian candidates' campaign strategies have converged over time because the technocratic approach introduced in 1994 has been repeated in subsequent PSDB campaigns and more gradually adopted in those of the PT. The consolidation of norms within the tight-knit Brazilian community of campaign

---

[33] *Folha de São Paulo*, October 16, 2010.
[34] *Folha de São Paulo*, August 17, 2010; *Folha de São Paulo*, August 21, 2010; *Folha de São Paulo*, August 23, 2010; *Folha de São Paulo*, October 6, 2010.

professionals has been the crucial mechanism in this process. In the aftermath of
the 1994 election, Brazilian political consultants widely embraced the technocratic approach to electioneering used during Cardoso's first presidential campaign, particularly his emphasis on specific proposals and policy competence.
A preference for policy-centric strategies was not the inevitable product of professionalization; in Chile, the opposite has occurred. However, once established
as the standard operating procedure among Brazilian political consultants, the
technocratic model has spread across the political spectrum as campaign professionals have gone on to advise presidential candidates from both the PT and
the PSDB.

Professional norms were a key mechanism of success contagion in Brazil
not only because there was a tight-knit community of campaign consultants in
which they could develop, but also because the perceived ideological distance
between Cardoso and the PT made outright imitation unlikely. In contrast to the
situation in Chile, where Lavín's strategists saw the governing Concertación as
having borrowed the Right's economic model and shifted to the center, Cardoso
came from a left-wing background and moved decisively to the right while in
office. Directly imitating his approach to the 1994 campaign would have been
anathema to PT leaders because Cardoso was viewed as a traitor to the Left.
Even the effort to hire political consultants who had previously worked for
right-wing candidates generated substantial opposition within the PT, whose
leaders did not fully heed their advice until 2002. However, embracing "professional" recommendations from consultants was ultimately an easier pill to
swallow than copying the strategy of a bitter foe.

The influence of political consultants in Brazilian campaigns has produced
frictions not only on the left but also within the center-right PSDB. In the presidential elections of 2002, 2006, and 2010, important leaders of the PSDB and
other allied parties objected to the strategy designed by campaign professionals, and they proposed alternative approaches that would have reduced the
policy focus of each campaign. Given such internal disagreements, consultants'
ability to impose their preferred strategies on dissenting politicians has been
an important factor underlying strategic inertia on the right-hand side of the
political spectrum. In each instance, internal dissidents were marginalized and
their preferences ignored, even though there were plausible reasons to consider
these alternative suggestions.

For its part, the case of the PT illustrates an important enabling factor for
the process of success contagion: a primary commitment to winning elections.
In 1998, despite having won the battle against party factions that opposed the
participation of mainstream advertising strategists, Lula and his inner circle
ultimately abandoned the technocratic approach recommended by these professional advisors. Their reasons for doing so included a historical commitment to denouncing the neoliberal economic model – in their mind, the cause
of the current economic crisis – and also an effort to better prepare the terrain
for future elections. In 2002, by contrast, Lula and his campaign team were

fully committed to modifying the PT's traditional discourse in order to win the election. The party's accumulated subnational administrative experience was arguably an important factor in this change of heart, predisposing its leaders to policy-centric campaign appeals and also giving them an appreciation of the value of holding executive office.

Finally, Brazil highlights the importance of governing success in establishing a model of campaign strategy that other candidates will adopt in the future. In contrast to Chile, the first direct presidential election after democratization in Brazil did not initiate a process of success contagion because the victorious candidate, Fernando Collor, was a clear failure in office. In the lead-up to the 1994 election, campaign professionals detected a popular rejection of Collor's neopopulism and an aversion to candidates who were reminiscent of the former president, and they recommended against a similar strategy. Hence, it was unlikely that any major candidate in next election would adopt a strategy that had become associated with such a spectacular case of political failure.

4

Limited Contagion and Inward-Oriented Reactions in Peru

A foreign electoral observer visiting Peru during its 2006 presidential campaign might well have been impressed by how different major candidates' strategies were from one another. Centrist candidate Alan García, president from 1985 to 1990, appealed for a second term by emphasizing a number of specific proposals and by utilizing the organizational structure of his American Popular Revolutionary Alliance (Alianza Popular Revolucionaria Americana, APRA) party as a major vehicle for reaching voters. On the right, Lourdes Flores of the National Unity coalition prioritized direct connections to voters and sought to empathize with their concerns rather than promising to solve their problems. And on the left, Ollanta Humala mounted a neopopulist bid for the presidency that sought to capitalize upon popular resentment with the wealthy and the political class, in stark contrast to the unity appeals of his two opponents.

If the foreign observer making note of these diverse approaches had visited Peru during previous presidential elections, she might also have been struck by how little had changed since Peru's transition to democracy in 1980. In contrast to the patterns in Chile and Brazil, the evolution of electoral campaigning in Peru has not led to convergence on a unique national strategy. Rather than becoming more similar over time, campaign strategies in Peru's 2006 election were as different from one another as they were in the 1980s.

The argument that Peruvian candidates have failed to converge upon a single dominant campaign strategy stands in contrast to many analyses of electoral politics and party system dynamics in Peru, which have tended to emphasize the recurrence of neopopulism following Alberto Fujimori's victory in the 1990 election. Scholars have pointed to the continuity of Fujimori's electoral strategies in his 1995 and 2000 reelection campaigns (Roberts and Arcé 1998; Schmidt 2000; Conaghan 2005), the imitation of Fujimori's organizational tactics by other candidates during the 1990s (Levitsky and Cameron 2003), and

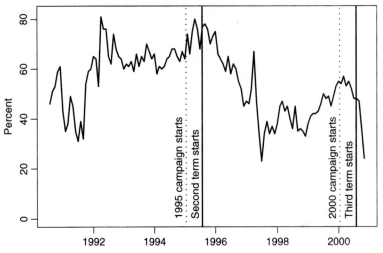

FIGURE 4.1. Approval of President Alberto Fujimori.

even the prevalence of Fujimori-style campaigns after his fall from power in 2000 (Roberts 2006; Weyland 2006b). Roberts (2006) goes so far as to apply the label "serial populism" to Peruvian politics from the 1990s on.

Existing arguments tell an important part of the story of how the campaign strategies of Peruvian presidential candidates have evolved since 1990. In several ways, the explanations they advance are compatible with the theory of success contagion. From 1990 to 2000, I argue that Peru experienced a limited form of success contagion with respect to the linkage dimension of campaign strategy. Fujimori's particular approach to political organization – crafting personal electoral vehicles to compete in each election, emphasizing direct linkages during his campaigns, and distancing himself from established intermediaries – was imitated by opposition candidates of varying ideological stripes during the 1990s. This outcome is consistent with the theory of success contagion, given that Fujimori enjoyed high approval ratings during his first two terms in office, particularly at the time of his 1995 reelection campaign (Figure 4.1). Fujimori himself also repeated his 1990 electoral strategy in the 1995 and 2000 campaigns, in keeping with the argument that one's own success tends to produce strategic inertia.

After Fujimori fled the country for exile in Japan in November 2000, neopopulism did not disappear from the Peruvian political scene. Alejandro Toledo in 2001 and Ollanta Humala in 2006 both ran for president using strategies quite similar to that of Fujimori in 1990. Yet the recurrence of neopopulism in Peru has been limited to these two candidacies, and to a particular segment of the political spectrum – an anti-establishment space left open by the demise of traditional Left parties that competed under the banner of the United Left (Izquierda Unida, IU) in the 1980s. Traditional parties are admittedly weak in

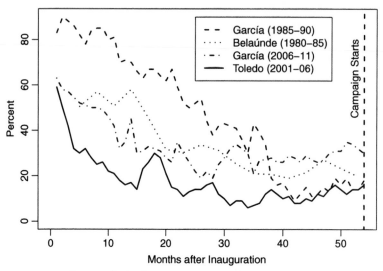

FIGURE 4.2. Approval of Select Peruvian Presidents.

present-day Peruvian politics, but this organizational weakness has not left the political scene wide open to newcomers in each presidential election. Rather, a familiar set of presidential contenders has emerged in the post-Fujimori era, with most major candidates running for president repeatedly between 2001 and 2011, and also having previously held office at the national level. Instead of choosing their strategies through the simple logic of occupying space in the political system, they have drawn upon this prior experience.

Fujimori's downfall thus put an end to the process of strategic contagion that had taken place in during the 1990s, returning Peru to a very different pattern of political evolution. The broader trend in Peruvian politics is one in which presidents have repeatedly been seen as failures in office. As illustrated by Figure 4.2, every Peruvian president besides Fujimori has seen his approval ratings fall dramatically over time, to no more than 30 percent by the start of the next electoral campaign. A decline in popularity is to be expected for even the most successful leaders, but the Peruvian figures stand in contrast to those of presidents Aylwin in Chile and Cardoso in Brazil, both of whom had over 50 percent approval at the time of the next election.

The widespread public repudiation of incumbent Peruvian presidents has occurred for a variety of reasons. During the 1980s, presidents Belaúnde and García were unpopular largely because of their inability to solve the country's two most pressing problems: hyperinflation and the Shining Path terrorist insurgency. Inflation rates and deaths from terrorist violence increased over the course of each presidential term, peaking just before the next election. In the 2000s, Peru enjoyed an economic boom under Toledo and Alan García's second term, with annual GDP growth averaging 5.7 percent between 2002 and

2006, and above 7 percent from 2006 to 2011. Poverty rates also fell steadily, from 55 percent at the start of Toledo's government to 31 percent at the end of García's. However, the uneven distribution of these economic gains, a weak and ineffective state, and various personal and political scandals under both presidents severely damaged their popularity while in office (Schmidt 2007; Taylor 2007; Levitsky 2011; Sanchez-Sibony 2012).

In the context of repeated governing failures, most Peruvian presidential candidates have chosen their campaign strategies not by reaching across the ideological spectrum to adopt an opponent's approach but rather through an inward-oriented process of responding to previous errors within their own party or political camp. Sometimes, as in the campaigns of APRA's Alan García, these inward-oriented reactions allow for a sort of strategic fine-tuning, modifying certain aspects of one's prior approach while maintaining others intact. In other cases, especially among candidates of the Peruvian Right, inward-oriented reactions tend to produce strategic zigzags over time. In this pattern, candidates shift between successive extremes of cleavage priming and unity appeals, policy focus and emphasis on image, and recourse to direct linkages versus greater use of party intermediation. Strategic zigzags can occur not only from one election to the next but also within the course of a single campaign.

Because Peru's repeated governing failures have prompted most candidates to choose their campaign strategies through inward-oriented reactions, politicians across the ideological spectrum have failed to converge upon a common approach to electioneering. This continued strategic diversity makes the Peruvian case an important theoretical counterpart to Chile and Brazil, which have witnessed convergence on unique national models of campaign strategy over time. Fujimori's successful presidency in the 1990s did initiate such a convergence process, but this episode ended with his downfall in 2000 and the return of parties and candidates who had been active in Peruvian politics during the 1980s. The broader lesson of the Peruvian case is that long-term strategic convergence is unlikely to occur in cases of repeated governing failure. When candidates choose their strategies in successive elections through inward-oriented reactions, there is no single force pushing them all in the same direction.

In the first section of this chapter, I examine Fujimori's neopopulist campaign in Peru's 1990 election and the contagion of Fujimori's direct linkage strategy to opposition candidates during the ensuing decade. The second section looks at the electoral bids of Alejandro Toledo in 2001 and Ollanta Humala in 2006, outsiders who kept the neopopulist strategy alive by occupying space on the anti-establishment side of the political spectrum. In the third section, I examine inward-oriented reactions to prior successes and failures by Mario Vargas Llosa and Lourdes Flores on the right and by APRA's Alan García on the center-left. The fourth section tests the argument by looking at the campaign strategies of the two major candidates in 2011, Keiko Fujimori and Ollanta Humala. Here, I show that Peruvian politics does not necessarily involved "serial populism"; even candidates and political movements that were closely associated with this strategy in the past can move away from it via inward-oriented reactions.

LIMITED SUCCESS CONTAGION: ALBERTO FUJIMORI AND NEOPOPULISM, 1990–2000

From 1990 to 2000, Peru experienced a limited form of success contagion, with major presidential candidates increasingly circumventing existing intermediary organizations and relying upon disposable parties built from scratch for the campaign. The first candidate to campaign in such a fashion was Alberto Fujimori, who ran a neopopulist bid for the presidency in Peru's 1990 election. By effectively controlling inflation and the Shining Path terrorist insurgency, Fujimori garnered impressive levels of public approval during his first term, prompting his opponents in the 1995 and 2000 elections to imitate his direct linkage strategy. Fujimori also employed similar strategies in each of his reelection bids. Because of the authoritarian nature of Peru's political regime during most of this period, success contagion did not extend to the cleavage-priming dimension of campaign strategy. On the whole, though, candidates' strategies in 1995 and 2000 are consistent with success contagion because they became more similar at a time when public opinion considered Fujimori a success.

Alberto Fujimori, 1990: The Rise of a Neopopulist Outsider

Neopopulism, a political strategy defined by the use of direct linkages and cleavage priming, was first introduced to Peru by Alberto Fujimori in the 1990 presidential election. An academic with no prior political background, Fujimori launched a new political movement in 1988 with the support of several university colleagues. The party that he founded, Cambio 90 (Change 90), had little *raison d'être* beyond his own candidacy, and he avoided forming any visible ties to existing political parties and interest groups. After more than a year of laboring in obscurity, Fujimori's candidacy took off in the month before the April 8 election, where he finished second to right-wing novelist Mario Vargas Llosa by a margin of 29–33 percent (Figure 4.3). During the runoff, he sought to polarize the race by priming ethnic and class cleavages, casting himself as a defender of the people against the wealthy white elite represented by his opponent. Fujimori's neopopulist strategy paid off in the second round, where he defeated Vargas Llosa with 63 percent of the valid vote.

From its inception, Fujimori's 1990 campaign sought to bypass traditional intermediary organizations, such as established parties and interest groups, in favor of alternative forms of linkage. The initial grassroots base for the movement was provided by evangelical Christian pastors and small businessmen. Clergy who were sympathetic to Fujimori's message of morality in politics went

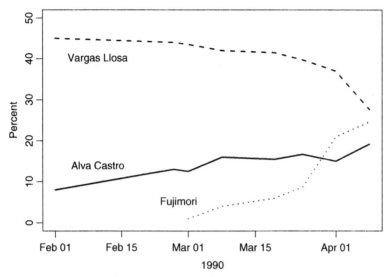

FIGURE 4.3. Intended Vote in Peru's 1990 Election.

door to door to proselytize on his behalf and gather signatures to register the new party (author's interviews, García and Vílchez). During the movement's early days, evangelical churches effectively served as the "party offices of Cambio 90" (Gutiérrez Sánchez 2000), with numerous pastors lending their home or work addresses to be used for the distribution of advertising material. A second important support base consisted of small-scale entrepreneurs and informal workers (author's interview, San Román). Truck drivers helped with the distribution of advertising material in rural areas, and bus and taxi drivers in Lima agreed to put up Cambio 90 posters and flyers in their vehicles (Schmidt 1996; Bowen 2000). The two vice presidential slots on Fujimori's slate were filled with representatives of these communities: Carlos García, president of the National Evangelical Council of Peru, and Máximo San Román, head of the Peruvian National Small Business Federation.

In the campaign for the runoff, Fujimori sought to circumvent even these relatively uninstitutionalized forms of intermediation, privileging person-to-person connections with individual voters. After the first-round vote, Fujimori quickly distanced himself from the evangelicals, removing them from the leadership of numerous rural campaign committees (author's interview, García). He also made little effort to organize the groundswell of new supporters. In the days after the first-round vote, the crowd of people trying to sign up as volunteers at Cambio 90's Lima headquarters was so large that police had to intervene to keep order.[1] Yet there was no effort to integrate these newcomers into any formal structure or give them organized tasks like distributing flyers.

[1] *La República*, April 11, 1990.

According to his Lima campaign manager, Fujimori "didn't even want to orga-nize the political party itself, because he didn't want any pressure from a party" (author's interview, Salgado). Rather, he emphasized his direct connections to voters, epitomized by the second-round campaign slogan "a president like you" (*un presidente como tú*).

In addition to favoring direct linkages, Fujimori's campaign can be consid-ered neopopulist because of his use of cleavage-priming appeals. In the first round, Fujimori's messages were strictly positive, emphasizing national unifica-tion and consensus-building. Once he had qualified for the runoff and become a serious contender for the presidency, however, Fujimori began to emphasize his own ethnic background (he was the son of Japanese immigrants) as well as that of his running mates, and to criticize Vargas Llosa as a representative of the wealthy, white Lima elite (Rospigliosi 1990: 39; Cameron 1994: 135).[2] This message was particularly prevalent in his speeches at rallies during the month of May. In his first public campaign activity of the second round, a visit to Lima shantytowns, Fujimori lashed out at rich residents of San Isidro and Miraflores, two wealthy neighborhoods in the capital, and claimed that "politicians and the powerful classes have left us only misery and neglect."[3] Reporting on the same event, *Caretas* noted that his aggressive and classist tone was a stark contrast to the unity appeals of the first round.[4] Similarly, in a May 9 rally in Lima's Villa El Salvador shantytown, Fujimori "defined the electoral contest...as a confrontation between whites and darks" (Vargas Llosa 1993: 560).

Fujimori, 1995 and 2000: Continued Neopopulism through Strategic Inertia

Fujimori stands out among modern Peruvian presidents in terms of his gov-erning success during the 1990s – measured both by accomplishments such as controlling inflation and terrorist violence, and by the high public approval that he achieved. Fujimori's first five years in office represent the only contem-porary instance of a Peruvian president becoming more popular over the course of his term (Figure 4.1). His second period was less positively evaluated, due to an economic slowdown, opposition to his bid for a third term, and the wan-ing positive effect of having tamed inflation and terrorist violence in the early 1990s. However, Fujimori still enjoyed over 50 percent approval at the start of his second reelection campaign in January 2000. Some of this positive public opinion – especially the twenty percentage-point improvement since December 1998 – can be attributed to Fujimori's manipulation of the mass media (Fowks 2000; Conaghan 2005). Nonetheless, Fujimori can be considered a successful

[2] San Román was of partial indigenous descent, and second vice presidential candidate Carlos García was Afro-Peruvian.

[3] *La República*, May 6, 1990.

[4] *Caretas*, May 7, 1990.

neopopulist president during his first two terms in office, especially compared to the spectacular failure of Fernando Collor in Brazil.

As a successful incumbent, Fujimori's approach to his 1995 and 2000 reelection campaigns involved substantial strategic inertia. In terms of linkage, Fujimori avoided institutionalizing his support base and sought out direct personal contact with voters. During the first several years of his presidency, Fujimori essentially "eviscerated" Cambio 90, purging it of both former allies and dissidents (Conaghan 2005: 52). For the 1992 constituent assembly elections, he created a new personal electoral vehicle, New Majority (Nueva Mayoría, NM), whose president described it as "a group of independents who collaborate with President Fujimori" (Roberts 2006: 95). Fujimori ran for reelection in 1995 on a ticket that combined the remnants of Cambio 90 with the new NM, before going on to create a third independent movement, Let's Go Neighbor (Vamos Vecino), in 1998. For the 2000 election, Fujimori established yet another personal electoral vehicle, the Peru 2000 National Independent Front. Peru 2000 was so lacking in grassroots capacity that Fujimori had to resort to a massive forgery operation to generate the signatures necessary to register the new party.

Rather than utilizing parties as a form of intermediation during his reelection campaigns, Fujimori sought out direct personal contact with the people. Apart from his extensive presence on television, the president's main connection with voters during the 1995 and 2000 campaigns occurred through the inauguration of public works such as schools and highways (Mauceri 1997; Roberts and Arcé 1998). In his travels around the country to preside over ribbon-cutting ceremonies, Fujimori spoke explicitly about the value of direct democracy that put the executive in contact with the people (Schmidt 2000: 108). In the final weeks before the first round of the 2000 election, Fujimori supplemented the public works inaugurations with a series of image-centric rallies, the highlight of which involved the president dancing to the technocumbia tune "Ritmo del Chino."[5]

During the 1995 and 2000 campaigns – and indeed, throughout his entire 10-year presidency – Fujimori also resorted to cleavage-priming appeals. While no longer able to unite the people against Vargas Llosa, the economic elite, and their supposedly sinister plans for market reform, the president continually lashed out against existing parties and interest groups. As Roberts (1995: 98) argues, Fujimori "portrayed Peru's political establishment as a privileged, self-reproducing dominant class that threatened to block the implementation of economic reforms while placing partisan interests above the public good." As with Collor's 1989 campaign in Brazil, part and parcel of Fujimori's efforts to establish direct ties to the people in 1995 and 2000 was a demonization of the "partyarchy" supposedly represented by other candidates. He thus

---

[5] Literally, "Rhythm of the Chinaman." Fujimori embraced the epithet "el chino," commonly used in Peru to refer to anyone of Asian descent.

continued with the neopopulist strategy of trying to unite "the people" in a struggle against a common enemy, but began to define this enemy as the "political class" rather than the oligarchy he had criticized in the 1990 campaign.

In sum, in the 1995 and 2000 elections, Fujimori repeated the formula with which he had initially triumphed in 1990 – an outcome consistent with the argument that one's own success leads to strategic inertia. Despite the inherent differences between running as a challenger and as an incumbent, or the contrast between his limited financial resources in 1990 and the spoils of office that he illegally leveraged in 1995 and 2000, Fujimori's two reelection efforts were similar with respect to the defining features of neopopulism.

The Opposition, 1995 and 2000: The Contagion of Direct Linkage Strategies

Fujimori's extralegal efforts to perpetuate his power qualify Peru as a case of electoral authoritarianism during most of the 1990s, and as argued in Chapter 1, there is not a strong expectation of success contagion in such cases.[6] When elections are not democratic, the campaign strategies of opposition candidates may effectively be chosen for them in certain respects, either by the incumbent government's restrictions on campaigning or by the fact that only certain strategies (e.g., unity appeals) are logical ways to defeat a powerful authoritarian regime. Nonetheless, there is strong evidence that a limited form of success contagion took place in Peru in the 1990s. During a period in which Fujimori enjoyed high approval ratings and could clearly be judged an example of governing success, opposition candidates in both 1995 and 2000 emulated his strategy of circumventing established parties, interest groups, and other forms of traditional intermediation and crafting personal electoral vehicles that facilitate direct appeals to voters.

Existing studies of Peruvian politics have noted a convergence in candidates' organizational strategies during the 1990s and have characterized this process in a manner quite similar to the theory of success contagion. Gutiérrez Sanín (2005) argues that post-1990 politics in Peru has involved a new form of contagion – similar to but distinct from Duverger's contagion from the left – which is characterized by the decline of party organization and the rise of media politics. For Levitsky and Cameron (2003: 10–11), "Fujimori's [governing] success suggested that established party labels and organizations were no longer necessary for (and might be a hindrance to) a successful political career." They maintain that the model of disposable parties was generalized during the 1990s "as politicians of all ideological stripes borrowed Fujimori's organizational strategy." Peruvian analysts have advanced similar interpretations. Rospigliosi (1994),

---

[6] Peru can be considered a democratic regime until Fujimori's closure of Congress in 1992, and an electoral authoritarian regime (Schedler 2006) thereafter.

for instance, argues that the rise of outsider candidates in the 1995 election was spurred on by the positive evaluation of Fujimori.

The campaign strategies of opposition candidates in 1995 and 2000 were consistent with these arguments about the contagion of Fujimori's anti-party stance and recourse to direct linkages. In 1995, Fujimori's major opponent was Javier Pérez de Cuéllar, a former Secretary-General of the United Nations, who ran on the ticket of the newly created Union for Peru (Unión por el Perú, UPP). An initial effort to name Pérez de Cuéllar as the candidate of a united opposition, led by traditional parties APRA, Popular Alliance (Alianza Popular, AP), and the Popular Christian Party (Partido Popular Cristiano, PPC), was stymied by his reluctance to form an alliance with established interests. Pérez de Cuéllar's reading of the previous presidential election was that Fujimori's independent stance provided a crucial advantage over Vargas Llosa (Schmidt 2000; Conaghan 2005: 90). As an organization, UPP had much in common with Fujimori's personal electoral vehicles. The party was pulled together solely for the election, becoming a leader or candidate depended upon personal connections to its founder, there was little programmatic agreement among those who belonged, and there was not much impetus to build the party in the long term (Sanborn and Panfichi 1996: 49–50; Levitt 1998).

The 2000 election saw a similar recourse to direct linkages, with all three major opposition candidates relying on the support of personal electoral vehicles. The first serious challenger to Fujimori was Alberto Andrade, a former PPC politician who had formed the independent movement We are Lima (Somos Lima) in his successful bid for the Lima mayorship in 1995, then renamed the party We are Peru (Somos Perú) prior to 2000 (Carrión 2000; Roberts 2006). Luís Castañeda Lossio, a second candidate to emerge as a challenger to Fujimori in 2000, had similarly resigned his membership in AP and formed a personal electoral vehicle known as the National Solidarity Party (Partido de Solidaridad Nacional).

Alejandro Toledo, who ultimately qualified for the runoff with Fujimori and then boycotted the second round in protest of unfair conditions, was supported by his own personal electoral vehicle. Toledo had originally founded Possible Country (País Posible) to support his 1995 presidential bid. However, Toledo was unable to gather enough signatures to register the party in 1995 and was forced to run with the support of a different group. In the years before the 2000 election, Toledo sought to refound his own political movement under the new name Possible Peru (Perú Posible, PP). Still lacking the grassroots capacity for a registration drive, PP resorted to forging an estimated 77 percent of the signatures that it presented to the electoral authorities (Caro 2004). According to his former press secretary, Toledo treated PP as his personal fiefdom during the lead-up to the 2000 election, overruling party militants' suggestions for congressional candidates and accepting only those who could contribute large sums of money (Zúñiga Mourao 2006: 68–70, 97–98). PP did not play much of an intermediary role in the campaign; Zúñiga Mourao (2006: 63) describes Toledo's direct, personal contact with supporters as the key component of his electoral strategy.

In sum, the electoral efforts of major opposition candidates in both 1995 and 2000 illustrate success contagion with respect to the linkage dimension of campaign strategy. In response to Fujimori's electoral success in 1990, and governing success thereafter, Pérez de Cuéllar, Andrade, Castañeda, and Toledo all sought to emulate the president's organizational strategy of crafting personal electoral vehicles and establishing direct connections to voters. On the whole, success contagion during the 1990s did not affect other dimensions of campaign strategy, a fact that is arguably due to the nondemocratic nature of the regime during this period. In confronting a powerful authoritarian regime, unity rather than cleavage-priming appeals are an obvious choice, as they were for the Chilean opposition in the 1988 plebiscite. Pérez de Cuéllar was particularly concerned with casting himself as a unity candidate in 1995; while maintaining his distance from established parties, he did not lash out at them as Fujimori regularly did.

PARTY SYSTEM COLLAPSE, NEOPOPULISM, AND "AVAILABILITY OF SPACE" ARGUMENTS

After having engineered a second reelection and weathered the scandal relating to Peru 2000's signature forgery, Fujimori's regime finally began to unravel in mid-September 2000 after the surfacing of a video in which his intelligence chief, Vladimiro Montesinos, was shown bribing a PP legislator to join the progovernment bloc in Congress. Over the next two months, the press began to expose the massive web of corruption that had propped up the Fujimori regime, and the president's once-impressive levels of support began to crumble. In a mid-November survey, Fujimori's approval rating had plummeted to 23 percent, down from 48 percent at the time of his third inauguration in July. On November 17, Fujimori resigned the presidency by fax from a hotel in Tokyo. The newly appointed leader of Peru's Congress became interim president, with new elections scheduled for April 2001.

Both Fujimori's presidency in the 1990s and his downfall in 2000 brought about significant changes in the configuration of Peruvian electoral politics. The party system that emerged in Peru after its return to democracy in 1980 was already showing signs of stress by the end of the decade, with the rise of an independent political movement led by Vargas Llosa. As described in the previous section, Fujimori intensified his attack on traditional parties after his 1990 victory, and candidates challenging his reelection emulated his strategy of privileging direct linkages via personal electoral vehicles. As a result, Peru's once-dominant traditional parties fell to combined vote shares of less than 10 percent in the 1995 and 2000 presidential elections (Tuesta Soldevilla 2001). Numerous analyses published during or shortly after this period identified a collapse of Peru's traditional party system (Cameron 1994, 1997; McClintock 1994; Tuesta Soldevilla 1995; Schmidt 1996; Tanaka 1998, 2006; Levitsky and Cameron 2003; Kenney 2003, 2004; Dietz and Myers 2007; Crabtree 2010; Seawright 2012).

There has been somewhat greater debate about the configuration of the party system after Fujimori's departure. In both the 2001 and 2006 elections, two of three major candidates were members of traditional parties that had seemed to disappear during the 1990s – Alan García of APRA, and Lourdes Flores of the PPC (the latter running as part of the National Unity coalition that also included several newer political movements). For some analysts, these elections suggested a partial resurgence of Peru's party system from the 1980s (Kenney 2003; Meléndez 2009; Boas 2010). Following the 2011 election, when APRA withdrew its candidate and the PPC failed to field one at all, consensus shifted toward the interpretation that Peru's traditional party system had truly and permanently collapsed (Levitsky 2011, 2013; Meléndez 2011; Tanaka 2011).

The demise of traditional parties in Peru is often thought to have implications for the campaign strategies that have predominated since Fujimori's departure – in particular, creating an empty political space that a series of neopopulist outsiders have been able to occupy. Levitsky and Cameron (2003: 25) argue that the collapse of Peru's party system generated a large mass of floating voters without partisan commitments, which has facilitated the rise of outsider candidates seeking to capture this temporary base of support in successive electoral contests. Roberts (2006) characterizes Peruvian politics since 1990 as a case of "serial populism" because party system collapse has freed up space for successive neopopulist outsiders and none of these politicians has forged new, durable cleavages around which a party system could be structured. In a similar vein, Weyland (2006: 35–36) considers neopopulism the "default option" in Peruvian politics because of persistent organizational weakness, and he predicts its recurrence.

I argue that the use of neopopulist strategies in the period after Fujimori's departure has been more limited than implied by these existing studies, and that there has actually been substantial strategic diversity among major presidential contenders from 2001 to 2011. Many candidates have continued to utilize the sorts of direct linkages that predominated during the 1990s, but García's campaigns in 2001 and 2006 drew upon an existing party structure to a significant extent, while Keiko Fujimori's 2011 campaign relied on intermediated linkages via a new one. An even greater level of strategic diversity was evident in terms of policy focus and cleavage priming, with some candidates, particularly Humala, making radical changes in their approach to successive campaigns. In the post-Fujimori era, neopopulism per se has been restricted to Toledo's campaign in 2001 and Humala's in 2006. In their 2011 presidential bids, these same politicians employed different strategies, underscoring the limits of the "serial populism" argument.

In order to understand the reasons for strategic diversity after Fujimori's demise, it is necessary to consider an important change in Peruvian electoral politics that has been largely overlooked in studies of party system collapse: the emergence of a familiar cast of characters who compete in successive presidential elections. In 1995 and 2000, major challengers to Fujimori were either complete newcomers to electoral politics (Toledo and Pérez de Cuéllar) or had run for office only at the municipal level (Castañeda and Andrade). From 2001 to 2011, by contrast, the only major presidential bids by newcomers to electoral politics were those of Ollanta Humala in 2006 and Pedro Pablo Kuczynski in 2011.[7] Others were former presidents (García in 2001 and 2006, and Toledo in 2011), repeat presidential candidates (Toledo in 2001, Flores in 2006, and Humala in 2011), or had served one or more terms in Congress (Flores in 2001 and Keiko Fujimori in 2011). In contrast to 1995 and 2000, there were no defectors from established parties after Fujimori's demise, nor repeat presidential candidates who crafted a new party for each election. While Peru's political scene is often thought to be dominated by a series of outsiders, the outsiders of the 2000s have stuck around and become established players on the electoral scene, gaining experience with successive presidential bids.

The consolidation of a new "political class" in Peru means that, despite the apparent collapse of traditional *parties*, political space has not been wide open in recent presidential elections. Rather, space has been filled by politicians with prior experience in electoral politics at the national level. As I will argue in the next section, this continuity of personnel, combined with repeatedly poor performance by elected presidents, has allowed strategic diversity to persist in Peruvian politics long after democratization. Rather than reaching across the ideological spectrum to embrace the approach of an opponent, most presidential candidates since 2001 have returned to a long-standing pattern of choosing their electoral strategies through inward-oriented reactions to their own prior success and failures, which typically leads them in different directions from one another.

Neopopulism, of course, has not disappeared from the Peruvian electoral scene. The reasons this approach was employed by Toledo in 2001 and Humala in 2006 have much to do with the sorts of "availability of space" arguments that been advanced previously. I argue that there *was* available political space in Peru's party system in 2001 and 2006, but only on the anti-establishment side of the political spectrum – a space originally occupied by Peru's partisan Left in the 1980s. Unlike the Center, with Alan García, and the Right, with Lourdes Flores, this anti-establishment space was not quickly reoccupied by career politicians after the demise of Fujimori. No politician or party with ties to the United Left coalition of the 1980s participated in the 2000 or 2001 elections, and in 2006,

---

[7] In this discussion of "major" candidates, I include two – Kuczynski and Toledo in 2011 – who received less than 20 percent of the valid vote in the first round and thus did not meet the selection criteria for full inclusion in the study.

three such candidates (Diez Canseco, Moreno, and Villarán) garnered only 1.4 percent of the valid vote. In 2001 and 2006, there was space for a newcomer to electoral politics – or relative newcomer, as one would have to classify Toledo in 2001 – to campaign as a neopopulist on the anti-establishment side of the political spectrum.

In the following sections, I examine the neopopulist campaigns of Alejandro Toledo in 2001 and Ollanta Humala in 2006, focusing on the anti-establishment space vacated by the partisan Left. Regardless of whether they ultimately govern on the left, or even occupy the leftmost position in terms of campaign proposals, neopopulist outsiders are anti-establishment candidates because their campaigns seek to unify the people in a struggle against the "powers that be." Hence, candidates with varying economic policy stances – such as Toledo, who did not oppose Peru's market-oriented economic model, and Humala, who did – can occupy the same political niche in successive elections. One youth organizer who was involved in both Toledo's and Humala's campaigns described the latter's rise to prominence in exactly these terms: Toledo "left open a very large space" that could be filled by Humala, who was also "occupying the same space that Fujimori occupied in 1990" (author's interview, Meza). Each of these candidates shared an outsider status and a rejection of the status quo represented by the incumbent president – discredited traditional politicians in 1990, corrupt authoritarianism in 2000–2001, or neoliberalism in 2006.

The recurrence of neopopulism in Peru has been facilitated not only by the existence of floating voters without loyalty to established parties but also by the presence of "floating militants" – people who will not only vote for the outsider of the day but also participate in an impromptu organizational structure supporting his campaign. Some of the key individuals who ran Fujimori's campaign at the local level in 1990 went on to do the same work for Toledo in 2000–2001 and Humala in 2006. The availability of floating militants is particularly important in a country where campaigns still include a major territorial component. Floating militants allow neopopulist outsiders to throw together a political movement that can mobilize people to attend rallies, among other important tasks. Yet neopopulists also fail to institutionalize the support of these floating militants, thus leaving them available as an impromptu organizational base for the next neopopulist outsider who comes along.

Neopopulist candidates in Peru have also made important use of cleavage-priming appeals, capitalizing upon popular discontent with social and economic marginalization. The manner in which they do so is consistent with an effort to occupy available space in the political system. Campaign advisors to both Toledo and Humala specifically recommended *against* cleavage-priming appeals and sought to craft messages of national unity in the parts of the campaign over which they had greater influence – particularly, television commercials. This stance shows that divisive campaigning has failed to gain broad legitimacy among campaign professionals in Peru. Yet in areas of the campaign less

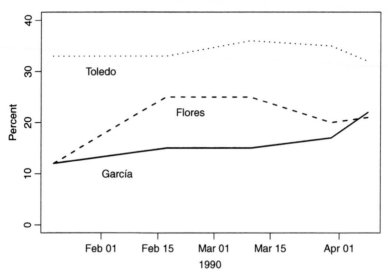

FIGURE 4.4. Intended Vote in Peru's 2001 Election.

controlled by their advisors – primarily speeches at public rallies – Toledo and Humala actively employed a cleavage-priming approach.

Alejandro Toledo, 2001: Neopopulism with Ethnic Appeals

As the primary challenger to Fujimori in 2000 and the leader of popular opposition to his third-term government, Toledo was well positioned as a candidate in 2001. The frontrunner in opinion polls throughout the race, Toledo seemed most likely to face center-right candidate Lourdes Flores in the runoff until a last-minute surge by Alan García (Figure 4.4). García narrowed the gap in the second-round campaign, though Toledo was ultimately elected president by a margin of 53–47 percent.

As in the 2000 campaign, Toledo drew upon the support of his personal electoral vehicle PP, which had continued to grow in size, somewhat chaotically, in the intervening months. Toledo's 2001 campaign manager estimated that 100,000 people were involved with PP at its height during that year's election, but this support was poorly organized in comparison to APRA (author's interview, C. Bruce). According to press spokesman Fernando Rospigliosi (author's interview), "there were [local] committees, but it was...the typical thing in Peru, people who see a candidate with possibilities and jump on board because they think they can get something out of it." Significantly, much of this support was drawn from people who had previously stood behind Fujimori. According to a Chilean consultant who worked on Toledo's campaign, "what Perú Posible had at that moment was a spontaneous structure...that principally embodied the disillusionment with Fujimori. Many people who supported Toledo were people who supported Fujimori at some point during his government. And so they replicated the system of *fujimorista* organization in that campaign, in favor of Toledo" (author's interview, Forch).

Ethnic identity was an important part of Toledo's appeal in the 2001 campaign, as it had been in 1995 and 2000 (Madrid 2011; Raymond and Arce 2011). Toledo's advisors always recommended that the candidate emphasize ethnicity in a positive fashion, portraying himself as someone who could bring together the country after the divisiveness of the Fujimori years. In television advertising, and in other elements of campaign strategy influenced by professionals, Toledo stressed a message of national unity, epitomized by the slogan "a government of all the races" (*un gobierno de todas las sangres*) (author's interview, E. Bruce).

Beyond the careful control of his advisors, however, Toledo's rally speeches in 2001 often took on a more confrontational tone, actively embracing ethnic cleavages. This approach was particularly prominent during March and April, when Toledo was under fire for various personal scandals. At one rally, Toledo said "we are so close, and for that reason the little snobs (*pituquitos*) from Miraflores have become frightened. They are afraid of the people coming to power. Let them have their money. Let them have their influence. I have my people, by God!" In other speeches, Toledo cast his opponent Flores as the candidate of the rich and himself as the candidate of the poor and denounced a conspiracy to bring down the *cholo* (a term for someone of partial indigenous ancestry).[8] Probably the most infamous cleavage-priming appeal during the 2001 campaign was delivered by Toledo's wife at a rally in Huaraz, defending him against the recent personal scandals: "We haven't thrown ourselves [into this campaign] to be cannon fodder, so that the little white boys from Miraflores can have freedom of the press to defame and to lie … Is that what we fought for? No, you Lima snobs! … Hear me well, you little Limeños who are so afraid of the Peruvian people. My *cholo* is healthy and sacred" (Moura 2001).

Once inaugurated as president in July 2001, Toledo made little effort to institutionalize his base of electoral support, thus permitting PP to quickly fizzle once his political fortunes began to decline. As in Fujimori's case, Toledo's failure to institutionalize support would facilitate this base of disillusioned militants being captured by a future neopopulist seeking to succeed him.

Ollanta Humala, 2006: Neopopulist Nationalism

In the 2006 election, the outsider candidate who emerged as best positioned to mobilize frustration with Toledo and opposition to the status quo was Ollanta Humala, a retired army officer. Humala initially approached leaders of Peru's

[8] *La República*, March 14, 2001; *Caretas*, March 22, 2001; *La República*, March 23, 2001; *El Comercio*, March 24, 2001.

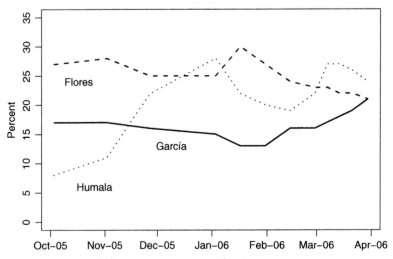

FIGURE 4.5. Intended Vote in Peru's 2006 Election.

traditional left-wing parties, making plans to join forces with an eye toward
the 2011 election (author's interview, Breña). However, as he rose in opinion
polls as a possible candidate for 2006 (Figure 4.5), Humala decided to run on
his own with the support of his hastily assembled Peruvian Nationalist Party
(PNP). This move shows that Humala was not necessarily averse to working with established parties, but rather adopted an anti-party stance once he
realized he had begun to fill a space that the traditional Left could no longer
occupy.

Once he had broken with the traditional Left parties, Humala's campaign
relied heavily on direct rather than intermediated linkages. As in the case of
Fujimori's and Toledo's personal electoral vehicles, Humala's PNP had little
grassroots capacity for such tasks as a registration drive. After failing to obtain
enough signatures to put the PNP on the ballot, Humala approached UPP,
which already enjoyed official status and was willing to formally support his
candidacy.[9] Even after incorporating the existing UPP, the coalition supporting
Humala had little *raison d'être* beyond his candidacy. As its official symbol for
the ballot, it chose a pot, or *olla*, because it would permit alliterative campaign
phrases such as "the *olla* is Ollanta" (author's interview, Méndez).

While lacking formal party organization, Humala picked up much of the
floating militant support that had previously gone to Toledo. Vladimir Meza
(author's interview), a former youth activist from Toledo's campaign, estimated

---

[9] UPP was Pérez de Cuéllar's party in 1995, but the former diplomat broke with the movement
after the election. UPP subsequently became a "party for rent" with little ideological or political
identity, supporting a variety of candidates with different political orientations in 2000, 2001,
and 2006 (Haya de la Torre 2006).

that 80–90 percent of PP youth leaders had shifted their support to Humala in 2006 and gotten informally involved in the campaign. Like his predecessors, however, Humala showed no inclination to institutionalize this floating militant support; few collaborators had been assigned formal positions of responsibility, which contributed to an ineffective campaign structure. According to Meza, "in each province, there are two or three groups that are extremely divided, and they fight amongst themselves every day. Each one conducts its own campaign, and each one focuses that campaign as it sees fit."

Humala's campaign was also similar to Toledo's in its juxtaposition of a national unity message in television advertising and a confrontational, cleavage-priming message in rally speeches. Humala's slogans for the first and second round – "Love for Peru" and "Future for Everyone" – sought to equate his nationalist ideology with the universal values such as patriotism. In one television spot, Humala explained that "we are all nationalists, we who love Peru." Many of these advertisements were particularly light in tone, with images of smiling supporters and upbeat music. This television advertising strategy, oriented primarily toward the press and the upper and middle classes in Lima, sought to make Humala more palatable to sectors that were naturally skeptical of his candidacy (author's interviews, Méndez and Pucci).

Humala agreed to the positive, unity-oriented campaign only reluctantly (author's interview, Méndez), and much of his discourse in rallies was openly confrontational, priming cleavages between rich and poor or between the people and the political class. Instead of mirroring his advertising strategy in rally speeches, Humala referred to politics as a sewer and told businessmen to go to hell.[10] At a rally in late March, he said that his "discourse is one of confrontation with the economic powers" and that his rivals "are those old, macerated politicians, that are now gray-haired and pot-bellied, who want to maintain poverty and unemployment."[11] In his closing rally, Humala referred to the president and members of Congress as "the morally collapsed political class," and said he would fight against "the dictatorship of the interests of the great economic groups."[12] Similar appeals could be found in one of Humala's television spots, made independently of the advertising strategists who favored positive messages. In it, the candidate claimed that "the Right, the oligarchy, and the traditional political class have no project for the country. They are an interest group, and the only thing that concerns them is preserving their privileges and wealth."

In sum, both Toledo's campaign in 2001 and Humala's campaign in 2006 show that the recurrence of neopopulism in Peru has been facilitated by the availability of space on the anti-status quo side of the political spectrum. At the base level, Toledo's and Humala's personal electoral vehicles drew upon many

[10] *Caretas*, March 23, 2006.
[11] *Caretas*, March 30, 2006.
[12] *El Comercio*, April 6, 2006; *La República*, April 6, 2006.

of the same floating militants that had initially been supporters of Fujimori –
and, during an earlier era, might have been involved with the partisan Left. In
each case, campaign professionals recommended that the candidate convey a
message of national unity and avoid divisive appeals. However, both candidates
followed such recommendations only in their television commercials and seized
opportunities to prime cleavages during their speeches at campaign rallies.

INWARD-ORIENTED REACTIONS: APRA AND THE RIGHT

Neopopulist outsiders constitute an important phenomenon in post-Fujimori
Peru: Toledo's neopopulist campaign helped him win the presidency in 2001,
and Humala's nearly did so in 2006. Yet the phenomenon of true outsiders
occupying empty space has effectively been limited to these two candidacies.
Political space has not been occupied by *parties* to the same extent that it was
in the 1980s; APRA, the PPC, and Toledo's PP all failed to field presidential
candidates when their leaders were ineligible to run for immediate reelection
(Toledo in 2006 and García in 2011) or had been tarnished by recent scandals
(Flores in 2011). Yet the presence of established *politicians* in the political field –
Flores and García in both 2001 and 2006, and Humala, Toledo, and Keiko
Fujimori in 2011 – has effectively prevented other outsiders from occupying
their niches.

I argue that the strategies adopted by major candidates in Peru's 2001 and
2006 elections can only be fully understood by combining the "open space"
perspective with the theory of success contagion. Success contagion argues that
when one president after another is a failure in office, future candidates will
select their strategies through inward-oriented reactions to prior experiences
within their own party or political camp. Such an inward-oriented approach
was already well established before Fujimori's presidency. Alan García's 1985
campaign was a clear reaction to the shortcomings of APRA's strategy in the
1980 election. Likewise, Mario Vargas Llosa's 1990 campaign was largely a
reaction to his diagnosis of the failings of former right-wing political candidates, and his strategy in the runoff responded directly to perceived errors of
his own first-round effort.

As politicians with a prior history in electoral politics, most presidential
candidates in post-Fujimori Peru have chosen strategies not by simply trying
to fill an existing political space but rather by reacting to perceived errors of
the past. The political discontinuity brought about by Fujimori's departure
effectively put an end to the broader convergence on direct linkage strategies that had taken place in 1995 and 2000. Meanwhile, Flores's and García's
candidacies in 2001 and 2006 marked the return of candidates, advisors, and
political parties that had acquired substantial prior experience in presidential
election campaigns. The pattern of inward-oriented reactions that had characterized the evolution of campaign strategies in the 1980s thus resumed after
Fujimori's departure. Despite the substantial attention that scholars have paid

to the recurrence of neopopulism in the 1990 and 2000s, inward-oriented reactions are an even more prevalent phenomenon, having begun prior to the Fujimori period and also influencing the strategies of most major candidates from 2001 to 2011.

Inward-oriented reactions are crucial for explaining why convergence in campaign strategies has not occurred in Peru as it has in Chile and Brazil. Because they are not responding to the same external stimulus, but rather to entirely different internal ones, the strategies of major candidates from APRA and the Right have neither become more similar to one another over time nor come to approximate the strategies of neopopulist outsiders like Toledo and Humala.

THE RIGHT: OVERREACTIONS AND STRATEGIC ZIGZAGS

On the right, inward-oriented approaches to the choice of campaign strategy have tended to result in dramatic shifts over time between different strategic extremes, often within the course of a single campaign. This zigzag pattern has been facilitated by a high degree of factionalism within campaign teams. As soon as a particular course of action begins to falter, with a candidate declining in the surveys or performing worse than expected in the first round of an election, there is typically an internal rival maneuvering to "sell" the candidate on a radically different strategy. On their own, such internal divisions do not generate inward-oriented approaches to campaign strategy or a pattern of strategic zigzags. Factionalism has also been common in other cases examined in this study, including Chile's Concertación and Brazil's Party of Brazilian Social Democracy (Partido da Social Democracia Brasileira, PSDB), but the factions consistently winning internal arguments have been those advocating an already legitimated model of electioneering. In countries like Peru, which lacks such a model, "anything goes" in terms of campaign strategy; there is no reason for a candidate not to try a radically different approach if the previous one produced less than satisfactory results.

In this section, I examine two major examples of strategic zigzags produced by inward-oriented reactions on the right. In 1990, right-wing intellectual Mario Vargas Llosa launched a campaign that was unprecedented in terms of its technocratic policy focus. Yet after failing to obtain a first-round victory that would offer a mandate for his bold reforms, Vargas Llosa abruptly reversed course in the second round, downplaying his proposals and acting the role of traditional politician as he inaugurated public works paid for by his party's philanthropic arm. His campaign also began to prime religious and racial cleavages, contradicting the strictly unity-oriented approach of the first round.

In 2001 and 2006, Lourdes Flores's campaigns evidenced a similar series of reactions to perceived errors. After having presented herself in 2001 as a somewhat stiff and formal politician without much charisma but with a command of policy details, she embarked on a multiyear effort to recast herself as an apolitical candidate who was close to the people and shared an intimate understanding of their concerns. The first several months of Flores's 2006 campaign thus employed the same personalistic strategy that has become commonplace in Chile. Yet as Flores began to lose ground in the polls about one month before the first round of the election, she quickly shifted course, embracing a more "political" image and launching a series of specific policy commitments during the final few weeks of her campaign.

Mario Vargas Llosa, 1990: From Technocratic Idealism to Pork-Barrel Politics

Mario Vargas Llosa, a distinguished novelist and intellectual of libertarian political leanings, founded the Liberty Movement in 1987 to defend free-market policies, reinvigorate Peru's beleaguered political Right, and mount a challenge to president Alan García, who had just announced plans to nationalize Peru's banking system. Though he had long expressed skepticism of traditional politics, Vargas Llosa ultimately entered into an alliance with two traditional parties, AP and the PPC, to form the Democratic Front (Frente Democrático, FREDEMO) in Peru's 1990 presidential election. Vargas Llosa held a comfortable lead in the polls throughout most of the first-round campaign. However, Fujimori's last-minute surge robbed Vargas Llosa of his desired absolute majority and spelled a likely defeat in the second round, since Fujimori could easily pick up the votes of those who had opposed Vargas Llosa on ideological grounds.

Vargas Llosa chose to structure his campaign around a detailed government program. Inspired by the writings of Hernando de Soto and the notion of popular capitalism, the candidate not only proposed a series of liberal solutions to the hyperinflation that plagued Peru in the late 1980s but also embarked upon a pedagogical project to educate Peruvians about the free market and convince them that the principles and policies he defended would improve their lives in tangible ways. His television advertising was thus heavily focused on policy. The campaign adopted inflation as its signature policy area, with a goal of reducing the annual rate to less than 10 percent within a year, and a series of advertisements featured FREDEMO economists explaining why this policy target was an important and realistic one. Overall, an estimated 60.7 percent of Vargas Llosa's first-round television advertising time focused on policy, and much of this (27.8 percentage points) was devoted to the policies he would implement as president (Table 4.1).[13]

Vargas Llosa's devotion to his government program colored nearly all of the strategic decisions made during the first round of the campaign, even contributing to actions that were politically inexpedient. In choosing a foreign

---

[13] Summary statistics regarding television advertising in Peru reflect actual broadcast time only in 2006 and 2011. For prior years, they represent estimates, as discussed in Appendix A.

TABLE 4.1. *Mario Vargas Llosa's Television Advertising, 1990 (Round 1)*

Policy focused	60.7
Specific proposals	11.3
General proposals	16.5
Achievements	2.2
Criticism	10.0
Diagnosis	20.6
Not policy focused (jingles, image, or other)	39.3
Cleavage priming	0.0
No cleavage priming	100.0

Note: Entries are percentages of estimated total advertising time.

campaign consultant, Vargas Llosa and his team "were reluctant to accept the involvement of an American firm because of their emphasis on image, color, and excess emotion, and not on pedagogy, which was our obsession" (Vargas Llosa 1991: 127–128). When early surveys showed that voters were attracted to the candidate's personality and character, the campaign sought to shift public opinion toward support for his program of reforms instead (Vargas Llosa 1991: 36). In negotiating an electoral coalition with leaders of AP and the PPC, Vargas Llosa was willing to cede slots on the legislative list, but "in the government plan I would not make concessions. The only reason I wanted to be president was *those* reforms" (Vargas Llosa 1993: 390).

Second-Round Reversal
Vargas Llosa interpreted his failure to obtain an outright victory in the first round of the election as a crushing defeat, prompting a drastic reversal of strategy in the campaign for the runoff. Setting aside many of his initial preferences, he approached the second-round campaign with a willingness to try whatever alternative approach was recommended by his advisors from the U.S.-based firm Sawyer/Miller (author's interviews, Cruchaga and Ghersi). The strategy ultimately adopted was a stark departure from Vargas Llosa's first-round campaign with respect to both policy focus and cleavage.

First and foremost, the second round of Vargas Llosa's campaign completely abandoned his earlier emphasis on proposals. While the first round had involved extensive policy-focused television advertising, the few commercials aired in the runoff campaign said nothing about Vargas Llosa's proposals (author's interview, Llosa).[14] Instead, they sought to criticize Fujimori for his ties to APRA and Alan García. Other than charging that Fujimori had no

---

[14] I analyzed fifty-nine distinct Vargas Llosa spots from the first round of the election, but was only able to locate two from the runoff. No advertising was broadcast prior to the final two weeks of the second-round campaign (*La República*, May 18, 1990), and little appears to have been broadcast thereafter.

government program, Vargas Llosa's second-round advertising did not discuss policy at all.

Instead of focusing on proposals, Vargas Llosa's second-round campaign embraced the type of activity he had always derided as the province of traditional politicians: inaugurating public works in poor neighborhoods. The candidate's daily schedule was reoriented to include numerous visits to shantytowns, primarily in the periphery of Lima, where he would make personal contact with poor people and promote the Liberty Movement's new Social Action Program (Programa de Acción Social, PAS). Rather than a proposal for a Vargas Llosa presidency, the PAS consisted of neighborhood improvement projects completed and inaugurated during the campaign itself, including sports fields, reservoirs, public markets, irrigation canals, roads, sewage systems, and electrification. Projects were funded out of the campaign budget as well as donations from Peruvian businessmen, foreign countries, and international organizations (Vargas Llosa 1993: 539, 544). Officially, the PAS was described as an effort to alleviate problems of nutrition, health, and employment for those who would be hardest hit by economic adjustment (Vargas Llosa 1993: 543–544).[15] In reality, this public works–style spending seemed to have little to do with softening the impact of market reform.

The logic behind the PAS is striking in its deviation from the policy focus and rejection of traditional politics that had inspired Vargas Llosa's entire political career. Several Liberty Movement founders who had played key roles in the first round, including Cruchaga and Ghersi, were opposed to the strategic shift. As Cruchaga (author's interview) put it, Vargas Llosa "had spoken very logically about a change in direction that meant adopting liberal policies, that meant less paternalism and more stimulating people to take the initiative. And how did he end up? Like Santa Claus!" Yet such objections from within the campaign team were largely ignored during the second round.

Vargas Llosa's runoff campaign also differed dramatically from his earlier strategy because it engaged in cleavage-priming attacks on his rival Fujimori. In the first round, Vargas Llosa had always maintained a positive stance toward his fellow candidates. In the second, however, he reluctantly accepted the advice of his Sawyer/Miller consultants that attacks on Fujimori would be necessary (Vargas Llosa 1993: 539–540). Officially, the strategy was to focus on Fujimori's lack of a government program, his ties to Alan García and the APRA government, and his possible tax evasion in prior real estate dealings. However, priming religious and ethnic cleavages also constituted a semiofficial campaign strategy, with decisions along these lines implemented behind the candidate's back (author's interview, Llosa).[16] On May 25, newspaper *La República*

---

[15] *El Comercio*, May 9, 1990, and May 25, 1990.

[16] Much of the religious polarization in the second round is also attributable to the Catholic Church independently campaigning against Fujimori because of his ties to evangelicals (Vargas Llosa 1993: 546–547).

reproduced a letter from the Liberty Movement committee in the department of Cusco, calling for an "underground campaign" with various cleavage-priming elements. These included "explaining the invasion of Japanese immigrants, with the eventual consequence of displacing the Peruvian people from a variety of activities." The letter also called for distributing an "anonymous flyer about the danger [posed by] the Catholic world and [celebrating] the advance of evangelist and other sects." The flyer would presumably be attributed to pro-Fujimori evangelicals to reinforce the stereotype that he and his supporters were anti-Catholic. Vargas Llosa (1993: 550) admits that after the election, "I was made aware that youth from Mobilization, of the Libertad Movement, had gone around towns and markets pretending to be evangelicals supporting Fujimori and speaking of the plague of the Catholics."

The multidimensional strategic shift between Vargas Llosa's first- and second-round campaign constitutes an inward-oriented reaction to the less-than-stellar results of the April 8 election. Rather than embracing an existing model of campaign strategy, Vargas Llosa's second-round campaign simply sought to do something radically different than what it had done in the past. The magnitude of change between the two rounds was facilitated by internal divisions within the campaign team. Advisors who favored the policy-centered approach lost influence after the first round. Meanwhile, the advice of Vargas Llosa's foreign consultants, which had often been ignored in the first part of the campaign, was now more carefully heeded. Less is known about the reasons for the cleavage-priming attacks in the second round, but it is possible that the newly empowered Sawyer/Miller consultants – much more comfortable with negative campaigning than the candidate himself – also encouraged this particular tactic.

Shifting to an attack strategy in the runoff might be partially attributable to the difference between a first-round campaign where Vargas Llosa was the frontrunner and a second round in which he became the underdog. Yet competitive incentives of this sort cannot explain Vargas Llosa's abandoning a heavy emphasis on policy, which was his primary motivation for entering politics in the first place. In the second round, Fujimori was trying to stake out a position as the "anti-shock" candidate, criticizing Vargas Llosa's proposed economic reform, yet major questions had arisen about his policy preparedness and whether he had any proposals of his own. A scheduled press conference in mid-April at which Fujimori was planning to present his new program was cancelled with the dubious excuse that he had gotten food poisoning the night before, and the official program was not actually released until more than a month later.[17] Explicitly contrasting Vargas Llosa's detailed plans with Fujimori's lack thereof might have been a more logical response to the competitive pressures of the second round.

---

[17] *La República*, April 18, 1990; *El Comercio*, May 20, 1990.

Lourdes Flores, 2001 and 2006: On-Again, Off-Again Personalism

Like Vargas Llosa's 1990 presidential campaign, the 2001 and 2006 campaigns of Lourdes Flores, candidate of the center-right National Unity (Unidad Nacional, UN) coalition, illustrate a series of inward-oriented reactions, with stark strategic shifts in reaction to perceived errors of the past. Flores was a longtime member of the PPC who had been elected to Congress in 1990 on FREDEMO's list and reelected twice on her own party's ticket; she also launched a short-lived presidential bid in 1995. In the lead-up to the 2001 election, Flores decided to run for president with the support of UN, a new alliance that brought together the PPC and two smaller center-right movements. The PPC remained the effective backbone of UN, and Flores retained her PPC membership; the reason to create the coalition was largely to circumvent the elite image that had become attached to the party's name (author's interview, Becerra).

Despite the initial move to distance Flores from an elite image, similar efforts were not effectively carried through the campaign itself. Flores's campaign activities tended toward large rallies rather than events that would bring her into closer contact with everyday people. According to one campaign strategist, "she didn't understand how important the market, the street, and the neighborhood were" (author's interview, Muro). Similarly, Flores's television advertising sought to reach out to voters programmatically, with a series of spots discussing job creation, decentralization, education, corruption, and agriculture. According to her head advertising strategist in 2001, Flores came across in these ads as distant and formal, with the image of an upper-class lawyer – a problem that the campaign failed to recognize at the time (author's interview, Echegaray).

Seeking Closeness to the People in 2006

After Flores's third-place finish behind Toledo and García in the first round of the 2001 election, her close advisors decided that she had been seen as too distant from the people and too much of a snob (*pituca*). To prepare for her 2006 presidential campaign, she would need a complete overhaul of her image so that she came across as someone who could empathize with the concerns of the poor.

Flores's political strategy in the lead-up to the 2006 election was a personalistic one – the strategy that has become commonplace among both Left and Right in Chile, but was being deployed in earnest for the first time in a Peruvian presidential campaign. In the five years between the two elections, Flores made regular weekend trips to towns around the country, meeting with small groups of people. PPC Vice President Raúl Castro (author's interview) described the strategy as "situating Lourdes among the people, popularizing her message, [and] changing what had been the traditional image of people from the PPC." Two years before the 2006 election, Flores started working with a Colombian campaign consultant, Gloria Isabel Ramírez, who reinforced the strategy of bringing Flores closer to the people. In particular, Ramírez came up with the idea for a series of "Lourdes listens to you" seminars, in which Flores served as a sounding block for the concerns of common people during her trips around the country.

In keeping with this closeness strategy, Flores's preferred activities during the first several months of the 2006 campaign were small-scale visits to markets and door-to-door canvassing of poor neighborhoods, rather than large, traditional rallies. As with Lavín's 1999 campaign in Chile, Flores's approach involved a "doubly direct" linkage strategy: she sought to establish direct personal connections with specific people and then multiply them through the television coverage of these events. In a February 2006 training session for UN's regional campaign managers, which I attended by invitation, communication strategist Abel Aguilar explained that any one of these events might only involve direct personal contact with 50–200 people, but that "what's important is the amplification of that activity that we achieve via the press and via the media. Because there, they are saying that Lourdes...gets close to the people, she understands their problems, she listens to people. This has been the common denominator of the last two years." In these visits, it was considered important to portray Flores as being close to the most generic possible representation of "the people," rather than any organized group that expressed a particularistic demand. While UN politicians were pushing for Flores to meet with fishermen, taxi drivers, people who wanted water for their shantytown, or organizers of neighborhood soup kitchens, consultant Ramírez rejected this advice, considering such meetings too political (author's interview, Confidential).

Flores's strategy also echoed the personalism of Chilean candidates by maintaining a distance from parties and traditional politicians. In this regard, she and her communication strategists sought to avoid what they interpreted as the major flaw of Vargas Llosa's 1990 campaign: letting the party's congressional candidates crowd out the message and the image of the presidential candidate.[18] UN thus prohibited its congressional candidates from running television advertisements and also limited their appearance at presidential campaign events.[19] The leaders of UN's constituent parties, principally the PPC, were also prevented from appearing as spokesmen who could rebut attacks on Flores by other candidates (author's interview, Aguilar). In early January, when Alan García began casting Flores as the candidate of the rich, the PPC Vice President stepped up to denounce this "dirty war" in the media, but was quickly sidelined by consultant Ramírez (author's interview, Castro).

---

[18] Because of Peru's open list proportional representation system, candidates for Congress compete not only with those from another party but also with those on their own slate. Each one is assigned a unique candidate number, which voters must remember and enter on the ballot in order to vote for him or her. This system provides an extra incentive to gain individual media exposure – particularly in Lima, where each list contained thirty-seven candidates in 2006.

[19] *La República*, February 22, 2006.

With respect to policy focus, Flores's personalistic strategy meant that demonstrating familiarity with people's problems and making vague statements about the future should take the place of specific proposals. At the February 2006 training seminar that I attended, Aguilar explained to the regional campaign managers that "closeness implies that she knows what the people need... This is a campaign without promises. Lourdes does not promise anything; Lourdes listens and commits herself to work tirelessly for those desires." Walks through poor neighborhoods and visits to public markets for one-on-one interaction were conducive to this strategy of listening to people's problems without making a lot of bold pronouncements.

The personalistic strategy that Flores employed during the majority of the 2006 campaign was a direct reaction to the perceived failures of 2001. In the previous campaign, according to Aguilar, "she played the role of the lawyer, efficient, very Lima-centric, very urban, a little distant from the people, a little bit of a know-it-all, and that did not connect with the people" (author's interview, Aguilar). Since presenting Flores as a formal, professional woman was not successful in the prior campaign, strategists sought to do the opposite in 2006 by creating the perception of empathy.

Strategic Shift During the First Round

Despite Flores's steadfast commitment to personalism during several years of preparatory campaigning and the first two months of the campaign proper, she abruptly abandoned this approach a month before the election in favor of traditional campaign events, specific policy commitments, and intermediation by fellow party leaders. Toward the end of February, as rivals were cutting into her lead, Flores began to listen to previously sidelined PPC leaders who were demanding a more "political" strategy (author's interview, Aguilar). On March 8, at a large rally in Lima, Flores unveiled her Commitment to the People, a list of ten specific proposals that included the promise of 650,000 new jobs per year during her five-year term.[20] The jobs promise began to feature prominently in her television advertising, which had previously been more oriented toward diagnosis of challenges and generic discussion of future policy. Traditional politicians also reappeared; Flores was now asking all of UN's congressional candidates in Lima to go house to house to communicate the new set of proposals.[21] Several days later, a PPC vice president announced that the campaign would be implementing a number of changes, including more rallies and the reintroduction of political spokesmen.[22]

Both the initial choice of a personalistic strategy for 2006 and the later abandonment of this approach resulted from inward-oriented assessments of what had gone wrong in the past – either in the 2001 election or in the first

[20] *El Comercio*, March 9, 2006.
[21] *El Comercio*, March 10, 2006.
[22] *El Comercio*, March 16, 2006.

several months of the 2006 campaign. Empathy-oriented personalism was a new strategy in Peruvian politics; Flores clearly was not copying this model from a previous candidate. Rather, her advisors emphasized that their initial approach to the 2006 campaign was a reaction to Flores's loss in 2001. And when Flores began to decline in the surveys in March 2006, the campaign shifted yet again in response to another perceived error. Flores's electoral strategies in these elections thus illustrate the pattern of strategic zigzags that can result when candidates' innovations in campaigning respond only to an interpretation of their own prior successes or failures.

APRA: TOWARD STRATEGIC FINE-TUNING

As with right-wing candidates in Peru, the evolution of APRA's approach to electoral campaigning has also been driven by an inward-oriented strategy of reacting negatively to perceived failures of the past. Between 1980 and 1990, APRA's strategy in presidential election campaigns resembled more of the zigzag pattern that has been characteristic of the Peruvian Right. Villanueva's 1980 campaign was sectarian, party-oriented, and focused on policy; García's 1985 campaign reversed each of these characteristics. Alva Castro's bid in 1990, while not discussed here in detail, was largely a counterreaction to García's 1985 campaign and a return to the sort of strategy Villanueva had employed in 1980 (author's interview, Salcedo). García's return from exile to compete in the 2001 and 2006 presidential elections, however, allowed a distinct pattern to emerge. Rather than overreacting to perceived errors of the past, García was able to fine-tune his earlier strategy. His ability to do so was facilitated by the renewed unity and discipline of his party in the 2000s, as well as García's own prior electoral experience and the continuity of many of his advisors throughout his political career.

Armando Villanueva, 1980: A Sectarian Mass Party Campaign

Following the death of its founder Víctor Raúl Haya de la Torre in August 1979, APRA was forced to confront a struggle for leadership succession while also preparing for the May 1980 elections. The party leader who emerged as presidential candidate, Armando Villanueva, favored a confrontational and sectarian approach, seeking to mobilize APRA's core supporters by priming the long-standing APRA/anti-APRA cleavage. APRA's campaign discourse "was sharp and moralistic: one is either with God or the Devil" (Oviedo 1981: 92). Television advertising appealed to "APRA or anarchy"; Villanueva warned that efforts to overthrow his future government would lead to civil war and that, like former Chilean president Salvador Allende, he would fight against a military coup to the death (Oviedo 1981: 108).

Villanueva's campaign was also strikingly focused on the party as a whole, rather than on himself as an individual. Out of twenty-four campaign-related television broadcasts aired by the party between January and May 1980, Villanueva appeared in only eleven, typically in conjunction with other APRA leaders (Oviedo 1981: 114–115). In comparison, Villanueva's major rival on the right, Fernando Belaúnde, appeared in fourteen of the nineteen programs his party broadcast during the same period, and he was typically featured alone (Oviedo 1981: 90–91). Villanueva's campaign jingle, "APRA is the Road" (*El APRA es el Camino*), was also party rather than candidate centric, and the accompanying television spot featured a chorus of APRA youth rather than images of the candidate himself (author's interview, Salcedo). Summing up the communication strategy of the campaign, an APRA advertising strategist noted that "the party not only predominated; its communication also focused on its own history and its own ideas" (author's interview, Otero).

Finally, Villanueva's campaign had a relatively high level of policy focus. In Oviedo's assessment (1981: 103), "a good dose of promises filled [APRA's] arguments about what should be." Concrete proposals included eliminating university entrance exams and ensuring the admission of all high school graduates, free primary and secondary education, implementing price controls and subsidies for food items, creating a Social Security Institute and Social Security Bank, guaranteeing social security at birth, and improving access to drinking water throughout Lima. Villanueva's message to Peruvians, particularly the lower classes, was that an APRA government would improve their lives in numerous tangible ways.

Villanueva's traditional mass party campaign succeeded in mobilizing the historical APRA vote, but the candidate was unable to mount a serious challenge to his major opponent, former president Fernando Belaúnde. Although APRA had gained the largest share of votes (41.7 percent of those validly cast) in the 1978 constituent assembly election, Villanueva lost the 1980 election to Belaúnde by a margin of 58.1–35.2 percent. This disappointing result prepared the stage for a reassessment of APRA's strategy and a reorientation of the party by Alan García in the early 1980s.

Alan García, 1985: An Image-Centric, Catch-All Campaign

The political project that brought Alan García to power in 1985 was entirely a reaction to the perceived errors of Villanueva's 1980 campaign. In 1980, García had embraced Villanueva's confrontational, sectarian stance, arguing on television that "who is not with APRA is anti-APRA" and defending his participation in APRA's violent "shock force" (Oviedo 1981: 99, 111). By the time of his 1985 campaign for the presidency, however, García's approach was the polar opposite of Villanueva's: inclusive, nonpartisan, vague on policy, and focused on his own personal image. Commenting on this shift, his longtime advisor Hugo Otero (author's interview) said that "he learned from that defeat [in 1980] ... I think that he understood that APRA should leave behind the era of the catacombs, where, like the entombed Christians, they thought of themselves as God's chosen people." Otero, who also participated in Villanueva's campaign and was responsible for much of its sectarian content, highlighted a similar reaction on his own part: "I lived through all of that, and I think that as a young person, I was very impacted by the mistake."

The most characteristic feature of García's 1985 campaign was his embrace of a new image of openness and a nondivisive message. The campaign adopted inclusive slogans such as "APRA extends its hand to you" and "my commitment is to all Peruvians." Rather than casting APRA as the savior of the nation, García appealed to patriotism and national pride. As his campaign jingle, he chose the popular waltz "My Peru," whose opening line was "I am proud to be Peruvian, and I am happy." The campaign's main television commercial ended with García announcing that "I am the candidate of APRA, but my commitment is to Peru and to all Peruvians." APRA's traditional party hymns, including the *marsellesa* with its images of struggle against imperialism, were carefully kept out of the presidential campaign. According to one APRA advertising strategist, "what changed is that APRA went from a situation of pride in its traditions and its symbols to a de-partisanization of the campaign" (author's interview, Salcedo).

García also avoided emphasizing class cleavages. While reaffirming his commitment to labor issues, he would often characterize organized labor as elitist. His discourse shunned class distinctions and generally referred to Peruvians as individuals or as "the people" rather than as members of specific social classes (Sanborn 1991: 293, 340).

In addition, García's campaign departed from Villanueva's by virtue of its "studied ambiguity on policy details" (Sanborn 1991: 336). Although APRA's national planning commission announced during the campaign that it was working on a government program, the actual document was not released until after the election.[23] Nor did proposals feature prominently in television advertising. In the sample of García's 1985 spots examined for this study, there was no mention of proposals, either general or specific. Policy discussion only took up 25.6 percent of the estimated total broadcast time (Table 4.2). Most of this policy content (16.8 percentage points) involved a diagnosis of current problems, such as the poor state of national industry; a somewhat smaller proportion (6 percentage points) criticized the government for its mismanagement of the economy. The closest García got to proposals in these commercials was saying "I raise my voice to defend the jobs of Peruvians."

In his speeches at rallies, García did engage in somewhat greater discussion of specific proposals, such as the expansion of the Agrarian Bank to increase credit for peasant farmers. Much of the policy discussion at rallies, however, involved criticism of problems under the current Belaúnde government rather than describing what García would do as president. According to newspaper coverage of the campaign, intangible ideas, such as promising a "nationalist,

[23] *Caretas*, April 17, 1985.

TABLE 4.2. *Alan García's Television Advertising, 1985*

Policy focused	25.6
Specific proposals	0.0
General proposals	0.0
Achievements	2.8
Criticism	6.0
Diagnosis	16.8
Not policy focused (jingles, image, or other)	74.4
Cleavage priming	0.0
No cleavage priming	100.0

Note: Entries are percentages of estimated total advertising time.

democratic, and popular government," were predominant in García's speeches. Summarizing the candidate's communication strategy, Fernando Tuesta Soldevilla (1985) argued that "APRA ... is appealing to theatricality before ideology, the image before the word, the slogan before the program."

In terms of linkage, García's 1985 campaign represented somewhat greater continuity, in that the party continued to serve an important intermediary function. Local party committees played a crucial role in García's 350 campaign rallies – publicizing each event, mobilizing participants, securing a stage and sound system, and accomplishing other logistical tasks (author's interview, Cuestas). In between the candidate's visits, local committees continued to carry out mini-rallies, distribute propaganda, and teach people how to vote (Sanborn 1991: 353). Members of the various APRA-affiliated sectoral groups, such as unions and student organizations, campaigned within their own sector and also contributed to the general campaign in their district (author's interview, Cuestas).

Yet García's campaign also sought to reach out to nonparty members through a new, campaign-specific linkage structure known as Independents with Alan. Independents with Alan was organized at a more micro-level than the party, with designated representatives for particular neighborhood blocks in Lima. This structure facilitated recruitment into the network; block representatives were likely to know their neighbors' political leanings and could readily identify potential supporters, and new recruits did not have to leave their neighborhood to sign up as campaign volunteers. Person-to-person campaigning by block representatives was also quite effective, since political independents tended to be more receptive to casual conversations with a known and trusted neighbor or work associate than to proselytizing by a party member (author's interview, LaNatta).

In sum, García's inward-oriented reaction to the failed effort of 1980 produced a campaign strategy that was quite different from Villanueva's – unity oriented, generic in terms of policy, and drawing on multiple forms of linkage. García's 1985 strategy was not an imitation of any particular prior example; rather, it was a negative reaction to a previous APRA campaign in which he and his advisors had participated. In this sense, it represents the same sort of inward-oriented reaction as the strategic shifts by Vargas Llosa in 1990 and Flores in 2006.

Alan García, 2001 and 2006: Fine-Tuning the APRA Campaign Strategy

After the fall of Fujimori, Alan García's repeat presidential bids in 2001 and 2006 involved a second reorientation, this time with respect to his 1985 strategy. While still conveying a message of unity and drawing on multiple forms of linkage, these campaigns differed radically from the first in terms of policy focus. In place of the policy-vague approach of 1985, García's 2001 and 2006 campaigns emphasized a series of specific proposals, while also seeking to claim credit for various achievements during his prior government. The nature of this shift – a fine-tuning process, involving a change in a single dimension of campaign strategy – was not inevitable. García might well have adopted a neopopulist strategy in 2001 like his opponent Toledo, priming cleavages and not bothering with intermediate linkage via the APRA party structure. However, the unity and discipline of his party and campaign team, and the absence of competing factions of advisors trying to "sell" the candidate on alternative approaches, facilitated a more modest revision of his earlier strategy.

Following a disastrous term as president in the 1980s, exile throughout most of the 1990s, and charges of corruption during his former presidency, García's second-place finish in 2001 and victory in 2006 constitute a stunning political comeback. García returned to Peru in January 2001 just in time to launch a campaign for the presidency, after Peru's Supreme Court ruled that the statute of limitations on his corruption charges had run out.[24] While his return generated great excitement among the APRA faithful, he initially stood at only 12 percent in the polls, and 65 percent of voters said that they would never support him. Yet García rose steadily in vote intention during the ensuing two-and-a-half months of first-round campaigning, narrowly beating Lourdes Flores to qualify for the runoff with Alejandro Toledo (Figure 4.4). In the first round of the 2006 election, García delivered a similarly impressive come-from-behind performance, again narrowly edging out Lourdes Flores to qualify for the runoff (Figure 4.5). In that campaign, he defeated Ollanta Humala by a margin of 53–47 percent and was elected to a second term as president.

García's emphasis on policy in his 2001 and 2006 campaigns makes sense only as an inward-oriented reaction, not as contagion across the ideological spectrum. Previous policy-oriented presidential campaigns in Peru, such as that of Vargas Llosa in 1990, had always fared poorly and should not have prompted emulation. However, García's close advisors in 2001 and 2006 – particularly longtime image advisor Hugo Otero – had worked closely with him

---

[24] *La República*, January 19, 2001.

during the 1985 campaign and ensuing presidency and were intimately familiar with the shortcomings of his earlier strategy. If one were to ask "what went
wrong" in García's initial foray into politics, a key part of the answer would be
that his image-centric 1985 campaign in no way prepared public opinion for
such radical moves as attempting to nationalize the banking system. Repeating
the same electoral strategy in 2001 or 2006 would do little to assuage concerns
about how he would govern during a second term.

In both the 2001 and 2006 elections, García's campaign presented a series
of tangible, center-left proposals that sought to scale back Fujimori's more radical market reforms and reaffirm some of the policy achievements of the prior
APRA government. Many of these commitments concerned labor rights, such
as requiring employers to respect the eight-hour workday and pay workers for
overtime, or eliminating temporary service contracts that restricted employees'
benefits. Others included expanding the length of the school day, reducing the
rates charged by public utilities, and offering agricultural development loans
though a revamped Agrarian Bank. In 2006, García unveiled the new Sierra
Exportadora initiative, a major proposal to stimulate export agriculture in the
Peruvian highlands, which was the subject of a short policy book published
during the campaign (García 2005). In the second round, García introduced a
"Water for Everyone" proposal, pledging to deliver drinking water to 500,000
residents of Lima shantytowns during his first six months in office.[25] His proposals also included specific initiatives for young voters, such as reserving government jobs for the top ten graduates of each Peruvian public university, or
requiring that 30 percent of each party's candidates for city council be younger
than 29.[26]

García's television advertising in 2001 and 2006 shows evidence of his campaign's strong emphasis on policy. While only an estimated 25.6 percent of his
1985 television advertising had been devoted to policy, this figure ranged from
43.4 percent to 69.5 percent across the first and second rounds of the 2001 and
2006 campaigns (Table 4.3). In the commercials analyzed from 1985, García
did not discuss his policy intentions at all; in 2001 and 2006, specific proposals occupied large shares of his total advertising time. Compared to other
campaigns in Peru, García's first-round campaigns in each election were highly
policy focused; in the second round of each, he intensified the strategy.

In contrast to 1985, the focus on García's personal image in 2001 and 2006
never came at the expense of policy focus. There was substantial emphasis on
show and charisma in these two campaigns; García garnered significant media
attention for singing and dancing at his rallies and in certain television spots.
But press coverage of these campaigns also frequently remarked on the policy-
centric nature of his appeals. *Caretas* noted that even before his return from
exile in 2001, García had begun making regular media appearances to advance

[25] *El Comercio*, June 4, 2006.
[26] *El Comercio*, April 22, 2006.

TABLE 4.3. *Alan García's Television Advertising, 2001 and 2006*

	2001 Round 1	2001 Round 2	2006 Round 1	2006 Round 2
Policy focused	43.4	69.5	46.6	51.4
Specific proposals	18.6	29.1	24.8	47.0
General proposals	6.5	1.6	3.9	0.6
Achievements	0.8	24.6	0.3	0.0
Criticism	4.4	0.0	3.2	0.6
Diagnosis	13.1	14.2	14.4	3.2
Not policy focused (jingles, image, or other)	56.6	30.5	53.4	48.6
Cleavage priming	0.0	0.0	0.5	0.0
No cleavage priming	100.0	100.0	99.5	100.0

Note: Entries are percentages of estimated (2001) or actual (2006) total advertising time.

specific proposals for the upcoming campaign, from revitalizing the Agrarian Bank to reducing fees for telephone service.[27] In 2006, *El Comercio* reported that during a meeting with APRA youth in Arequipa, García "explained to them, as if he were a professor in front of his students, the APRA proposal and his position in terms of foreign capital."[28] Summarizing candidates' first-round strategies, the same newspaper noted that "the APRA candidate concentrated his time on offering 45- to 60-minute-long rallies to expound upon his government plan."[29]

In other respects, García's 2001 and 2006 campaigns were more similar to that of 1985. As in his first contest, García continued to convey a message of inclusiveness, national unity, and universal values such as patriotism. In the campaign for the runoff in 2001, García adopted the slogan "The Consensus-Building President" (*Presidente de la Concertación*). In his second-round closing rally that year, he promised to "carry the flag of national unity to the government, because in this difficult and dramatic hour, we need all of the political forces, organizations, institutions, and civil society to come together."[30]

In 2006, García reiterated the theme of national unity, though in a manner that involved greater confrontation with his primary opponent Ollanta Humala. After Venezuelan president Hugo Chávez publicly criticized García, voiced support for Humala, and threatened to cut off diplomatic relations in the event of a García victory, García sought to rally nationalistic sentiment in favor of his candidacy. One of García's most frequently broadcast second-round spots began with a clip of Chávez expressing support for Humala and

[27] *Caretas*, January 18, 2001.
[28] *El Comercio*, March 22, 2001.
[29] *El Comercio*, April 9, 2001.
[30] *El Comercio*, June 1, 2001.

then announced that the electoral choice boiled down to "Chávez or Peru." While more confrontational than the tone he had adopted in 2001, García's anti-Chávez message in 2006 was similar in its call for national unity. Rather than emphasizing cleavages within the country, García sought to unite the people against an external villain.

In terms of linkage, García's 2001 and 2006 campaigns also marked strategic continuity. As in 1985, he relied on both party intermediation and alternative, campaign-specific linkage structures in an effort to reach out to supporters. His performance in 2001 and 2006 was not only an impressive personal comeback but also signaled a resurgence of the APRA party structure that had lain dormant for much of the 1990s. While APRA candidates for president and Congress had fared poorly in the 1995 and 2000 elections – possibly because of strategic voting for the candidates most likely to defeat Fujimori and his legislative lists – partisan enthusiasm was notably reinvigorated by García's return to Peru in January 2001. Reporting on his first Lima rally during the 2001 campaign, newsweekly *Caretas* (February 1, 2001) remarked that "with the arrival of Alan García, APRA has once again become a mass phenomenon after being orphaned for almost ten years. It has once again shown organization and discipline, and one cannot deny that a large part of the Lima contingent was made up of youth."

In the years following García's return, APRA was able to regain much of its old organizational strength (author's interview, Nava). During the 2006 campaign, party officials estimated that APRA had between 500,000 and 600,000 registered members, the same number as in the mid-1980s (Sanborn 1991: 342; author's interviews, Garrido Lecca and Pinedo). It was also actively recruiting and training new youth members around the country via a training camp held regularly at the national headquarters in Lima (author's interview, Pinedo).

In addition to reinvigorating the party itself, García's 2001 and 2006 campaigns made use of alternative linkage structures similar to those employed in 1985. In 2001, Independents with Alan was reestablished under the name Everyone for Peru, with some of the same individuals taking on similar leadership roles (author's interview, LaNatta). In addition, a new García-centered youth group, Youth with Alan, was created in 2001 to incorporate young voters who wanted to get involved in the campaign without joining APRA and participating in the party's youth organization. Youth with Alan played a particularly important linkage role during the 2006 campaign with such activities as canvassing, wall painting, and staffing campaign tents at Lima beaches on summer weekends to reach out to other youth (author's interview, Pinedo).[31]

In order to ensure strong attendance at his campaign events in 2006, García drew upon these multiple forms of linkage. To mobilize attendance at a rally in Lima the week before the first-round vote, APRA relied on campaign-specific

---

[31] *Caretas*, February 23, 2006.

volunteers to distribute flyers to the general population, as well as party militants to bring in organized groups such as sanitation workers.[32] For the organization of his second-round closing rally, García relied upon 300 members of Youth with Alan, 200 general volunteers, and 1,000 district-level party leaders.[33]

García's 2006 campaign similarly combined intermediated and direct linkage strategies in its efforts to reach social groups with specific sectoral interests. The campaign approached some poorly organized groups, such as taxi drivers, largely as individuals. Campaign volunteers would visit drivers while they were waiting at taxi cues, talk to them about García's proposals for pensions and auto insurance, and offer an automobile air freshener in the shape of an APRA star (author's interview, Benza Pflucker). Yet García's campaign also benefited from APRA's longtime affiliation with the Confederation of Peruvian Workers (Confederación de Trabajadores Peruanos, CTP), which still maintains formal representation within the party. The CTP participated in the 2006 campaign, with activities such as a demonstration outside the Venezuelan ambassador's residence to protest Hugo Chávez's public statements against García.

In contrast to the dramatic, multidimensional shifts that have characterized the trajectory of right-wing electoral strategies in Peru, García's most recent campaigns did not involve a wholesale reversal of his earlier approach. Neither did he shift course between 2001 and 2006, or between the first and second rounds of either campaign. Rather, in the second round of each election, he intensified a strategy that, in comparison to 1985, was already highly focused on policy. While García's strategic fine-tuning still constitutes an inward-oriented reaction to his initial approach to winning the presidency, it was more disciplined and successful than the inward-oriented reactions of other candidates.

A major reason for García's more moderate adjustment to his earlier strategy concerns the absence of competing factions of advisors trying to "sell" the candidate on alternative approaches. The discipline of APRA's party leadership and the continuity of García's inner circle throughout his political career have ensured that there are few "pretenders to the power behind the throne," who might stand a chance of gaining influence if they could convince the candidate to shift course. In a less disciplined campaign or party, García's loss to Toledo in the second round of the 2001 election, or his decline in the polls during January–February of 2006, might have been seized upon by a dissident advisor calling for a different strategy. Other plausible alternatives did exist. Given the negative image of parties in general, and the ignominious history of reserving state jobs for APRA partisans during García's prior administration, he might well have chosen to circumvent the party machinery

---

[32] *La República*, April 2, 2006.
[33] *La República*, May 30, 2006.

altogether in 2001, relying strictly on direct linkages and adopting an anti-party stance. García might also have sought to prime class cleavages in that election, contesting Toledo's efforts to win lower-class votes through ethnic appeals. But in García's campaign teams, and in APRA more broadly, the existence of longtime collaborators and the loyalty with which they are rewarded prevented strategists hawking new ideas from replacing one another in rapid succession.

TESTING THE ARGUMENT: INWARD-ORIENTED REACTIONS
IN 2011

Peru's 2011 election is a further example of major candidates choosing strategies that departed radically from their own or their party's prior approach, while also differing from those of their competitors. The 2011 campaign in Peru started with a wide field of contenders, but the top two finishers in the first round were from movements with an anti-establishment history – Ollanta Humala, the losing candidate from 2006, and Keiko Fujimori, an incumbent congresswoman and daughter of ex-president Alberto Fujimori. Either candidate had the potential to campaign as a neopopulist and might have done so if their strategic dictum had simply been to occupy available political space. Yet both candidates were also able to draw upon prior experience during the 2011 campaign. Rather than embracing neopopulism, each made major changes to the prior *fujimorista* or *humalista* campaign strategy, a pattern consistent with inward-oriented reactions.

Ollanta Humala's strategy for 2011 was nearly the opposite of what it had been in 2006. In his first bid for the presidency, Humala had been vague in terms of his policy intentions, especially in the first round. The approach in 2006, according to one strategist, was "to develop a totally emotional campaign" rather than to make rational arguments or focus on proposals (author's interview, Méndez). In the second round, policy focus increased substantially, but only because Humala concentrated on the diagnosis of existing problems and criticism of García's prior record. In his television advertising, emphasis on proposals remained low in both rounds, as summarized in Table 4.4. The same was true of rallies and comments to the press, where he typically referred to a number of intangible objectives, such as "refounding the Republic" and establishing a "new division of power."

In 2011, Humala's campaign was, first and foremost, about proposals. In place of the vague policy discussion of 2006, Humala focused on the details of programs such as Pensión 65 (state-supported pensions for the elderly), Cuna Más (free childcare for working mothers), SAMU (mobile emergency medical service), and Beca 18 (scholarships for youth), along with his plans to raise the minimum wage to 750 soles and extend the conditional cash transfer program Juntos. Humala consistently emphasized policy in all facets of the campaign. In comments to the press, when asked what was different about his second run for

TABLE 4.4. *Ollanta Humala's Television Advertising, 2006 and 2011*

	2006 Round 1	2006 Round 2	2011 Round 1	2011 Round 2
Policy focused	13.7	53.3	62.6	44.7
Specific proposals	0.0	2.9	12.8	7.5
General proposals	5.9	3.9	14.4	4.2
Achievements	0.0	0.0	0.0	0.8
Criticism	5.9	15.9	0.0	0.0
Diagnosis	2.0	30.6	35.4	32.2
Not policy focused (jingles, image, or other)	86.3	46.7	37.4	55.3
Cleavage priming	0.3	0	0	0
No cleavage priming	99.7	100.0	100.0	100.0

Note: Entries are percentages of total advertising time.

the presidency, Humala and his advisors emphasized the detailed proposals.[34] In a debate just before the first-round vote, he used nearly all of his time – even that allocated for asking questions of other candidates – to describe his specific plans.[35] In Humala's television advertising, proposals accounted for 27 percent of his total advertising time in the first round, and 12 percent in the second round – both much higher than in 2006.[36]

Humala also abandoned the cleavage priming of 2006, explicitly adopting a nonconfrontational approach in 2011. This was true not only of his television advertising – already almost entirely positive in the last campaign – but also of his speeches at rallies and comments to the press, where he had previously conveyed his divisive campaign appeals. Facing a combative interviewer from *El Comercio* (April 18, 2011), an establishment newspaper that was highly critical of Humala, he stuck to the nonconfrontational message: "In this campaign, I have not engaged in attacks or aggression because I don't want to polarize, I don't want us to return to 2006, when society was polarized to the point of aggression and, in the end, it came down to a choice between the lesser of two evils." Within the campaign team, Humala's conciliatory stance was somewhat controversial; numerous advisors favored a return to cleavage-priming approach of 2006, especially at points when the candidate seemed to stagnate in the surveys (León 2011). Yet Humala stuck with his unity-oriented message throughout the 2011 campaign.

Part of the reason for Humala's policy emphasis and nonconfrontational stance is the involvement of political consultants from Brazil's PT who had

[34] *El Comercio*, February 14, 2011; *La República*, March 8, 2011, and March 25, 2011.
[35] *La República*, April 4, 2011.
[36] Humala broadcast more than twice as much advertising in the second round, so the amount devoted to proposals, though lower in a relative sense, was nearly identical in absolute terms.

previously worked on Lula's presidential campaigns. Luis Favre and Valdemir Garreta led a team of Brazilian consultants that started working with Humala prior to his launching the campaign in mid-December 2010. In terms of policy, they recommended that Humala's campaign convey "clear proposals with brand names" (León 2011: 50). The policy details of programs such as Pensión 65 and Cuna Más were already in Humala's government plan, but their names, the way they were packaged, and the concrete manner in which they were presented owed much to the Brazilian consultants. Favre, Garreta, and their team also consistently advocated a nonconfrontational approach; they sought to "de-Humala-ize" the candidate, softening his radical image from 2006.

Given the central role of campaign professionals, one might be tempted to attribute Humala's strategic about-face to his blindly following the advice of foreign experts rather than to an explicit inward-oriented reaction. Yet hiring consultants from Brazil's PT was almost certainly not done with a simple desire to professionalize the campaign, but rather to do for Humala what political consultants had helped do for Lula: lower resistance to his candidacy among middle-class voters by emphasizing the details of his proposals and conveying a nonconfrontational message. In other words, the decision to hire the Brazilians in the first place and to heed their advice was likely due to an inward-oriented reaction to Humala's prior campaign.

The campaign of Humala's second-round opponent, Keiko Fujimori, also involved substantial strategic shifts vis-à-vis prior *fujimorista* campaigns. Fujimori engaged in none of the cleavage-priming attacks on the political class that had been her father's pedigree. Her campaign was aggressively critical of her major opponent Humala, but it also called for social unity, or "building bridges among Peruvians" as she put it in one of her first television advertisements. Keiko Fujimori's campaign was also heavily focused on policy. This was a notable change from Alberto Fujimori's image-centric campaigns of the 1990s, and also from 2006, when *fujimorista* congresswoman Martha Chávez ran for president largely as a stand-in for Alberto Fujimori (who was, at the time, in Chile awaiting extradition to Peru). Chávez's television advertisements were replete with slogans such as "Martha is the *chino* and the *chino* is Martha," but they said little about her policy intentions. In contrast, Keiko Fujimori's television advertising was very policy centric, especially in the second round, and it primarily centered on her proposals (Table 4.5).

Most significantly, Keiko Fujimori's campaign sought to do something that, in Alberto Fujimori's day, had been politically anathema: draw on intermediated linkages through an organized party. Part of Fujimori's campaign strategy for 2011 was to build up partisan structures within the *fujimorista* movement (Urrutía 2011a: 4). Though *fujimorismo* began as an explicitly disorganized current within society, it now has youth groups, mothers' clubs, and a party leaders' school that holds regular meetings. The movement's formal structure also maintains ties to autonomous base-level organizations, such as a network of soup kitchens in poor neighborhoods (Urrutía 2011b; Levitsky 2013).

TABLE 4.5. *Keiko Fujimori's Television Advertising, 2011*

	Round 1	Round 2
Policy focused	58.1	78.5
Specific proposals	13.3	55.9
General proposals	37.7	5.2
Achievements	2.8	0.0
Criticism	1.0	0.0
Diagnosis	3.3	17.4
Not policy focused (jingles, image, or other)	41.9	21.5
Cleavage priming	0	0
No cleavage priming	100.0	100.0

Note: Entries are percentage of total advertising time.

Fujimorismo's grassroots capacity allowed it to gather 1 million signatures, more than legally required, to register Keiko Fujimori's new party label in 2010 – a notable contrast to Peru 2000's need to resort to signature forgery a decade before. These intermediated linkages were also used to great effect during the campaign proper, with volunteers knocking on doors and handing out calendars with the candidate's image (Urrutía 2011a).

In 2011, therefore, both major candidates in Peru continued the pattern of strategic zigzags, running campaigns that differed significantly from their own prior efforts or those of their copartisans. Humala and Fujimori's campaigns also differed from one another – while both emphasized policy and avoided priming cleavages, Fujimori sought to build intermediated linkages, while Humala continued to rely on a personal electoral vehicle. Quite significantly, neither Humala nor Fujimori campaigned as neopopulists, even though Alberto Fujimori had occupied this space in the 1990s and Humala had done so in 2006.

CONCLUSION

The evolution of presidential election campaign strategies in Peru has followed a different course than in Chile and Brazil, with major candidates failing over the long term to converge upon a single national model of electioneering. Rather, the evolution of campaign strategies has followed a number of distinct paths. As summarized in Figure 4.6, the majority of these outcomes are consistent with the theory of success contagion as laid out in Chapter 1. Only the neopopulist campaigns of the 2000s – Toledo in 2001 and Humala in 2006 – clearly contradict the theory, since they took place after the demise of Fujimori's neopopulist government.

Following Fujimori's victory in the 1990 election, he was able to govern successfully for ten years, with approval ratings substantially higher than the norm for Peruvian presidents. Consistent with the theory of success contagion,

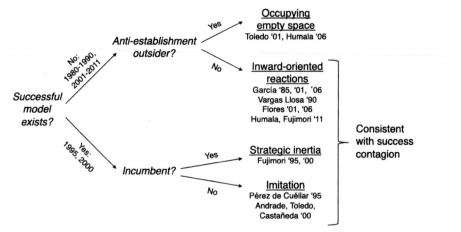

FIGURE 4.6. Campaign Strategies in Peru.

Fujimori's initial electoral victory and positively evaluated terms in office generated strategic inertia; his strategies in the reelection bids of 1995 and 2000 were similar to that of his 1990 campaign. Fujimori's success also generated a form of imitation among opposition candidates across the political spectrum, who copied the president's organizational strategy by distancing themselves from existing forms of intermediation and crafting new personal electoral vehicles for their campaigns. Strategic convergence in the 1990s was limited to the linkage dimension of campaign strategy, in part because of the authoritarian nature of Fujimori's regime. Nonetheless, the strategies of Peruvian candidates did become more similar to one another during this decade.

Peru's limited process of success contagion during the 1990s came to an end after Fujimori's downfall, so the recurrence of neopopulist strategies in 2001 and 2006 has to be explained by a distinct mechanism. Many scholars have emphasized the collapse of Peru's traditional parties in the early 1990s and the large space that they left available for capture by improvised outsider candidates. Yet "available space" has not been wide open to outsiders since Fujimori's demise; multiple politicians with substantial prior experience in national-level electoral politics have contested every election since 2001. Empty space has remained only on the anti-establishment side of the political spectrum, a niche originally occupied by the partisan Left in the 1980s. Available space has thus allowed for a single major neopopulist candidate in certain elections – Toledo in 2001 and Humala in 2006 – who relied upon direct linkages and primed cleavages in an effort to unify "the people" in a struggle against a common enemy. Their efforts were facilitated by the availability of a large mass of floating voters, as well as "floating militants" – citizens who are willing to provide organizational support for the anti-status quo candidate of the day.

Despite the attention paid to imitating Fujimori in the 1990s and occupying available space in the 2000s, the most prominent trend in Peruvian campaign strategies has involved inward-oriented reactions. Since Peru's 1980 transition to democracy, every president has had dismal approval ratings at the start of the campaign to replace him – including Fujimori, whose support plummeted prior to his resigning the presidency in November 2000. In the absence of a clear example of both successful electioneering and successful governance, presidential candidates from Alan García to Lourdes Flores to Ollanta Humala have chosen campaign strategies through an inward-oriented process of reacting to their own prior errors.

Inward-oriented reactions can take on two distinct patterns, depending on the level of factionalism within candidates' campaign teams. On the right, with numerous groups of advisors struggling for influence within the campaign, there has always been an internal dissident maneuvering to "sell" the candidate on a radically different strategy whenever the current one begins to falter. Hence, candidates have tended to overreact to prior errors, generating a pattern of strategic zigzags over time. For APRA, the multiple candidacies of Alan García and the continuity of his major advisors throughout his political career prevented the same sort of recurrent zigzag pattern. Rather, García was able to fine-tune his electoral strategy over time, making more minor alterations to his 1985 approach for the campaigns of 2001 and 2006.

On the whole, Peru is an important negative case for the theory of success contagion. Without a model of campaign strategy that is legitimated by a successful governing experience, major candidates are unlikely to converge on a common approach to electioneering. Rather, the coexistence of neopopulist outsiders occupying available space and inward-oriented reactions among candidates with prior experience has meant that campaign strategies were no more similar to one another in the 2000s than they were in 1980.

5

Success Contagion and Presidential Campaigns in Comparative Perspective

The types of appeals candidates present to voters and the means by which they mobilize support carry great import for the quality of new democracies around the world. Electoral strategies matter for whether citizens exercise real influence over the political agenda, versus responding in a plebiscitarian fashion to options presented by politicians. Campaign styles affect whether people participate enthusiastically in democratic politics or whether levels of apathy and abstention remain high. The nature of campaigns helps determine whether elected officials can be held accountable for their promises, versus claiming a right to govern at will based on a vague mandate of "change." Approaches to campaigning also have implications for the ability of the victorious candidate to govern effectively once in office.

Despite the substantive importance of electoral campaigns in new democracies, political scientists have not offered a satisfactory explanation for how and why campaign strategies evolve over time. Existing arguments about the changing nature of electoral campaigns tend to emphasize cross-national convergence in candidates' strategies and techniques. Claims of Americanization posit convergence on a model of campaigning developed in the United States, through either the diffusion of an American example or the international activities of U.S.-based political consultants. Arguments about the modernization of electioneering maintain that the nature of campaigning passes through the same set of stages in democracies around the world, and that countries should end up with similar electoral campaigns once they have acquired sufficient democratic experience. These theoretical perspectives mirror the focus on cross-national convergence inherent in earlier arguments such as Duverger's (1959) "contagion from the left" and Epstein's (1967) "contagion from the right."

Yet the cases of Chile, Brazil, and Peru illustrate that cross-national convergence has been limited to particular technologies of campaigning or

competitive tactics and has not affected campaign strategies at the more fundamental level of linkages, cleavage priming, and policy focus. The use of internal
polls and focus groups for message definition has now become commonplace
in these three countries, and professionals are routinely hired to conduct campaign research using these techniques, as well as to produce television advertising. However, professionalization or the use of modern technologies has not
meant that candidates in multiple countries always adopt the same strategies.
In Brazil, candidates routinely campaign with a high policy focus, whereas in
Chile, they typically place much less emphasis on policy details. Chilean and
Brazilian campaigns may be similar in terms of linkage and cleavage priming,
but on these dimensions, Peru presents a contrasting example. The presidential
campaigns of the American Popular Revolutionary Alliance (Alianza Popular
Revolucionaria Americana, APRA) have long drawn upon intermediated linkages via the party machinery and allied organizations, while Keiko Fujimori's
campaign also did so in 2011. Meanwhile, a series of neopopulist outsiders
have sought support by emphasizing fundamental divisions in society.

In order to explain the very different patterns of presidential campaigning
that have developed in Chile, Brazil, and Peru since their transitions to democracy, this study has developed a theory of *success contagion*, which focuses on
candidates' adherence to models of campaign strategy that have been legitimated by successful episodes of democratic governance. In this concluding
chapter, I move beyond the specific countries in which the theory was developed, testing its applicability to other third-wave democracies. The first section
reviews the theory of success contagion, using examples from Chile, Brazil,
and Peru to illustrate the mechanisms of imitation, professional norms, strategic inertia, failure avoidance, and inward-oriented learning. It then examines a
series of alternative explanations for the observed cross-national variation. In
the second section, I draw upon secondary literature to examine the evolution
of campaign strategies in ten additional new democracies: Argentina, Benin,
Ecuador, Ghana, Honduras, Mali, Nicaragua, the Philippines, South Korea, and
Uruguay. In seven of these countries, the evolution of campaign strategies since
democratization is consistent with the predictions of success contagion, and an
eighth country, Ecuador, provides partial support. The major exceptions, South
Korea and the Philippines, serve to confirm certain limitations to the theory
that were posited in Chapter 1, such as its difficulty in explaining campaign
dynamics when there is limited organizational continuity from one election to
the next. I conclude with a review of the implications of campaign strategy for
the quality of democracy in Chile, Brazil, Peru, and elsewhere.

REVIEWING THE THEORY OF SUCCESS CONTAGION

The theory of success contagion holds that major candidates, regardless of ideological orientation, are likely to adopt the first victorious campaign strategy subsequently legitimated by a successful term in office for the elected

president. The contagion of this model can occur through two distinct mechanisms: outright imitation of prior strategies and the consolidation of norms within national communities of campaign professionals. Success contagion also implies a corollary: failure avoidance. Strategies that lead to electoral victory may be delegitimated by ensuing failure in office, prompting future candidates to avoid them. And when one president after another proves to be highly unpopular, candidates are likely to choose strategies through an inward-oriented process of reacting to previous errors within their own political camp.

In instances of success contagion, candidates' convergence on particular national models of campaign strategy creates isomorphic outcomes, just as organizations often converge upon forms and procedures that are similar to those of their peers (DiMaggio and Powell 1983). A central claim of the isomorphism literature is that actors are motivated to seek legitimacy. Such behavior has been identified in a number of empirical realms, but it has a particularly prominent place in studies of competing firms, where deviating from established norms is often thought to negatively impact upon a company's performance (Lieberman and Asaba 2006). In Chapter 1, I argued that legitimacy concerns are likely to play at least as large a role in presidential elections as in competition among firms. The appropriateness of candidates' actions may be even more highly scrutinized than that of firms in the marketplace, due to the compressed time frame of a campaign, the smaller number of relevant actors, and the heightened media attention. Moreover, if voters disapprove of departure from the range of legitimate strategies, their sanction (in the form of lost votes or declining poll standings) will be effected much more immediately than the impact of public opinion on a firm's sales. Consumers do not go to the marketplace en masse, in a comparable fashion to that of voters on election day.

Imitation, Professional Norms, and Strategic Inertia

A first mechanism through which success contagion can occur concerns the imitation of prior electoral strategies. As with managers of firms or public bureaucracies, presidential candidates and their close political advisors are likely to imitate the strategies of those among their peers who are most successful and prestigious – the winners of previous elections that went on to maintain a positive public image in office. The role of imitation as a mechanism of contagion across the ideological spectrum can be seen most clearly in the campaign of right-wing candidate Joaquín Lavín in Chile's 1999 election. Lavín's strategy of communicating closeness to the people and an empathy with their concerns (and thus, utilizing direct linkages and maintaining a low policy focus) was specifically inspired by the prior efforts of the center-left Concertación. When success contagion takes place through outright imitation, a strategy is copied directly from one's opponents on the other side of the ideological spectrum.

The consolidation of professional norms about appropriate campaigning can also play a key role in this process of strategic diffusion. Strategies that were successful in previous elections and become associated with prestigious incumbents are likely to be institutionalized as norms or best practices within a country's community of campaign professionals and subsequently reinforced through training seminars, conferences, and the publication of how-to manuals. Once a particular strategy becomes standard operating procedure, it can readily spread across the political spectrum as these professionals are employed by candidates of varying ideological stripes. Success contagion via professional norms is an indirect rather than a direct mechanism because it does not involve candidates and their advisors explicitly copying the tactics of a predecessor. Rather, they adhere to the recommendations of professionals whose standard approach incorporates a strategy initially introduced by the other side.

Professional norms constitute the key mechanism of success contagion in Brazil. Lula and his close circle of advisors did not specifically seek to imitate the strategy of Fernando Henrique Cardoso, the victor of the 1994 election, in the same manner that Lavín aimed to copy the Concertación's prior campaign strategy in Chile. Rather, Lula and the Workers' Party (Partido dos Trabalhadores, PT) gradually heeded the advice of mainstream Brazilian political consultants, who consistently advocated the same type of strategy that Cardoso had used to win in 1994. Instead of being transmitted directly from right to left, therefore, the predominant campaign strategy in Brazil diffused across the ideological spectrum indirectly, first being embraced by a nonpartisan community of campaign professionals and only later being adopted by Brazil's major presidential candidate on the left.

Two factors influence whether imitation or professional norms is likely to be the predominant mechanism of strategic contagion in a given country. On the supply side, the importance of norms increases when there is a sufficiently large, well-integrated community of campaign professionals. Federalism, a prior history of electoral contestation (either before or during authoritarian rule), and a large and well-developed economy are all important for sustaining the initial growth of a political consulting industry. In Brazil, each of these factors has supported the emergence of a strong community of campaign consultants, allowing professional norms to serve as the major mechanism of success contagion. In Chile, the situation is somewhat less favorable for campaign consultants, and there is less of a well-developed professional community. Here, norms have played a role in success contagion, but they are not the primary mechanism.

On the demand side, the importance of imitation increases when politicians of Left and Right do not see themselves as fundamentally different from one another. The greater the perceived distance from the president who introduced a successful strategy, the more likely that future candidates on the other side of the political spectrum will be reluctant to copy it, either for fear of betraying their ideological roots or because they think it simply will not work for them. In Chile, where the Concertación had embraced the Right's economic model and governed from the center, Lavín's campaign advisors had no qualms about strategic mimicry; politicians from the governing coalition were political adversaries but not ideological foes. In Brazil, Cardoso was much more of a bitter enemy for the PT, having come from the left but shifted to the right during his campaign and subsequent government. Directly imitating Cardoso's strategy would have been a difficult pill to swallow; following similar advice from nonpartisan campaign professionals was more palatable.

Imitation and professional norms facilitate strategic contagion to the other side of the ideological spectrum, but for convergence to occur, the party introducing an initially successful approach must also stick with it in the future. Therefore, strategic inertia is a third mechanism for explaining why the strategies of presidential candidates might become more similar over time. If a particular strategy worked well in the past, it is less likely to be questioned in the future. This dynamic is shown quite clearly by the campaigns of the Chilean Left in 1989 and 1993, which avoided cleavage priming, privileged direct linkages, and limited policy focus in a manner quite similar to that of the campaign for the "No" option in the 1988 plebiscite. Similarly, Lula repeated a number of characteristics of his 1989 campaign in 1994 because his previous approach had been seen as a fairly successful one.

Even when certain strategists propose an alternative course of action, the advisors who designed an initially successful approach are likely to be empowered in the future and better able to marginalize internal dissidents. In Chile's 1999 election, Concertación strategists who had been involved in prior presidential campaigns were able to convince Ricardo Lagos to return to the coalition's tried-and-true strategy in the second round. Likewise, José Serra and Geraldo Alckmin, candidates of the center-right PSDB in Brazil's 2002 and 2006 elections, both ignored the protests of important political advisors and stuck steadfastly to the strategies recommended by the campaign professionals who had gained great authority after Cardoso's electoral victories in 1994 and 1998. Because of this dynamic, the PSDB did not alter its strategies in 2006 or 2010 even after Serra's loss in the 2002 presidential election.

Failure Avoidance and Inward-Oriented Reactions

The corollary of success contagion via imitation, professional norms, or strategic inertia is that candidates will actively avoid a campaign strategy associated with a disgraced incumbent, even if that strategy was seen as contributing to his or her prior electoral victory. Campaign strategists are likely to perceive that voters will not make the same mistake twice, being seduced by someone who seeks to woo them with a similar appeal. Thus, they will counsel candidates in the next election to avoid moves that could associate them with the style of the current (or recently ousted) president.

The phenomenon of failure avoidance can be seen most clearly in the Brazilian case by comparing the writings of campaign professionals both before and after Fernando Collor's downfall in 1992. As discussed in Chapter 3, prior to Collor's impeachment, consultants tended to express admiration for the anti-establishment stance that he had used to win in 1989. In the lead-up to the 1994 election, however, they clearly recommended against any approach that would be reminiscent of Collor's prior campaign strategy.

In countries where one president after another is unsuccessful in office, candidates are unlikely to converge upon a single campaign strategy. Lacking a model of successful electioneering combined with successful governing, they are instead likely to choose their strategies through an inward-oriented process of reacting to prior errors within their own party or political camp. Drawing different lessons from these previous efforts, the candidates of contrasting ideological tendencies may move in different directions from one campaign to the next, even leapfrogging each other in successive elections.

Peru, with its pattern of repeated failures in office, is a prime example of inward-oriented reactions. On the right-hand side of the political spectrum, candidates have often made dramatic changes in multiple aspects of campaign strategy from one election to the next, or even between successive rounds of a single election. The result has often been a zigzag pattern of alternating between different strategic extremes rather than settling on a single approach and adhering to it in multiple campaigns.

While serving as a case of repeated failure and inward-oriented learning over the long term, Peru also presents a partial example of success contagion during the 1990s. In the 1995 and 2000 elections, at a time when incumbent president Alberto Fujimori enjoyed high approval ratings, those challenging his reelection imitated his strategy of circumventing established intermediary organizations, crafting personal electoral vehicles, and generally privileging direct linkages.

Once Left and Right have converged upon a common approach to electioneering, they are likely to stick with it in the future, as witnessed in both Brazil and Chile. However, strategic convergence can be dislodged by a major change in a country's party system that interrupts the continuity of parties and political forces competing in presidential elections. In Peru, Fujimori's removal from office in 2000 was much more than the personal failure of a single politician; it constituted the fall of an authoritarian regime and brought major changes to the country's electoral dynamics. Traditional party politicians like Alan García and Lourdes Flores saw their prospects reinvigorated in 2001 and 2006, while *fujimorismo* was unable to mount a serious challenge in either election (though it rebounded in 2011). Strategic convergence in Peru thus ended after Fujimori's demise.

Weighing Alternative Explanations

After initially describing the distinct patterns of electioneering in Chile, Brazil, and Peru, Chapter 1 examined a number of alternative explanations for their strategic diversity. Now that that theory of success contagion has been applied in detail to these countries, it is worth revisiting this question of alternative explanations, leveraging evidence that was presented in Chapters 2–4.

Success contagion implies a certain degree of contingency in the evolution of campaigning in any given country, since the diffusion of a particular electoral strategy depends upon the governing performance of the president elected to office, and failure can occur for any number of reasons. In this regard, the theory can be distinguished from a model in which each country has a largely predetermined optimal campaign strategy, and candidates independently settle upon this "best" approach through individual trial-and-error experimentation. Pierson (2004: 94) has likened this causal model to a frog in a pond hopping among lily pads where one is coated with superglue; the endpoint is fully determined in advance even though the path to get there and the duration of the journey are not. This rival perspective might argue, for example, that technocratic strategies are optimal for modern Brazilian candidates, and that Left and Right were likely to discover this fact eventually, regardless of the fate of any particular candidate or government. By contrast, success contagion emphasizes a contingent process whereby convergence on a technocratic approach depended on the failure of Collor's government and the success of Cardoso's, and it implies that the outcome would have been different if Collor – like his fellow neopopulist, Fujimori – had been a popular president.

Alternative explanations for cross-national variation in campaign strategies that adhere to the "lily pad" model are likely to focus on the different factors that might determine which approach works best in a given country, including institutional or structural variables, historical context, and the distribution of voter preferences. For an explanation focused on Chile, Brazil, and Peru, some of these factors can be ruled out a priori. As noted in Chapter 1, these countries are similar on a number of institutional variables that might be expected to influence campaign strategies, such as the majority runoff formula for presidential elections, concurrent legislative elections (with a few exceptions), and, during the period under study, compulsory voting. Structural variables such as levels of education or inequalities among social classes or ethnicities also do not map onto prevailing patterns of campaigning in a way that might independently explain the outcome.

The major institutional variable that correlates with observed cross-national differences in campaigning is immediate presidential reelection, which has been permitted in Brazil since 1998 but is banned in Chile and – outside of the Fujimori period – also in Peru. This institutional feature might explain the greater policy focus of Brazilian campaigns: incumbents running for reelection should naturally focus on their first-term accomplishments, and challengers may be more likely to criticize them on policy grounds. There does seem to be a "reelection effect" on the degree to which Brazilian campaigns emphasize policy – Cardoso and Lula both focused more on policy when running for their second term than for their first. However, their first successful campaigns also involved substantially more policy emphasis than one sees in Chile. Moreover, Chile does permit nonimmediate reelection, and Frei's 2009 campaign for a nonconsecutive second term was still broadly consistent with the Chilean norm of deemphasizing policy.

Comparing the campaigns of incumbent cabinet members running for president offers further evidence that differences in policy focus between Chile and Brazil cannot simply be attributed to the notion that immediate presidential reelection gives Brazilian candidates a record to defend. Cardoso in Brazil in 1994 and Bachelet in Chile in 2005 were both incumbent ministers of popular governments, whereas Serra in Brazil in 2002 and Lagos in Chile in 1999 were incumbent ministers of less popular governments. In both cases, the policy focus of the Brazilian candidates was substantially higher. Bachelet surely could have gotten more mileage out of her previous accomplishments as health and defense minister under Lagos, but following the established model of campaign strategy in Chile, she put much more emphasis on her identification with the people and empathy with their concerns.

If structural and institutional variables do not seem to account for cross-national differences in campaign strategy, perhaps the unique historical circumstances of each country do so. One might posit, for instance, that the different outcomes in Chile and Brazil simply constitute negative reactions to case-specific factors – the extreme technocracy of Chile's military regime that led voters to tire of policy-centric political messages, versus Brazil's recurrent hyperinflation that made the public yearn for a capable administrator. Certainly, these sorts of contextual variables influenced the strategy of Chile's Concertación in 1988 and 1989 and of Cardoso in Brazil's 1994 election. However, the campaign strategy ultimately adopted in these cases was not predetermined by background variables. Within the Concertación, a number of important political leaders insisted that the campaign for the "No" in the 1988 plebiscite place emphasis on policy and confrontation rather than emotion and national reconciliation. If not for the presence and influence of the social scientists from CIS, the strategy of this campaign could easily have been a different one.

Moreover, there is no clear one-to-one mapping between context and campaign strategy across Chile, Brazil, and Peru. Hyperinflation and extant political corruption may have inspired Cardoso to stress policy details in 1994, but these same conditions in 1989 led Collor to cast himself as an anti-establishment outsider who said little about his policy intentions. Likewise, Peru's 1990 election, which was also fought out in the context of hyperinflation and corruption charges against the incumbent government, saw Fujimori advance few proposals, while Vargas Llosa adopted a highly technocratic approach.

A different alternative explanation might invoke the Downsian notion that parties and candidates simply respond rationally to the preferences of voters and that the distribution of those preferences is what should determine optimal campaign strategies. Thus, one might posit that strategic convergence in Chile and Brazil is simply driven by candidates appealing to the median voter, who holds different preferences with respect to the policy focus of campaigns in each country. The fact that convergence does not happen immediately but rather takes place over several electoral cycles might be attributed to the advent of better surveys and focus groups, allowing candidates to respond to voters' preferences once they have accurately measured them. Meanwhile, the lack of convergence in Peru might be attributed to a different distribution of voter preferences that does not allow for a unique equilibrium.

Yet invoking a Downsian logic as an alternative explanation requires problematic assumptions that go well beyond standard spatial theory. If the median voter theorem is to explain the outcomes described in this study, one must believe that voters have preferences not only over a single left-right policy dimension but also over high versus low policy focus, the presence or absence of cleavage priming, and intermediated versus direct linkages. The combination of these distinct sets of preferences implies a complicated multidimensional space where the simple convergence outcome of the median voter theorem would not apply.

The notion that candidates can respond mechanically to voter preferences over policy focus, cleavage priming, and form of linkage also makes unrealistic assumptions about how accurately such preferences can be measured or how readily campaign research translates into campaign strategy. Using surveys to query public opinion about policy issues is a straightforward process, and it is not hard for candidates to identify those valence issues that top the list of voters' concerns or to locate the median stance on position issues. However, it is much more difficult to determine how detailed the public wants a candidate's proposals to be or whether voters want to see fundamental societal divisions emphasized during the campaign. In the cases examined in this study, strategic decisions with respect to linkage, cleavage priming, and policy focus could rarely be read directly off of the results of surveys or focus groups. Rather, groups of advisors within a candidate's campaign team routinely advanced different strategic recommendations based on divergent interpretations of the same research. In each instance, the side that tended to win these internal disputes was the one whose recommended approach was consistent with the prevailing campaign strategy, as determined by success contagion.

If a model of country-specific optimal campaign strategies seems to lack explanatory power, one might posit that there are best approaches only for certain types of parties and candidates in each country, such as those on the left. In Chapter 1, I argued that broad structural explanations for the moderation of the Left, such as the end of the Cold War and the decline of organized labor, cannot explain why Brazilian candidates shifted to the center by emphasizing policy details while Chilean candidates did so by saying little about policy at all. Yet the electoral challenges faced by Brazil's PT and Chile's Concertación have not been identical. The PT began its life in the 1980s as an avowedly socialist party, and Lula ran for president three times before he was ultimately elected in 2002. The Concertación, by contrast, adopted a moderate stance in its first electoral contest and was successful from the start. Perhaps the PT needed to emphasize policy detail to convince voters of its ideological moderation and preparedness to govern, whereas the Concertación had a record of moderate governance that already spoke for itself.

An explanation focused on the different electoral challenges facing the Left in Chile and Brazil, however, ignores the similarities between the Concertación and the PT before they were both elected. Lula was certainly criticized by his opponents during the 1990s for harboring supposedly radical policy intentions or having little administrative experience. But in Chile's 1988 plebiscite, the Concertación was ruthlessly attacked for the failures of the Allende government, and the military regime insisted that all of its policy achievements would be erased if the Left were to return to power. And in the 1989 presidential election, Büchi specifically accused Aylwin of having a secret government program that had been negotiated with the Concertación's far-left parties and would be revealed only after the election. Yet in both campaigns, the Chilean Left placed very little emphasis on its proposals. Thus, an argument focusing on the electoral challenges facing the Left cannot explain why the Concertación acted differently from Lula in similar circumstances.

In a related vein, one might also propose that the absence of cleavage priming in Chile and Brazil is simply a product of the prior radicalization of the Left, which learned from experience in the 1970s–1990s that emphasizing class divisions is not an effective way to get elected or to govern once in office. Yet nothing in the logic of this explanation could account for the reluctance of the Chilean Right to prime religious cleavages in the 1999 and 2005 elections. The lesson that politicians and political consultants in Chile have drawn from the 1988 plebiscite is that polarization and open conflict of any sort – not just class or ideological polarization – are not appropriate strategies for presidential campaigns.

The fate of the Left and broader party system dynamics are certainly not irrelevant to the choice of electoral strategies in Latin America. As argued in Chapter 4, the demise of the traditional partisan Left in Peru is a key factor in the recurrence of neopopulism, as it has created unoccupied space on the anti-establishment side of the political spectrum that opportunistic outsiders have been able to occupy on a repeated basis. Yet this dynamic, distinct from the logic of success contagion, only partially explains the choice of campaign strategies in Peru. Centrist and right-wing candidates – including former neopopulists like Humala in 2011 – choose their approaches through inward-oriented reactions, according to the theory. And the survival of the partisan Left in Chile and Brazil, which might explain why these countries' campaign dynamics differ from those of Peru, cannot account for why they differ from one another.

TESTING THE GENERALITY OF SUCCESS CONTAGION

The theory of success contagion advanced in this study was developed inductively based on an analysis of presidential election campaigns in Chile, Brazil, and Peru through 2005–2006. The next round of presidential elections, in 2009–2011, tested the theory's predictions for each case. As explained in Chapter 1, the logic of success contagion should also apply more broadly, describing presidential candidates' strategies in other cases of third-wave transition from authoritarian rule. In this section, I draw upon secondary literature to test the theory's predictions in ten additional countries: Argentina, Benin, Ecuador, Ghana, Honduras, Mali, Nicaragua, the Philippines, South Korea, and Uruguay.

Characterizing additional cases solely on the basis of secondary literature is obviously a more limited enterprise than was possible with the analysis of Chile, Brazil, and Peru. When relying on other scholars' assessments – for example, characterizing a campaign as policy centric – one cannot always be certain of their metrics or point of reference. Moreover, due to the spottiness of secondary literature, in no case was it possible to score campaign strategies for all three dimensions – linkage, cleavage priming, and policy focus – and for every major candidate since democratization. Because of these limitations, the discussion below focuses on those dimensions of campaign strategy that are more consistently discussed in the secondary literature on each country, and also those for which multiple analysts tend to agree in their assessments. Finally, while an analysis of secondary literature allows us to say whether the evolution of some aspects of campaign strategy is consistent with the predictions of success contagion, it is generally insufficient to uncover the mechanisms, such as imitation of prior example, by which contagion may have occurred.

Taking these limitations into consideration, the results of this test are encouraging for the theory of success contagion. Four out of ten countries – Benin, Ghana, Mali, and Nicaragua – present evidence of candidates either converging on the campaign strategy of a successful former president or jointly adhering to strategies legitimated by a transitional government. Three additional countries – Argentina, Uruguay, and Honduras – are primarily cases of repeated governing failures in which candidates have not converged on common strategies. Rather, as predicted by the theory of success contagion, they show evidence of strategic zigzags, a pattern consistent with inward-oriented reactions to perceived failures of the past. Finally, the evolution of presidential campaign strategies in Ecuador, the Philippines, and South Korea contradicts the predictions of success contagion in important respects (though Ecuador also provides partial support). These cases serve to confirm several previously posited limitations to the scope of success contagion, such as its difficulty in characterizing campaign dynamics when there is little continuity of parties or individual candidates across successive elections.

Benin, Mali, and Ghana: Ethnic Diversity without Cleavage Priming

While much of Africa has struggled with political instability since democratization in the 1990s, several African countries have witnessed a series of successful presidential terms. As predicted by the theory of success contagion, major candidates in Benin, Mali, and Ghana have converged on the first political strategy legitimated by a successful governing experience, the key feature of which is an avoidance of cleavage priming. Significant cleavages exist in each of these countries. In Benin and Ghana, aggregate electoral returns and individual survey data show substantial ethnic, regional, and religious variation in the support bases of different presidential candidates (Nugent 1999; Creevey et al. 2005; Fridy 2007; Battle and Seely 2010; Takyi et al. 2010; Ichino and Nathan 2013). Ethnic voting patterns are less prevalent in Mali, but experimental research has shown that coethnicity boosts citizens' evaluation of a hypothetical candidate (Dunning and Harrison 2010). Since none of these countries has mandatory voting, mobilizing one's base by priming ethnic cleavages could be an attractive electoral strategy. I argue that candidates have refrained from doing so because of the legitimacy that has become attached to national unity appeals.

Benin and Mali

Presidential candidates in Benin have avoided playing the ethnic card since the transition to democracy (Gisselquist 2008: 808). In the country's first three post-democratization elections, the major presidential candidates were former transitional Prime Minister Nicéphor Soglo (victorious in 1991) and former dictator Mathieu Kérékou (the winner of the 1996 and 2001 elections). In 1991, Kérékou's campaign proposed a semipresidential system as a way of averting tribalism (Heilbrunn 1993: 295), and in 1996, he explicitly cast himself as a national unity candidate (Dissou 2002). In designing a field experiment to be carried out during the 2001 election, Wantchekon (2003: 409, n. 19) rejected the idea of asking Soglo and Kérékou to prime ethnic cleavages in their stump speeches, noting that "purely ethnic messages would be too disconnected from [their] campaign strategies." In 2006, political newcomer Thomas Boni Yayi, of mixed ethnic and religious heritage, made similarly broad, consensus-seeking appeals in his bid for the presidency (Battle and Seely 2010: 51; Souaré 2011: 77; Bleck and van de Walle 2012: 1401). And in 2011, the main candidate contesting Boni Yayi's reelection bid was supported by a multiparty coalition with the name "Union Builds the Nation" (Souaré 2011: 77).

In a similar fashion, presidential candidates in Mali have consistently avoided priming ethnic cleavages during electoral campaigns. Alpha Oumar Konaré won the 1992 presidential election on the basis of a national unity platform (Boyer 1992: 42). There was not much of a campaign for Konaré's reelection in 1997, since the opposition staged a boycott out of protest over supposedly unfair conditions (Smith 1997; Sborgi 1998). However, Konaré adopted an inclusive approach in his negotiations with the opposition during this episode; he sought to prevent the boycott "in accordance with his style ... proposing the possibility of a large coalition cabinet immediately after the elections" (Sborgi 1998: 466–467). In the 2002 election, independent opposition candidate Amadou Toumani Touré launched a successful bid to succeed

Konaré, and he won reelection to a second term in 2007. Like his predecessor, Touré's campaigns placed an emphasis on national unity and eschewed ethnic appeals (Baudais and Sborgi 2008; Bleck and van de Walle 2012: 1401; van Vliet 2013).

Democracy was interrupted in Mali in 2012, following an uprising against Touré's government by ethnic Tuareg rebels, a military coup against Touré for his poor handling of the Tuareg insurgency, and the subsequent incursion of foreign Islamist fighters who occupied much of the country's North. The election scheduled for April 2012 was thus postponed until July 2013. Yet the ethnic tensions that gave rise to Mali's 2012 crisis did not translate into cleavage-priming campaign strategies in that election. On the contrary, Ibrahim Boubacar Keïta won the 2013 election with a campaign that promised to "revive dialogue between all the sons of our nation" ("Mali: IBK Wins" 2013: 19811), and another candidate "argue[d] for inter-communal dialogue with representatives from all communities as well as armed groups" (Wing 2013: 485).

A key reason candidates in Benin and Mali avoid priming cleavages concerns the national conferences that inaugurated their transitions to democracy and the role these conferences played in legitimizing unity-oriented political strategies. In Benin, in the face of rising anti-government protest, Kérékou convened a national conference in 1990 to represent "all the vital forces of the nation" and discuss details of a transition to multiparty rule (Heilbrunn 1993; Nzouankeu 1993; Nwajiaku 1994; Robinson 1994). The conference unexpectedly declared itself a sovereign transitional authority, proceeding to suspend the constitution, dissolve the National Assembly, appoint an interim government, and call elections for the following year. As a result of this process, the body that ruled Benin during its transition to democracy was broadly representative of different groups in society, including different ethnicities (Seely 2005). Consistent with the notion of success contagion, Seely (2005: 362) has argued that "the legacy of transitions in the early 1990s shaped the boundaries of appropriate political debate and strategy today" and enshrined a spirit of national unity and consensus in electoral politics. Benin's first successful government was its transitional government, and the strategy of cooperation that characterized this initial governing experience effectively removed cleavage priming from the range of legitimate strategies in subsequent electoral campaigns.

In Mali, a similar national conference, which was explicitly modeled on Benin's, inaugurated the transition to democracy and lent legitimacy to a political strategy of consensus and reconciliation (Nzouankeu 1993; Clark 2000). As in Benin, this experience is likely to have influenced candidates' strategies, starting with the inaugural presidential election. Moreover, after the founding election, Mali's president Konaré went on to govern in the inclusive manner that he had promised during his 1992 campaign. He successfully negotiated an end to the 1990–1995 Tuareg rebellion, and he pursued administrative decentralization, both as an olive branch to the rebels and also to build broad-based support in other parts of the country (Smith 2001). By the end of his second term,

73 percent of Malians approved of Konaré's performance (Bratton, Coulibaly, and Machado 2001). It was thus unlikely that any major candidate would deviate from the national unity strategy that both Konaré and the national conference had helped to legitimate.

Ghana

Ghana is a more conventional case of success contagion, with major candidates employing different strategies from one another in the first election but subsequently converging after the first successful presidency. Ghana's transition to democracy began when authoritarian incumbent J. J. Rawlings agreed to hold democratic elections in 1992 and presented himself as the candidate of the National Democratic Congress (NDC). The NDC's campaign in this inaugural election sought to preserve peace among different ethnic and regional groups (Nugent 1995: 245). In contrast, Adu Boahen of the National Patriotic Party (NPP) ran a dirty and divisive campaign that focused on ethnic cleavages and made racial attacks against Rawlings, whose father was from Scotland and whose mother was a member of Ghana's Ewe minority (Nugent 1995: 244–245).

While its initial efforts to challenge the ruling NDC sought to exploit ethnic cleavages, Ghana's NPP subsequently shifted to a strategy of national unity during the latter half of the 1990s (Dickovick 2008). In the years since, playing down ethnic rivalries has been a common feature of both major parties' campaigns (Arthur 2009: 46; Kelly 2009: 446; Whitfield 2009: 640). Following upon Rawlings' first term, whose success is indicated by the fact that he won reelection with 57 percent of the vote, the NPP and its presidential candidate John Kufuor avoided ethnic appeals in the 1996 campaign. Jeffries (1998: 191) notes that there was no regional or ethnic pattern to electioneering in 1996; both Rawlings and Kufuor relied on appeals to voters' economic interests rather than ethnic identities. Likewise, in 2000, the NPP sought an image of ethnic inclusiveness by choosing a Muslim from northern Ghana as Kufuor's running mate (Gyimah-Boadi 2001), and it "campaigned vigorously to dispel the notion that it was a 'tribal party'" (Oelbaum 2004: 251). In 2008, both major candidates "tended to stay above the fray, emphasizing their campaign promises" and "preached against ethnic politicization and pledged a peaceful election" (Daddieh 2009: 644). In 2012, NDC candidate John Dramani Mahama pledged to be "the needle that will sew the cloth of Ghana together" (Burke 2012). After Mahama won a narrow first-round victory and the NPP alleged fraud, its decision to contest the result through a judicial process rather than inciting violence "showcased the Ghanaian political culture of tolerance that is distinct in Africa" (Kwarteng 2014: 90).

Ghanaian candidates' adherence to a national unity strategy is not quite as clear-cut as in Mali and Benin, and there is disagreement regarding the characterization of recent elections. Some scholars highlight instances of divisive ethnic appeals during runoff campaigns in 2000 and 2008 (Gyimah-Boadi 2001:

108; Frempong 2001: 149, 156; Oelbaum 2004; Arthur 2009: 61; Bowers 2009; Gyimah-Boadi 2009: 143). However, others emphasize the absence of cleavage priming in these elections, especially in comparison to recent campaigns in Côte d'Ivoire, Kenya, and Zimbabwe (Nugent 2001: 426; Daddieh 2009; McConnell 2009). Meanwhile, an electoral observer mission blamed the media rather than politicians for inciting ethnic tensions in the 2008 runoff, crediting one of the candidates with calling for a civil tone (Commonwealth Observer Group [2009]: 43). Ultimately, interpretations may hinge on whether one examines Ghanaian campaigns in comparative perspective, where cleavage priming is minimal, or vis-à-vis prior elections in the same country, where even isolated instances of ethnic divisiveness might seem worthy of emphasis.

Nicaragua: The Sandinistas' Embrace of National Unity Appeals

Among Latin American cases, Nicaragua provides an example of success contagion similar to that of Ghana, in which candidates differed in their approaches to early elections but ultimately converged upon a strategy in which they avoid priming cleavages. In 1990, Daniel Ortega of the Sandinista National Liberation Front (Frente Sandinista de Liberación Nacional, FSLN) ran for reelection against Violeta Barrios de Chamorro, the candidate of the National Opposition Union (Unión Nacional Opositora, UNO). The opposition to the Sandinistas specifically chose Chamorro as a symbolic unity candidate because of the widespread respect for her martyred husband, who was assassinated by the Somoza dictatorship in the 1970s. Her campaign portrayed her as the mother who would reunite the fractured Nicaraguan family (Robinson 1992; Kampwirth 1998; Anderson and Dodd 2005). In contrast, Ortega's campaign relied on cleavage priming; it was arrogant, belligerent, triumphalist, and sought to link UNO to the Somoza supporters that the Sandinista revolution had overthrown (Barnes 1992, 1998: 83).

Chamorro won the 1990 election and went on to serve six years as a popular president, ending her term with a 70 percent approval rating (Anderson and Dodd 2002: 84). In each of his subsequent campaigns for the presidency, Ortega has adhered to the strategy that Chamorro employed in 1990, casting himself as a national unity candidate rather than priming class cleavages. In the 1996 election, Ortega stressed moderation, alliance building, and reconciliation; he used the slogan "Government for All," and his television spots conveyed "feel-good messages promising to unite all Nicaraguans" (McCoy and McConnell 1997: 77; Patterson 1997; Barnes 1998). Likewise, in the 2001, 2006, and 2011 elections, Ortega avoided confrontation and emphasized the concepts of peace, love, reconciliation, and national unity (Anderson and Dodd 2002, 2005; Stahler-Sholk 2003: 542; Cupples and Larios 2005: 329; McConnell 2007; Ortega Hegg 2007; Kampwirth 2008; Cupples 2009: 113; Gooren 2010; Feinberg 2011; Pérez-Baltodano 2012). For a politician considered to be part of Latin America's leftist resurgence, Ortega's campaigns have been a far cry from the cleavage-priming discourse of Venezuela's Hugo Chávez or Bolivia's Evo Morales.

Right-wing candidates have also generally avoided priming cleavages in their efforts to defeat Ortega. Arnoldo Alemán did run a polarizing campaign in 1996, seeking to tie Ortega to the societal conflict of the 1980s and criticizing the Sandinistas' militant union base (Patterson 1997; Barnes 1998). Subsequent right-wing candidates, however, have been less divisive. During the 2001 campaign, in the months after the September 11 terrorist attacks in the United States, Enrique Bolaños sought to smear Ortega by pointing out his ties to Arab leaders (Cupples and Larios 2005) – a strategy that may have been dirty, but did not attempt to divide Nicaraguans in any way. Similarly, most criticism of Ortega in 2006 and 2011 focused on issues other than social divides – his alleged reliance on donations from Hugo Chávez and his efforts to circumvent a constitutional prohibition on reelection (Vargas 2006: 170; Pérez-Baltodano 2012: 217). These campaigns, while bitterly fought, did not seek to divide Nicaraguans along class lines.

Argentina, Honduras, and Uruguay: Governing Failures and Inward-Oriented Reactions

Among third-wave democracies in Latin America, which typically were forced to implement difficult economic reforms soon after their transitions from authoritarian rule, successful governance has been much more the exception than the rule. In the context of multiple unpopular presidencies in Argentina, Honduras, and Uruguay, there has been no long-term convergence in campaign strategies. Rather, these countries have witnessed back-and-forth strategic shifts from one election to the next, with different candidates sometimes moving in opposite directions from one another – a pattern consistent with inward-oriented reactions to prior errors within one's own party or political camp.

Post-democratization presidents have not been uniformly unpopular in Argentina, Honduras, and Uruguay; each country has had several leaders that garnered much higher approval ratings than their peers. These include Carlos Menem, Néstor Kirchner, and Cristina Fernández de Kirchner in Argentina; Carlos Flores and Ricardo Maduro in Honduras; and Tabaré Vázquez and José Mujica in Uruguay. Hence, in each country, there is the possibility of observing short-term convergence in campaign strategies amidst a broader pattern of inward-oriented reactions and strategic diversity, as in Peru. The theoretical expectation for convergence is strongest in the case of Carlos Menem, who was only the second president after democratization in Argentina and took office at a time when other candidates were more likely to be uncertain about how to campaign effectively. We do, in fact, see evidence of a short-term process of success contagion during the 1990s, following Menem's first term. In the other cases, either there is no evidence or only weak evidence of convergence, or the successful presidencies have been too recent to fully assess how other candidates have reacted.

Argentina

From 1983 to 1989, Argentina witnessed strategic reversals by major presidential candidates from both the Justicialist Party (Partido Justicialista, PJ, also known as the Peronists) and the Radical Civic Union (Unión Cívica Radical, UCR), a pattern consistent with inward-oriented reactions by each party. In the country's first post-democratization election, Raúl Alfonsín of the UCR ran a campaign with relatively low policy focus. Of his thirteen major spots, only four contained specific policy commitments (Borrini 2003: 296–298). After six years of disastrous government by Alfonsín, which ended in hyperinflation and riots that forced the president from office six months early, UCR candidate Eduardo Angeloz ran a campaign with a strong policy emphasis (Waisbord 1995: 49–50, 79). The first phase of his television advertising focused on his accomplishments as governor, and the second phase on his program of government, with substantial emphasis on specific proposals (Borrini 2003: 131–132). Angeloz's running mate justified this approach as a reaction to Alfonsín's failure in office, saying that "society no longer sees Alfonsín as the man that led its fight for achieving a democratic system, but rather as the president that should offer solutions to concrete problems" (Borrini 2003: 125).

A comparable strategic shift – yet in the opposite direction – can be seen on the part of the PJ. In 1983, PJ candidate Ítalo Luder ran a very party-oriented campaign in which "the candidate was just a detail, a mere electoral requirement" (Waisbord 1995: 30). Intermediated linkages, from the Peronist machine itself to affiliated labor unions, played a key role in Luder's electoral efforts. According to Waisbord (1995: 30), "the Peronists also believed that the election was about ideas and not candidates," implying a policy-focused appeal. In 1989, the strategy of PJ candidate Carlos Menem differed from that of Luder on both of these dimensions. Rather than emphasizing policy detail, Menem's campaign made only vague references to a "salariazo" (big wage increase) and "productive revolution" (Packenham 1994: 14; Germano and Dell Oro 2000: 19; Teichman 2001: 114). The Peronist party itself also played a relatively minor role in Menem's campaign, which "relied on the candidate's direct contact with the electorate" and presented him as an apolitical outsider with ties to individual voters (Waisbord 1995: 41, 46).

Menem effectively gained control of inflation once in office, and he was a popular incumbent by the time of the 1995 election, prompting imitation of his previous campaign strategy. Argentina's 1995 election thus provides evidence of strategic convergence. None of the major candidates in this race placed much emphasis on policy. Rather, "the electoral campaign was remarkable for its subdued tone and the almost total lack of debate of substantive issues: the emphasis was on style and personalities" (Szusterman 1996: 113; see also Falcoff 1995; Perry 1995). In addition, opposition candidates felt compelled to imitate Menem's strategy of direct linkage via the mass media by appearing on popular talk shows, "some of them visibly uncomfortable but willing to fulfill their obligations as media-centric politicians" (Borrini 2003: 150). The major political coalition challenging Menem's reelection – FREPASO, made up of disaffected Peronists and other critics of market reform – had little party apparatus and relied primarily on direct media linkages of this sort (Canton and Jorrat 2002).

Adherence to Menem's former campaign strategy continued in the 1999 election, even though the president's popularity had declined somewhat by the end of his second term. Opposition candidate Fernando de la Rua, representing an alliance between UCR and FREPASO, sought to distance himself from Menem as an individual and from his flashy political style. But de la Rua's campaign contained few promises (Levitsky 2000) and was not any more policy centric than Menem's previous efforts. Of his major television spots, only five contained policy commitments; the other sixteen mostly focused on his image of honesty and good governance (Borrini 2003). The campaign of the Peronist candidate, Eduardo Duhalde, was similar, with four spots conveying proposals, two discussing prior achievements, and nine making no reference to policy (Borrini 2003).

Consistent with the theoretical argument in Chapter 1, it was not until a severe crisis brought about a major change in the country's party system that strategic diversity returned to Argentina's electoral campaigns. In December 2001 and January 2002, a worsening economic recession and default on the peso led to massive protests and the resignation of four successive presidents in a matter of weeks. The UCR, Argentina's major anti-Peronist party, took the blame for the crisis and virtually collapsed in its aftermath, leaving opponents of Peronism without partisan representation for the first time since the 1940s (Levitsky and Murillo 2008). Peronism itself was also fragmented, with three Peronist candidates representing different factions of the movement in the 2003 presidential election. In the aftermath of the 2001–2002 crisis, presidents Néstor Kirchner and Cristina Fernández de Kirchner constructed a reordered Peronist coalition that included a number of UCR politicians, further decimating Argentina's oldest political party (Etchemendy and Garay 2011).

Following Argentina's 2001–2002 crisis and consequent party system realignment, presidential candidates ceased to adhere to the strategy that Menem introduced in 1989. In the 2003 election, third-place candidate Ricardo López Murphy presented a number of specific proposals about public works, tax reform, and fiscal reform, and he "deviated radically from the country's traditional political culture" by emphasizing the rule of law and denouncing clientelism and personalism (Sánchez 2005: 466).[1] For their part, the Kirchners' campaigns in the 2000s departed from Menem's standard approach of

[1] Menem, also a candidate in this election, was just as vague about policy intentions as he had been in previous contests (Sánchez 2005).

prioritizing direct linkages. After his victory in the 2003 election, Néstor Kirchner focused on building a new base of organized political support, bringing labor unions and a growing mass movement of unemployed persons (the *piqueteros*) into his coalition. These intermediated forms of linkage went on to play a key role in the 2007 and 2011 campaigns of his wife and successor, Cristina Fernández de Kirchner (Levitsky and Murillo 2008; Etchemendy and Garay 2011; Calvo and Murillo 2012), in combination with empathy appeals and direct connections to the people (Annunziata 2012: 79).

Néstor Kirchner and Cristina Fernández de Kirchner both garnered high approval ratings in their first terms (Levitsky and Murillo 2008; Catterberg and Palanza 2012), raising the possibility of a new round of success contagion. However, the lopsided nature of these contests – Fernández de Kirchner won by 22 percentage points in 2007 and 37 points in 2011 – might also limit the potential for strategic contagion, since opposition candidates had no reasonable expectation of winning. Unfortunately, analysis of the Argentine campaigns of 2007 and 2011 has focused much more on Fernández de Kirchner than on the opposition, so it is hard to score the strategies of other candidates in these elections.

Honduras

Honduras is a straightforward case of repeated governing failure in which most presidents since the transition to democracy have been repudiated by public opinion, and candidates have not converged upon a common approach to electioneering. Between 1981 and 1997, four successive presidents from both the Liberal Party (Partido Liberal, PL) and the National Party (Partido Nacional, PN) ended their terms with low levels of popularity. Roberto Suazo Córdova (PL, 1982–1986) suffered because of his cooperation with the Reagan administration's foreign policy and his efforts to engineer a second term (Rosenberg 1989; Paz Aguilar 1990). José Azcona Hoyo (PL, 1986–1990) ended up unpopular for having presided over worsening inflation, unemployment, and debt (*Por Qué Perdió el Partido Liberal* 1990). Rafael Leonardo Callejas Romero (PN, 1990–1994) was widely repudiated by the end of his term for his economic austerity measures and numerous allegations of corruption (Salomón 1994; Ruhl 1998; Sieder 1998). Carlos Roberto Reina (PL, 1994–1998) was unpopular because of poor economic performance; his successor from his own party, Carlos Roberto Flores Facussé, explicitly ran against him ("Carlos Roberto Flores Facussé" 2004).

In the context of repeated governing failures, the presidential campaign strategies of the PL and PN started out similar to one another but diverged over time. In 1985, both major candidates relied upon their parties' campaign organizations – that is, intermediated linkages – to stimulate turnout in the countryside (McDonald and Ruhl 1989). In addition, they campaigned with a relatively low policy focus, emphasizing "efficient and honest government and [other] vagaries that mean nothing" (Fiallos 1986: 72; see also Molina Chocano

1992: 105). Both sides were also similar in that they avoided cleavage priming and employed positive, unity-oriented slogans such as "a new dawn" and "the great national hope" (Molina Chocano 1992).

From this common approach in the mid-1980s, candidates of the PL and PN began to deviate in different ways during subsequent presidential election campaigns, a pattern consistent with inward-oriented reactions to perceived errors of the past. In 1989, the PL's Carlos Roberto Flores Facussé ran a candidate-centered campaign that relied upon direct linkages and sought to circumvent party authorities (*Por Qué Perdió el Partido Liberal* 1990: 50). This strategy differed from the intermediated linkages used by his predecessor. Likewise, in 1993, Oswaldo Ramos Soto of the PN employed an anti-communist, cleavage-priming strategy against his PL opponent, in contrast to the PN's less divisive approach to the 1985 campaign (Salomón 1994).

After four unpopular presidents from 1981 to 1997, Honduras had two that were judged successful by public opinion: Carlos Roberto Flores Facussé (PL, 1997–2001) and Ricardo Maduro Joest (PN, 2001–2005) (Díaz 2001; Booth and Aubone 2008). This raises the possibility of strategic convergence during the 2000s. However, the expectation of success contagion is not particularly strong in this case. Both parties had contested four presidential elections prior to 2001, gaining campaign experience that would reduce their level of uncertainty and limit incentives to adopt an opponent's strategies.

In effect, the pattern of strategic zigzags continued into the 2000s, suggesting ongoing inward-oriented reactions by candidates of both parties. Between 2001 and 2005, the PL and PN virtually flip-flopped in terms of their strategies. In the 2001 election, PL candidate Rafael Pineda Ponce sought to prime cleavages against his opponent, casting himself as a man of the people with rural, indigenous roots, and criticizing the rich, modern city dwellers represented by his opponent (Meza 2002: 32–33, 38–40). His campaign also focused very little on proposals (Meza 2002: 27–28, 31, 62). Meanwhile, PN candidate Ricardo Maduro Joest avoided responding in kind to his opponent's cleavage-priming attacks, instead placing emphasis on detailed proposals (Meza 2002: 45–46, 56–58, 62).

In 2005, the strategies of the PL and PN candidates were virtually the opposite of those that they had employed in 2001. The PN's Porfirio Lobo Sosa failed to present a government program, and "his discourse and electoral offerings were weak and underdeveloped, so his campaign was based more on confrontation than proposals" (*Elecciones Generales 2005* 2006). Lobo's campaign strategy was also described as "fear-inducing and dictatorial," suggesting a cleavage-priming approach (*Elecciones Generales 2005* 2006: 54). Meanwhile, Manuel Zelaya Rosales of the PL conveyed "a message of hope and national reconciliation" (*Elecciones Generales 2005* 2006: 54) that differed from the divisive strategy of his party's last presidential candidate. Zelaya also based his campaign around a clearly defined and well-developed program of government (*Elecciones Generales 2005* 2006: 49).

Though Honduras's 2009 presidential campaign was overshadowed by the coup that removed Zelaya from office earlier that year, strategic zigzags are also evident in this election. The PN's Lobo called for a grand national dialogue and sought to downplay social tensions resulting from Zelaya's ouster, which contrasted with Lobo's own cleavage-priming approach in 2005. Meanwhile, PL candidate Elvin Santos ran a more divisive campaign that was critical of Zelaya and his supporters (Malkin 2009a, 2009b; Álvarez Araya 2010).

Uruguay

As in the case of Honduras, Uruguay's electoral campaigns have been characterized by strategic zigzags amidst a series of failed presidencies from the 1980s to the 2000s. Julio María Sanguinetti of the Colorado Party (1985–1990) had an approval rating below 20 percent by the end of his first term (González 1990: 67; González 1995). Luís Alberto Lacalle of the National Party (1990–1995) was similarly unpopular by the start of the next electoral campaign (González 1995). During Sanguinetti's second term (1995–2000), his approval rating ranged from 25 percent to 30 percent, brought down by the effects of the global economic crisis (Canzani 2000; Cason 2000). Jorge Batlle of the Colorado Party (2000–2005) also presided over poor economic performance and had less than 10 percent approval at the time of the next election (Canzani 2005: 69).

In this context of repeated governing failures, the evolution of candidates' campaign strategies is consistent with the pattern of inward-oriented reactions. Between Uruguay's first two post-transition elections, all major political parties reversed their strategies in important respects. In 1984, the Colorado Party adopted a government program that was deliberately vague, and its presidential campaign focused on personality and abstract ideas such as "change" (Gillespie 1985: 20; Mieres 1985: 116; Gillespie 1991). By contrast, the 1989 campaign of Colorado candidate Batlle emphasized policy goals that had not been achieved under President Sanguinetti (González 1990: 83). For the National Party, the 1984 campaign of left-leaning Alberto Sáenz de Zumarán relied on cleavage priming and "a political line of radical opposition" to the outgoing military regime (Mieres 1985; Gillespie 1986: 227; Rial 1986; Alcántara Sáez and Crespo Martínez 1992: 125). In 1989, however, National Party candidate Luís Alberto Lacalle abandoned "the permanent reference to divisions, in exchange for another [message] that sought the cooperation of all Uruguayans" (González 1990: 93). Finally, the 1984 campaign of the left-wing Broad Front drew heavily upon intermediated linkages, including party militants organized into base communities, the labor and student movements, and cooperatives (Gillespie 1985, 1986; Mieres 1985: 121, 123). In the next presidential election, the Front privileged advertising over and above these intermediated linkages, and it chose to underutilize its mobilizational capacity (González 1990: 100; Mieres 1990).

Subsequent presidential campaigns have seen similar back-and-forth strategic shifts by Uruguayan political parties, particularly with respect to policy focus. In 1994, former Colorado president Sanguinetti was elected to a second term following a campaign that emphasized his proposals and prior achievements (Finch 1995: 234; Espíndola 2001). This approach contrasted with the low policy focus of Sanguinetti's 1984 campaign. In the next election, Colorado Party candidate Jorge Batlle deviated from his predecessor's policy-focused strategy, running an emotional campaign that emphasized his family background and personal characteristics (Cason 2000; Espíndola 2001). De Amas and Cardarello (2000: 116) specifically characterize Batlle's 1999 strategy as a reaction to previous failures, given that he had lost the last four presidential elections with a programmatic and proposal-oriented message. On the National Party side, the 1994 campaign of Alberto Volonté adopted an "emotional electioneering style" (Finch 1995: 235), in contrast to the "painful commitment to specific measures" of the National Party's 1984 campaign (Gillespie 1991: 202; see also Gillespie 1985: 20).

The campaigns of the Broad Front during the 1980s and 1990s also evolved in a manner consistent with inward-oriented reactions. In 1989, the Broad Front's presidential campaign involved an "almost total disappearance of concrete proposals" (González 1990: 106; see also Gillespie 1986 on the 1984 campaign). In 1999, however, Vázquez's presidential campaign emphasized his performance as mayor of Montevideo and also his detailed plans for the future, particularly with respect to tax policy (Espíndola 2001; Moreira 2004: 64). Cason (2000: 94) even concludes that "the Left erred in being too specific about its proposed policies" in this election. Over the same period, the campaigns of the Colorado and National Parties were both shifting back and forth in terms of policy focus, so it is difficult to attribute the Broad Front's change in strategy to imitation of either of its opponents.

After a long series of unpopular presidents, Tabaré Vázquez (2005–2010) and José Mujica (2010–2015) of the Broad Front broke with the pattern of their predecessors, finishing their terms with approval ratings of 70 percent and 60 percent, respectively (Altman and Buquet 2015). As with Honduras, there is the possibility that candidates might converge upon the strategies that elected these popular governments, though expectations of contagion would be stronger if the first successful presidency had been in the 1980s.

In Uruguay, there is some evidence to suggest that candidates may be converging on an approach legitimated by Vázquez and Mujica's presidencies. Over the course of four campaigns from 1999 to 2014, Vázquez and Mujica avoided priming cleavages and emphasized proposals and policy competence (Cason 2000: 94; Espíndola 2001; Moreira 2004: 64; Canzani 2005; Altman and Castiglioni 2006; Altman 2010; Garcé 2010; Mieres 2012; Altman and Buquet 2015). By contrast, candidates from the Colorado and National Parties used cleavage-priming strategies in the 1999, 2004, and 2009 elections, especially when attacking their leftist opponents (de Amas and Cardarello 2000;

Espíndola 2001; Moreira 2004: 67; Buquet 2005; Canzani 2005; Garcé 2010; Altman 2010; Mieres 2011). In 2009, for instance, the National Party's Luís Alberto Lacalle referred to the poor as being dirty and lazy and ran a Cold War–style spot accusing Mujica, a leftist guerrilla during the 1960s–1970s, of having ties to current criminal activity (Altman 2010; Garcé 2010; Mieres 2011: 38–39). Yet in 2014, National Party candidate (and Lacalle's son) Luís Lacalle Pou "made a drastic change to the strategy followed by his father five years prior, replacing strong criticism with a positive message" (Altman and Buquet 2015). Lacalle Pou's approach in 2014 might reflect imitation of the Broad Front's successful example, yet it could also result from an inward-oriented reaction. Observing future elections would help to determine if Uruguayan candidates have actually converged on positive, unity-oriented campaigns.

Ecuador, South Korea, and the Philippines: The Limits to Success Contagion

While seven of the ten countries examined in this section illustrate patterns of electioneering that are broadly consistent with success contagion, the three remaining countries – Ecuador, South Korea, and the Philippines – present at least partially disconfirming evidence. In each country, some of the campaign strategies employed in recent elections contradict what we would expect based on the success or failure of initial governing experiences. However, these three countries share certain characteristics that set them apart from the others examined in this section and serve to confirm several limitations to the scope of success contagion. All three have personality-centered party systems in which there is little organizational continuity from one election to the next, a characteristic that makes success contagion less likely to apply. Moreover, both Ecuador and the Philippines deviate from the predictions of success contagion largely because of the presence of a series of neopopulist outsiders in recent elections. As in Peru, the partial or total collapse of a country's traditional party system may create unoccupied space that neopopulist candidates are able to fill on a repeated basis, regardless of whether this campaign strategy was ever legitimated by a successful governing experience.

Ecuador
Ecuador is a mixed case with respect to success contagion, presenting confirming evidence during the 1980s when its traditional party system was largely intact, but contradicting this theory in more recent elections. During the first several presidential campaigns after its transition to democracy, Ecuadorian candidates converged on a policy-centric campaign strategy. In the words of Villavicencio (1988: 14–15), "since 1978, the two great winners of the second rounds of the election...have maintained the constant tactic of using electoral offers; in other words, the possible, reliable, and believable proposal." In 1978, victorious left-wing candidate Jaime Roldós "conceived of the action of government within ideological and programmatic channels condensed in the

21 points of his electoral platform" (Argones 1985: 102).[2] In 1984, right-wing candidate León Febres Cordero won the runoff with a campaign that emphasized "Bread, Housing, Jobs" and other specific promises (Argones 1985: 146; Villavicencio 1988: 20–21). By the time of the 1988 election, both major candidates were focusing on policy (Villavicencio 1988). Rodrigo Borja placed substantial emphasis on his government program and sought to present himself as a statesman surrounded by qualified specialists (Montúfar 1990: 170). His opponent Abdalá Bucaram also oriented his campaign around proposals, though these were much more demagogic and contradictory than Borja's (Montúfar 1990: 169; Freidenberg 2003: 395).

Ecuadorian candidates' strategic convergence during the 1980s is consistent with the logic of success contagion, since the politician originally associated with the policy-centric campaign strategy, Jaime Roldós, was a fairly popular president. Just before Roldós died in a plane crash in May 1981, 44 percent approved of his performance in office; this figure had been as high as 58 percent only several months prior ("Aprobación al Presidente Sube con Caso Colombia" 2008). At the time of the 1984 election, Roldós was remembered very positively; a majority of Ecuadorians thought that the country would be better off if he were still president (Argones 1985: 127). Success contagion would thus predict convergence on the strategy of Roldós's 1978 campaign, as we see with respect to policy focus during the 1980s.

Though there is evidence of success contagion in Ecuador at a time when its traditional party system was largely intact, this pattern broke down following party system collapse in the 1990s. During the 1980s, Abdalá Bucaram's personality-centered Ecuadorian Roldosist Party (Partido Roldosista Ecuatoriano, PRE) shared the stage with three traditional parties, the Social Christian Party (Partido Social Cristiano, PSC), Democratic Left (Izquierda Democrática, ID), and Popular Democracy (Democracia Popular, DP). Together, these four parties captured approximately half to three-quarters of the vote in congressional elections from 1984 to 2002 (Pachano 2006: 106; Sánchez 2008: 326). Yet each party was at least partially discredited by the low popularity and poor performance of the president it put into office during this period – Febres Cordero (PSC, 1984–1988), Borja (ID, 1988–1992), Bucaram (PRE, 1996–1997), and Jamil Mahuad (DP, 1998–2000). After falling out of favor, none of these parties was granted a second chance by voters; their presidential candidates placed no better than fourth in the 2002, 2006, 2009, and 2013 elections.

The collapse of Ecuador's traditional party system effectively put an end to the strategic convergence of the 1980s. By all accounts, recent campaigns in Ecuador have varied with respect to policy focus. In 2002, independent candidate Lucio Gutiérrez ran for office with only a vague campaign platform (Quintero 2005: 127). His anti-establishment successor, Rafael Correa, made

---

[2] Roldós's major opponent on the right, Sixto Durán, avoided specific proposals (Villavicencio 1988: 20).

much more specific policy commitments during the 2006 campaign, particularly in the second round (Conaghan 2007a; Echeverría 2007; León 2007).
Like Argentina, therefore, Ecuador supports the argument that a major party
system change can dislodge strategic convergence.

While the campaigns of recent Ecuadorian presidential candidates have varied in terms of policy focus, they have converged in a very different way that
cannot be accounted for by the theory of success contagion. In 2002, 2006,
2009, and 2013, major candidates of both Right and Left employed neopopulist
strategies, priming cleavages and relying on direct linkages. In 2002, Gutiérrez
ran for president with the support of a personal electoral vehicle and adopted an
anti-corruption discourse that sought to prime the cleavage between the people
and the political class (Quintero 2005; Sánchez 2008: 327). His major opponent on the right, Álvaro Noboa, ran on the ticket of his own personal electoral
vehicle, emphasizing traditional ideological cleavages with an anti-communist
discourse (Quintero 2005). Likewise, the 2006 election pitted Noboa, using a
similar strategy, against Correa, who founded his own Proud Sovereign Country
Movement, sought out direct connections to voters, and aimed to exploit popular dissatisfaction with the country's political and economic elite (Conaghan
2007a, 2007b, 2008; Sánchez 2008: 327; de la Torre and Conaghan 2009).
Correa, Gutiérrez, and Noboa all competed against one another again in 2009
and 2013, employing similar strategies as in their previous bids (Bowen 2010;
Freidenberg 2011; de la Torre 2013). The second-place candidate in 2013,
Guillermo Lasso, would not fit the neopopulist characterization, but like his
competitors, he relied on direct linkages and was supported by a personal electoral vehicle (de la Torre 2013).

The recurrence of neopopulism in recent Ecuadorian elections contradicts
the theory of success contagion because convergence on this strategy began
well before a neopopulist president had served a successful term in office. The
first major candidate to run as a neopopulist outsider was Bucaram, who competed in several presidential elections and won in 1996 (Burbano de Lara 1992;
de la Torre 1994, 1999, 2000; Freidenberg 2003). Yet Bucaram was perhaps
Ecuador's clearest example of governing failure since its transition to democracy. After fewer than six months in office, Congress voted to remove him from
the presidency on the grounds of "mental incapacity," and he went into exile to
escape corruption charges. Gutiérrez, elected in 2002, was also removed from
office by a congressional vote after massive anti-government demonstrations
in 2005. Correa marks an exception – he has enjoyed consistently high levels
of public approval (Basabe-Serrano and Martínez 2014) – but convergence on
neopopulism was well established prior to that point.

In sum, the initial contagion of policy-centric campaign appeals and the
departure from this strategy after the collapse of Ecuador's traditional party
system are both consistent with the logic of success contagion. However,
candidates' convergence on neopopulist strategies in 2002 and 2005 presents
a greater problem for the theory, since it happened well before Correa's

successful neopopulist presidency. The recurrence of neopopulism in Ecuador seems to adhere to a similar logic as in Peru, whereby the demise of traditional parties opens up space in the party system for opportunistic outsiders who prime cleavages and utilize direct linkages. As Ecuador was a case of complete rather than partial party system collapse, neopopulists were able to occupy this available space across the political spectrum in 2002, 2006, 2009, and 2013.

The Philippines

The Philippines is similar to Ecuador in that the theory of success contagion is contradicted by the rise of neopopulist outsiders in recent elections. The 1998 presidential election in the Philippines was won by Joseph "Erap" Estrada, a neopopulist former movie star. Adopting the slogan "Erap for the Poor," he described himself as an outcast of the Philippine elite and openly criticized rich and middle-class voters who did not support him (Laquian and Laquian 1998: 111; Case 1999; Rood 2002: 158). He also made a direct appeal to the masses, privileged face-to-face campaigning, and ran on the ticket of his own personal electoral vehicle, the Party of the Filipino Masses (Laquian and Laquian 1998; Rood 2002: 155). Midway through his term as president, Estrada was impeached on corruption charges and forced from office by a popular uprising. However, fellow movie star Fernando Poe, Jr. launched a similar neopopulist bid for the presidency in 2004 (Rogers 2004; Teehankee 2010), and Estrada himself returned as a candidate in 2010, repeating his strategy from 1998. Meanwhile, Manny Villar resurrected the largely defunct Nacionalista Party as a personal vehicle for his own populist bid in 2010, criticizing the elite and casting himself as one of the masses (Teehankee 2010; Thompson 2010). Neopopulism in the Philippines has been limited to the left-hand side of the political spectrum – neither Jose de Venecia, Gloria Macapagal-Arroyo, nor Benigno Aquino sought to prime cleavages in their 1998, 2004, and 2010 campaigns – but it has become a crucial feature of Philippine electoral politics in recent years.

The theory of success contagion would not predict the rise of neopopulist outsiders in the Philippines because the first president to serve a successful term in office did not employ such a strategy. In 1986, Corazon Aquino, the widow of a former senator and key opposition figure, became president after an electoral campaign that sought to unify the country against dictator Ferdinand Marcos (Crisostomo 1987). In 1992, Aquino's successor, Fidel V. Ramos, similarly emphasized national unity and his own role in the struggle to oust Marcos (Crisostomo 1997: 196–198). Aquino's success or failure in office is somewhat difficult to score, but Ramos was unambiguously successful as president and enjoyed high approval ratings in the lead-up to the 1998 election (Bolongaita 1999; Case 1999; Montinola 1999; Social Weather Stations 2007).[3] Thus,

---

[3] Aquino's presidency was dogged by corruption scandals and has been described as a failure (Fontaine 1992; Timberman 1992), and her popularity declined over the course of her term.

Estrada's cleavage-priming approach in 1998 deviated from the unity-oriented campaign strategy that should have been legitimated by either Aquino's or Ramos's term in office.

Though the recurrence of neopopulism in the Philippines contradicts the theory of success contagion, a focus on "available space" in the Philippine party system helps explain this phenomenon. In a similar fashion to Peru, space became available on the left-hand side of the Philippine political spectrum after 1986, and neopopulist outsiders stepped in to fill the void in recent elections. Throughout much of the twentieth century, the Philippine partisan Left participated actively in electoral politics (Quimpo 2005: 7–8). During the 1972–1986 Marcos regime, however, the newly founded Communist Party of the Philippines (CPP) rejected electoral participation in favor of an armed insurrectionary strategy. After Marcos's fall, the CPP and other new Left groups remained ambivalent about electoral politics; many of them accepted elections as an instrument through which they could accumulate forces for class struggle but did not participate wholeheartedly (Quimpo 2005). As a result, the traditional partisan Left never established much of an electoral foothold in the new Philippine democracy, and it has been virtually absent at the presidential level, leaving ample space for neopopulist outsiders to prime class cleavages.[4]

South Korea

South Korea is a final case in which the evolution of campaign strategies is not well explained by success contagion. Since its transition from authoritarian rule in 1987, South Korea has witnessed repeated governing failures, and each president has been highly unpopular by the end of his term. Roh Tae Woo (1987–1992) had the lowest approval rating of any previous Korean president by the time of the next election (Lee and Glasure 1995). Kim Young Sam (1992–1997) ended his term with single-digit approval thanks to the Asian economic crisis (Park 1998). Kim Dae Jung (1997–2002) suffered from influence-peddling and corruption scandals and was "largely discredited" by 2002 because of North Korea's acquisition of nuclear weapons (H. Y. Lee 2003; Walker and Kang 2004). Roh Moo Hyun (2002–2007) had become one of Korea's most unpopular presidents by the end of his term, largely because of his inability to translate economic growth into lower inequality (Armstrong

---

However, she still had more approval than disapproval by the eve of the 1992 campaign (Social Weather Stations 2007).

[4] An unusual feature of the Philippine electoral system may also help to explain Estrada's neopopulist campaign in 1998. Philippine presidents and vice presidents are elected separately, rather than on the same ticket. Estrada initially launched a presidential bid in the 1992 election, but later withdrew to run for vice president, winning by a large margin. At the time of the 1998 election, therefore, Estrada was also a popular incumbent, and he had won in 1992 using a very different strategy than Ramos. Under such circumstances, it seems logical that Estrada would repeat his successful formula from 1992.

2008: 126; Hahm 2008; Hundt 2008; Lie and Kim 2008). Finally, Lee Myung-Bak (2007–2012) had fairly weak support throughout his presidency, thanks to numerous scandals and an unpopular foreign policy stance; his approval rating had dropped to 20 percent by the time of the next election (Sohn and Kang 2013).

In the context of repeated governing failures, the theory of success contagion would predict inward-oriented reactions and continued strategic diversity among parties and candidates. Yet most of the literature on electoral campaigns in South Korea emphasizes the continuity of political strategies during the post-dictatorship period and similarities rather than differences in the approaches of competing candidates. In Korea's highly personalized political system, direct linkages prevail, and parties have not served as an important form of intermediation for any candidate. Rather, parties are "more akin to personal entourages than to public institutions" (Hahm 2008: 130), and "leading political personalities have viewed parties as disposable vehicles for their personal electoral ambitions" (Heo and Stockton 2005: 685; see also Armstrong 2008; Hundt 2008; Kang and Jaung 1999; Steinberg and Shin 2006). Roh Moo Hyun, whose linkage strategy is often considered innovative due to his reliance on an Internet-based support group in 2002 (Cho 2003; H. Y. Lee 2003), was nonetheless consistent with this strategy of utilizing direct linkages and running a highly personalized campaign.

Cleavage priming is also relatively uncommon in Korean presidential campaigns. The electoral support base for major parties and political figures often varies substantially across different parts of the country, reflecting South Korea's deep regional divides (Kang 2003). Yet existing analyses of specific campaigns present few examples of presidential candidates priming regional cleavages for electoral gain. Rather, they describe numerous cases in which candidates specifically cast themselves as national unity figures in an effort to overcome a regionally concentrated base of support (Han 1988; Lee 1990: 76; Lee 1995: 57; Park 2002: 134; Cho 2003; H. W. Lee 2003; Hahm 2008). The one exception to candidates' avoidance of cleavage priming concerns the 1992 campaign of Kim Young Sam, who used "red scare" tactics against his left-wing opponent Kim Dae Jung (Lee 1993; Lee 1995; Park 2002: 136).[5]

Finally, Korean electoral campaigns tend to have a low policy focus and lack debate on substantive issues. Rather, candidates' electoral appeals typically center on the nature of the regime, political leadership, and abstract national objectives – a feature that has been attributed to the personality-centered rather than programmatic nature of parties (Park 2002: 136). In 2002, for instance, both Lee Hoi Chang and Roh Moo Hyun focused their campaigns on principles,

---

[5] Park (2002: 145) suggests that priming regional cleavages is a common tactic in Korean campaigns. Yet I found no specific examples of such cleavage priming in presidential elections. It may be a more common tactic in legislative or regional races that do not target the entire national electorate.

making it difficult for voters to distinguish between their platforms (H. W. Lee 2003). This pattern may be changing – Lee Myung-Bak in 2007, and both major candidates in 2012, placed greater emphasis on specific economic proposals (Hundt 2008; Kwon 2010; Sohn and Kang 2013; H. Kim 2014; Y. Kim 2014). However, even if candidates are now converging on policy-centered campaigns, the change cannot be attributed to success contagion since there have been no popular incumbents.

In sum, presidential election campaigns in Korea have tended to involve strategic continuity and common approaches among competing candidates, in contrast to the zigzags and diversity of approaches predicted by success contagion. The most likely explanation concerns the continuity of major political figures from the pre- to post-dictatorship period. As Heo and Stockton (2005: 683) have argued, "in Korea, democracy did not bring new competitors into the party system and Koreans selected from the same menu as they had historically. The extant political personalities were powerful enough to block the emergence of new political actors, so the party system configuration changed little." Both Kim Young Sam (a major candidate in 1987 and 1992) and Kim Dae Jung (who ran in 1987, 1992, and 1997) were key politicians during the pre-dictatorship period. Kim Dae Jung had previously run for president in 1971, and Kim Young Sam was a longtime member of the National Assembly, first elected in 1954. Hence, the politicians who dominated Korean presidential elections in the decade after democratization likely brought with them well-established campaign strategies and techniques from the previous democratic era. They would have been less likely to seek out new approaches through any of the mechanisms related to success contagion. In no other country examined in this study was there anywhere near as much continuity of major political figures from pre- to post-dictatorship.[6]

Reviewing and Assessing the Evidence

On the whole, the test of success contagion conducted in this section is encouraging for the theory. As summarized in Table 5.1, its predictions are supported in seven out of ten countries, and partially supported in an eighth. In Benin, Mali, Ghana, and Nicaragua, major presidential candidates converged upon national unity strategies and have avoided priming cleavages in their electoral campaigns. Strategic convergence in each of these countries can be linked to

---

[6] Chile did see some continuity in terms of the parties that dominated electoral politics before and after the period of military rule. However, there was less continuity of individual politicians than in Korea. Of the major figures involved in the transition process, only Patricio Aylwin had previously run for elected office. Almost all the leaders of the partisan Right in Chile's new democracy had been students or young professionals, rather than seasoned politicians, prior to the 1973 coup.

TABLE 5.1. *Testing Success Contagion*

Country	Theory Supported	Candidates Converge	Summary of Argument
Benin	Yes	Yes	Transition govt. legitimates unity strategies
Mali	Yes	Yes	Transition govt. legitimates unity strategies
Ghana	Yes	Yes	Successful govt. legitimates unity strategies
Nicaragua	Yes	Yes	Successful govt. legitimates unity strategies
Argentina	Yes	Yes: 1990s	Repeated failure → inward-oriented reactions
		No: 1980s, 2000s	Contagion ends with party system change
Uruguay	Yes	No	Repeated failure → inward-oriented reactions
Honduras	Yes	No	Repeated failure → inward-oriented reactions
Ecuador	Partially	Yes	Contagion ends with party system change Open space → recurrent neopopulism
The Philippines	No	No	Open space → recurrent neopopulism
South Korea	No	Yes	Political continuity pre-/post-dictatorship limits theory's applicability

the legitimating role of either the successful transition government or the first successful elected government. Three additional cases – Argentina, Uruguay, and Honduras – show evidence of back-and-forth shifts in campaign strategy that suggest inward-oriented reactions. As predicted by the theory of success contagion, we see this particular zigzag pattern in countries where there have been repeated governing failures. Argentina also illustrates strategic convergence during the 1990s, following Menem's successful first term in office. Finally, Ecuadorian candidates converged on a strategy of high policy focus in the 1980s, an outcome that is also consistent with success contagion. Only after the collapse of Ecuador's party system does the theory become less useful for explaining campaign dynamics.

Though the evolution of presidential campaign strategies in Ecuador, the Philippines, and South Korea contradicts the predictions of success contagion in important ways, each of these countries has one or more features that should make the theory less likely to apply. In South Korea, democratization in 1987 implied much less of an electoral tabula rasa than in other countries examined in this study. On the contrary, its transition to democracy marked the return of politicians who had played a key role in the previous democratic era and had even run for president in the past. Rather than being uncertain about the process of electioneering, they were likely to have developed their own reliable approaches prior to the interruption of democratic rule. They would thus have much less incentive to choose new strategies through any of the mechanisms related to success contagion.

The Philippines lies at the other end of the spectrum of political continuity. Democratization marked a clear break from the parties and personalities who had dominated elections in the previous democratic era, but it did not bring any new regularity to electoral politics. The two-party system of the pre-dictatorship period was replaced with a system of excessive fluidity. Existing parties in the Philippines are largely the fiefdoms of a few powerful individuals, and dissenting elites routinely craft personal electoral vehicles when they cannot secure the nomination of established parties. This characteristic – largely shared with Peru – has meant that there is little organizational continuity from one election to the next. Yet in contrast to Peru, the Philippines has also seen little *individual* continuity across elections. From 1986 to 2010, the only major repeat candidacy was that of Joseph Estrada in 1998 and 2010. As discussed in Chapter 1, the theory of success contagion is less likely to apply when there is neither organizational nor individual continuity from one election to the next, since there is less potential for learning over time.

Finally, both Ecuador and the Philippines have seen significant political space opened up within their party systems, either by the reluctance of the partisan Left to embrace electoral competition or by the withering of traditional parties on both sides of the ideological spectrum. These are countries with high levels of inequality falling along class and ethnic lines, which provides fertile ground for neopopulist outsiders to gain electoral support by priming cleavages and preying upon dissatisfaction with the status quo. As long as sufficient space has been made available in the country's party system, therefore, it appears that neopopulism can be repeated by at least one major candidate in each election, even if this political strategy has never produced a successful government. Moreover, it is possible for multiple candidates to converge on neopopulist strategies through a process distinct from success contagion, as has happened in Ecuador.

Ecuador presents an important contrast with Peru: the former has seen repeat candidacies by neopopulist outsiders who do *not* change their strategies, whereas in the latter, most candidates running a second time make major strategic modifications. The difference may lie in the extent to which traditional parties and politicians met their demise in each country. In Peru, even if one considers traditional *parties* to have collapsed, traditional party *politicians* were major candidates in both 2001 and 2006. As such, they were much less likely to adopt the neopopulist strategy of running against the system. In Ecuador, by contrast, there were no traditional party politicians among the major candidates in 1998, 2002, 2006, 2009, or 2013. Ecuador's party system collapse was more definitive than that of Peru, and it created more space across the ideological spectrum – not only on the left – for neopopulist outsiders. Correa, Gutiérrez, and Noboa have also been able to play off one another in successive contests, each casting himself as defender of the people against the threat posed by one or both opponents and the social currents they represent. The phrase "serial populism" (Roberts 2006) – conveying the notion of a self-sustaining political dynamic favoring anti-establishment outsiders – much more aptly describes recent electoral dynamics in Ecuador than in Peru.

The cases of Ecuador, South Korea, and the Philippines, therefore, allow us to confirm one stated limitation to the scope of success contagion and also formulate several others. As discussed in Chapter 1, success contagion is less likely to apply where there has been little organizational as well as individual continuity in electoral politics since a country's transition to democracy. We can also add that the theory may not hold when there is a high degree of continuity between the pre- and post-dictatorship periods in terms of the specific politicians running for office. Finally, success contagion may not apply when all or part of a country's traditional party system has collapsed, leaving space for neopopulist outsiders who mobilize support by priming cleavages and making direct appeals to the public.

CAMPAIGN STRATEGIES AND THE QUALITY OF DEMOCRACY

At the outset of this study, I argued that presidential campaign strategies are substantively important because of their implications for the quality of democracy, an umbrella concept that embodies notions such as participation, representation, and patterns of future governance. In conclusion, it is worth revisiting these earlier claims about the broader repercussions of campaign strategies, drawing upon specific evidence from Chile, Brazil, and Peru.

In Chile, the Concertación's approach to the 1988 plebiscite campaign inaugurated a style of politics that has been described as "democracy by agreement," with pervasive consensus-seeking among political elites and little room for the participation of organized intermediary groups (Siavelis 2008). Just as Concertación candidates have relied on direct linkages and sought to circumvent unions, social movements, and grassroots-level political party structures during electoral campaigns, Concertación governments from 1990 to 2010 granted these entities little input into major policy decisions. In negotiating a tax reform package in 1990, for instance, Concertación leaders largely ignored the input of organized civil society (Boylen 1996). Moreover, politicians' avoidance of cleavage-priming confrontation in both electoral appeals and subsequent governing has meant that issues related to the divergent interests of different social groups are largely absent from the political agenda. Where a policy issue enjoys consensus among political elites of Right and Left, such as targeted social spending to reduce extreme policy, the Concertación was able to make major strides. However, it made little progress from 1990 to 2010 on those issues that get to the heart of class divides, such as increasing the tax burden on the wealthy in order to address high rates of inequality (Fairfield 2010, 2015).

Though democracy by agreement has allowed for impressive economic growth and political stability in Chile, it has also contributed to a growing sense of popular alienation with politics. In the 2008 Latinobarómetro, Chile had the lowest score among eighteen Latin American countries on an index of political participation. It was also the country where people were most skeptical that they could change things in their lives through either the act of voting or participating in public protests (Latinobarómetro 2008: 97–98).

Paradoxically, Chile seems to be stuck in a situation where the elite-dominated, top-down style of politics that is so alienating to citizens is also the only one that allows for effective governance. In her 2005–2006 presidential campaign, Michelle Bachelet sought to respond to this popular dissatisfaction, emphasizing her distance from traditional political parties and her desire to empower individual people rather than political elites. Yet the style of politics she established during her "citizen campaign" complicated subsequent attempts to govern. Bachelet's anti-party stance during the election translated into strained relations with congressional legislators, even from her own coalition. In preparing policy initiatives in several key areas – education, pensions, and electoral system reform – Bachelet created advisory committees without any input from party leaders. Unsurprisingly, party leaders proceeded to reject the committees' proposals (Navia 2008). The result was significant delay or legislative stalemate in each of these areas – a sharp contrast with the normal efficiency of democracy by agreement.

Despite skepticism in opinion polls about the efficacy of popular protest, Chilean students took to the streets in massive numbers in 2011–2012 to demand changes to a largely privatized and expensive educational system that limits opportunities for the middle class, along with increased taxes on the wealthy to fund greater educational spending. Though protestors criticized the response of the newly inaugurated center-right Piñera government as inept, slow, and insufficient, their efforts eventually helped pressure the government to pass a permanent corporate tax increase (Fairfield 2015a). Yet the fact that this reform could only be achieved through massive popular mobilization speaks to the shortcomings of a style of electoral politics where social conflict and policy focus are minimized. Neither tax nor educational reform figured prominently in the 2009–2010 presidential campaign. With inequality squarely on the political agenda after the student protests, Bachelet's 2013 campaign did propose a further corporate tax increase that was later enacted during her second presidency, but this departure from electoral politics as usual was due primarily to the student mobilizations temporarily shifting actors' strategic calculus (Fairfield 2015a, 2015b). Under democracy by agreement, battles over major social issues may be fought out in the streets, but they are much less frequently waged in the electoral arena.

In Brazil, candidates' convergence on policy-focused electoral appeals has had clear positive implications for accountability and democratic representation, which one can appreciate by comparing efforts at market reform under Collor and Cardoso. In 1989, Collor ran for office primarily by emphasizing change, moral renewal, and a new style of politics rather than a specific policy platform. Yet immediately after taking office, he implemented drastic shock therapy measures that in no way had been foreshadowed by his campaign, such as freezing 70–80 percent of Brazil's liquidity for eighteen months (Weyland 2002: 115–116). Had this policy intention been made clear before the runoff, voters might well have opted for Lula, who was only narrowly defeated. In contrast, Cardoso's policy-centric campaign in Brazil's 1994 election sought and achieved a clear mandate for his ensuing reform agenda. Though elements of Cardoso's reforms remain unpopular – in particular, charges of corruption in the privatization of state firms – none of the policies he implemented could be cast as "neoliberalism by surprise" (Stokes 2001).

The move away from cleavage priming has been more of a mixed bag for Brazilian democracy, with some clear benefits but also certain drawbacks. Collor's confrontational rhetoric and attacks on the political class helped him win the 1989 election, but by maintaining a similar stance in office, he ended up with few political allies and encountered governing difficulties (Schneider 1991; Weyland 1993; Panizza 2000). Given Brazil's highly fragmented party system, no single party stands a chance of gaining a majority in Congress; even pre-electoral coalitions must typically be expanded after the president takes office in order to gain a reliable base of support for his policies. "Coalitional presidentialism" – the standard approach to governing in Brazil – is facilitated by campaigns that do not prime cleavages, such as those of Cardoso in the 1990s and Lula in the 2000s. Though the bargains used to build these coalitions are often distasteful, and sometimes illegal (Samuels 2008), governing through political give-and-take between elected legislators and the president is arguably preferable to Collor's modus operandi of enacting major policies through unilateral decree (Lamounier 2003).

At the same time, the abandonment of cleavage priming by the Left has meant important issues that deserve a place in public debate have largely remained off the policy agenda. While in opposition, the PT had long championed an "inversion of priorities" – governing in a manner that would benefit subaltern groups by helping to transform the conditions that produced their marginalization (Samuels 2013). Chief among these policy goals was agrarian reform, given the highly concentrated nature of wealth and landholdings in Brazil. Yet as the PT shifted toward a less divisive campaign rhetoric, it placed much less emphasis on this issue. Governing has followed the approach of the 2002 campaign rather than the party's historical commitments; the Lula government did little to address inequality in land tenure (Carter 2010). Certainly, the PT government's policies have improved the lives of many of Brazil's poor, by raising the minimum wage, improving access to consumer credit, and redistributing income through the conditional cash transfer program Bolsa Família. However, these policies do not address some of the major structural causes of poverty.

Lula's shift away from intermediated linkages has also contributed to a narrowing of the political agenda. Had Lula won the 1989 election, he might well have shifted to the center once in office, as has often been the case with elected leftist politicians. However, traditional popular-sector allies such as the Landless Rural Workers' Movement and the Unified Workers' Central, which played a large role in the 1989 campaign, would have been in a stronger position to demand that their concerns remain at the top of the PT's governing agenda. By contrast, Lula's victorious 2002 campaign relied much more heavily on direct linkages. Owing less of a campaign debt to traditional civil society allies, he had greater freedom to ignore their primary demands while in office.

It should be underscored that the elite-dominated, top-down style of governance that one finds in Chile, and to a lesser extent in Brazil, is not the inevitable product of convergence in campaign strategies per se. Rather, it results from convergence on a style of electioneering that deemphasizes cleavages, circumvents intermediated linkages, and, in the case of Chile, minimizes policy content. There may be exceptions to these trends – Nicaragua, despite the limited cleavage priming in presidential campaigns, has not witnessed the same narrowing of the political agenda as one sees in Brazil and Chile (Levitsky and Roberts 2011). However, the general pattern seems to be that when major battles between competing interests are deemphasized during the campaign, they are also unlikely to be taken up after the election.

Given the failure of Peruvian candidates to adopt a common approach to electioneering, the evolution of campaign strategies in this country has very different implications for the quality of democracy than in Chile or Brazil. The lack of strategic convergence in Peru, combined with the recurrent candidacies of neopopulist outsiders, has meant that presidential elections present voters with a much broader array of options. Citizens are consequently much more engaged during electoral periods than in many other Latin American countries. In the 2006 Latinobarómetro survey, Peru had the second-highest level of electoral participation in Latin America, with 88 percent reporting that they voted in the recent presidential contest (Latinobarómetro 2006: 20). During campaigns, Peruvians attend the rallies of major candidates in much greater numbers, and with much more visible enthusiasm, than in neighboring Chile and Brazil.

However, the aspect of Peruvian elections that tends to generate such enthusiastic participation – the presence of neopopulist outsiders among the field of major candidates, significantly raising the stakes of each contest – has also created major problems for Peruvian democracy. The nature of neopopulist appeals, pledging a resolution to the myriad injustices suffered by Peru's poor, indigenous population, creates often unrealistic expectations of radical change. Alejandro Toledo suffered a dramatic loss of support and recurrent popular protests against his government after shifting from a cleavage-priming campaign to a market-oriented economic policy that boosted inequality (Taylor 2007). On the other hand, a neopopulist who went on to govern in the divisive manner that he campaigned – as Ollanta Humala might have done if he had won in 2006 rather than in 2011 – could create an entirely different set of problems. In Peru's fragmented party system, no neopopulist has any hope of winning a single-party legislative majority, so an intransigent stance in office would likely lead to policy immobilism.

The electoral polarization generated by neopopulist campaigns can have negative consequences for governance even when a less divisive opponent is the winner. After Peru's bitterly fought 2006 election, García attributed his victory to the support of more moderate, middle- and upper-class voters in Lima and the coast, not to the poorer populations in the Amazon and Southern highlands who overwhelmingly voted for Humala. Consequently, he interpreted his mandate as serving middle-class and business interests by maintaining existing market-friendly economic policies without pursuing any significant income redistribution. Though García and his historically center-left party arguably had the opportunity to address Peru's entrenched inequality, the divisiveness of the election in which he triumphed may have encouraged him not to do so. The result was significant social unrest, including violent protests against García's government, despite impressive macroeconomic performance (Cameron 2011).

After reviewing the broad ramifications of candidates' campaign strategies in Chile, Brazil, and Peru, it should be clear that they can matter for more than just the outcome of an election. In this context, it is important to understand how and why the campaign strategies of presidential candidates in new democracies can evolve in such different directions over time. The value of the theory of success contagion is that it provides a clear, flexible, yet also falsifiable framework for answering this question. By explaining how politicians approach the public in a bid for their support, and why they do so differently in different national contexts, we ultimately gain a better understanding of three fundamental aspects of politics – the relationship between elites and citizens, the role of societal divisions versus national unity, and the policy agendas that will take future governments down alternative paths.

APPENDIX A

Methodology for the Content Analysis of Television Advertising

This Appendix contains methodological details on the content analysis of television advertising from presidential election campaigns in Chile, Peru, and Brazil. As discussed in Chapter 1, the results of this content analysis, in conjunction with other data, are used to measure the policy focus and cleavage-priming dimensions of different candidates' campaigns.

TELEVISION ADVERTISING FORMATS

Chile, Brazil, and Peru differ somewhat in the form of television advertising allowed during electoral campaigns. In Chile and Brazil, candidates are not allowed to purchase ads; instead, they receive blocks of government-sponsored airtime which run simultaneously on all broadcast television channels during the thirty to sixty days before the first-round vote and two to three weeks before the second-round vote. Individual programs are typically between two and ten minutes long, depending on the number of contenders and, in Brazil, the size of each candidate's congressional delegation.[1] In recent elections, Peru has also allocated free time to presidential candidates, but it also permits paid advertising, which is far more prominent. The typical campaign ad in Peru, therefore, is a thirty-second spot interspersed among commercial advertisements.

In Chile and Brazil, the same presidential advertisements are broadcast nationally. In Peru, candidates may buy ads in local media markets, though such targeting is rare in presidential elections. Campaign advertising programs in Brazil are aired both at mid-day and during prime time, though broadcasts in

---

[1] Since 1996, Brazil has also allowed fifteen-, thirty-, and sixty-second campaign spots to be aired for free at various times throughout the day. I did not examine these spots because (a) they are often included as segments in the longer broadcasts, and (b) they are only available for part of the period under study.

these time slots are often quite similar, and campaigns always treat the prime-time slot as more important. In Chile, presidential campaign advertising typically alternates between a mid-day and a prime-time slot on successive days.

The relevant population for the content analysis consists of all campaign advertising on national broadcast television aired by the presidential candidates listed in Table 1.3 (Chapter 1), with the exception of those from Peru's 1995 and 2000 elections. I was able to acquire and analyze the vast majority of this material. Advertising from the 2009–2011 electoral cycle was obtained from the major candidates' YouTube channels; for the 2005–2006 campaigns, I recorded it directly. For earlier years, I obtained copies of videos from a variety of archival sources, which are listed in the Acknowledgments.

In Brazil, I analyzed only the evening electoral broadcasts, following existing studies (e.g., Porto and Guazina 1999; Porto 2007). Viewership for daytime electoral broadcasts is lower, and Brazilian campaign strategists consider this advertising space less important than the prime-time broadcast; often, the daytime slot simply repeats the previous night's program. I was able to obtain most of the evening broadcasts for every major candidate since 1989; in no case was I missing more than 25 percent of episodes, and in most cases, the figure was closer to 5 percent. For candidates who had broadcast more than four hours of advertising in any one election, I analyzed a systematic random sample of half of the episodes from that campaign (i.e., every other episode with a random start). In other cases, I analyzed all episodes.

In Chile, I obtained all broadcasts (daytime and prime time) for major candidates except for the first four days of Büchi's advertising in 1989. I analyzed all of this material, except for the 1988 plebiscite, in which I analyzed a systematic random sample of half of the episodes. In contrast to Brazil, there is no strong justification for excluding daytime broadcasts in Chile. In elections without a concurrent legislative race (1999–2000, and the second-round elections in 2006 and 2010), presidential candidates receive free television advertising in both time slots, and they typically repeat programs. In all other elections, however, legislative and presidential candidates alternate daytime and evening slots on successive days, and candidates generally produce different programs for each slot.

In Peru, I analyzed all spots I was able to obtain. Because of the nature of campaign advertising in Peru – broadcast at various times throughout the day and on different channels – it is more difficult to assess the completeness of this collection. For the most recent two elections, I was able to check the collection against data on spots aired in Lima from the tracking firm MediaCheck. For 2006, I am missing only a handful of spots aired two to four times. For 2011, the collection is more spotty but still includes the majority of candidates' advertisements. For earlier years, I have no independent source of verification, but since I obtained most of these spots directly from the advertising producers themselves, the collection should be fairly comprehensive.

CODING PROCEDURE

Following Porto's approach for Brazil (Porto and Guazina 1999; Porto 2007), I used a combination of the appeal and the segment as the recording unit. Segments typically change with a change in speaker, but within individual segments, there may be multiple distinct appeals. For example, a candidate might criticize the incumbent government for its failure to control inflation (one appeal) and then discuss his own policy proposals in that area (a second appeal). Spots, because they are shorter than free electoral broadcasts, contain fewer distinct segments or appeals. Across all content analyzed, the average length of a unit was twenty-two seconds.

A common coding scheme was used for the analysis of all three countries. The principal categories that are relevant to this book's argument include whether the segment was devoted to policy (versus image, ideology, values, partisan affiliation, jingles, or the conduct of the campaign itself) and whether it engaged in cleavage priming. Among segments devoted to policy, relevant subcategories include whether the appeal conveyed criticism, an acclaim, or diagnosis; whether it concerned the future, present, or past; and whether the policy discussion was specific or general. Appendix B describes these categories in greater detail. For policy-related segments, I also coded the specific policy area being discussed.

SUMMARY STATISTICS

The summary statistics presented in this study give the percentage of a candidate's total advertising time that falls into the categories and subcategories listed above. In the text and tables, I use the term "proposals" to refer to acclaims about future policy, and "achievements" for acclaims about past or present policies. In calculating summary statistics, I weight each coded unit according to its elapsed time, as well as the frequency or estimated frequency with which the corresponding spot or episode was broadcast. In Brazil and Chile, data on broadcast frequency can be readily obtained because broadcasts occur at a specific time of day on all channels. In Peru, such data are more difficult to come by since spots air at different times on different channels. For the 2006 and 2011 elections, I use data from the tracking firm MediaCheck, which gives broadcast frequency for all campaign spots on all over-the-air television stations in Lima. For the 2001 election, I use the frequency with which each spot appeared in an archival collection of daily recordings of morning and evening news broadcasts during the campaign, housed at the Instituto Prensa y Sociedad in Lima. For earlier elections, I assume that broadcast frequency is inversely proportional to length; a thirty-second spot is broadcast twice as often as a 60-second spot.

TABLE A.1. *Results of Inter-Coder Reliability Testing*

Coding Decision	Country/Coder					
	Chile A	Chile C	Brazil B	Brazil C	Peru A	Peru C
Policy focus (yes vs. no)	88%	70%	82%	89%	92%	85%
Policy: acclaims vs. criticism vs. diagnosis	84%	59%	80%	54%	82%	28%
Policy acclaims: future vs. past/present	54%	100%	96%	95%	58%	83%
Future policy acclaims: specific vs. general	100%	67%	59%	67%	86%	100%
Cleavage priming (yes vs. no)	100%	99%	96%	99%	99%	99%

Note: Entries are percentages of segments where coding agrees with the author's decisions.

This is an approximation to actual practice – longer spots are almost always broadcast less frequently because of the greater cost of larger blocks of television time.

To be certain that my conclusions about the evolution of Peruvian campaign strategies do not depend on the differential weighting strategies for earlier versus more recent spots, I generated a version of Figure 1.3 in which all spots – not only those prior to 2001 – were weighted inversely proportional to length. The same general pattern is evident.

INTER-CODER RELIABILITY

To test reliability, I had three research assistants recode samples of advertising from each country using written coding instructions (Appendix B) and a coding sheet (Appendix C). Like me, coders were proficient speakers of the relevant languages but not natives of Chile, Peru, or Brazil, ensuring that they would not bring extensive background knowledge to bear in their coding decisions. After an initial training session for each coder, I randomly sampled one video for each candidate and election year in Chile and Brazil, and two videos for each candidate and election year in Peru, from among those that the coder had not yet seen. A first round of reliability testing took place in 2010 and excluded material from the 2009–2011 elections, which had not yet been analyzed. A second round, with a new coder and a fresh, nonoverlapping sample, took place in 2015 and covered all elections in the analysis. In terms of elapsed time, the material subject to intercoder reliability testing amounted to 7.9 percent of all content analyzed for Brazil and Chile, and 20.8 percent for Peru.

Intercoder reliability statistics are presented in Table A.1. I focus on those coding decisions that are directly relevant to the analysis presented in the book. For instance, coders categorized every policy segment as specific or general, but I only make use of this distinction in the case of future policy acclaims (i.e., proposals), so I present statistics for this subset. For most categories and subcategories, agreement is 80 percent or better, which is generally consider acceptable (Neuendorf 2002: 143). Coders nearly always achieved this reliability threshold for the main categories used in the analysis, policy focus and cleavage priming. Most instances of less-than-satisfactory agreement involve subcategories of policy-focused appeals and are suggestive of coder idiosyncracies. For example, coder C had difficulty distinguishing diagnosis from acclaims and criticism, but the other coders for each country had no trouble with this category. Likewise, coder A had trouble distinguishing the timing (future versus past/present) of policy acclaims, but others did not. Only with respect to general versus specific future policy acclaims in Brazil did both coders working on a country obtain less-than-satisfactory results. I excluded policy areas from the intercoder reliability testing since they are referenced only infrequently in the analysis.

APPENDIX B

Coding Instructions for Reliability Testing

TO BE CODED FOR ALL SEGMENTS

Policy, Jingle/Opening/Closing/Transitional, Image, or Other

Policy involves any issue that a government deals with by passing laws or issuing decrees, or the task of governing in general. Discussion of policy often mentions the relevant policy area (e.g., jobs, taxes, environment, crime, etc.) but may also be generic or implied (e.g., "he'll get things done" or "they were in office for ten years and didn't solve any problems"). Policy can include policy-relevant activities outside of government, for example, a candidate talking about how he used to conduct research on economic policy at a private think tank or used to work as a lawyer challenging the government on human rights cases.

If there is only a brief mention of a policy issue, but the segment is mostly about something else, don't code it as policy. For instance, "come to a rally this weekend and show your support for Pablo's efforts to create jobs! Plaza de Armas, 7 p.m., etc." is primarily about the campaign itself, and thus falls into the *other* category as described below, even though job creation is briefly mentioned.

Image segments are about politicians as people, rather than policy. They include biographical information on the candidate, as long as this does not discuss policy (e.g., "he was born in a small town in the mountains" is about image, but "he was elected mayor at age 25 and presided over an unprecedented expansion of public housing" is about policy). They include segments introducing the candidate's family. They include mentions of positive traits (honesty, intelligence, creativity, experience, commitment to family) or negative traits about someone being criticized (liar, ruthless, etc.). They also include segments claiming that the candidate identifies with or empathizes with certain groups (e.g., "I represent the workers and will fight for them," "I understand the concerns of farmers and fisherman") or with "the people" in general (e.g., "Roberto is the candidate of the people"), without discussing policy issues relevant to them. Identification messages of this sort are sometimes used in attacks as well; these also count as image related (e.g., "my opponent is the candidate of the rich").

Jingle, Opening, Closing, or Transitional: Jingles are campaign songs that express general themes, slogans, and ideas. Code a segment as a jingle only if it is the main thing going on in the segment. For example, if the music of a jingle is playing in the background while a voice-over discusses policy proposals, code what the voice-over is saying. Opening, closing, or transitional segments come at the start or end of a spot, or between separate components of a longer mini-program; they are typically short in duration and convey generic messages such as slogans (e.g., "the candidate of change"), logos, how to vote for the candidate (e.g., "vote for number 3"), etc. Segments whose main purpose seems to be humor or entertainment also fall into this category.

You may encounter songs that, rather than expressing general themes, slogans, and ideas, are about a particular policy area, the candidate's biography, etc. In this case, code the segment in the corresponding category rather than as a jingle.

Other includes anything that doesn't fall into the categories above. Some things that you may encounter, and which should be classified in this category, include:

- Segments about the *campaign or election* itself: reporting poll numbers about intended vote, announcing upcoming rallies, discussing a successful rally, criticizing an opponent for unfair tactics, urging monetary donations, discussing the campaign advertising itself, etc. Includes video footage from a rally or a campaign event – though if that footage is of the candidate speaking, you should code what he/she is saying. Also includes statements about the meaning of the election, such as "this Sunday is the election, the day when the people speak, exercising their right to choose the politicians who will work for them for the next four years."
- Segments that are primarily about *values/concepts/emotions*: unity, freedom, change, hope, equality, patriotism, peace, justice, opportunity, etc. These also include negative values/concepts/emotions: fear, chaos, etc.
- Segments primarily about *party affiliation*: for example, the leader of the Christian Democratic Party saying he endorses Candidate A for president. This subcategory also includes affiliation with a prior military regime.
- Segments primarily about *ideology*: for example, a candidate discussing what nationalism means, or attacking an opponent for being a closet communist.
- Segments tying a candidate to some disgraced public figure. The message could be explicit, or it could be more subtle, such as news footage of this public figure endorsing the candidate.
- Generic expressions of support or intended vote without giving a reason why ("I'm voting for Pablo," "I support Pablo").

Divisive or Not Divisive

Divisive[1] segments explicitly place the candidate or his/her opponent on one side of a significant social divide: rich versus poor, workers versus economic elite, "the people" versus "the political class," left versus right, white versus indigenous, competing religious identities, etc. A statement such as "I represent the working people, not the bankers" would fall into this category. However, simply emphasizing that "I am looking out for the concerns of the workers" would not qualify because the candidate might also claim to have the interests of the bankers at heart. An attack on one's opponent such as "he is the candidate of the rich" does count as divisive because the implication is that the opponent does not represent the poor or middle class.

Not divisive refers to any segment not in the above category.

TO BE CODED ONLY FOR POLICY SEGMENTS

Past, Present, or Future

Present includes the time frame of the current electoral campaign, so something like "yesterday the president raised interest rates by 10%" counts as present. *Past* is anything prior to the current campaign, and *future* runs from election day onward. Future includes any mention of promises, proposals, or a plan or program of government, even if discussed in the past or present tense, since these are about future policy (e.g., "my proposals include ..." or "yesterday I introduced my government plan").

Criticism, Praise, or Framing

Criticism involves a negative message about a political opponent or enemy – typically, an opposing candidate, a political party, or an incumbent or prior government (or just "the government"). Criticism does not simply describe a problem; it must assign blame to a target. Sometimes attacks only vaguely specify a target (e.g., "they had their chance to govern and didn't accomplish anything") but this would still count as criticism.

Praise[2] involves a positive message, typically about the candidate himself/ herself but sometimes about an incumbent or prior government, a political party, the vice presidential candidate, one of the candidate's advisors, etc. Praise involves someone, or some institution, getting or taking credit. Sometimes this is explicit (e.g., "when I am president, I am going to lower taxes") and sometimes it is more vague (e.g., "we are going to improve education").

---

1 "Divisive" is the equivalent of "cleavage-priming" in the main text.
2 "Praise" is the equivalent of "acclaims" in the main text.

Framing[3] involves discussion of a particular policy area without engaging in criticism or praise. This can include diagnosis of the policy situation in a particular area (e.g., "we are facing the worst hyperinflation in a decade" or "crime rates have never been lower"). Even though such statements may reflect negatively or positively upon the current government, they should not be counted as criticism or praise unless someone or some institution is given blame or credit. Other examples of framing include dramatic reenactments (such as showing someone getting mugged) or common people telling a story (e.g., a mother talks about trying to afford medicine for her sick child) in order to introduce a particular policy area. Statements that identify needs (e.g., "we need to make sure that students can afford college") without claiming them as actual policy goals or priorities also count as framing.

General or Specific

General policy segments discuss issues or identify goals, accomplishments, or failures without much detail on how they were or will be achieved (e.g., "I am going to improve healthcare," "as governor, I improved healthcare," "healthcare has never been as bad as it was under President Rodríguez," or "many families are struggling with healthcare").

Specific policy segments include detailed information, such as about how a goal will be achieved or why a particular policy counts as a failure (e.g., "I am going to introduce a discounted low-income prescription drugs program," "under my opponent's plan, the cost of some life-saving medications will triple," or "the Drugs for Seniors program has given millions of retirees access to medications, but it doesn't go far enough").

---

3 "Framing" is the equivalent of "diagnosis" in the main text.

APPENDIX C

Coding Sheet for Reliability Testing

Segment 1

   0:00 to 0:10

Choose one:

   [ ] 1. Policy
   [ ] 2. Jingle, opening, closing, or transitional
   [ ] 3. Image
   [ ] 4. Other

Choose one:

   [ ] 1. Divisive   [ ] 2. Not divisive

For policy, choose one:

   [ ] 1. Past   [ ] 2. Present   [ ] 3. Future

For policy, choose one:

   [ ] 1. Criticism   [ ] 2. Praise   [ ] 3. Framing

For policy, choose one:

   [ ] 1. Specific   [ ] 2. General

References

Abrahamson, Eric. 1991. "Managerial Fads and Fashions: The Diffusion and Rejection of Innovations." *Academy of Management Review* 16, 3: 586–612.

Abrahamson, Eric and Lori Rosenkopf. 1993. "Institutional and Competitive Bandwagons: Using Mathematical Modeling as a Tool to Explore Innovation Diffusion." *Academy of Management Review* 18, 3: 487–517.

Alcántara Sáez, Manuel and Ismael Crespo Martínez. 1992. *Partidos Políticos y Procesos Electorales en Uruguay (1971–1990)*. Madrid: Fundación Centro Español de Estudios de América Latina.

Alencar, Kennedy. 2006. "Análise: Iguais na TV, Lula e Alckmin se Anulam." *Folha de São Paulo* August 15.

Allamand, Andrés. 1999. *La Travesía del Desierto*. Santiago: Aguilar.

Almarza, Rafael. 1989. "En la Provincia." In *La Campaña del No Vista por Sus Creadores*. Santiago: Ediciones Melquíades, pp. 51–54.

Almeida, Alberto Carlos. 2006. *Por Que Lula? O Contexto e as Estratégias Que Explicam a Eleição e a Crise*. Rio de Janeiro: Editora Record.

Almeida, Jorge. 2002. *Marketing Político: Hegemonia e Contra-hegemonia*. São Paulo: Fundação Perseu Abramo/Xama.

Altman, David. 2010. "The 2009 Elections in Uruguay." *Electoral Studies* 29: 533–536.

Altman, David and Aníbal Pérez-Liñán. 2002. "Assessing the Quality of Democracy: Freedom, Competitiveness, and Participation in 18 Latin American Countries." *Democratization* 9, 2: 85–100.

Altman, David and Daniel Buquet. 2015. "Uruguay 2014: Not Much of a Change in a Changing Country." *Electoral Studies* 38: 101–106.

Altman, David and Rossana Castiglioni. 2006. "The 2004 Uruguayan Elections: A Political Earthquake Foretold." *Electoral Studies* 25: 147–154.

Álvarez Araya, Óscar. 2010. "Honduras: Las Elecciones Como vía de Salida a la Crisis Política." ARI no. 11/2010, Real Instituto Elcano.

Anderson, Leslie E. and Lawrence C. Dodd. 2002. "Nicaragua Votes: The Elections of 2001." *Journal of Democracy* 13, 3: 80–94.

Anderson, Leslie E. and Lawrence C. Dodd. 2005. *Learning Democracy: Citizen Engagement and Electoral Choice in Nicaragua, 1990–2001*. Chicago: University of Chicago Press.

Angell, Alan, Maria D'Alva Kinzo, and Diego Urbaneja. 1992. "Latin America." In David Butler and Austin Ranney (eds.), *Electioneering: A Comparative Study of Continuity and Change*. New York: Oxford University Press, pp. 43–69.

Angell, Alan and Benny Pollack. 2000. "The Chilean Presidential Elections of 1999–2000 and Democratic Consolidation." *Bulletin of Latin American Research* 19: 357–378.

Annunziata, Rocío. 2012. "Hacia un Nuevo Modelo del Lazo Representativo? La Representación de Proximidad en las Campañas Electorales de 2009 y 2011 en Argentina." In Isidoro Cheresky and Rocío Annunziata (eds.), *Sin Programa, Sin Promesa: Liderazgos y Procesos Electorales en Argentina*. Buenos Aires: Prometeo Libros, pp. 45–87.

"Aprobación al Presidente Sube con Caso Colombia." 2008. CEDATOS/Gallup International. Available at: www.cedatos.com.ec/contenido.asp?id=51 (accessed on January 19, 2009).

Argones, Nelson. 1985. *El Juego del Poder: De Rodríguez Lara a Febres Cordero*. Quito: Corporación Editora Nacional.

Armstrong, Charles. 2008. "Contesting the Peninsula." *New Left Review* 51: 115–135.

Arriagada, Genaro. 1989. "Prólogo." In *La Campaña del No Vista por Sus Creadores*. Santiago: Ediciones Melquíades, pp. xii–xviii.

Arthur, Peter. 2009. "Ethnicity and Electoral Politics in Ghana's Fourth Republic." *Africa Today* 56, 2: 45–73.

Auth, José. 1994. "Elecciones Presidenciales y Parlamentarias de 1993." *Estudios Públicos* 54: 339–361.

Azevedo, Clovis Bueno de. 1995. *A Estrela Partida ao Meio*. São Paulo: Entrelinhas.

Bachelet, Michelle. 2005. "Estoy Contigo: Programa de Gobierno." [Santiago].

Baim, Joel A. C., Stan Xiao Li, and John M. Usher. 2000. "Making the Next Move: How Experiential and Vicarious Learning Shape the Locations of Chains' Acquisitions." *Administrative Science Quarterly* 45: 766–801.

Baker, Andy, Barry Ames, and Lucio R. Renno. 2006. "Social Context and Campaign Volatility in New Democracies: Networks and Neighborhoods in Brazil's 2002 Elections." *American Journal of Political Science* 50(2): 382–399.

Baloyra, Enrique A. and John D. Martz. 1979. *Political Attitudes in Venezuela: Societal Cleavages and Political Opinion*. Austin, TX: University of Texas Press.

Barnes, William A. 1992. "Rereading the Nicaraguan Pre-Election Polls in the Light of the Election Results." In Vanessa Castro and Gary Prevost (eds.), *The 1990 Elections in Nicaragua and Their Aftermath*. Boulder, CO: Rowman & Littlefield, pp. 41–128.

Barnes, William A. 1998. "Incomplete Democracy in Central America: Polarization and Voter Turnout." *Journal of Interamerican Studies and World Affairs* 40, 3: 63–101.

Barozet, Emmanuelle. 2003. "Movilización de Recursos y Redes Sociales en los Neopopulismos: Hipótesis de Trabajo Para el Caso Chileno." *Revista de Ciencia Política* 23, 1: 39–54.

Bartolini, Stefano and Peter Mair. 1990. *Identity, Competition, and Electoral Availability: The Stabilisation of the European Electorates 1885–1985*. New York: Cambridge University Press.

Basabe-Serrano, Santiago and Julián Martínez. 2014. "Ecuador: Cada Vez Menos Democracia, Cada Vez Más Autoritarismo...Con Elecciones." *Revista de Ciencia Política* 34, 1: 145–170.

Battle, Martin and Jennifer C. Seely. 2010. "It's All Relative: Modeling Candidate Support in Benin." *Nationalism and Ethnic Politics* 16: 42–66.

Baudais, Virginie and Enrico Sborgi. 2008. "The presidential and parliamentary elections in Mali, April and July 2007." *Electoral Studies* 27, 4: 769–773.

Berrier Sharim, Karina. 1989. *Derecha Regimental y Coyuntara Plebiscitaria: Los Casos de Renovación Nacional y la UDI*. Santiago: Programa de Jóvenes Investigadores, Servicio Universitário Mundial (WUS–Chile).

Bleck, Jaimie and Nicolas van de Walle. 2012. "Valence Issues in African Elections: Navigating Uncertainty and the Weight of the Past." *Comparative Political Studies* 46, 11: 1394–1421.

Blumler, Jay G. and Dennis Kavanagh. 1999. "The Third Age of Political Communication: Influences and Features." *Political Communication* 16: 209–230.

Boas, Taylor C. 2005. "Television and Neopopulism in Latin America: Media Effects in Brazil and Peru." *Latin American Research Review* 40, 2: 27–49.

Boas, Taylor C. 2007. "Conceptualizing Continuity and Change: The Composite-Standard Model of Path Dependence." *Journal of Theoretical Politics* 19, 1: 33–54.

Boas, Taylor C. 2009. "Varieties of Electioneering: Presidential Campaigns in Latin America." Ph.D. Dissertation, University of California, Berkeley.

Boas, Taylor C. 2010. "Varieties of Electioneering: Success Contagion and Presidential Campaigns in Latin America." *World Politics* 62, 4: 636–675.

Boas, Taylor C. 2013. "Mass Media and Politics in Latin America." In Jorge I. Domínguez and Michael Shifter (eds.), *Constructing Democratic Governance in Latin America*, 4th edn. Baltimore, MD: Johns Hopkins University Press, pp. 48–77.

Boas, Taylor C. 2015. "Voting for Democracy: Campaign Effects in Chile's Democratic Transition." *Latin American Politics and Society* 57, 2: 67–90.

Bolongaita, Emil P., Jr. 1999. "The Philippines: Consolidating Democracy in Difficult Times." *Southeast Asian Affairs* 26: 237–252.

Booth, John A. and Amber Aubone. 2008. "Las elecciones de 2005 y la participación electoral en Honduras en perspectiva regional comparada." In Manuel Alcántara Sáez and Fátima García Díez (eds.), *Elecciones y política en América Latina*. Mexico City: Instituto Electoral del Estado de México/Miguel Ángel Porrúa, pp. 41–73.

Borrini, Alberto. 2003. *Cómo se Vende un Candidato: Un Siglo de Campañas Políticas en la Argentina*. Buenos Aires: La Crujía.

Boushey, Graeme. 2010. *Policy Diffusion Dynamics in America*. New York: Cambridge University Press.

Bowen, James D. 2010. "Ecuador's 2009 Presidential and Legislative Elections." *Electoral Studies* 29: 186–189.

Bowen, Sally. 2000. *El Expediente Fujimori: El Perú y su Presidente 1990–2000*. Lima: Perú Monitor.

Bowers, Emily. 2009. "Ghanaians Vote in Constituency to Decide Presidency." *Bloomberg News*, January 2.

Bowler, Shaun and David M. Farrell. 2000. "The Internationalization of Campaign Consultancy." In Thurber and Nelson (eds.), pp. 153–174.

Boyer, Allison. 1992. "An Exemplary Transition." *Africa Report* 37, 4: 40–42.

Boylen, Delia. 1996. "Taxation and Transition: The Politics of the 1990 Chilean Tax Reform," *Latin American Research Review* 31, 1: 7–31.

Bratton, Michael, Massa Coulibaly, and Fabiana Machado. 2001. "Popular Perceptions of Good Governance in Mali." Afrobarometer Paper no. 9.

Braun, Dietmar and Fabrizio Gilardi. 2006. "Taking 'Galton's Problem' Seriously: Towards a Theory of Policy Diffusion." *Journal of Theoretical Politics* 18, 3: 298–322.

Bruhn, Kathleen. 2004. "The Making of the Mexican President, 2000: Parties, Candidates, and Campaign Strategy." In Domínguez and Lawson (eds.), pp. 123–156.

Bruhn, Kathleen. 2009. "López Obrador, Calderón, and the 2006 Presidential Campaign." In Domínguez, Lawson, and Moreno (eds.), pp. 169–188.

Bruhn, Kathleen. 2015. "Chronicle of a Victory Foretold: Candidates, Parties, and Campaign Strategies in the 2012 Mexican Presidential Election." In Domínguez, Greene, Lawson, and Moreno (eds.), pp. 32–62.

Buquet, Daniel. 2005. "Elecciones Uruguayas 2004–2005: De la Vieja Oposición a la Nueva Mayoría." In Daniel Buquet (ed.), *Las Claves del Cambio: Ciclo Electoral y Nuevo Gobierno 2004/2005*. Montevideo: Ediciones de la Banda Oriental, pp. 11–26.

Burbano de Lara, Felipe. 1992. "Populismo, Democracia, y Política: El Caso de Abdalá Bucaram." In Blasco Peñaherrera, Alfredo Castillo, Alejandro Moreano, Marco Proaño, Amparo Menéndez-Carrión, Felipe Burbano, Iván Fernández, and Carlos de la Torre E. (eds.), *Populismo*. Quito: Instituto Latinoamericano de Investigaciones Sociales, Fundación Friedrich Ebert, pp. 119–141.

Burke, Laura. 2012. "Ghana Election, a Democracy Test." *Yahoo! News*, December 6.

Burns, Lawton R. and Douglas R. Wholey. 1993. "Adoption and Abandonment of Matrix Management Programs: Effects of Organizational Characteristics and Interorganizational Networks." *Academy of Management Journal* 36, 1: 106–138.

Calvo, Ernesto and M. Victoria Murillo. 2012. "Argentina: The Persistence of Peronism." *Journal of Democracy* 23, 2: 148–161.

Cameron, Maxwell A. 1994. *Democracy and Authoritarianism in Peru: Political Coalitions and Social Change*. New York: St. Martin's Press.

Cameron, Maxwell A. 1997. "Political and Economic Origins of Regime Change in Peru: The Eighteenth Brumaire of Alberto Fujimori." In Maxwell A. Cameron and Philip Mauceri (eds.), *The Peruvian Labyrinth: Polity, Society, Economy*. University Park, PA: Pennsylvania State University Press, pp. 37–69.

Cameron, Maxwell A. 2011. "Peru: The Left Turn That Wasn't." In Steven Levitsky and Kenneth M. Roberts (eds.), *The Resurgence of the Latin American Left*. Baltimore, MD: Johns Hopkins University Press, pp. 375–398.

Campusano S., Mauricio. 2005. "Estrategia Para Ampliar Votación: Piñera Exhibe Apoyo de Grupo de Falangistas." *El Mercurio* December 14.

Canton, Darío and Jorge Raúl Jorrat. 2002. "Presidential Voting in Argentina, 1995 and 1999." *International Journal of Public Opinion Research* 14, 4: 413–427.

Canzani, Agustín. 2000. "Mensaje en Una Botella: Analizando las Elecciones de 1999–2000." In *Elecciones 1999/2000*. Montevideo: Ediciones de la Banda Oriental, pp. 237–263.

Canzani, Agustín. 2005. "Cómo Llegar a Buen Puerto: Un Análisis Desde la Opinión Pública de la Trayectoria Electoral del EPFA." In Daniel Buquet (ed.), *Las Claves del*

Cambio: Ciclo Electoral y Nuevo Gobierno 2004/2005. Montevideo: Ediciones de la Banda Oriental, pp. 63–86.

"Carlos Roberto Flores Facussé." 2004. *Encyclopedia of World Biography*. Detroit, MI: Thomson Gale.

Caro, Carolina. 2004. "La Corrupción Vuelve a Perú." *Americaeconomía.com*, December 30.

Carothers, Thomas. 1999. *Aiding Democracy Abroad: The Learning Curve*. Washington, DC: Carnegie Endowment for International Peace.

Carothers, Thomas. 2006. *Confronting the Weakest Link: Aiding Political Parties in New Democracies*. Washington, DC: Carnegie Endowment for International Peace.

Carrión, Julio F. 2000. "La Campaña Electoral y la Opinión Pública en el Perú Actual." Paper presented at the International Congress of the Latin American Studies Association, Miami, FL, March 16–18.

Carter, Miguel. 2010. "The Landless Rural Workers' Movement and Democracy in Brazil." *Latin American Research Review* 45 (Special Issue): 186–217.

Case, William. 1999. "The Philippine Election in 1998: A Question of Quality." *Asian Survey* 39, 3: 468–485.

Cason, Jeffrey. 2000. "Electoral Reform and Stability in Uruguay." *Journal of Democracy* 11, 2: 85–98.

Catterberg, Gabriela and Valeria Palanza. 2012. "Argentina: Dispersión de la Oposición y el Auge de Cristina Fernández de Kirchner." *Revista de Ciencia Política* 32, 1: 3–30.

Centellas, Miguel. 2007. "From 'Parliamentarized' to 'Pure' Presidentialism: Bolivia after October 2003." Paper presented at the annual meeting of the Midwest Political Science Association, Chicago, IL, April 12–15.

Centeno, Miguel Ángel. 1993. "The New Leviathan: The Dynamics and Limits of Technocracy." *Theory and Society* 22, 3: 307–335.

Centeno, Miguel Ángel. 1994. *Democracy within Reason: Technocratic Revolution in Mexico*. University Park, PA: Pennsylvania State University Press.

Cho, Kisuk. 2003. "Continuity and Change in the 2002 Presidential Election." *Korea Journal* 43, 2: 109–128.

CIS. 1987. "Dignidad: Una Estrategia Para Ganar la Democracia." Informe no. 3, November.

CIS. 1988. "Una Opción Democrática Enérgica y Segurizante: Orientaciones Ante los 'Indecisos'." Informe no. 9, May.

Clark, Andrew F. 2000. "From Military Dictatorship to Democracy: The Democratization Process in Mali." In R. James Bingen, David Robinson, and John M. Staatz (eds.), *Democracy and Development in Mali*. East Lansing; MI: Michigan State University Press, pp. 251–264.

Collier, David and James Mahoney. 1996. "Insights and Pitfalls: Selection Bias in Qualitative Research." *World Politics* 49, 1: 56–91.

Collier, David, James Mahoney, and Jason Seawright. 2004. "Claiming Too Much: Warnings about Selection Bias." In Henry E. Brady and David Collier (eds.), *Rethinking Social Inquiry: Diverse Tools, Shared Standards*. Lanham, MD: Rowman & Littlefield, pp. 85–102.

Collier, Ruth Berins. 2001. "Populism." In Neil J. Smelser and Paul B. Baltes (eds.), *International Encyclopedia of Social and Behavioral Sciences*. New York: Elsevier, pp. 11813–11816.

Commonwealth Observer Group. [2009]. *Ghana Parliamentary and Presidential Elections, 7 December 2008, and Presidential Run-off Election, 28 December 2008.* London: Commonwealth Secretariat.

Conaghan, Catherine M. 2005. *Fujimori's Peru: Deception in the Public Sphere.* Pittsburgh, PA: University of Pittsburgh Press.

Conaghan, Catherine M. 2007a. "Ecuador's Gamble: Can Correa Govern?" *Current History* 106, 697: 77–82.

Conaghan, Catherine M. 2007b. "The 2006 Presidential and Congressional Elections in Ecuador." *Electoral Studies* 26: 823–828.

Conaghan, Catherine M. 2008. "Ecuador: Correa's Plebiscitary Presidency." *Journal of Democracy* 19, 2: 46–60.

Correa, Enrique. 1989. "La Oportunidad Democrática." In *La Campaña del No Vista por Sus Creadores.* Santiago: Ediciones Melquíades, pp. 159–162.

Crabtree, John. 2010. "Democracy without Parties ? Some Lessons from Peru." *Journal of Latin American Studies* 42: 357–382.

Creevey, Lucy, Paul Ngomo, and Richard Vengroff. 2005. "Party Politics and Different Paths to Democratic Transitions: A Comparison of Benin and Senegal." *Party Politics* 11, 4: 471–493.

Crisostomo, Isabelo T. 1987. *Cory: Profile of a President.* Boston, MA: Branden Publishing Co.

Crisostomo, Isabelo T. 1997. *Fidel V. Ramos: Builder, Reformer, Peacemaker.* Quezon City: J. Kriz Publishing Enterprise.

Cupples, Julie. 2009. "Rethinking Electoral Geography: Spaces and Practices of Democracy in Nicaragua." *Transactions of the Institute of British Geographers* 34: 110–124.

Cupples, Julie and Irving Larios. 2005. "Gender, Elections, Terrorism: The Geopolitical Enframing of the 2001 Nicaragian Elections." *Political Geography* 24: 317–339.

da Silva, Luiz Inácio Lula. 2002. "Programa de Governo 2002." [São Paulo]: Partido dos Trabalhadores.

Daddieh, Cyril Kofie. 2009. "The Presidential and Parliamentary Elections in Ghana, December 2008." *Electoral Studies* 28: 642–647.

de Amas, Gustavo and Antonio Cardarello. 2000. "Del 'Sentimiento' a la Razón. La Estrategia Discursiva de Batlle de Abril a Noviembre." In *Elecciones 1999/2000.* Montevideo: Ediciones de la Banda Oriental, pp. 111–140.

de la Torre, Carlos. 1999. "Neopopulism in Contemporary Ecuador: The Case of Bucaram's Use of the Mass Media." *International Journal of Politics, Culture and Society* 12, 4: 555–571.

de la Torre, Carlos. 2000. *Populist Seduction in Latin America: The Ecuadorian Experience.* Athens, OH: Ohio University Center for International Studies.

de la Torre, Carlos. 2013. "Technocratic Populism in Ecuador." *Journal of Democracy* 24, 3: 33–46.

de la Torre, Carlos and Catherine Conaghan. 2009. "The Hybrid Campaign: Tradition and Modernity in Ecuador's 2006 Presidential Election." *International Journal of Press/Politics* 14, 3: 335–352.

de la Torre Espinosa, Carlos. 1994. "Las Imágenes Contradictorias de Abdalá: Discursos y Culturas Políticas en las Elecciones de 1992." *Ecuador Debate* 32: 54–64.

Deephouse, David L. 1999. "To Be Different, or to Be the Same? It's a Question (and Theory) of Strategic Balance." *Strategic Management Journal* 20: 147–166.

Delios, Andrew, Ajai S. Guar, and Shige Makino. 2008. "The Timing of International Expansion: Information, Rivalry and Imitation among Japanese Firms, 1980–2002." *Journal of Management Studies* 45, 1: 169–195.

Di Palma, Giuseppe. 1972. "Conclusion." In Giuseppe Di Palma (ed.), *Mass Politics in Industrial Societies: A Reader in Comparative Politics.* Chicago, IL: Markham Publishing Company, pp. 394–411.

Diamond, Larry and Leonardo Morlino (eds.) 2005. *Assessing the Quality of Democracy.* Baltimore, MD: Johns Hopkins University Press.

Díaz, Miguel. 2001. "Honduras Alert: President-elect Vows to Fight Crime." In *Hemisphere Focus: 2001–2002.* Washington, DC: Center for Strategic and International Studies.

Dickovick, J. Tyler. 2008. "Legacies of Leftism: Ideology, Ethnicity, and Democracy in Benin, Ghana, and Mali." *Third World Quarterly* 29, 6: 1119–1137.

Dietz, Henry A. and David J. Myers. 2007. "From Thaw to Deluge: Party System Collapse in Venezuela and Peru." *Latin American Politics & Society* 49, 2: 59–86.

DiMaggio, Paul J. and Walter W. Powell. 1983. "The Iron Cage Revisited: Institutional Isomorphism and Collective Rationality in Organizational Fields." *American Sociological Review* 48: 147–160.

Dimenstein, Gilberto and Josias de Souza. 1994. *A História Real: Trama de uma Sucessão.* São Paulo: Editora Ática.

Dissou, Machioudi. 2002. *Le Bénin et l'épreuve démocratique: Leçons des élections de 1991 à 2001.* Paris: L'Harmattan.

Domínguez, Jorge I. and Chappell Lawson (eds.) 2004. *Mexico's Pivotal Democratic Election: Candidates, Voters, and the Presidential Campaign of 2000.* Stanford and La Jolla, CA: Stanford University Press/Center for U.S.-Mexican Studies, University of California, San Diego.

Domínguez, Jorge I., Chappell H. Lawson, and Alejandro Moreno (eds.) 2009. *Consolidating Mexico's Democracy: The 2006 Presidential Campaign in Comparative Perspective.* Baltimore, MD: Johns Hopkins University Press.

Domínguez, Jorge I., Kenneth F. Greene, Chappell H. Lawson, and Alejandro Moreno (eds.) 2015. *Mexico's Evolving Democracy: A Comparative Study of the 2012 Elections.* Baltimore, MD: Johns Hopkins University Press.

Downs, Anthony. 1957. *An Economic Theory of Democracy.* New York: Harper & Row.

Dulio, David A. 2004. *For Better or Worse? How Political Consultants Are Changing Elections in the United States.* Albany, NY: State University of New York Press.

Dunning, Thad and Lauren Harrison. 2010. "Cross-Cutting Cleavages and Ethnic Voting: An Experimental Study of Cousinage in Mali." *American Political Science Review* 104, 1: 21–39.

Duverger, Maurice. 1959. *Political Parties: Their Organization and Activity in the Modern State,* 2nd edn. New York: John Wiley & Sons, Inc.

Echeverría, Julio. 2007. "La Democracia Difícil: Neopopulismo y Antipolítica en Ecuador." *Revista de Ciencias Sociales* 27: 27–35.

Elecciones Generales 2005: Monitoreo y Análisis Desde la Sociedad Civil. 2006. Tegucigalpa: Centro de Investigación y Promoción de los Derechos Humanos.

Elkins, Zachary and Beth Simmons. 2005. "On Waves, Clusters, and Diffusion: A Conceptual Framework." *Annals of the American Academy of Political and Social Science* 598: 33–51.

Epstein, Leon D. 1967. *Political Parties in Western Democracies*. New York: Praeger.

Espíndola, Roberto. 2001. "No Change in Uruguay: The 1999 Presidential and Parliamentary Elections." *Electoral Studies* 20: 649–657.

Etchemendy, Sebastián and Candelaria Garay. 2011. "Argentina: Left Populism in Comparative Perspective, 2003–2009." In Steven Levitsky and Kenneth M. Roberts (eds.), *The Resurgence of the Latin American Left*. Baltimore, MD: Johns Hopkins University Press, pp. 283–305.

Eulau, Heinz and Kenneth Prewitt. 1973. *Labyrinths of Democracy: Adaptations, Linkages, Representation, and Policies in Urban Politics*. New York: Bobbs-Merrill Company, Inc.

Fairfield, Tasha. 2010. "Business Power and Tax Reform: Taxing Income and Profits in Chile and Argentina." *Latin American Politics and Society* 52, 2: 37–71.

Fairfield, Tasha. 2015a. *Private Wealth and Public Revenue in Latin America: Business Power and Tax Politics*. New York: Cambridge University Press.

Fairfield, Tasha. 2015b. "Structural Power in Comparative Political Economy: Perspectives from Policy Formulation in Latin America." *Business and Politics* 17, 3: 411–442.

Falcoff, Mark. 1995. "The 1995 Argentine Elections: Pre-Election Report #1." Western Hemisphere Election Study Series, Vol. 13, Study 3. Washington, DC: Center for Strategic and International Studies.

Farrell, David. 1996. "Campaign Strategies and Tactics." In Lawrence LeDuc, Richard Niemi, and Pippa Norris (eds.), *Comparing Democracies: Elections and Voting in Global Perspective*. Thousand Oaks, CA: Sage, pp. 160–183.

Farrell, David. 1998. "Political Consultancy Overseas: The Internationalization of Campaign Consultancy." *PS: Political Science and Politics* 31, 2: 171–176.

Feinberg, Richard. 2011. "Daniel Ortega and Nicaragua's Soft Authoritarianism." *Foreign Affairs*, November 2. Available at: www.foreignaffairs.org/articles/nicaragua/2011-11-02/daniel-ortega-and-nicaraguas-soft-authoritarianism (accessed on September 27, 2015).

Ferraz, Francisco. 2003. *Manual Completo de Campanha Eleitoral*. 2nd edn. Porto Alegre: L&PM Editores.

Ferreira, Roger. [1998]. "Os Labirintos do Voto: A Reeleição de Fernando Henrique Vista por Dentro." Manuscript.

Fiallos, Aníbal Delgado. 1986. *Honduras Elecciones 85: Más Allá de la Fiesta Cívica*. Tegucigalpa: Editorial Guaymuras.

Figueiredo, Ney Lima. 2002 [1994]. *Jogando Para Ganhar: Marketing Político: Verdade e Mito*. 2nd edn. São Paulo: Geração Editorial.

Figueiredo, Ney Lima and José Rubens de Lima Figueiredo, Jr. 1990. *Como Ganhar uma Eleição: Lições de Campanha e Marketing Político*. São Paulo: Cultura Editores Associados.

Figueiredo, Rubens and Ricardo Ribeiro. 1999. "La Elección Presidencial de 1998 en el Brasil: La Campaña de la Reelección." In Frank Priess and Fernando Tuesta Soldevilla (eds.), *Campañas Electorales y Medios de Comunicación en América Latina*. Buenos Aires: Centro Interdisciplinario de Estudios sobre el Desarrollo Latinoamericano, Konrad Adenauer Stiftung, pp. 81–134.

Filho, Expedito. 1994. *Fernando Henrique Cardoso: Crônica de uma Vitória*. Rio de Janeiro: Editora Objetiva.

Finch, Henry. 1995. "The Uruguayan Election of 1994." *Electoral Studies* 14, 2: 232–236.

Fontaine, Roger W. 1992. "The Philippines: After Aquino." *Asian Affairs* 19, 3: 170–190.

Fowks, Jacqueline. 2000. *Suma y Resta de la Realidad: Medios de Comunicación y Elecciones Generales 2000 en el Perú*. Lima: Freidrich Ebert Stiftung.

Francia, Peter L. and Paul S. Herrnson. 2007. "Keeping It Professional: The Influence of Political Consultants on Candidate Attitudes toward Negative Campaigning." *Politics & Policy* 35, 2: 246–272.

Freidenberg, Flavia. 2003. *Jama, Caleta y Camello: Las Estrategias de Abdalá Bucaram y del PRE para Ganar las Elecciones*. Quito: Corporación Editora Nacional.

Freidenberg, Flavia. 2011. "Ecuador 2009: Las Elecciones que Consolidan el Cambio del Sistema de Partidos." In Manuel Alcántara Sáez and María Laura Tagina (eds.), *América Latina: Política y Elecciones del Bicentenario (2009–2010)*. Madrid: Centro de Estudios Constitucionales y Políticos, pp. 63–96.

Frempong, A. Kaakyire Duku. 2001. "Ghana's Election 2000: The Ethnic Undercurrent." In Joseph R. A. Ayee (ed.), *Deepening Democracy in Ghana: Politics of the 2000 Elections*, Vol. 1. Accra: Freedom Publications Ltd., pp. 141–159.

Fridy, Kevin S. 2007. "The Elephant, Umbrella, and Quarreling Cocks: Disaggregating Partisanship in Ghana's Fourth Republic." *African Affairs* 106: 281–305.

Gallagher, Michael, Michael Laver, and Peter Mair. 1992. *Representative Government in Western Europe*. San Francisco, CA: McGraw Hill.

Garcé, Adolfo. 2010. "Uruguay 2009: De Tabaré Vázquez a José Mujica." *Revista de Ciencia Política* 30, 2: 499–535.

García, Alan. 2005. *Sierra Exportadora*. Lima: n.p.

Garretón M., Manuel Antonio. 1989. "Popular Mobilization and the Military Regime in Chile: The Complexities of the Invisible Transition." In Susan Eckstein (ed.), *Power and Popular Protest: Latin American Social Movements*. Berkeley, CA: University of California Press, pp. 259–277.

Garretón Merino, Manuel Antonio. 1993. "La Renovación Ideológica Chilena." In Gustavo Cuevas Farren (ed.), *La Renovación Ideológica en Chile: Los Partidos y Su Nueva Visión Estratégica*. Santiago: Instituto de Ciencia Política, Universidad de Chile, pp. 19–27.

Gerber, Elisabet. 2006. *Comunicación y Política: Análisis de la Campaña Presidencial de Michelle Bachelet*. Santiago: Freidrich Ebert Stiftung.

Germano, Carlos and Jorge Dell Oro. 2000. "Las Elecciones Presidenciales de 1999." In Fundación Konrad Adenauer (ed.), *Trastienda de Una Elección*. Buenos Aires: Temas Grupo Editorial, pp. 13–32.

Gibson, Edward L. 1992. "Conservative Electoral Movements and Democratic Politics: Core Constituencies, Coalition Building, and the Latin American Electoral Right." In Douglass A. Chalmers, Maria do Larmo Campello de Souza, and Atilio Boron (eds.), *The Right and Democracy in Latin America*. Westport, CT: Greenwood Publishing, pp. 13–42.

Gilardi, Fabrizio. 2010. "Who Learns from What in Policy Diffusion Processes?" *American Journal of Political Science* 54, 3: 650–666.

Gilardi, Fabrizio. 2012. "Transnational Diffusion: Norms, Ideas, and Policies." In Walter Carlsnaes, Thomas Risse, and Beth Simmons (eds.), *Handbook of International Relations*, 2nd edn. Thousand Oaks, CA: Sage, pp. 453–477.

Gillespie, Charles G. 1985. "Electoral Stability, Party System Transformation, and Redemocratization: The Uruguayan Case in Comparative Perspective." Presented at the conference on "Recent Electoral Changes in the Americas," Center for Iberian and Latin American Studies, University of California, San Diego, February 21–22.

Gillespie, Charles G. 1986. "Activists and Floating Voters: The Unheeded Lessons of Uruguay's 1982 Primaries." In Paul W. Drake and Eduardo Silva (eds.), *Elections and Democratization in Latin America, 1980–1985*. San Diego, CA: Center for Iberian and Latin American Studies/Center for U.S.-Mexican Studies/Institute of the Americas, University of California, San Diego, pp. 215–244.

Gillespie, Charles G. 1991. *Negotiating Democracy: Politicians and Generals in Uruguay*. New York: Cambridge University Press.

Gisselquist, Rachel M. 2008. "Democratic Transition and Democratic Survival in Benin." *Democratization* 15, 4: 789–814.

Glick, David M. 2013. "Safety in Numbers: Mainstream-Seeking Diffusion in Response to Executive Compensation Regulations." *Quarterly Journal of Political Science* 8: 95–125.

Glick, David M. and Zoe Friedland. 2014. "How Often Do States Study Each Other? Evidence of Policy Knowledge Diffusion." *American Politics Research* 42, 6: 956–985.

Godoy, Eduardo de, Cláudio Barreto, Carlos Sarno, and Eduardo Safira. 2000. "Mesa 1 – A Campanha Eleitoral na Mídia em 1998." In Antonio Albino Canelas Rubim (ed.), *Mídia e Eleições de 1998*. Salvador: Editoria Universitária Facom/UFBA, pp. 263–298.

González, Luís E. 1995. "Continuity and Change in the Uruguayan Party System." In Scott Mainwaring and Timothy R. Scully (eds.), *Building Democratic Institutions: Party Systems in Latin America*. Stanford, CA: Stanford University Press, pp. 138–163.

González, Rodolfo. 1990. *Elecciones 1989*. Montevideo: Celadu.

Gooren, Henri. 2010. "Ortega for President: The Religious Rebirth of Sandinismo in Nicaragua." *European Review of Latin American and Caribbean Studies* 89: 47–63.

Graham, Carol. 1992. *Peru's APRA: Parties, Politics, and the Elusive Quest for Democracy*. Boulder, CO: Lynne Rienner Publishers.

Graham, Erin R., Charles R. Shipan, and Craig Volden. 2013. "The Diffusion of Policy Diffusion Research in Political Science." *British Journal of Political Science* 43, 3: 673–701.

Grandi, Rodolfo, Alexandre Marins, and Eduardo Falcão. 1992. *Voto é Marketing...o Resto é Política*. São Paulo: Edições Loyola.

Graziano, Francisco. 1995. *O Real na Estrada: A Campanha de Fernando Henrique à Presidência*. São Paulo: Editora Paulicéia.

Greenberg, Stanley B. 2009. *Dispatches from the War Room: In the Trenches with Five Extraordinary Leaders*. New York: St. Martin's Press.

Greene, Kenneth F. 2011. "Campaign Persuasion and Nascent Partisanship in Mexico's New Democracy." *American Journal of Political Science* 55, 2: 398–416.

Greenwood, Royston, Roy Suddaby, and C. R. Hinings. 2002. "Theorizing Change: The Role of Professional Associations in the Transformation of Institutionalized Fields." *Academy of Management Journal* 45, 1: 58–80.

Grossmann, Matt. 2009. "Going Pro? Political Campaign Consulting and the Professional Model." *Journal of Political Marketing* 8, 2: 81–104.

Grossmann, Matt. 2012. "What (or Who) Makes Campaigns Negative?" *American Review of Politics* 33, 1: 1–22.

Guanaes, Nizan. 2001. "Prefácio." In Duda Mendonça, *Casos e Coisas*. São Paulo: Globo, pp. 11–12.

Guillén, Mauro F. 2002. "Structural Inertia, Imitation, and Foreign Expansion: South Korean Firms and Business Groups in China, 1987–1995." *Academy of Management Journal* 45, 3: 509–525.

Gutiérrez Sánchez, Tomás. 2000. *El "Hermano" Fujimori: Evangélicos y Poder Político en el Perú del '90*. Lima: Ediciones AHP (Archivo Histórico del Protestantismo Latinoamericano).

Gutiérrez Sanín, Francisco. 2005. "Deconstruction without Reconstruction? The Case of Peru (1978–2004)." Working Paper no. 63, Crisis States Programme, Development Research Centre, London School of Economics.

Gyimah-Boadi, E. 2001. "A Peaceful Turnover in Ghana." *Journal of Democracy* 12, 2: 103–117.

Gyimah-Boadi, E. 2009. "Another Step Forward for Ghana." *Journal of Democracy* 20, 2: 138–152.

Hacker, Jacob. 2004. "Privatizing Risk without Privatizing the Welfare State: The Hidden Politics of Social Policy Retrenchment in the United States." *American Political Science Review* 98, 2: 243–260.

Hagopian, Frances. Forthcoming. *Reorganizing Political Representation in Latin America: Parties, Program, and Patronage in Argentina, Brazil, Chile, and Mexico*. New York: Cambridge University Press.

Hagopian, Frances, Carlos Gervasoni, and Juan Andres Moraes. 2009. "From Patronage to Program: The Emergence of Party-Oriented Legislators in Brazil." *Comparative Political Studies* 42, 3: 360–391.

Hahm, Chaibong. 2008. "South Korea's Miraculous Democracy." *Journal of Democracy* 19, 3: 128–142.

Han, Sung-Joo. 1988. "South Korea in 1987: The Politics of Democratization." *Asian Survey* 28, 1: 52–61.

Harding, James. 2008. *Alpha Dogs: The Americans Who Turned Political Spin into a Global Business*. New York: Farrar, Straus, and Giroux.

Haunschild, Pamela and Anne S. Miner. 1997. "Modes of Interorganizational Imitation: The Effects of Outcome Salience and Uncertainty." *Administrative Science Quarterly* 42: 472–500.

Haveman, Heather A. 1993. "Follow the Leader: Mimetic Isomorphism and Entry into New Markets." *Administrative Science Quarterly* 38, 4: 593–627.

Hawkins, Kirk. 2003. "Populism in Venezuela: The Rise of Chavismo." *Third World Quarterly* 24, 6: 1137–1160.

Hawkins, Kirk. 2010. *Venezuela's Chavismo and Populism in Comparative Perspective*. New York: Cambridge University Press.

Haya de la Torre, Agustín. 2006. "Perú: La Persistencia de Los Outsiders y Los Retos Para la Democracia." *Nueva Sociedad* (Special edition), March.

Heichel, Stephan, Jessica Pape, and Thomas Sommerer. 2005. "Is There Convergence in Convergence Research? An Overview of Empirical Studies on Policy Convergence." *Journal of European Public Policy* 12, 5: 817–840.

Heilbrunn, John R. 1993. "Social Origins of National Conferences in Benin and Togo." *Journal of Modern African Studies* 31, 2: 277–299.

Henisz, Witold J. and Andrew Delios. 2001. "Uncertainty, Imitation, and Plant Location: Japanese Multinational Corporations, 1990–1996." *Administrative Science Quarterly* 46, 3: 443–475.

Heo, Uk and Hans Stockton. 2005. "The Impact of Democratic Transition on Elections and Parties in South Korea." *Party Politics* 11, 6: 675–688.

Herrnson, Paul S. 1988. *Party Campaigning in the 1980s*. Cambridge, MA: Harvard University Press.

Hill, Kim Quaile and Patricia A. Hurley. 1999. "Dyadic Representation Reappraised." *American Journal of Political Science* 43, 1: 109–137.

Holzinger, Katharina and Christoph Knill. 2005. "Causes and Conditions of Cross-national Policy Convergence." *Journal of European Public Policy* 12, 5: 775–796.

Hundt, David. 2008. "Korea – Squandering a Mandate for Change?" *Australian Journal of International Affairs* 62, 4: 497–512.

Huneeus, Carlos. 2001. "La Derecha en el Chile Después de Pinochet: El Caso de la Unión Demócrata Independiente (UDI)." Working Paper no. 285, Kellogg Institute, University of Notre Dame.

Huneeus, Carlos. 2003. "A Highly Institutionalized Political Party: Christian Democracy in Chile." In Scott Mainwaring and Timothy R. Scully (eds.), *Christian Democracy in Latin America: Electoral Competition and Regime Conflicts*. Stanford, CA: Stanford University Press, pp. 121–161.

Hunter, Wendy and Timothy J. Power. 2007. "Rewarding Lula: Executive Power, Social Policy, and the Brazilian Elections of 2006." *Latin American Politics and Society* 49, 1: 1–30.

Hurley, Patricia A. and Kim Quaile Hill. 2003. "Beyond the Demand-Input Model: A Theory of Representational Linkages." *Journal of Politics* 65, 2: 304–326.

IBGE (Instituto Brasileiro de Geografia e Estatística). 1998. *Pesquisa Mensal de Emprego*. Brasília: IBGE, June.

Ichino, Nahomi and Noah L. Nathan. 2013. "Crossing the Line: Local Ethnic Geography and Voting in Ghana." *American Political Science Review* 107, 2: 344–361.

ILO (International Labour Organization). 2006. *2006 Labour Overview: Latin American and the Caribbean*. Lima: ILO/Regional Office for Latin America and the Caribbean.

Inglehart, Ronald. 1984. "The Changing Structure of Political Cleavages in Western Society." In Russell Dalton, Scott Flanagan, and Paul Beck (eds.), *Electoral Change in Advanced Industrial Democracies*. Princeton, NJ: Princeton University Press, pp. 25–69.

Iten, Marco and Sérgio Kobayashi. 2002. *Eleição: Vença a Sua! As Boas Técnicas do Marketing Político*. São Paulo: Ateliê Editorial.

Jeffries, Richard. 1998. "The Ghanaian Elections of 1996: Towards the Consolidation of Democracy?" *African Affairs* 97, 387: 189–208.

Johnson, Dennis W. 2001. *No Place for Amateurs: How Political Consultants Are Reshaping American Democracy*. New York: Routledge.

Johnson, Jason. 2012. *Political Consultants and Campaigns: One Day to Sell*. Boulder, CO: Westview Press.

Johnston, Richard, André Blais, Henry E. Brady, and Jean Crête. 1992. *Letting the People Decide: Dynamics of a Canadian Election*. Stanford, CA: Stanford University Press.

Kampwirth, Karen. 1998. "Feminism, Antifeminism, and Electoral Politics in Postwar Nicaragua and El Salvador." *Political Science Quarterly* 113, 2: 259–279.

Kampwirth, Karen. 2008. "Abortion, Antifeminism, and the Return of Daniel Ortega: In Nicaragua, Leftist Politics?" *Latin American Perspectives* 35, 6: 122–136.

Kang, David C. 2003. "Regional Politics and Democratic Consolidation in Korea." In Samuel S. Kim (ed.), *Korea's Democratization*. New York: Cambridge University Press, pp. 161–180.

Kang, Won-Taek and Hoon Jaung. 1999. "The 1997 Presidential Election in South Korea." *Electoral Studies* 18: 599–608.

Karch, Andrew. 2007. "Emerging Issues and Future Directions in State Policy Diffusion Research." *State Politics and Policy Quarterly* 7, 1: 54–80.

Katz, Richard S. and Peter Mair. 1995. "Changing Models of Party Organization and Party Democracy: The Emergence of the Cartel Party." *Party Politics* 1, 1: 5–28.

Kay, Bruce H. 1996. "'Fujipopulism' and the Liberal State in Peru, 1990–1995." *Journal of Interamerican Studies and World Affairs* 38, 4: 55–98.

Keck, Margaret E. 1992. *The Workers' Party and Democratization in Brazil*. New Haven, CT: Yale University Press.

Kelly, Bob. 2009. "The Ghanaian Election of 2008." *Review of African Political Economy* 36, 121: 441–450.

Kenney, Charles D. 2003. "The Death and Rebirth of a Party System, Peru 1978–2001." *Comparative Political Studies* 36, 10: 1210–1239.

Kenney, Charles D. 2004. *Fujimori's Coup and the Breakdown of Democracy in Latin America*. Notre Dame, IN: University of Notre Dame Press.

Kern, Montague. 1989. *30-Second Politics: Political Advertising in the Eighties*. New York: Praeger.

Key, V. O., Jr. 1961. *Public Opinion and American Democracy*. New York: Alfred A. Knopf.

Kim, Hyejin. 2014. "A Link to the Authoritarian Past? Older Voters as a Force in the 2012 South Korean Presidential Election." *Taiwan Journal of Democracy* 10, 2: 49–71.

Kim, Youngmi. 2014. "The 2012 Parliamentary and Presidential Elections in South Korea." *Electoral Studies* 34: 326–330.

Kirchheimer, Otto. 1966. "The Transformation of Western European Party Systems." In Joseph LaPalombara and Myron Wiener (eds.), *Political Parties and Political Development*. Princeton, NJ: Princeton University Press, pp. 177–200.

Kitschelt, Herbert. 2000. "Linkages between Citizens and Politicians in Democratic Polities." *Comparative Political Studies* 33, 6/7: 845–879.

Kitschelt, Herbert. 2012. *Research and Dialogue on Programmatic Parties and Party Systems*. Stockholm: International Institute for Democracy and Electoral Assistance.

Kitschelt, Herbert, Kirk A. Hawkins, Juan Pablo Luna, Guillermo Rosas, and Elizabeth Zechmeister. 2010. *Latin American Party Systems*. New York: Cambridge University Press.

Kitschelt, Herbert and Daniel Kselman. 2013. "Economic Development, Democratic Experience, and Political Parties' Linkage Strategies." *Comparative Political Studies* 46, 11: 1453–1484.

Kitschelt, Herbert and Steven I. Wilkinson. 2007. *Patrons, Clients, and Policies: Patterns of Democratic Accountability and Political Competition*. New York: Cambridge University Press.

Knutsen, Oddbjørn and Elinor Scarbrough. 1995. "Cleavage Politics." In Jan W. Van Deth and Elinor Scarbrough (eds.), *The Impact of Values*. New York: Oxford University Press, pp. 492–523.

Kotscho, Ricardo. 2006. *Uma Vida de Repórter: Do Golpe ao Planalto*. São Paulo: Companhia das Letras.

Kramer, Michael. 1996. "Rescuing Boris." *Time* 148, 4 (July 15): 28–37.

Kuntz, Ronald A. 1985. *Marketing Político: Manual de Campanha Eleitoral*. São Paulo: Global Editora.

Kwarteng, Charles. 2014. "Swords into Ploughshares: The Judicial Challenge of Ghana's 2012 Presidential Election Results." *The Round Table: The Commonwealth Journal of International Affairs* 103, 1: 83–93.

Kwon, Hyeok Yong. 2010. "Economic Perceptions and Electoral Choice in South Korea: The Case of the 2007 Presidential Election." *The Pacific Review* 23, 2: 183–201.

Lamounier, Bolívar. 2003. "Brazil: An Assessment of the Cardoso Administration." In Jorge I. Domínguez and Michael Shifter (eds.), *Constructing Democratic Governance in Latin America*, 2nd edn. Baltimore, MD: Johns Hopkins University Press, pp. 269–291.

Langston, Joy. 2009. "The PRI's 2006 Presidential Campaign." In Domínguez, Lawson, and Moreno (eds.), pp. 152–168.

Laquian, Aprodicio and Eleanor Laquian. 1998. *Joseph Ejercito "Erap" Estrada: The Centennial President*. Vancouver: Institute of Asian Research, University of British Columbia.

Latinobarómetro. 2006. *Informe Latinobarómetro 2006*. Santiago: Corporación Latinobarómetro.

Latinobarómetro. 2008. *Informe 2008*. Santiago: Corporación Latinobarómetro.

Lawson, Chappell and James A. McCann. 2005. "Television News, Mexico's 2000 Elections and Media Effects in Emerging Democracies." *British Journal of Political Science* 35: 1–30.

Lawson, Kay. 1980. "Political Parties and Linkage." In Kay Lawson (ed.), *Political Parties and Linkage: A Comparative Perspective*. New Haven, CT: Yale University Press, pp. 3–24.

Lawson, Kay. 1988. "When Linkage Fails." In Kay Lawson and Peter H. Merkl (eds.), *When Parties Fail: Emerging Alternative Organizations*. Princeton, NJ: Princeton University Press, pp. 13–38.

Ledeneva, Alena V. 2006. *How Russia Really Works: The Informal Practices That Shaped Post-Soviet Politics and Business*. Ithaca, NY: Cornell University Press.

Lee, Aie-Rie and Yong U. Glasure. 1995. "Party Identifiers in South Korea: Differences in Issue Orientations." *Asian Survey* 35, 4: 367–376.

Lee, Hong Yung. 1993. "South Korea in 1992: A Turning Point in Democratization." *Asian Survey* 33, 1: 32–42.

Lee, Hong Yung. 2003. "South Korea in 2002: Multiple Political Dramas." *Asian Survey* 43, 1: 64–77.

Lee, Hyeon-Woo. 2003. "Issues and Campaign Strategies in the 2002 Presidential Election." *Korea Journal* 43, 2: 146–171.

Lee, Manwoo. 1990. *The Odyssey of Korean Democracy: Korean Politics, 1987–1990*. New York: Praeger.

Lee, Manwoo. 1995. "South Korea's Politics of Succession and the December 1992 Presidential Election." In James Cotton (ed.), *Politics and Policy in the New Korean State: From Roh Tae-Woo to Kim Young-Sam*. New York: St. Martin's Press, pp. 35–65.

León, Carlos. 2011. "'Nosotros Nos Equivocamos Menos': Vida, Muerte y Resurrección Electoral de Ollanta Humala." In Carlos Meléndez (ed.), *Post-candidatos: Guía Analítica de Sobrevivencia Hasta las Próximas Elecciones*. Lima: Mitín Editores, pp. 43–88.

León, Osvaldo. 2007. "Ecuador: Elecciones, Medios, y Democracia." *Chasqui* 97: 50–55.

Levitsky, Steven. 2000. "The 'Normalization' of Argentine Politics." *Journal of Democracy* 11, 2: 56–69.

Levitsky, Steven. 2011. "A Surprising Left Turn." *Journal of Democracy* 22, 4: 84–94.

Levitsky, Steven. 2013. "Peru: The Challenges of a Democracy without Parties." In Jorge I. Domínguez and Michael Shifter (eds.), *Constructing Democratic Governance in Latin America*, 4th edn. Baltimore, MD: Johns Hopkins University Press, pp. 282–315.

Levitsky, Steven and Maxwell A. Cameron. 2003. "Democracy without Parties? Political Parties and Regime Change in Fujimori's Peru." *Latin American Politics and Society* 45, 3: 1–33.

Levitsky, Steven and Kenneth M. Roberts. 2011. "Latin America's 'Left Turn': A Framework for Analysis." In Steven Levitsky and Kenneth M. Roberts (eds.), *The Resurgence of the Latin American Left*. Baltimore, MD: Johns Hopkins University Press, pp. 1–28.

Levitsky, Steven and María Victoria Murillo. 2008. "Argentina: From Kirchner to Kirchner." *Journal of Democracy* 19, 2: 16–30.

Levitsky, Steven and Lucan Way. 2010. *Competitive Authoritarianism: Hybrid Regimes after the Cold War*. New York: Cambridge University Press.

Levitt, Barbara and James G. March. 1988. "Organizational Learning." *Annual Review of Sociology* 14: 319–340.

Levitt, Barry S. 1998. "Parties and Politicians in Contemporary Peru: Exploring New Forms of Electoral Representation." Paper presented at the annual meeting of the Latin American Studies Association, Chicago, IL, September 24–26.

Lie, John and Andrew Eungi Kim. 2008. "South Korea in 2007: Scandals and Summits." *Asian Survey* 48, 1: 116–123.

Lieberman, Evan S. 2005. "Nested Analysis as a Mixed-Method Strategy for Comparative Research." *American Political Science Review* 99, 3: 435–452.

Lieberman, Evan S. 2009. *Boundaries of Contagion: How Ethnic Politics Have Shaped Government Responses to AIDS*. Princeton, NJ: Princeton University Press.

Lieberman, Marvin B. and Shigeru Asaba. 2006. "Why Do Firms Imitate Each Other?" *Academy of Management Review* 31, 2: 366–385.

Lijphart, Arend. 1999. *Patterns of Democracy: Government Forms and Performance in Thirty-Six Countries*. New Haven, CT: Yale University Press.

Lima, Marcelo O. Coutinho de. 1988. *Marketing Eleitoral: Para Não Desperdiçar Recursos*. São Paulo: Ícone.

Linz, Juan J. 1994. "Presidential or Parliamentary Democracy: Does It Make a Difference?" In Juan Linz and Arturo Valenzuela (eds.), *The Failure of Presidential Democracy: Comparative Perspectives*, Vol. 1. Baltimore, MD: Johns Hopkins University Press, pp. 3–87.

Luna, Juan Pablo. 2014. *Segmented Representation: Political Party Strategies in Unequal Democracies*. New York: Oxford University Press.

Luttbeg, Norman R. 1968. "Political Linkage in a Large Society." In Norman R. Luttbeg (ed.), *Public Opinion and Public Policy: Models of Political Linkage*. Homewood, IL: Dorsey Press, pp. 1–9.

Madrid, Raúl. 2011. "Ethnic Proximity and Ethnic Voting in Peru." *Journal of Latin American Studies* 43: 267–297.

Maggetti, Martino and Fabrizio Gilardi. 2015. "Problems (and Solutions) in the Measurement of Policy Diffusion Mechanisms." *Journal of Public Policy*. doi:10.1017/S0143814X1400035X.

Maggiotto, Michael A. and Gary D. Wekkin. 2000. *Partisan Linkages in Southern Politics: Elites, Voters, and Identifiers*. Knoxville, TN: University of Tennessee Press.

Mainwaring, Scott, Ana María Bejerano, and Eduardo Pizarro Leongómez. 2006. "The Crisis of Democratic Representation in the Andes: An Overview." In Scott Mainwaring, Ana María Bejerano, and Eduardo Pizarro Leongómez (eds.), *The Crisis of Democratic Representation in the Andes*. Stanford, CA: Stanford University Press, pp. 1–44.

Mainwaring, Scott and Timothy R. Scully. 2003. "The Diversity of Christian Democracy in Latin America." In Scott Mainwaring and Timothy R. Scully (eds.), *Christian Democracy in Latin America: Electoral Competition and Regime Conflicts*. Stanford, CA: Stanford University Press, pp. 30–63.

Malfitani, Chico. 2001. Comments at roundtable discussion "Profissionais do Marketing Político," Conference on "Mídia e Marketing Político no Processo Eleitoral," Pontifícia Universidade Católica de São Paulo, August 24.

"Mali: IBK Wins." 2013. *Africa Research Bulletin* 50, 8: 19810–19811.

Malkin, Elisabeth. 2009a. "Fate of Ousted Leader Clouds Election Result in Honduras." *New York Times*, November 30.

Malkin, Elisabeth. 2009b. "Weary of Political Crisis, Honduras Holds Election." *New York Times*, November 28.

Mancini, Paolo. 1999. "New Frontiers in Political Professionalism." *Political Communication* 16: 231–245.

Manhanelli, Carlos Augusto. 1988. *Estratégias Eleitorais: Marketing Político*. São Paulo: Summus.

Manhanelli, Carlos Augusto. 1992. *Eleição é Guerra: Marketing para Campanhas Eleitorais*. São Paulo: Summus.

Manin, Bernard. 1997. *The Principles of Representative Government*. New York: Cambridge University Press.

Mark, David. 2006. *Going Dirty: The Art of Negative Campaigning*. Lanham, MD: Rowman & Littlefield.

Markun, Paulo. 1989. *Como Perder as Eleições (Ou Táticas e Estratégias para Evitar Que Isso Aconteça)*. São Paulo: Feeling Editorial.

Matheus, Carlos. 1998. "Pesquisa e Povo: O Eleitor, Esse Desconhecido." In Cid Pacheco, Isavel Cristina Alencar de Azevedo, and Lucia Ferreira Reis (eds.), *Voto é Marketing?* Rio de Janeiro: Irradiação Cultural, pp. 78–84.

Mauceri, Philip. 1997. "Return of the Caudillo: Autocratic Democracy in Peru." *Third World Quarterly* 18, 5: 899–911.

Mayobre, José Antonio. 1996. "Politics, Media, and Modern Democracy: The Case of Venezuela." In Swanson and Mancini (eds.), pp. 227–245.

Mayorga, René Antonio. 1997. "Bolivia's Silent Revolution." *Journal of Democracy* 8, 1: 142–156.

McClintock, Cynthia. 1994. "Presidents, Messiahs, and Constitutional Breakdowns in Peru." In Juan Linz and Arturo Valenzuela (eds.), *The Failure of Presidential Democracy*. Baltimore, MD: Johns Hopkins University Press, pp. 360–395.

McConnell, Shelley A. 2007. "Nicaragua's Turning Point." *Current History* 106, 697: 83–88.

McConnell, Tristan. 2009. "Ghana's New President: Africa's Symbol of a Working Democracy." *Christian Science Monitor,* January 8.

McCoy, Jennifer L. and Shelley A. McConnell. 1997. "Nicaragua: Beyond the Revolution." *Current History* 96, 607: 75–80.

McDonald, Ronald H. and J. Mark Ruhl. 1989. *Party Politics and Elections in Latin America*. Boulder, CO: Westview Press.

McFaul, Michael. 1996. "Time: Scoop or Dupe?" *Moscow Times,* July 17.

Medeiros, Alexandre. 1994. *Nos Bastidores da Campanha: Luiz Inácio Lula da Silva: Crônica de um Sonho*. Rio de Janeiro: Editora Objetiva.

Meléndez, Carlos. 2009. "La Insistencia de los Partidos. Una Aproximación sobre la Permanencia de los Partidos Políticos Tradicionales en los Países Andinos." In Martín Tanaka (ed.), *La Nueva Coyuntura Crítica en los Países Andinos*. Lima: Instituto de Estudios Peruanos/IDEA Internacional, pp. 21–48.

Meléndez, Carlos. 2011. "Post-Candidatos." In Carlos Meléndez (ed.), *Post-candidatos: Guía analítica de sobrevivencia hasta las próximas elecciones*. Lima: Mitín Editores, pp. 9–20.

Méndez, Roberto, Oscar Godoy, Enrique Barros, and Arturo Fontaine Talavera. 1989. "Por Qué Ganó el No?" *Estudios Públicos* 33: 83–134.

Mendonça, Duda. 2001. *Casos e Coisas*. São Paulo: Globo.

Meseguer, Covadonga. 2005. "Policy Learning, Policy Diffusion, and the Making of a New Order." *Annals of the American Academy of Political and Social Science* 598: 67–82.

Meseguer, Covadonga. 2009. *Learning, Policy Making, and Market Reforms*. New York: Cambridge University Press.

Meza, Víctor (ed.) 2002. *Proceso Electoral 2001: Monitoreo Desde la Sociedad Civil*. Tegucigalpa: Centro de Documentación de Honduras.

Mieres, Pablo. 1985. "Los Partidos Uruguayos y el Sistema Político: Imágenes y Desafíos del Presente." In *De la Tradición a la Crisis: Pasado y Presente de Nuestro Sistema de Partidos*. Montevideo: Ediciones de la Banda Oriental, pp. 113–141.

Mieres, Pablo. 1990. "Un Sistema de Partidos en Transición. Notas Preliminares a Propósito de los Resultados de las Elecciones Nacionales de 1989." *Cuadernos del CLAEH* 53: 5–22.

Mieres, Pablo. 2011. "Las Campañas Electorales en Chile y Uruguay, Continuidad y Alternancia." Presented at the Spanish Congress of Political Science, Murcia, September.

Mieres, Pablo. 2012. "Las Candidaturas Vicepresidenciales en las Campañas Electorales: El Caso de Uruguay 2009." Presented at the 4th Uruguayan Congress of Political Science, Montivideo, November.

Miguel, Luis Felipe. 1998. "O Campeão da União: O Discurso de Fernando Henrique Na Campanha de 1994." *Comunicação e Política* 5, 1: 49–82.

Miguel, Luis Felipe. 2000. *Mito e Discurso Político: Uma Análise a Partir da Campanha Eleitoral de 1994*. Campinas/São Paulo: Editora da Unicamp/Imprensa Oficial.

Miguel, Luis Felipe. 2003. "A Eleição Visível: A Rede Globo Descobre a Política em 2002." *Dados – Revista de Ciências Sociais* 46, 2: 289–310.

Miller, Danny and Ming-Jer Chen. 1994. "Sources and Consequences of Competitive Inertia: A Study of the U.S. Airline Industry." *Administrative Science Quarterly* 39, 1: 1–23.

Molina Chocano, Guillermo. 1992. "Elecciones y Consolidación Democrática en Honduras en la Última Década." In *Una Tarea Inconclusa: Elecciones y Democracia en América Latina: 1988–1991*. San José: Instituto Interamericano de Derechos Humanos/Centro de Asesoría y Promoción Electoral, pp. 96–116.

Montes, Carlos. 1989. "El Vals ante la Barricada." In *La Campaña del No Vista por Sus Creadores*. Santiago: Ediciones Melquíades, pp. 37–42.

Montinola, Gabriella R. 1999. "The Philippines in 1998: Opportunity amid Crisis." *Asian Survey* 39, 1: 64–71.

Montúfar, César M. 1990. "Ecuador: Elecciones Presidenciales de 1988." *Revista Mexicana de Sociología* 52, 4: 155–176.

Morales, Mauricio and Rodrigo D. Bugueño. 2002. "La UDI Como Expresión de la Nueva Derecha en Chile." *Instituciones y Desarrollo* 12–13: 317–347.

Moreira, Contanza. 2004. *Final del Juego: Del Bipartidismo Tradicional al Triunfo de la Izquierda en Uruguay*. Montevideo: Ediciones Trilce.

Morgan, Jana. 2011. *Bankrupt Representation and Party System Collapse*. University Park, PA: Pennsylvania State University Press.

Moura, Ricardo. 2001. "Perú Imposible: O 'Los Apus Han Hablado.'" *El Opiniado* 42 (June 4). Available at: nuestraimagen.ws/opinionado/opi42.html (accessed on September 27, 2015).

Navia, Patricio. 2008. "Top-Down and Bottom-Up Democracy in Latin America: The Case of Bachelet in Chile." *Stockholm Review of Latin American Studies* 3: 119–130.

Navia, Patricio. 2009. *El Díscolo*. Santiago: Random House Mondadori.

Navia, Patricio and Alfredo Joignant. 2000. "Las Elecciones Presidenciales de 1999: La Participación Electoral y el Nuevo Votante Chileno." In *Nuevo Gobierno: Desafíos de la Reconciliación, Chile 1999–2000*. Santiago: FLACSO–Chile, pp. 119–144.

Negrine, Ralph and Stylianos Papathanassopoulos. 1996. "The 'Americanization' of Political Communication: A Critique." *Harvard International Journal of Press/Politics* 1, 2: 45–62.

Neuendorf, Kimberly A. 2002. *The Content Analysis Guidebook*. Thousand Oaks, CA: Sage.

Norris, Pippa. 2000. *A Virtuous Circle: Political Communication in Postindustrial Societies*. New York: Cambridge University Press.

Nugent, Paul. 1995. *Big Men, Small Boys and Politics in Ghana: Power, Ideology, and the Burden of History, 1982–1994*. New York: Pinter.

Nugent, Paul. 1999. "Living in the Past: Urban, Rural, and Ethnic Themes in the 1992 and 1996 Elections in Ghana." *Journal of Modern African Studies* 37, 2: 287–319.

Nugent, Paul. 2001. "Winners, Losers, and Also Rans: Money, Moral Authority and Voting Patterns in the Ghana 2000 Election." *African Affairs* 100: 405–428.

Nwajiaku, Kathryn. 1994. "The National Conference in Benin and Togo Revisited." *Journal of Modern African Studies* 32, 3: 429–447.

Nyhan, Brendan and Jacob M. Montgomery. 2015. "Connecting the Candidates: Consultant Networks and the Diffusion of Campaign Strategy in American Congressional Elections." *American Journal of Political Science* 59, 2: 292–308.

Nzouankeu, Jacques Mariel. 1993. "The Role of the National Conference in the Transition to Democracy in Africa: The Cases of Benin and Mali." *Issue* 21, 1–2: 44–50.

O'Donnell, Guillermo. 1994. "Delegative Democracy." *Journal of Democracy* 5: 55–69.

O'Donnell, Guillermo. 2004. "Human Development, Human Rights, and Democracy." In Guillermo O'Donnell, Jorge Vargas Cullell, and Osvaldo M. Iazzetta (eds.), *The Quality of Democracy: Theory and Applications*. Notre Dame, IN: University of Notre Dame Press, pp. 9–92.

Oelbaum, Jay. 2004. "Ethnicity Adjusted? Economic Reform, Elections, and Tribalism in Ghana's Fourth Republic." *Commonwealth & Comparative Politics* 42, 2: 242–273.

Oliveira, Jorge. 2006. *Campanha Política: Como Ganhar Uma Eleição: Regras e Dicas*. São Paulo: A Girafa.

Oppenheimer, Bruce I. 1996. "The Representational Experience: The Effect of State Population on Senator-Constituency Linkages." *American Journal of Political Science* 40, 4: 1280–1299.

Ortega Hegg, Manuel. 2007. "Nicaragua 2006: El Regreso del FSLN al Poder." *Revista de Ciencia Política* Special volume: 205–219.

Ostiguy, Pierre. 1997. "Peronismo y Antiperonismo: Bases Socioculturales de la Identidad Política en la Argentina." *Revista de Ciencias Sociales* 6: 133–213.

Otaño, Rafael. 1995. *Crónica de la Transición*. Santiago: Planeta.

Oviedo, Carlos. 1981. *Manejos de la Propaganda Política*. Lima: Promotores, Consultores, y Asesores Andinos SRL/Centro de Documentación e Información Andina.

Oxhorn, Philip. 1994. "Where Did All the Protesters Go? Popular Mobilization and the Transition to Democracy in Chile." *Latin American Perspectives* 21, 3: 49–68.

Pachano, Simón. 2006. "Ecuador: The Provincialization of Representation." In Scott Mainwaring, Ana María Bejerano, and Eduardo Pizarro Leongómez (eds.), *Crisis of Democratic Representation in the Andes*. Stanford, CA: Stanford University Press, pp. 100–131.

Packenham, Robert A. 1994. "The Politics of Economic Liberalization: Argentina and Brazil in Comparative Perspective." Working Paper no. 206, Helen Kellogg Institute for International Studies, University of Notre Dame.

Panebianco, Angelo. 1988. *Political Parties: Organization and Power.* New York: Cambridge University Press.

Panizza, Francisco. 2000. "Neopopulism and Its Limits in Collor's Brazil." *Bulletin of Latin American Research* 19: 177–192.

Park, Chan Wook. 2002. "Elections in Democratizing Korea." In John Fuh-sheng Hsieh and David Newman (eds.), *How Asia Votes.* New York: Seven Bridges Press, pp. 118–146.

Park, Tong Whan. 1998. "South Korea in 1997: Clearing the Last Hurdle to Political-Economic Maturation." *Asian Survey* 38, 1: 1–10.

Patterson, Henry. 1997. "The 1996 Elections and Nicaragua's Fragile Transition." *Government and Opposition* 32: 380–398.

Paz Aguilar, Ernesto. 1990. "Elecciones en Honduras: Entre el Marasmo y la Ilusión." In *Cuadernos Liberales*, Vol. 2. Tegucigalpa: Instituto de Educación Política del Partido Liberal de Honduras, pp. 90–99.

Pérez-Baltodano, Andrés. 2012. "Nicaragua: Democracia Electoral Sin Consenso Social." *Revista de Ciencia Política* 32, 1: 211–228.

Perloff, Richard M. and Dennis Kinsey. 1992. "Political Advertising as Seen by Consultants and Journalists." *Journal of Advertising Research* May/June: 53–60.

Perry, William. 1995. "The 1995 Argentine Elections: Pre-Election Report #2." Center for Strategic and International Studies, Western Hemisphere Election Study Series, Vol. 13, Study 4.

Pierson, Paul. 2004. *Politics in Time: History, Institutions, and Social Analysis.* Princeton, NJ: Princeton University Press.

Plasser, Fritz. 2000. "American Campaign Techniques Worldwide." *Harvard International Journal of Press/Politics* 5, 4: 33–54.

Plasser, Fritz and Gunda Plasser. 2002. *Global Political Campaigning: A Worldwide Analysis of Campaign Professionals and Their Practices.* Westport, CT: Praeger.

Poguntke, Thomas. 2002. "Party Organizational Linkage: Parties without Firm Social Roots?" In Kurt Richard Luther and Ferdinand Müller-Rommel (eds.), *Political Parties in the New Europe: Political and Analytical Challenges.* New York: Oxford University Press, pp. 43–62.

Pollack, Marcelo. 1999. *The New Right in Chile, 1973–1997.* New York: St. Martin's Press.

Por Qué Perdió el Partido Liberal: Anatomía de una Derrota. 1990. Tegucigalpa: Instituto de Educación Política del Partido Liberal de Honduras.

Porto, Mauro Pereira. 2007. "Framing Controversies: Television and the 2002 Presidential Election in Brazil." *Political Communication* 24: 19–36.

Porto, Mauro Pereira and Liziane Soares Guazina. 1999. "A Política Na TV: O Horário Eleitoral da Eleição Presidencial de 1994." *Contracampo* 3: 5–33.

Posner, Paul W. 1999. "Popular Representation and Political Dissatisfaction in Chile's New Democracy." *Journal of Interamerican Studies and World Affairs* 40, 1: 59–85.

Posner, Paul W. 2004. "Local Democracy and the Transformation of Popular Participation in Chile." *Latin American Politics and Society* 46, 3: 55–81.

Prado, Antônio de Pádua, Jr. and José Augusto Guilhon Albuquerque. 1987. *ABC do Candidato (Marketing Político).* São Paulo: Editora Babel Cultural.

Puryear, Jeffrey M. 1994. *Thinking Politics: Intellectuals and Democracy in Chile, 1973–1988.* Baltimore, MD: Johns Hopkins University Press.

Quimpo, Nathan Gilbert. 2005. "The Left, Elections, and the Political Party System in the Philippines." *Critical Asian Studies* 37, 1: 3–28.

Quintero López, Rafael. 2005. *Electores Contra Partidos en un Sistema Política de Mandos.* Quito: Ediciones Abya-Yala.

Raymond, Christopher and Moisés Arce. 2011. "The Politicization of Indigenous Identities in Peru." *Party Politics* 19, 4: 555–576.

Raymond, Christopher and Brian M. Barros Feltch. 2014. "Parties, Cleavages and Issue Evolution: The Case of the Religious-Secular Cleavage in Chile." *Party Politics* 20, 3: 429–443.

Rial, Juan. 1986. "The Uruguayan Elections of 1984: A Triumph of the Center." In Paul W. Drake and Eduardo Silva (eds.), *Elections and Democratization in Latin America, 1980–1985.* San Diego: Center for Iberian and Latin American Studies/Center for U.S.-Mexican Studies/Institute of the Americas, University of California, pp. 245–271.

Roberts, Kenneth M. 1995. "Neoliberalism and the Transformation of Populism in Latin America: The Peruvian Case." *World Politics* 48, 1: 82–116.

Roberts, Kenneth M. 1998. *Deepening Democracy? The Modern Left and Social Movements in Chile and Peru.* Stanford, CA: Stanford University Press.

Roberts, Kenneth M. 2006. "Do Parties Matter? Lessons from the Fujimori Experience." In Julio F. Carrión (ed.), *The Fujimori Legacy: The Rise of Electoral Authoritarianism in Peru.* University Park, PA: Pennsylvania State University Press, pp. 81–101.

Roberts, Kenneth M. 2014. *Changing Course in Latin America: Party Systems in the Neoliberal Era.* New York: Cambridge University Press.

Roberts, Kenneth M. and Moisés Arcé. 1998. "Neoliberalism and Lower-Class Voting Behavior in Peru." *Comparative Political Studies* 31, 2: 217–246.

Robinson, Pearl T. 1994. "The National Conference Phenomenon in Francophone Africa." *Comparative Studies in Society and History* 36, 3: 575–610.

Robinson, William I. 1992. *A Faustian Bargain: U.S. Intervention in the Nicaraguan Elections and American Foreign Policy in the Post-Cold War Era.* Boulder, CO: Westview Press.

Rogers, Steven. 2004. "Philippine Politics and the Rule of Law." *Journal of Democracy* 15, 4: 111–125.

Rood, Steven. 2002. "Elections as Complicated and Important Events in the Philippines." In John Fuh-sheng Hsieh and David Newman (eds.), *How Asia Votes.* New York: Seven Bridges Press, pp. 147–164.

Rosenberg, Mark B. 1989. "Can Democracy Survive the Democrats? From Transition to Consolidation in Honduras." In John A. Booth and Mitchell A. Seligson (eds.), *Elections and Democracy in Central America.* Chapel Hill, NC: University of North Carolina Press, pp. 40–59.

Rospigliosi, Fernando. 1990. "Elecciones Generales, Perú: 8 de Abril y 10 de Julio de 1990." *Boletín Electoral Latinoamericano* 3: 32–40.

Rospigliosi, Fernando. 1994. "Caudillos Independientes." *Caretas,* October 6: 27.

Rottinghaus, Brandon and Irina Alberro. 2005. "Rivaling the PRI: The Image Management of Vicente Fox and the Use of Public Opinion Polling in the 2000 Mexican Election." *Latin American Politics and Society* 47, 2: 143–158.

Ruhl, J. Mark. 1998. "Honduras: Militarism and Democratization in Troubled Waters." Paper presented at the International Congress of the Latin American Studies Association, Chicago, IL, September 24–26.

Sabato, Larry J. 1981. *The Rise of Political Consultants: New Ways of Winning Elections*. New York: Basic Books.

Salomón, Leticia. 1994. *Democratización y Sociedad Civil en Honduras*. Tegucigalpa: Centro de Documentación de Honduras.

Samuels, David. 2004. "From Socialism to Social Democracy? Party Organization and the Transformation of the Workers' Party in Brazil." *Comparative Political Studies* 37, 9: 999–1024.

Samuels, David. 2008. "Brazil: Democracy under Lula and the PT." In Jorge I. Domínguez and Michael Shifter (eds.), *Constructing Democratic Governance in Latin America*, 3rd edn. Baltimore, MD: Johns Hopkins University Press, pp. 152–176.

Samuels, David. 2013. "Brazil: Democracy in the PT Era." In Jorge I. Domínguez and Michael Shifter (eds.), *Constructing Democratic Governance in Latin America*, 4th edn. Baltimore, MD: Johns Hopkins University Press, pp. 177–203.

San Francisco, Alejandro. 2003. "Political Parties and Democratic Transition in Chile 1989–2001: The Case of the Unión Democrática Independiente (UDI)." Paper presented at the Joint Session of Workshops, European Consortium for Political Research, Edinburgh, March 28–April 2.

Sanborn, Cynthia Ann. 1991. "The Democratic Left and the Persistence of Populism in Peru, 1975–1990." Ph.D. Dissertation, Harvard University.

Sanborn, Cynthia Ann and Aldo Panfichi. 1996. "Fujimori y las Raíces del Neopopulismo." In Fernando Tuesta Soldevilla (ed.), *Los Enigmas del Poder: Fujimori 1990–1996*. Lima: Fundación Friedrich Ebert, pp. 29–52.

Sanchez-Sibony, Omar. 2012. "The 2011 Presidential Election in Peru: A Thorny Moral and Political Dilemma." *Comparative Politics* 18, 1: 109–126.

Sánchez, Omar. 2005. "Argentina's Landmark 2003 Presidential Election: Renewal and Continuity." *Bulletin of Latin American Research* 24, 4: 454–475.

Sánchez, Omar. 2008. "Transformation and Decay: The De-institutionalisation of Party Systems in South America." *Third World Quarterly* 29, 2: 315–337.

Santa Rita, Chico. 2001. *Batalhas Eleitorais: 25 Anos de Marketing Político*. São Paulo: Geração Editorial.

Sartori, Giovanni. 1976. *Parties and Party Systems: A Framework for Analysis*. New York: Cambridge University Press.

Sborgi, Enrico. 1998. "Assessing Democracy in Mali: A Procedural Analysis." *Il Politico* 63, 3: 449–477.

Scammell, Margaret. 1999. "Political Marketing: Lessons for Political Science." *Political Studies* 47: 718–739.

Schedler, Andreas (ed.) 2006. *Electoral Authoritarianism: The Dynamics of Unfree Competition*. Boulder, CO: Lynne Rienner Publishers.

Schmidt, Gregory D. 1996. "Fujimori's 1990 Upset Victory in Peru: Electoral Rules, Contingencies, and Adaptive Strategies." *Comparative Politics* 28, 3: 321–354.

Schmidt, Gregory D. 2000. "Delegative Democracy in Peru? Fujimori's 1995 Landslide and the Prospects for 2000." *Journal of Interamerican Studies and World Affairs* 42, 1: 99–132.

Schmidt, Gregory D. 2007. "Back to the Future? The 2006 Peruvian General Election." *Electoral Studies* 26, 4: 813–819.

Schneider, Ben Ross. 1991. "Brazil under Collor: Anatomy of a Crisis." *World Policy Journal* 8, 2: 321–347.

Scotto, Gabriela. 2004. *As (Difusas) Fronteiras Entre a Política e o Mercado: Um Estudo Antropológico sobre Marketing Político, Seus Agentes, Práticas e Representações*. Rio de Janeiro: Relume Dumará.

Seawright, Jason. 2012. *Party-System Collapse: The Roots of Crisis in Peru and Venezuela*. Stanford, CA: Stanford University Press.

Seely, Jennifer C. 2005. "The Legacies of Transition Governments: Post-transition Dynamics in Benin and Togo." *Democratization* 12, 3: 357–377.

Séguéla, Jacques. 2000. *Le Vertige des Urnes*. Paris: Flammarion.

Shipan, Charles R. and Craig Volden. 2008. "The Mechanisms of Policy Diffusion." *American Journal of Political Science* 52, 4: 840–857.

Shirk, David A. 2009. "Choosing Mexico's 2006 Presidential Candidates." In Domínguez, Lawson, and Moreno (eds.), pp. 129–151.

Shugart, Matthew Soberg and John M. Carey. 1992. *Presidents and Assemblies: Constitutional Design and Electoral Dynamics*. New York: Cambridge University Press.

Siavelis, Peter M. 2008. "Chile: The End of the Unfinished Transition." In Jorge I. Domínguez and Michael Shifter (eds.), *Constructing Democratic Governance in Latin America*. 3rd edn. Baltimore, MD: Johns Hopkins University Press, pp. 177–208.

Sieder, Rachel. 1998. *Elecciones y Democratización en Honduras Desde 1980*. Tegucigalpa: Editorial Universitaria.

Silva, Patricio. 2001. "Towards Technocratic Mass Politics in Chile? The 1999–2000 Elections and the 'Lavín Phenomenon'." *European Review of Latin American and Caribbean Studies* 70: 25–39.

Simmons, Beth A., Frank Dobbin, and Geoffrey Garrett. 2008. "Introduction: The Diffusion of Liberalization." In Beth A. Simmons, Frank Dobbin, and Geoffrey Garrett (eds.), *The Global Diffusion of Markets and Democracy*. New York: Cambridge University Press, pp. 1–63.

Sluyter-Beltrão, Marília. 1992. "Interpreting Brazilian Telenovelas: Biography and Fiction in a Rural-Urban Audience." In Anamaria Fadul (ed.), *Serial Fiction in TV: The Latin American Telenovelas*. São Paulo: Universidade de São Paulo, pp. 63–76.

Smith, Zeric Kay. 1997. "Mali Election Update #5." Posting to H-AFRICA, May 7.

Smith, Zeric Kay. 2001. "Mali's Decade of Democracy." *Journal of Democracy* 12, 3: 73–79.

Social Weather Stations. 2007. "Net Satisfaction Ratings of Presidents: Philippines, May 1986 to June 2007." Available at: www.sws.org.ph/ind-pres.htm (accessed on January 21, 2009).

Sohn, Yul and Won-Taek Kang. 2013. "South Korea in 2012: An Election Year under Rebalancing Challenges." *Asian Survey* 53, 1: 198–205.

Souaré, Issaka K. 2011. "The 2011 Presidential Election in Benin: Explaining the Success of One of Two Firsts." *Journal of African Elections* 10, 2: 73–92.

Stahler-Sholk, Richard. 2003. "The Presidential and Legislative Elections in Nicaragua, 2001." *Electoral Studies* 22: 538–544.

Steinberg, David I. and Myung Shin. 2006. "Tensions in South Korean Political Parties in Transition: From Entourage to Ideology?" *Asian Survey* 46, 4: 517–537.

Stinchcombe, Arthur L. 1968. *Constructing Social Theories*. New York: Harcourt, Brace, & World.

Stokes, Susan C. 2001. *Mandates and Democracy: Neoliberalism by Surprise*. New York: Cambridge University Press.

Stokes, Susan C., Thad Dunning, Marcelo Nazareno, and Valeria Brusco. 2013. *Brokers, Voters, and Clientelism: The Puzzle of Distributive Politics*. New York: Cambridge University Press.

Suassuna, Luciano and Luiz Antônio Novaes. 1994. *Como Fernando Henrique Foi Eleito Presidente*. São Paulo: Editora Contexto.

Sunkel, Guillermo. 1989. "Las Encuestas de Opinión Pública: Entre el Saber y el Poder." Documento de trabajo no. 439, FLACSO–Chile, December.

Sunkel, Guillermo. 1992. *Usos Políticos de las Encuestas de Opinión Pública*. Santiago: FLACSO.

Sussman, Gerald. 2005. *Global Electioneering: Campaign Consulting, Communications, and Corporate Financing*. Lanham, MD: Rowman & Littlefield.

Sussman, Gerald and Lawrence Galizio. 2003. "The Global Reproduction of American Politics." *Political Communication* 20: 309–328.

Swanson, David L. and Paulo Mancini (eds.) 1996. *Politics, Media, and Modern Democracy: An International Study of Innovations in Electoral Campaigning and Their Consequences*. Westport, CT: Praeger.

Szusterman, Celia. 1996. "The 1995 Argentine Elections." *Electoral Studies* 15, 1: 109–16.

Takyi, Baffour K., Chris Opoku Agyeman, and Agnes Kutin-Mensah. 2010. "Religion and the Public Sphere: Religious Involvement and Voting Patterns in Ghana's 2004 Elections." *Africa Today* 56, 4: 63–86.

Tanaka, Martín. 1998. *Los Espejismos de la Democracia: El Colapso del Sistema de Partidos en el Perú*. Lima: Instituto de Estudios Peruanos.

Tanaka, Martín. 2006. "From Crisis to Collapse of the Party Systems and Dilemmas of Democratic Representation: Peru and Venezuela." In Scott Mainwaring, Ana María Bejerano, and Eduardo Pizarro Leongómez (eds.), *The Crisis of Democratic Representation in the Andes*. Stanford, CA: Stanford University Press, pp. 47–77.

Tanaka, Martín. 2011. "A Vote for Moderate Change." *Journal of Democracy* 22, 4: 75–83.

Taylor, Lewis. 2007. "Politicians without Parties and Parties without Politicians: The Foibles of the Peruvian Political Class, 2000–2006." *Bulletin of Latin American Research*, 26, 1: 1–23.

Teehankee, Julio C. 2010. "Image, Issues, and Machinery: Presidential Campaigns in Post-1986 Philippines." In Nathan Gilbert Quimpo and Yuko Kasuya (eds.), *The Politics of Change in the Philippines*. Manila: Anvil Publishing Inc., pp. 114–161.

Teichman, Judith A. 2001. *The Politics of Freeing Markets in Latin America: Chile, Argentina, and Mexico*. Chapel Hill, NC: University of North Carolina Press.

Thelen, Kathleen. 2003. "How Institutions Evolve: Insights from Comparative Historical Analysis." In James Mahoney and Dietrich Rueschemeyer (eds.), *Comparative Historical Analysis in the Social Sciences*. New York: Cambridge University Press, pp. 208–240.

Thelen, Kathleen. 2004. *How Institutions Evolve: The Political Economy of Skills in Germany, Britain, the United States, and Japan*. New York: Cambridge University Press.

Thompson, Mark R. 2010. "Populism and the Revival of Reform: Competing Political Narratives in the Philippines." *Contemporary Southeast Asia* 32, 1: 1–28.

Thurber, James A. and Candice J. Nelson (eds.) 2000. *Campaign Warriors: The Role of Political Consultants in Elections*. Washington, DC: Brookings Institution Press.

Timberman, David G. 1992. *The 1992 Philippine Elections: Putting Democracy to the Test*. New York: Asia Society.

Tironi, Eugenio. 1990. *La Invisible Victoria: Campañas Electorales y Democracia en Chile*. Santiago: Ediciones SUR.

Tironi, Eugenio. 2002. *El Cambio Está Aquí*. Santiago: La Tercera-Mondadori.

Tironi, Eugenio. 2010. *Radiografía de una Derrota, o Cómo Chile Cambió Sin Que la Concertación se Diera Cuenta*. Santiago: Uqbar Editores.

Tironi, Eugenio and Felipe Agüero. 1999. "¿Sobrevivirá el Nuevo Paisaje Político Chileno?" *Estudios Públicos* 54: 151–168.

Torcal, Mariano and Scott Mainwaring. 2003. "The Political Recrafting of Social Bases of Party Competition: Chile, 1973–95." *British Journal of Political Science* 33: 55–84.

Torquato do Rego, Francisco Gaudêncio. 1985. *Marketing Político e Governamental: Um Roteiro para Campanhas Políticas e Estratégias de Comunicação*. São Paulo: Summus Editorial.

Tuesta Soldevilla, Fernando. 1985. "La Estudiada Estrategia del APRA." *La República*, March 3.

Tuesta Soldevilla, Fernando. 1995. *Los Enigmas del Poder: Fujimori 1990–1996*. Lima: Fundación Friedrich Ebert.

Tuesta Soldevilla, Fernando. 2001. *Perú Político en Cifras: 1821–2001*. Lima: Fundación Friedrich Ebert.

Urrutía, Adriana. 2011a. "Hacer Campaña y Construir Partido: Fuerza 2011 y su Estrategia para (Re)legitimar al Fujimorismo a través de su Organización." *Argumentos* 5, 2.

Urrutía, Adriana. 2011b. "Que la Fuerza (2011) Esté Con Keiko: El Nuevo Baile del Fujimorismo." In Carlos Meléndez (ed.), *Post-candidatos: Guía Analítica de Sobrevivencia Hasta las Próximas Elecciones*. Lima: Mitín Editores, pp. 91–120.

Valenzuela, Arturo. 1995. "Chile: Origins and Consolidation of a Latin American Democracy." In Larry Diamond, Juan J. Linz, and Seymour Martin Lipset (eds.), *Politics in Developing Countries: Comparing Experiences with Democracy*, 2nd edn. Boulder, CO: Lynne Rienner, pp. 67–118.

Valenzuela, Arturo and J. Samuel Valenzuela. 1986. "Party Oppositions under the Chilean Authoritarian Regime." In J. Samuel Valenzuela and Arturo Valenzuela (eds.), *Military Rule in Chile: Dictatorship and Oppositions*. Baltimore, MD: Johns Hopkins University Press, pp. 184–229.

Valenzuela, Sebastián and Teresa Correa. 2007. "Madam or Mr. President? Chile's Michelle Bachelet, Press Coverage and Public Perceptions." Paper presented at the ILASSA Student Conference on Latin America, University of Texas, Austin, February 1–3.

van Vliet, Martin. 2013. "Mali: From Dominant Party to Platform of Unity." In Renske Doorenspleet and Lia Nijzink (eds.), *One-Party Dominance in African Democracies.* Boulder, CO: Lynne Rienner, pp. 143–168.

Vargas, Oscar-René. 2006. *Elecciones 2006: La Otra Nicaragua Posible.* Managua: Centro de Estudios de la Realidad Nacional (CEREN).

Vargas Llosa, Álvaro. 1991. *El Diablo en Campaña.* Madrid: El País/Aguilar.

Vargas Llosa, Mario. 1993. *El Pez en el Agua.* Madrid: Alfaguara.

Ventura Egoávil, José. 2002. *La Campaña Política: Técnicas Eficaces.* Lima: Escuela Mayor de Gestión Municipal.

Villavicencio, Gaitán L. 1988. "Las Ofertas Electorales y los Límites del Clientelismo." In *Ecuador 88: Elecciones, Economía, Estrategias.* Quito: Editorial El Conejo, pp. 11–33.

Waisbord, Silvio R. 1995. *El Gran Desfile: Campañas Electorales y Medios de Comunicación en la Argentina.* Buenos Aires: Editorial Sudamericana.

Waisbord, Silvio R. 1996. "Secular Politics: The Modernization of Argentine Electioneering." In Swanson and Mancini (eds.), pp. 207–225.

Walker, Scott and Kyung-Tae Kang. 2004. "The Presidential Election in South Korea, December 2002." *Electoral Studies* 23: 840–845.

Wantchekon, Leonard. 2003. "Clientelism and Voting Behavior: Evidence from a Field Experiment in Benin." *World Politics* 55: 399–422.

Weyland, Kurt. 1993. "The Rise and Fall of President Collor and Its Impact on Brazilian Democracy." *Journal of Interamerican Studies and World Affairs* 35, 1: 1–37.

Weyland, Kurt. 1996. "Neopopulism and Neoliberalism in Latin America: Unexpected Affinities." *Studies in Comparative International Development* 31, 3: 3–31.

Weyland, Kurt. 2001. "Clarifying a Contested Concept: Populism in the Study of Latin American Politics." *Comparative Politics* 34, 1: 1–22.

Weyland, Kurt. 2002. *The Politics of Market Reform in Fragile Democracies: Argentina, Brazil, Peru, and Venezuela.* Princeton, NJ: Princeton University Press.

Weyland, Kurt. 2005. "Theories of Policy Diffusion: Lessons from Latin American Pension Reform." *World Politics* 57: 262–295.

Weyland, Kurt. 2006a. *Bounded Rationality and Policy Diffusion: Social Sector Reform in Latin America.* Princeton, NJ: Princeton University Press.

Weyland, Kurt. 2006b. "The Rise and Decline of Fujimori's Neopopulist Leadership." In Julio F. Carrión (ed.), *The Fujimori Legacy: The Rise of Electoral Authoritarianism in Peru.* University Park, PA: Pennsylvania State University Press, pp. 13–38.

Whitefield, Stephen. 2002. "Political Cleavages and Post-Communist Politics." *Annual Review of Political Science* 5: 181–200.

Whitfield, Lindsay. 2009. "'Change for a Better Ghana': Party Competition, Institutionalization and Alternation in Ghana's 2008 Elections." *African Affairs* 108, 433: 621–641.

Wilson, Andrew. 2005. *Virtual Politics: Faking Democracy in the Post-Soviet World.* New Haven, CT: Yale University Press.

Wing, Susanna D. 2013. "Briefing: Mali: Politics of a Crisis." *African Affairs* 112, 448: 476–485.

World Bank. 2008. "World Development Indicators." Available at: http://datacatalog .worldbank.org (accessed on September 27, 2015).

Xia, Jun, Justin Tan, and David Tan. 2008. "Mimetic Entry and Bandwagon Effect: The Rise and Decline of International Equity Joint Venture in China." *Strategic Management Journal* 29: 195–217.

Youngers, Coletta A. 2000. *Deconstructing Democracy: Peru under President Alberto Fujimori*. Washington, DC: Washington Office on Latin America.

Zúñiga Mourao, Jenny. 2006. *Yo Conocí al Monstruo por Dentro*. Lima: Julio Verde del Campo.

Author's Interviews

Chile

Baraona, Pablo. Campaign manager, Büchi 1989. Santiago, June 21, 2007.

Benado, Camila. Press relations, Bachelet 2005. Santiago, September 26, 2005.

Bitar, Sergio. Campaign comanager, Bachelet 2005 (second round). Santiago, June 19, 2007.

Cordero, Gonzalo. Communication strategist, Lavín 1999 and Lavín 2005. Santiago, June 26, 2007.

Cortés, Flavio. Communication strategist, Frei 1993. Santiago, October 6, 2005.

de la Maza, Francisco. Campaign manager, Lavín 1999. Santiago, November 16, 2005.

Díaz, Francisco Javier. Speechwriter, Bachelet 2005. Santiago, October 7, 2005, and June 21, 2007.

Enríquez-Ominami, Marco. Advertising strategist, Lagos 1999 (first round). Santiago, June 8, 2007.

Figueroa, Carlos. Communication director, "No" 1988, Aylwin 1989, and Frei 1993; communication codirector, Lagos 1999. Santiago, December 20, 2005.

Forch, Juan Enrique. Television advertising, "No" 1988, Aylwin 1989, and Frei 1993. Santiago, December 19, 2005.

Galleguillos, Nany. Coordinator, Women with Bachelet, Bachelet 2005. Santiago, October 13, 2005.

García, Eugenio. Television advertising director, Lagos 1999 (second round). Santiago, December 15, 2005.

González, Eugenio. National coordinator, Büchi 1989; territorial operations, Lavín 1999. Santiago, June 12, 2007.

Gumucio, Manuela. Television advertising director, Lagos 1999 (first round). Santiago, November 16, 2005.

Guzmán, Eugenio. Strategist, Alessandri 1993 and Lavín 1999. Santiago, September 27, 2005.

Hinzpeter, Rodrigo. Campaign manager, Piñera 2005. Santiago, June 22, 2007.

Iriarte, Jorge. Advertising strategist, Lavín 1999. Santiago, January 11, 2006.

Jofré, René. Director of territorial operations, Bachelet 2005. Santiago, June 21, 2005.

Krauss, Fernando. Coordinator, Youth with Bachelet, Bachelet 2005. Santiago, October 3, 2005.

Larroulet, Cristián. Strategist, Büchi 1989, Lavín 1999, and Lavín 2005. Santiago, January 11, 2006.

Lorenzini, Pablo. Campaign coordinator, Maule region, Bachelet 2005. Santiago, November 15, 2005.

Mackenna, Jorge. Event organizer, Büchi 1989 and Lavín 1999. Santiago, January 23, 2006.

Montes, Carlos. Strategist, Lagos 1999 (second round). Santiago, November 23, 2005.

Moreno, Juan Pablo. Chief of staff, Lavín 1999 and Lavín 2005. Santiago, December 14, 2005.

Ominami, Carlos. Communication codirector, Lagos 1999 (first round). Santiago, June 21, 2007.

Pérez Yoma, Edmundo. Executive secretary, Frei 1993. Santiago, December 13, 2005.

Rivadeneira, Ignacio. Chief of staff, Piñera 2005. Santiago, September 23, 2005, and June 12, 2007.

Salcedo, José Manuel. Television advertising, "No" 1988, Aylwin 1989, Frei 1993, and Lagos 1999. Santiago, November 22, 2005.

Sepúlveda, Renato. Territorial operations, Lavín 1999 and Piñera 2005. Santiago, January 18, 2006.

Solari, Ricardo. Communication director, Bachelet 2005. Santiago, June 18, 2007.

Solis, Sergio. Coordinator, citizen network, Lagos 1999. Santiago, October 26, 2005.

Subercaseaux, Martín. Advertising strategist, Büchi 1989 and Lavín 1999. Santiago, November 17, 2005.

Tironi, Eugenio. Survey research and television advertising, "No" 1988; television advertising and speechwriting, Aylwin 1989; head communication strategist, Lagos 1999 (second round). Santiago, September 14, 2005.

Toloza, Cristián. Speechwriter, Frei 1993. Santiago, October 28, 2005.

Valdés, Juan Gabriel. Survey research and television advertising, "No" 1988. Belo Horizonte, Brazil, July 28, 2006.

Vinacur, Martín. Television advertising director, Bachelet 2005. Santiago, June 18, 2007.

Brazil

Abrão, José. Mobilization coordinator, Cardoso 1998. São Paulo, November 1, 2006.

Azevedo, Carlos. Television advertising director, Lula 1989 and Lula 1994. São Paulo, November 30, 2006.

Berni, José Roberto. Advertising strategist, Cardoso 1998 and Serra 2002. São Paulo, September 20, 2006, and October 30, 2006.

Bom, Djalma. Union organizer/fundraising, Lula 1989. São Bernardo do Campo, September 22, 2006.

Bornhausen, Jorge. President, Liberal Front Party (PFL), Cardoso 1994, Cardoso 1998, Serra 2002, and Alckmin 2006. Brasília, December 14, 2006.

Caldas Pereira, Eduardo Jorge. Strategic coordinator, Cardoso 1994; general coordinator, Cardoso 1998; communication strategist, Serra 2002; operational coordinator, Alckmin 2006. Rio de Janeiro, December 4, 2006.

Coimbra, Marcos. Survey research coordinator, Collor 1989; survey research, Lula 2006. Belo Horizonte, October 31, 2006.

Cotrim, Toni. Communication strategist, Lula 1989; advertising strategist, Lula 1998. São Paulo, August 18, 2006.

da Silva, Vicente Paulo. Union organizer, Lula 1989; president, Unified Workers' Central (CUT), Lula 1994. Brasília, November 9, 2006.

Dias, José Américo. Communication director, Lula 1989 and Lula 1998. São Paulo, August 24, 2006.

Dirceu, José. Secretary general, PT, Lula 1989; political coordinator, Lula 1998; campaign manager, Lula 2002. São Paulo, October 27, 2006.

Falcão, Rui. Communication strategist, Lula 1989; campaign comanager, Lula 1994. São Paulo, November 29, 2006.

Figueiredo, Marcus. Survey research and strategy, Cardoso 1994 and Cardoso 1998. Rio de Janeiro, October 11, 2006.

Godoy, Dudu. Advertising strategist, Lula 1998. São Paulo, August 25, 2006.

Gonzalez, Luiz. Marketing director, Alckmin 2006. São Paulo, November 29, 2006.

Greenhalgh, Luiz Eduardo. Campaign comanager, Lula 1994. Brasília, November 9, 2006.

Guerra, Sergio. Campaign manager, Alckmin 2006. Brasília, December 12, 2006.

Gushiken, Luiz. President, PT, Lula 1989; campaign manager, Lula 1998; communication strategist, Lula 2002. Brasília, November 9, 2006.

Kotscho, Ricardo. Press secretary, Lula 1989, Lula 1994, and Lula 2002. São Paulo, October 17, 2006.

Olsen, Orjan. Survey research, Cardoso 1994. São Paulo, August 30, 2006.

Pereira da Silva, Hamilton. Television advertising strategist, Lula 1989; agenda coordinator, Lula 1994. Brasília, October 7, 2006.

Pimenta da Veiga, João. President, PSDB, Cardoso 1994; political coordinator, Serra 2002. Brasília, November 10, 2006.

Pomar, Wladimir. Campaign manager, Lula 1989. Rio de Janeiro, October 10, 2006.

Prado, Antônio de Padua. Survey and focus group research director, Alckmin 2006. São Paulo, November 1, 2006.

Prado, Wander Bueno do. Logistics, Lula 1989 and Lula 1994. Santo André, October 23, 2006.

Ribeiro, Belisa. Television advertising director, Collor 1989. Rio de Janeiro, October 9, 2006.

Rodrigues, Rui. Television advertising, Cardoso 1994, Cardoso 1998, and Serra 2002. São Paulo, September 21, 2006.

Rosa e Silva, Cláudio Humberto. Press secretary and strategist, Collor 1989. Brasília, November 6, 2006.

Santos, Paulo de Tarso. Head advertising strategist, Lula 1989 and Lula 1994. São Paulo, August 28, 2006.

Seligman, Milton. General coordinator, Serra 2002. São Paulo, October 26, 2006.

Sokol, Markus. Communication coordinator, Lula 1994. São Paulo, October 17, 2006.

Vasconcelos, Paulo. Advertising strategist, Collor 1989. Belo Horizonte, October 31, 2006.

Venturi, Gustavo. Survey research, Lula 1998 and Lula 2006. São Paulo, November 29, 2006.

Peru

Aguilar, Abel. Communication strategist, Vargas Llosa 1990 and Flores 2006. Lima, February 13, 2006, and May 11, 2006.

Becerra, Luís. Political strategist, Flores 2001. Lima, March 21, 2006.

Benza Pflucker, Gaston. Strategist, García 2006. Lima, March 14, 2006.

Breña, Rolando. Leader, Communist Party of Peru – Red Homeland, Barrantes 1985. Lima, May 18, 2006.

Bruce, Carlos. Lima campaign manager, Toledo 2001. Lima, April 25, 2006.

Bruce, Eduardo. Communication strategist, Toledo 2001. Lima, February 3, 2006.

Castro, Raúl. Vice president, PPC, Flores 2006. Lima, June 9, 2006.

Confidential. Campaign leadership, Flores 2006. Lima, May 22, 2006.

Cruchaga, Miguel. General secretary, Libertad Movement, Vargas Llosa 1990. Lima, May 10, 2006.

Cuestas, Walter. Operational coordinator, García 1985. Lima, June 10, 2006.

Echegaray, Manuel. Communication strategist, Vargas Llosa 1990; head advertising strategist, Flores 2001. Lima, February 8, 2006, and April 19, 2006.

Forch, Juan Enrique. Communication strategist, Toledo 2001. Santiago, Chile, December 19, 2005, and June 22, 2007.

García, Carlos. Vice presidential candidate, Fujimori 1990. Lima, March 4, 2006.

Garrido Lecca, Hernán. Campaign manager, García 2006. Lima, March 14, 2006.

Ghersi, Enrique. Political and organizational strategist, Vargas Llosa 1990. Lima, May 30, 2006.

LaNatta, Augusto. Coordinator, Independents with Alan, García 1985; coordinator, Todos por el Perú, García 2001. Lima, April 19, 2006.

Llosa, Luís. Communication strategist, Vargas Llosa 1990. Lima, May 18, 2006.

Méndez, Pepe. Head advertising strategist, Humala 2006. Lima, March 20, 2006.

Meza, Vladimir. Head youth organizer, Toledo 2001; territorial operations, Humala 2006. Lima, April 24, 2006.

Muro, Krishna. Survey and focus group research, Flores 2001. Lima, February 10, 2006.

Nava, Luís. Personal secretary to Alan García, García 2001 and García 2006. Lima, May 2, 2006.

Otero, Hugo. Communication strategist, Villanueva 1980; head communication strategist, García 1985, García 2001, and García 2006. Lima, March 9, 2006.

Pinedo, Ricardo. Coordinator, Youth with Alan, García 2006. Lima, March 16, 2006.

Pucci, Alejandro. Communication strategist, Humala 2006. Lima, April 17, 2006.

Rospigliosi, Fernando. Press secretary, Toledo 2001. Lima, February 27, 2006.

Salcedo, Alfonso. Communication strategist, Villanueva 1980, García 1985, Alva Castro 1990, and Toledo 2001. Lima, March 22, 2006.

Salgado, Luz. Lima campaign manager, Fujimori 1990. Lima, April 25, 2006.

San Román, Máximo. Vice presidential candidate, Fujimori 1990. Lima, February 28, 2006.

Vílchez, Pedro. Territorial operations, Fujimori 1990. Lima, May 2, 2006.

Index

CPSIA information can be obtained at www.ICGtesting.com
Printed in the USA
LVOW07*0850130316

478919LV00003BA/5/P